UNLAWFUL TERRITORIAL SITUATIONS IN INTERNATIONAL LAW

Developments in International Law

VOLUME 55

The Titles published in this series are listed at the end of this volume.

Unlawful Territorial Situations in International Law

Reconciling Effectiveness, Legality and Legitimacy

ENRICO MILANO

With a Foreword
by
Christine Chinkin

MARTINUS NIJHOFF PUBLISHERS
LEIDEN / BOSTON

A C.I.P. Catalogue record for this book is available from the Library of Congress.

Printed on acid-free paper.

ISBN 90 04 14939 2
© 2006 Koninklijke Brill NV, Leiden, The Netherlands
Koninklijke Brill NV incorporates the imprints Brill Academic Publishers,
Martinus Nijhoff Publishers and VSP.

http://www.brill.nl

Printed and bound in The Netherlands.

Alla memoria del Professor Miele

'there is [not] always a clear and specific legal rule
readily applicable to every international situation,
but that every international situation
is capable of being determined as a matter of law'

Jennings and Watts, *Oppenheim's International Law*, 9th ed., Vol. 1, 13,
cit. in Judge Higgins' Dissenting Opinion, *Legality of the Threat or Use of*
Nuclear Weapons, Advisory Opinion, ICJ Reports 1996, 592.

TABLE OF CONTENTS

PREFACE AND ACKNOWLEDGMENTS

It is difficult to render justice to the many sources of inspiration for the present project. The decision to spend four years working on a doctoral thesis, and many months on refining the result of that work into a book, is inevitably inspired by many personal motives and external inputs that influence the early enterprises – and a Ph.D. is possibly the earliest enterprise - of an aspiring international lawyer. Trying to track them all down would result in a tedious exercise for the reader: I will therefore limit myself to mention the three most important, most significant and most influential on the final outcome.

The first motive has to do with the choice to take effectiveness as the conceptual focus of my analysis of unlawful territorial situations. I was studying for my bachelor in Padua back in 1996, and I had the fortune to have my first course in international law taught by Professor Alberto Miele. Professor Miele's provocative style, together with his emphasis - sometimes extreme - on a realistic and historically contextualised concept of international law, deeply shaped my way of looking at international law from the very beginning of my encounter with the subject. His particular attention for the concept of effectiveness as one of the traditional tenets of the international legal system led me to think often in the following years about its continued relevance in current international law. When time came to draft a research project for my Ph.D., the temptation to write a comprehensive doctoral treatise on the concept of effectiveness in international law was too strong to resist it only with my own forces. I was lucky enough to find myself in a British academic environment that would be naturally suspicious of purely theoretical or doctrinal work. Thus, the wise advice by many of the people surrounding me, and in particular by my supervisor Christine Chinkin, to evaluate the impact of the concept of effectiveness on a particular case-study or area of international law putting on the same level its theoretical elaboration and the analysis of relevant state and UN practice, at the same time avoiding the risks involved in a general theoretical work. I am most grateful for that advice, and, in retrospect, I can see how the exercise of focusing my analysis of the concept of effectiveness on a particular social and legal phenomenon helped me to fully grasp the different facets and implications involved in using the concept of effectiveness to understand any relevant area of international law. I am not sure Professor Miele would have particularly liked the development of my understanding of the role of effectiveness in international law; but, given his passion for teaching his students, I am sure that he would have fully appreciated the influence that his lectures had on my approach to international law. This book is dedicated to Alberto Miele, who departed from us too early and left some university classrooms in Padua strangely quiet.

The second reason is the enduring importance of unlawful territorial situations as pathological phenomena of the international society. The number of military interventions in the internal affairs of sovereign states in the post-cold war era has increased, and so has the complexity of the claims put forward and of the involvement of international institutions in their management. While the last few years have seen a strong attention by international lawyers towards alleged breaches of Article 2(4) of the UN Charter, much less attention has been devoted to the effects produced by such interventions upon the 'victim' state. Article 2(4)'s main function is arguably to protect the 'territorial integrity or political independence' of states, and the aims and effects of military interventions often undermine states' territorial sovereignty well after the cessation of the hostilities. Questions of occupation and withdrawal have been at the centre of the dispute in many of the current international crises, including Iraq, Palestine, Cyprus, Lebanon. Again, whereas international lawyers have focused on the conduct of the occupying forces and the application of human rights law and international humanitarian law to that conduct, or, also often, on the overall settlement of those disputes, little attention has been devoted to the question of the legality or illegality of the occupation itself, as if the choice to occupy or not was exclusively an issue of policy. The point here is not that the former concerns are not important, on the contrary, but that the occupation of a territory by foreign forces is not simply a matter of policy, but an important legal question as well; indeed, a legal question that is worth full investigation, as it involves some of the fundamental legal norms of the international community to which international lawyers should be fully committed.

Finally, the third main source of inspiration lies in the every day reality of being on the receiving end of the world of media and, very often, of politics. I have always found the language used to describe political and territorial disputes involving a pattern of foreign occupation, be it Palestine, Lebanon, Cyprus, Western Sahara, East Timor or Iraq, politically charged, descriptively inaccurate and analytically biased. The subjective language of the media and of politicians has lent positive connotations to the foreign presences of military forces on disputed territories, by designating them as 'international presence', 'multinational force', 'peace-keeping mission', 'humanitarian mission', 'temporary presence' or, alternatively, has thrown them under a negative light, by designating them as 'foreign occupation', 'forcible occupation', 'military occupation' or simply 'occupation'. The clashing narratives of the parties in the dispute and the biased narratives of many of the media represent, and have represented, to my eyes, the perfect recipe for reproducing the conflict endless times. I thought, and I think, that one of the contributions that international law might give to the analysis and resolution of those disputes would be to provide a common and neutral ground and language in which to articulate claims and pretensions. A shared narrative might become the only way to move away from conflict to dialogue and solution.

This awareness led me to think of the concept of unlawful territorial situation: something broader, and at the same time stricter, than a regime of occupation as defined by Article 42 of the Regulations annexed to the 1907 Hague Convention; a regime of foreign presence without a proper legal basis, whose definition would not necessarily require the existence of a military occupation, as, for instance, was the case for the South African *Bantustans*, and could also include territorial regimes established by competent international organisations. Going back to the basics of the law, i.e. the legality or illegality of the territorial situation, would also contribute to return to the law one its main original functions, i.e. to provide a criterion on which to determine whether a certain social phenomenon or social conduct is in accordance or not with the legal norms. With all the rigidity and internal rhetoric that such exercise might imply, and with all its unfashionable flavour, the re-discovery of one of the original functions of the law was in the present author's mind the kind of exercise that would show the full essence and value of international law in disputes over territory and sovereignty, and one of the dignified roles international lawyers can play in those disputes. On the other hand, using the concept of effectiveness as the main analytical device would help me avoid a mechanist application of the law and consider the endogenous role of power into the law, both as a creator and device of application of positive law, and as a 'magic box' where the 'illegal' may be transformed into the 'legal'. It was in this latter respect that I could fully appreciate the role of legitimacy as a *trait-d'union* between effectiveness and legality.

The book represents an updated and revised version of the Ph.D. thesis defended in London on 10 June 2004. I am most grateful to my supervisor Christine Chinkin for her invaluable academic advice and personal encouragement throughout my years at the London School of Economics. I wish to thank the two examiners Nigel White and Matthew Craven for their detailed feedback and constructive criticism, which importantly contributed to the refinement of my thesis and to its transformation into the present book. Attila Tanzi's generous suggestions and feedback must be also acknowledged: they were instrumental to publishing parts of the thesis in the form of articles and the whole thesis in the present form of a book. Section 7 of Chapter 5 is indeed a revised version of the article 'Territorial Disputes, Wrongful Occupations and State Responsibility: Should the International Court of Justice Go the Extra Mile?' published in *The Law and Practice of International Courts and Tribunals* 3 (2004), 509-541; section 4 of Chapter 6 is a revised version of the article 'Security Council Action in the Balkans: Reviewing the Legality of Kosovo's Territorial Status' published in *The European Journal of International Law* 14 (2003), 999-1022. Special thanks also go to the LSE, in particular the Law Department, for providing me with the necessary support and conditions to successfully complete my Phd. I am grateful to Timothy Barnett, Jesse Elvin, Beverley Neufeld, Tara Salmon and Stephen Tully for proof-reading and for language revision of the thesis.

Finally, I would like to thank especially my parents, Francesco and Mirna, and my brothers, Giuseppe and Marcello, for their personal and financial support. Much of the outcome is due to their patience. I am also indebted to Marcello and Roberta for providing the 'logistics' the many times I had to move out and into a new place. Patrizia's care, love and smiles were also invaluable; her determination and hard-working character were and still are a model to follow in all my enterprises.

E.M.
October 2005

FOREWORD

One of the most pervasive norms of the post-UN Charter world has been the prohibition of acquisition of territory through the use of force. A logical corollary of Article 2 (4) of the Charter the principle was enshrined in the Declaration on Friendly Relations between States and has been reiterated ever since by international institutions and within academic literature. But at the beginning of the 21st century there are many situations of territories occupied or managed by foreign forces, or by governments installed through the instrumentality of foreign forces – the Palestinian Occupied Territories, Kosovo, Northern Cyprus, Western Sahara, Iraq to name just a few. There are controversies over the legal status of the various territories and the applicable legal regime: some are unhesitatingly and almost universally accepted as illegal; others as illegal but legitimate; others as acquiring a *de facto* legality. Some territorial occupations have eventually been terminated, although as in the case of East Timor only through devastation and the shedding of much blood. The contexts of each situation are different, for example the duration, degree and purpose of occupation, the status of the foreign forces and the response of the particular territory's citizens. How to analyse these diverse situations in accordance with international law and how to reconcile the many conflicting legal arguments were the challenging questions Dr Milano sought to answer. In doing so, he took the brave decision to use as his framework the doctrine of effectiveness – a brave decision because the association of the doctrine with military and other forms of power has meant it has had little purchase with Anglo-American international lawyers since at least the Second World War, although scholars in civil law countries have continued to weigh its usefulness and place within international law. Dr Milano analyses the theoretical and practical significance of effectiveness and from this starting point examines the interplay between effectiveness, legality and that pragmatic halfway house, legitimacy, in contemporary unlawful territorial situations – a broader concept than occupation. In his conclusion he reflects on the ambiguous nature of effectiveness as a legal device placed both within and outside positive law, by looking at events in Iraq from 2003 onwards. This book is an absorbing and timely study of some of the major dilemmas of the contemporary international legal order. The intellectual merit of the PhD thesis on which it is based has already been recognised through the awards of the 2004 Alberico Gentili Prize and the 2005 Georg Schwarzenberger Prize. I am sure the book will be similarly acclaimed by scholars and practitioners of international law and relations.

Christine Chinkin
London School of Economics

TABLE OF ABBREVIATIONS

AC	Appeal Cases
AD	*Annual Digest of Public International Law Cases*
AJIL	*American Journal of International Law*
All ER	The All England Law Reports
ALR	Australian Law Reports
BYIL	*British Yearbook of International Law*
ECJ	European Court of Justice
ECHR	European Court of Human Rights
EEZ	Exclusive Economic Zone
EJIL	*European Journal of International Law*
EPIL	*Encyclopedia of Public International Law*
FLR	Federal Law Reports
GA	United Nations General Assembly
GYIL	*German Yearbook of International Law*
ICJ	International Court of Justice
ICTR	International Criminal Tribunal for Rwanda
ICTY	International Criminal Tribunal for the Former Yugoslavia
ICLQ	*International and Comparative Law Quarterly*
ILC	International Law Commission
ILM	*International Legal Materials*
ILR	*International Law Reports*
ITLOS	International Tribunal for the Law of the Sea
KA	Kumanovo Agreement
KLA	Kosovo Liberation Army
LJIL	*Leiden Journal of International Law*
LNTS	League of Nations Treaty Series
LoN	League of Nations
NAM	Non-Aligned Movement
NYIL	*Netherlands Yearbook of International Law*
PAIGC	African Party for the Independence of Guinea and Cape Verde
PCIJ	Permanent Court of International Justice
RGDIP	*Revue général de droit international public*
RIAA	Reports of International Arbitral Awards
SC	United Nations Security Council
SCOR	Security Council Official Records
TRNC	Turkish Republic of Northern Cyprus
UK	United Kingdom of Great Britain and Northern Ireland
UKTS	United Kingdom Treaty Series

UNBDC   Iraq-Kuwait United Nations
                     Boundary Demarcation Commission
UNCC   United Nations Compensation Commission
UNMIK   United Nations Mission in Kosovo
UNTAET   United Nations Transitional Administration
                     in East Timor
UNTS   United Nations Treaty Series
US   United States of America
USM   Union of Serbia and Montenegro
VCLT   1969 Vienna Convention on the Law of Treaties
ZaöRV   *Zeitschrift für ausländisches öffentlichen Recht und Völkerrecht*

TABLE OF CASES

ICJ Applications, Memorials and Pleadings

National

Australia

Canada

Israel

TABLE OF TREATIES AND OTHER INTERNATIONAL INSTRUMENTS

TABLE OF UN RESOLUTIONS AND DOCUMENTS

GA Resolutions

SC Records

Other UN Documents

CHAPTER 1

INTRODUCTION

Historians will tell us whether the war in Iraq has been the most momentous event of the beginning of the 21st century on the international arena. What cannot be doubted is that in its modern factual violence, in its post-modern justification, in its pragmatic, but, at the same time, moralistic rhetoric, in its swift and velocious conduct, in the *grandeur* of its revolutionary project, in its media attention and its public opinion reaction, the invasion of Iraq has epitomised the Western war of the new century. Belligerent parties of international lawyers have dug deep into the Charter's spirit and into the letter of Security Council resolutions to condemn the war as illegal and aggressive, or, alternatively, to provide the Emperor with dignified clothes. The present book does not pretend to add new elements to that discussion, however important and rich that was. In a sense, it wants to start from an even more foundational question of international law involved in the 2003 intervention, which has received less attention from international lawyers: the sovereignty and territorial integrity of Iraq.

When looking at the statements and official documents dealing with Iraq in the aftermath of the war, one cannot fail to observe the almost obsessive reference to Iraq's sovereignty and territorial integrity. Among the objectives of *Operation Iraqi Freedom*, the British Government spelled out the aim 'to preserve wider regional security, including by maintaining the territorial integrity of Iraq [...].'[1] On 8 April 2003, as Baghdad was about to fall, President George W Bush and Prime Minister Tony Blair stated that 'we plan to seek the adoption of new United Nations Security Council resolutions that would affirm Iraq's territorial integrity [...].'[2] United Nations (UN) Security Council (SC) Resolution 1483 adopted on 22 May 2003 did indeed reaffirm 'the sovereignty and territorial integrity of Iraq', despite recognising the authority of Coalition states over Iraq.[3] In the debate following the adoption of the resolution a number of countries - including Angola, Chile, Pakistan, Russia - explained their support for the resolution on the basis that it reaffirmed the territorial integrity and sovereignty of Iraq.[4] A few days before, the Administrator of the Coalition Provisional

---

[1] *British Military Campaign Objectives*, March 2003. Full text reproduced in House of Commons Research Paper, *The Conflict in Iraq*.
[2] Cit. in Bowers, 'Iraq: law of occupation', June 2003, 10, in House of Commons Research Paper 03/51.
[3] SC Res. 1483 (2003), Preamble.
[4] S/PV. 4761.

Authority (CPA) had issued Regulation n. 1, in which he spelled out the responsibility of the US Central Command to 'directly support the CPA by [...] maintaining Iraq's territorial integrity and security.'[5] Commentators confirmed their view over the question of the Iraqi sovereignty. For instance, Frederic Kirgis writing on SC Resolution 1483 stated that

> 'the fact that a country is occupied and is under the effective, but temporary, control of the occupying powers does not affect its continuing status as a sovereign state. Iraq remains a state as a matter of international law, with rights and obligations toward other sovereign states. The Security Council has imposed restrictions on some of those rights and obligations, and for the time being the occupying powers will act on behalf of Iraq in carrying them out, but Iraq's sovereignty under international law remains intact.'[6]

Other commentators agreed with this view.[7]

Adopting the perspective of common sense, we would find difficult to reconcile the presence of thousands of foreign troops on Iraqi soil, the exercise of a wide-ranging powers both at a civilian and a military level by foreign powers, the policy of 'de-baathification' of the Iraqi society by the occupying powers, with the fact that 21st Century international law assesses the territorial state of Iraq as that of a sovereign state whose territorial sovereignty was preserved in the year 2003. One is tempted into the conclusion that international law must be a strange and weak law, a law which prefers symbols and formulas, and uses words and concepts in a way exactly opposite to their original meaning. What the present book attempts to do is to shed light on this ambivalence permeating sovereignty discourse. It bridges the gap between the common idea of state sovereignty as synonymous with political independence and with exercise of supreme authority with regard to a certain territorial basis, and a formalistic idea of sovereignty and territorial integrity devoid of substantive meaning, as that that appears in Iraq in the immediate aftermath of the 2003 war. It does that because an international law which opts for either of the two extremes is an international law incapable of assessing and regulating territorial sovereignty. By choosing the former concept of national sovereignty, international law will always accept and recognise what is effective and real, in other words, it will recognise sheer power as it is; by choosing the latter, it will abstain from passing a judgement by simply invoking the abstract formula of 'territorial status'. The way the book bridges that gap is by considering the concept of unlawful territorial situation.

A preliminary definition of an unlawful territorial situation is a territorial state of affairs, which is established and pursued in defiance of international norms and

---

[5] CPA/REG/16 May 2003/01.
[6] Kirgis, 'Security Council Resolution 1483 on the Rebuilding of Iraq', in *ASIL Insights* May 2003, in <http://www.asil.org/insights/insigh107.htm>.
[7] E.g. Bowers, *supra* n. 2, 18-19.

principles. In particular, by using the category of territorial situation, the international lawyer can assess the legality of a territorial state of affairs with regard to international rules concerning states' and peoples' territorial sovereignty. Well-established legal rules and principles protecting territorial sovereignty against external occupations are the prohibition to change a peaceful *status quo* through the use of force, the principle of *uti possidetis*, the principle of self-determination, and the principle of territorial integrity. The assessment of unlawfulness is contextual, in the sense that the territorial situation can be analysed at a particular point in time regardless as to whether the formal status is contested or not. This is not to deny that the review of legality of a territorial situation may be often controversial, and the line between lawfulness and unlawfulness may appear blurred. In fact, this work shows how the interplay between those principles of legality and the legal protection of territorial sovereignty is much more complex than normally claimed, making a contextual assessment of legality often problematic. The principles of 'territorial legality' work at two distinct levels, one of source and preservation of territorial title, the other of protection of peoples' or states' territorial sovereignty, and the lack of a territorial title by the occupier does not necessarily result in a situation of territorial unlawfulness.

Furthermore, to avoid replacing a formalist approach, that of 'formal status', with another formalist approach, that of 'territorial illegality', the present project builds the normative framework for analysing territorial situations on the legal-normative concept of effectiveness. Effectiveness meant as the adaptation of the law to realities and *status quo* was considered until the 1970s one of the dominant principles of the international legal system. It was generally accepted that its prominent role was due to a conception of international law as a law of co-ordination of sovereign nations trying to maximise their self-interest. The lack of centralised enforcement mechanisms was also considered one of the main reasons why the principle of effectiveness played such a strong role. At present times, it is impossible to deny the simple fact that effectiveness is no longer a 'fundamental' or 'dominant' principle of the international legal system; however, it is also impossible to deny the enduring importance and relevance of the concept of effectiveness to a sound analysis of unlawful territorial situations, and its function in overcoming formalistic definitions of territorial sovereignty. The book proposes a possible reconciliation between effectiveness and the principles of legality mentioned above, by showing its nature as a device that can transform factual situations into law, if complemented and boosted by a process of 'legitimation' of originally unlawful territorial situations. It underlines how the international legal system, by tolerating the legitimation of effectiveness, may paradoxically preserve in the short term the internal coherence of the rule of law, at the same time gradually re-gaining influence over originally unlawful territorial situations. On the other hand, the present study warns of the dangers inherent in such a model of effectiveness and legitimacy beyond positive law, in terms of long term sustainability of a rule of law in the international society.

This introductory chapter preliminarily sets out the meaning of unlawful territorial situation as a legal category. It then looks at the concept of effectiveness, showing its problematic nature of device of transformation of social realities into law. It raises some preliminary questions on the more sinister nature of legitimacy as a catalyst of successful transformation of illegal effectiveness into lawful situations. Finally, it briefly describes the book's structure.

1. Defining unlawful territorial situations as a legal category

The definition of the international law category of 'unlawful territorial situation' should be addressed at the outset, as unlawful territorial situations represent the subject matter of the book. This is best done through an analysis of the three terms 'unlawful', 'territorial' and 'situation' in their separate and joint meaning, to spell out a general working definition.

A. Situation

The three terms are considered in the reverse, looking first at the term 'situation'. Its common literal meaning, as found in the Oxford Dictionary, varies from 'a place (with its surroundings) which is occupied by something', to a 'state of affairs' or, alternatively, a 'set of circumstances'.[8] It is quite interesting to notice that the former description corresponds, by and large, to the social phenomenon studied in this book. Moreover, the term 'situation' does not seem to entail in itself any distinctive legal meaning. In the UN Charter the term 'situation' is separated from the term 'dispute' in Articles 34 and 35, which deal with the peaceful settlement of disputes. In *Namibia*, the ICJ found the practice of the SC not to invite South Africa to participate in the discussion on the 'Situation in Namibia' in accordance with the procedural consequences of the distinction drawn in the Charter between the two concepts.[9] However, the Court has not tried to define the distinction, nor are SC meetings of much help in this respect. Doctrinal contributions have also tended to downplay the legal difference between the two, by stating that disputes may represent a sub-category of

---

[8] *The Oxford Paperback Dictionary – New Edition* (1994), 751.

[9] *Legal Consequences for States of the Continued Presence of South Africa in Namibia notwithstanding Security Council Resolution 276* (1970), Advisory Opinion, ICJ Reports 1971, 6, at 22-23. See, however, the US apparently contradictory practice of claiming Article 27 as a basis for justifying its abstention on the question of permission of entry into its national territory of members of the Southern Rhodesian regime. S/PV.2090 and comment by Tavernier, 'L'Année des Nations Unies' 24 *Annuaire française de droit international* (1978), 520.

situations, but in any case it is difficult to think of any 'situation' subject to a process of peaceful settlement according to Chapter VI and VII of the Charter, which is not a dispute too.[10] The qualification of the concept of 'situation' with the terms 'territorial' and 'unlawful' may shed some light on this debate.

B. Territorial situation

The concept of territorial situation is, perhaps unintentionally, illustrated by the European Court of Human Rights decision on admissibility in *Bankovic v. Belgium et al.*.[11] The applicants were citizens of the Federal Republic of Yugoslavia (FRY), whose relatives died as a result of NATO bombing of the Serbian Radio Television Centre in Belgrade on 23 April 1999. They claimed that each NATO country, which had taken part in the military actions in the FRY in 1999, should be held responsible for the breach of Article 2 (right to life), Article 10 (freedom of expression) and Article 13 (the right to an effective remedy) of the European Convention of Human Rights (ECHR). The main contentious point raised by the applicants was the jurisdiction *ratione personae* and *ratione loci* of the Court according to Article 1 of the ECHR.[12] They maintained that the criterion of effective control and effective situation in a foreign country developed by the same Court in *Loizidou* should be extended to include control over airspace, as it was exercised by NATO over the FRY in 1999.[13] The defendants counter-claimed that the term 'jurisdiction' in Article 1 should be interpreted in its ordinary public international law meaning, as entailing an exercise of general legal authority over certain people and territories. The rationale of *Loizidou* should be strictly linked to an exercise of territorial jurisdiction in a country already party to the ECHR.[14] It should not be extended, incurring the risk of considering NATO countries accountable under the ECHR for any kind of military operation abroad.[15] The Court agreed with this latter argument. It stated that 'the jurisdictional competence of a State is primarily territorial' and that 'a State may not actually exercise jurisdiction on the territory of another without the

---

[10] Conforti, *Le Nazioni Unite* (1986, 4th ed.), 167-168; Treves, 'La Prévention des Conflits Internationaux dans la Déclaration Adoptée en 1988 par l'Assemblée Géneral de l'O.N.U.' 34 *Annuaire française de droit international* (1988), 437; Tavernier, 'Article 27: Vote', in Cot, Pellet (eds.), *La Charte des Nations Unies* (1991, 2nd ed.), 505.

[11] *Bankovic et al. v. Belgium et al.*, European Court of Human Rights, Decision on Admissibility of Application no. 52207/99, 12 December 2001.

[12] Article 1 European Convention of Human Rights reads: 'The High Contracting Parties shall secure to everyone within their jurisdiction the rights and freedoms defined in Section I of [the] Convention.'

[13] *Loizidou v. Turkey (Merits)*, Judgement of 18 December 1996, ECHR Series A (1996-VI), 2219; *Bankovic*, *supra* n. 11, para. 47.

[14] *Ibidem*, para. 42.

[15] *Ibidem*, para. 44.

latter's consent, invitation or acquiescence, unless the former is an occupying State in which case it can be found to exercise jurisdiction in that territory, at least in certain respects.'[16] Based on this assumption, the Court dismissed the applicants' argument that control over airspace could amount to jurisdiction.[17]

A discussion of the wisdom of the Court's solution on the merits of the decision is beyond the purpose of the present project, however, the *Bankovic* decision is interesting from the perspective of defining the legal concept of 'territorial situation'. The concept can be equated to the exercise of territorial jurisdiction by a certain international person, normally a State, but possibly also an international organisation, a national liberation movement, and potentially even a terrorist group. It could be argued that the Court's approach in *Bankovic* depends on a restrictive definition of territory, which does not include airspace, nor possibly sea areas. However, it is clear that the concept of territory is here taken in a legal, rather than physical sense. It is the spatial framework within which a general legal authority is exercised.[18] It is difficult to think that control over airspace alone may result in the exercise of any general legal authority. The case of NATO in 1999 and the case of the US-UK no-fly zones in Iraq until 2003 seem to confirm the Court's view that air space control is a form of factual control, without the involvement of general legal authority. In this sense, it seems better to exclude instances of air space control from the scope of territorial situations. As for waters, it is undeniable that the control exercised by the State over its internal waters and over the territorial sea amounts to territorial jurisdiction. More controversial is the question whether the coastal state's legal prerogatives over the EEZ and the continental shelf can amount to an exercise of territorial jurisdiction: however, the letter and purpose of Articles 56 and 77 of 1982 United Nations Convention on the Law of the Sea seem to suggest that the jurisdictional rights are so specific, limited and functional to a defined number of economic, scientific and environmental activities that we can hardly talk about territorial jurisdiction. In conclusion, we can define a 'territorial situation' as a state of affairs where an international actor displays factual control *and* general legal authority over a certain territory.

---

[16] *Ibidem*, paras. 59-60.

[17] *Ibidem*, para. 76.

[18] When referring to 'legal authority', I do not refer to an authority exercised in accordance with the law, or, more specifically, in accordance with international law, but to an authority capable of displaying extensive juridical effects, regardless whether the legal basis is valid or invalid. However, the reader must be warned that terms like 'juristic' and 'juridical' are terms and concepts imported from civil law countries, therefore 'foreign' to the English legal terminology. Thus, I will avoid using those terms despite the ambiguity of the term 'legal', and refer the reader to the context in which the expressions 'legal basis', 'legal authority' and 'legal effects' are found, in order to understand their meaning.

Of course, such exercise of territorial jurisdiction is not necessarily exclusive and unconditional, but can be limited in time and in purpose. An example mentioned in *Bankovic* is the exercise of military administration, which is often accompanied by the parallel exercise of civil administration by local authorities or international authorities, such as in Kosovo. We may think of geographically even more limited territorial situations, such as those deriving from the concession of military bases to a foreign country in the state's own territory.[19] Last but not least, nothing precludes using interchangeably the expression 'territorial situation' and 'territorial status', when referring to a state of affairs, indeed a *status quo*, characterised by an effective display of legal authority over a certain territory.[20] However, it is here preferred 'territorial situation', as 'territorial status' often indicates the formal designation of a certain territory. Such formal designation – for instance, Non-Self-Governing Territory, Trusteeship Administration, province, international protectorate – may have consequences on the way international law defines the unlawfulness of a certain territorial situation. However, the two concepts should be differentiated. At any rate, when referring to this latter meaning of territorial status, the expression 'formal status' or 'formal territorial status' will be used for the sake of clarity, whereas 'territorial status' will be used synonymously with 'territorial situation'.

Finally, the concept of territorial situation should not be confused with the concept of territorial occupation, as the former is broader than the latter, and it encompasses it. The concept of territorial occupation is precisely defined in Article 42 of the Regulations annexed to the 1907 Hague Convention: '[t]erritory is considered occupied when it is actually placed under the authority of the hostile army. The occupation extends only to the territory where such authority has been established and can be exercised.'[21] This definition normally presupposes the existence of an armed conflict leading to the occupation, which is not necessarily present in territorial situations: on the other hand, many of the territorial situations analysed in the present book can be characterised as territorial occupations. Among the advantages of choosing the concept of territorial situation for the present study, rather than the concept of territorial occupation, is the fact that the former better lends itself to the analysis of

---

[19] This specific category of territorial situation is not analysed in this book. Of course, a foreign military base in a state's territory, such as the US military base of Guantanamo in Cuba, can be potentially included in the concept of unlawful territorial situation; however, that will depend on the specific terms of the agreement between the host state and the foreign country through which, usually, these arrangements are made.

[20] On the definition of *status quo* in international law see Grewe, 'Status quo', in Bernhardt (ed.), *EPIL* (2000) (Vol. IV), 687.

[21] The text of the 1907 Hague Convention and the other relevant instruments analysed in this section can be found in Schindler, Toman (eds.), *The Laws of Armed Conflict: a Collection of Conventions, Resolutions and Other Documents* (1981).

unlawfulness of territorial regimes, moving away from the question of application of international humanitarian law that will indeed depend on the coercive military control over a certain territory. Another important advantage is that the term 'territorial situation' is less politically charged than the term 'territorial occupation' and it helps situating the international law 'narrative' on a more neutral ground.

C. Unlawful territorial situation

The exercise of territorial jurisdiction, in other words of general legal authority over a certain territory, is normally accompanied by the presumption that the subject exercising such jurisdiction has a right to do so. This is due to the role that the concept of effectiveness has played in the way international law has developed its basic concepts. However, the presumption can be rebutted, and, in certain circumstances, the display of legal authority may not be complemented by a valid legal basis. In other words, the basis of those legal powers may be invalid under international law or in conflict with one or more international law norms. Thus, the definition of unlawfulness concerning territorial situations relates in principle to the right or the competence to rule over a certain territorial area, rather than the fact that such competence is exercised, or the way in which it is exercised. For instance, the adoption of SC Resolution 554 declaring the 1983 South-African constitution null and void, due to its discrimination between the white and Asian population, on the one hand, and the black population, on the other, indicates a situation of governmental illegitimacy, rather than of unlawfulness of the long-established South African state.[22] The *apartheid* regime, fully institutionalised through that constitution, affected the legality of that regime and constitutional framework, rather than the territorial situation as such, whose lawfulness was derived from the territorial competence of the state South Africa. The line between governmental illegitimacy and unlawfulness of the territorial situation can be more blurred, and the former can lead to the latter. In both the case of Southern Rhodesia and in the case of Transkei, the establishment of newly independent states was condemned by the international community due to the governmental racist structure, which in turn also affected the unlawfulness of the newly defined territorial situation.[23]

Unlawful territorial situations should be also kept conceptually distinct from territorial disputes. We can define a territorial dispute as a legal conflict between two or more international persons over the territory's attribution.[24] Whereas most

---

[22] SC Res. 554 (1984). Roth, *Governmental Illegitimacy in International Law* (1999), 243.

[23] SC Res. 216 (1965); GA Res. 3116 (XXVIII). Ziccardi Capaldo, *Le situazioni territoriali illegittime nel diritto internazionale* (1977), 67.

[24] I include in territorial disputes border disputes. In fact, whereas traditionally the doctrine had differentiated between the two (e.g. La Pradelle, *La frontière. Etude de Droit Internationale* (1928), 141-

of unlawful territorial situations are also territorial disputes, this is not necessarily so, as an unlawful occupation may not be always the subject of a dispute. The case of Kosovo shows this possibility.[25] Moreover, a territorial dispute does not necessarily involve an unlawful territorial situation: the occupying state may hold a lawful title or legal basis, or neither contenders may be in possession of the disputed territory.

The concept of unlawful territorial situation is a relatively unexplored subject. The question of territorial disputes and territorial sovereignty has, on the other hand, received considerable attention in international law. Malcom Shaw's *Title to Territory in Africa* and Marcelo Kohen's *Possession contestée et souveraineté territoriale* stand out as comprehensive monographs, which shed light on both the theoretical implications surrounding the law of territory and the practice of states and international tribunals.[26] These two studies incidentally deal with the question of unlawful occupation of territories, yet the definition of unlawful territorial situation shows how this notion differs from that of territorial disputes. The issue of unlawful territorial situations only covers one specific aspect of the law of territorial sovereignty, albeit a fundamental one: rather than the issue of title to territory, it deals with the legal protection of territorial sovereignty meant as effective exercise of territorial competence. James Crawford's *The Creation of States in International Law* also considered a series of legal issues which have direct implications for the question of unlawful territorial situations.[27] In fact, the concept of statehood represents the natural development and crystallisation of a territorial situation, exactly as modern legal conceptions of territorial sovereignty

---

143; Jennings, *The Acquisition of Territory in International Law* (1963), 12; Sharma, 'Boundary Dispute and Territorial Dispute: a Comparison' 10 *Indian Journal of International Law* (1970), 162), the ICJ in 1986 observed in *Burkina Faso/Mali* that the distinction between a territorial dispute concerning attribution to territory and frontier or border disputes 'is not so much a difference in kind but rather a difference of degree as to the way the operation in question is carried out. The effect of any delimitation, no matter how small the disputed area crossed by the line, is an apportionment of the areas of land lying on either side of the line. [...] Moreover, the effect of any judicial decision rendered either in a dispute as to the attribution of territory or in a delimitation dispute, is necessarily to establish a frontier' (*Case Concerning the Frontier Dispute* (Burkina Faso/Mali), ICJ Reports 1986, 554, at 563). See also on this issue, Kohen, *Possession contestée et souveraineté territoriale* (1997), 119-126.

[25] See *infra* Ch. 6, section 4.

[26] Shaw, *Title to Territory in Africa* (1986); Kohen, *supra* n. 24.

[27] Crawford, *The Creation of States in International Law* (1979).

are derived from the same legal conceptions of statehood.[28] Other contributions have dealt with individual cases of unlawful territorial situations or specific issues related to the concept. However, the only general contribution on unlawful territorial situations is that by Giuliana Ziccardi Capaldo.[29] Ziccardi Capaldo analysed the practice of the main political organs of the UN, the SC and the General Assembly (GA), in non-recognising territorial situations in defiance of emerging international norms, and showed how these emerging international norms affected the law of territory. The main conclusion reached by the author was that non-recognition cannot be derived from a general theory of invalidity, but rather it should be construed as a sanction.[30]

All these studies, to different extents, represent the main sources of inspiration for the development of a comprehensive and self-sustaining thesis on unlawful territorial situations. The book integrates an already impressive bulk of research undertaken on issues of territorial sovereignty, in order to elaborate a comprehensive reading of the concept of unlawful territorial situation through the lens of international law as it affects these phenomena in the beginning of the 21st century. In this sense, it builds on Ziccardi Capaldo's work to develop a comprehensive study, which includes most recent questions of territorial sovereignty such as the exercise of territorial competencies by the SC.[31] It is submitted that this is of the outmost importance, since unlawful occupations of territories, often dressed up in new guises, represent one of the enduring problems of the international society, and one where lately international law has appeared to play only a peripheral role.

2. Effectiveness and legitimacy in unlawful territorial situations: preliminary questions and hypotheses

The principle of effectiveness as juristic concept attracted a considerable amount of attention in the period between the 1950s and the 1970s in continental Europe. In common law countries its existence did not go unnoticed, but it was only considered with regard to specific legal issues, such as statehood or territorial disputes. At a later stage, its use and elaboration as a general concept of international law was abandoned. This is possibly due to the perception that international law had reached a stage of development, where its function was no

---

[28] See *infra* Ch. 3, section 2.
[29] Ziccardi Capaldo, *supra* n. 23. The book was published in Italian, but it also contains a final summary in the English language.
[30] *Ibidem*, 130. For the confirmation in the present book of Ziccardi Capaldo's conclusion see *infra* Ch. 5, section 2.
[31] See *infra* Ch. 6.

longer to accept social reality as it is, but rather to promote and occasionally impose common values and normative standards of international justice. In addition, there was a shift in positivist jurisprudence towards an increasingly pragmatic approach to the study of international law, and of the development of new theoretical approaches, broadly defined post-modern, which were suspicious about modernist concepts such as effectiveness.[32] However, the problematic questions related to the role of effectiveness in international law have occasionally re-emerged. It is worth noticing that Martti Koskenniemi ably caught the ambivalence between the concreteness and normativity of international law in *From Apology to Utopia*, stressing the importance of 'effectiveness discourse' in the elaboration of statehood and territorial sovereignty in international law.[33] Moreover, despite this lack of recent attention, the Commentary on the 2001 ILC Articles on State Responsibility talks about the 'the important role played by the principle of effectiveness in international law'.[34] Quite interestingly, Kreijen's recent study *State Failure, Sovereignty and Effectiveness* captures the enduring relevance of effectiveness as one of the foundational concept of the international legal system.[35] By looking at the phenomenon of state failure in Africa, the author takes a broader and normatively critical stance towards the neglect of effectiveness as one of the principal features of international law. He states that 'the abandonment of effectiveness disrupts the relationship between law and power that is central to the proper functioning of the norms in a decentralized legal order'.[36] Some of Kreijen's views will be discussed at a later stage, suffices it to say at this stage that it is hoped that the present book will also contribute to a renewed discussion over the role of effectiveness in contemporary international law.[37]

In the present project, effectiveness constitutes the main organising concept, in other words, it represents a methodological and theoretical tool used to read and interpret the issue of unlawful territorial situations in international law. This book re-considers effectiveness as a juristic concept, by looking at its doctrinal elaboration and at the functions of international law it can contribute to explain. By looking at its doctrinal elaboration, the book shows the ambiguities inherent in the concept of effectiveness itself, as a concept that can be both situated within positive law and outside this latter. It then focuses on its main object, unlawful territorial situations, to consider the extent to which effectiveness still plays a role

---

[32] See *infra* Ch. 2, section 3.7.

[33] Koskenniemi, *From Apology to Utopia: the Structure of the International Legal Argument* (1989).

[34] Crawford (ed.), *The International Law Commission's Articles on State Responsibility: Introduction, Text and Commentaries* (2002), 110.

[35] Kreijen, *State Failure, Sovereignty and Effectiveness* (2004).

[36] *Ibidem*, 3.

[37] *Infra*, Ch. 2, section 4.

with regard to that specific issue, and to assess its interaction with principles of substantive legality as they have developed post 1945. It argues that the concept of effectiveness is deeply entrenched in the ideas of statehood and territorial sovereignty, and that the substantive principles of legality developed after World War II arose as a limitation on effectiveness. Furthermore, the book shows how these principles of legality often work at an unsophisticated level due to the inherent strength of the concept of effectiveness, as they fail to dictate a full invalidity of unlawful territorial situations, and to decisively impact on the application of other legal norms and claims. Most importantly, the choice to focus on the phenomenon of *unlawful* territorial situations unveils a driving motive and foundational question behind the present study: the truly critical aspect of the concept of effectiveness is that of the violation of international law and the creation of new law as a result of that violation. To what extent, if any, does international law recognise the effects produced by its violations, and what is the exact relationship between the original violation and subsequent recognition of legal effects?

It is often asserted that international law, unlike domestic legal systems, lacks any centralised enforcement and amendment mechanism, which is why the action of facts on the legal order is congenital.[38] As a qualification to that assertion, it is here argued that such a difference of role of *die normative Kraft des Faktischen* between international law and national law is a quantitative one, rather than a qualitative one: it is not a necessary consequence of the decentralised system of enforcement and sanction that effectiveness plays a prominent role in international law; it is rather the case that a centralised system of enforcement and sanction typical of a domestic legal system tends to be more effective, therefore the acceptance of social reality is more mediated by the action of legal norms. Those who argue for the qualitatively different role of effectiveness in the two systems tend to confuse the structure of those legal systems, indeed qualitatively different, and the core of the question, i.e. the role of facts in relation to legal norms.

In a national legal system, any violation of the law is enforceable and sanctionable by a centralised authority, which is ostensibly in a situation of impartiality and supremacy in regard to the legal persons of that system. According to Kelsen, the state has a monopoly on the use of force and, as a corollary, the use of force in a national legal system is either a wrongful act or a sanction.[39] That makes the system of sanctions normally effective because of the

---

[38] See Krüger, 'Das Prinzip der Effektivität, oder: Über die besondere Wirklichkeitsnähe des Völkerrecht', in *Festschrift für Jean Spiropulos* (1957), 265, at 268-269; Shaw, *supra* n. 26, 18; Kreijen, *supra* n. 35, 372.

[39] Kelsen, *General Theory of Law and State* (1961).

structured system in which the system of sanctions is organised: the sanctions are part of a concrete order made of a formal constitution, a system of legislation, a system of sociological and institutional mechanisms, and in particular of a number of shared values between the members of the national community, which often leads to spontaneous compliance. Behind the idea of the modern state is indeed the idea of a social contract between the members of the community that decide to renounce to settle disputes between themselves by force, and delegate the authority to settle their disputes to a centralised system of institutions. Obedience to the law is ensured both by the threat of sanctions and by the belief in a number of shared values. However, far from the ideal or the functioning society, the working of legal sanctions in a domestic legal system may be poor despite the centralisation of the mechanisms: that may be the case when the number of violations to a given norm increase, and the costs of keeping a constant and effective sanction to that violation increase as well. In turn, the increasing number of breaches of the law may depend on the lack of recognition by the members of the community of the legitimacy of the authority of the state and the institutions representing it. That may ultimately result in a revolution, the law-making violation *par excellence*. Or, more simply, it may depend on the lack of recognition by the members of the community of the legitimacy of that specific norm. In this latter case, the legislator may reach the conclusion that the conduct by the private citizens, despite representing a violation of the existing law, displays representative patterns of new values that need to find normative protection: the state has at its disposal a centralised amendment procedure that creates new law according to the new factual situation; such new law may even 'legalise' retroactively the effects of the original violation. In other words, the concept of effectiveness has its place even in a national legal system, and it is the correspondence of factual behaviours with shared values and/or with practical reasons that may lead the legislator to the amendment or creation of new law.

In international law, the enforcement mechanism is mostly based on the concept of self-help, typical of a horizontal legal system. A violation of one state's rights by another state may give rise to legitimate counter-measures by the interested state or, in certain cases, the whole international community according to the substantive value of that right.[40] In other words, the enforcement of the law is up to the very same addressees of legal norms. Sometimes, it will be possible that states party to a dispute will agree to refer their dispute to a third party, such as an international judicial body, which may eventually ascertain the illegality of the parties' conduct and enforce the law by ordering a remedy. Furthermore, at the present stage of development of international law, the system presents

---

[40] Article 22, Article 48 and Article 54, ILC Articles on State Responsibility, in Crawford, *supra* n. 34.

instances of 'verticalisation', where sanctions present some of the features typical of a domestic legal system. In the field of international peace and security, when the SC ascertains a threat or breach of international peace and security in accordance with Article 39 of the Charter, it has the power to order sanctions under Article 41 which are legally binding for all member States: the system presents a vertical mechanism of decision-making and a horizontal mechanism of implementation.[41]

A decentralised system of enforcement and sanction is normally, but not necessarily, weaker than a centralised one. States, indeed, may decide not to enforce the law due to a number of reasons. These include the need of those affected by such violations to get away with their own breaches of the law; the fact that the interests at stake may merit no more than a verbal protest; the disproportion in military and economic power between the offended state and the one breaching international law; the impossibility to reach a decision on sanctioning the unlawful conduct in the organs which are competent for such action. One should not fail to observe the fact that the same reasons may apply to the enforcement of the law and the sanction of violations in a dysfunctional state with centralised institutions and mechanism. At any rate, if the wrongful act is not sanctioned, the new unlawful situation, if effective and stable, can produce legal effects that international law may recognise. Furthermore, similarly to what happens in a domestic legal system, effective realities determined by breaches of international law may determine the amendment of the existing law, in particular in those instances where a general consensus is found in international society, and a new legal regulation determines which normative values have to be attached to the new sociological reality. This is clear in the customary process, which is one of the two ordinary law-creating facts in international law.[42]

In conclusion, it is an empirical fact, rather than a theoretically proven necessity, that because of the lack of a system of compulsory jurisdiction, because of the lack a centralised system of amendment and enforcement, and because of the less cohesive nature of the international society, the concept of effectiveness has a more prominent role in international law than in a functioning and developed domestic legal system. A case that has been very much debated, and that will be studied in detail later in this book, shows some of the complex features that relation between effectiveness and validity of the law has in current

---

[41] This enforcement procedure has been put into effect only occasionally because of the SC inaction due to the political struggles between permanent members during the Cold War and in the post Cold War era, more recently in the cases of Kosovo in 1999 and Iraq in 2003.

[42] The Truman declaration and the US and Latin American claims and effective assertions of jurisdiction on the continental shelf in the 1940s and in the 1950s represent an example of what Charles De Visscher has defined *l'effectivité en action*, that is the law-amending and progressive nature of effectiveness in the customary process (*Les effectivité du droit international public* (1967), 67).

international law.[43] Despite the claim to a customary right of humanitarian intervention, the aerial bombardment of the FRY by NATO countries in 1999 represented for many international lawyers a breach of the existing laws on the use of force as set out in Chapter VII of the UN Charter.[44] Such illegality of NATO's military operations will be fully argued at the later stage, at this stage it is simply assumed.[45] In particular the breach of Article 2(4) of the Charter is normally considered a breach of a rule of *ius cogens*. A legal system strictly based on the principle *ex iniuria ius non oritur* as envisaged by Lauterpacht[46] would not have recognised the effects of the military agreement on the decommissioning of Yugoslav troops annexed to SC Resolution 1244.[47] The Vienna Convention on the Law of Treaties (VCLT), - which is binding on all NATO countries, except for the US and Turkey, and on the Union of Serbia and Montenegro (USM) and is further considered expression of customary law by those states who have not ratified it -, declares in Article 52 that 'a treaty is void if its conclusion has been procured by the threat or use of force in violation of the principles of international law embodied in the Charter of the United Nations.' The agreement should be therefore void and non-binding on the USM, which would therefore be entitled to maintain its previous territorial status in Kosovo. Therefore, we could consider the new *status quo* an illegal territorial situation, brought about by a grave breach of international law. However, SC Resolution 1244 appears to have recognised the new state of affairs by legalising instantaneously the new territorial status.[48] Resolution 1244 did not in fact legalise the intervention, which is never mentioned in the resolution; but it recognised the new territorial situation as set out in Annex 2, and it authorised

---

[43] *Infra* Ch. 6, section 4.

[44] For different approaches reaching the same conclusions on the unlawfulness of NATO intervention in the FRY see Brownlie, 'Kosovo Crisis Inquiry:Memorandum on the International Law Aspects', and Chinkin, 'The Legality of NATO's Action in the Former Republic of Yugoslavia (FRY) under International Law', 4th Report of the House of Commons Foreign Affairs Committee, as reprinted in 49 *ICLQ* (2000), 878; Cassese, '*Ex iniuria jus* oritur: Are We Moving towards International Legitimation of Forcible Humanitarian Countermeasures in the World Community' 10 *EJIL* (1999), 23; White, 'The legality of bombing in the name of humanity' 5 *Journal of Conflict and Security Law* (2000), 27. For different conclusions envisaging the development of a new customary rule allowing humanitarian intervention see Greenwood, 'International law and the NATO intervention in Kosovo', 4th Report of the House of Commons Foreign Affairs Committee, in 49 *ICLQ* (2000), 926.

[45] See *infra* Ch. 6, para. 4.2.4.

[46] Hersch Lauterpacht stated that 'to admit that, apart from well-defined exceptions, an unlawful act, or its immediate consequences may become *suo vigore* a source of legal right for the wrongdoer is to introduce into the legal system a contradiction which cannot be solved except by a denial of its legal character.' *Recognition in International Law* (1947), 421.

[47] Annex II to SC Res. 1244 (1999). See *infra* Ch. 6, section 4.2.1.

[48] SC Res. 1244 (1999).

under Chapter VII the establishment of a military security presence led by NATO.[49] What we seem to face here is an operation of effectiveness that adapts the law to the new sociological reality. Paradoxically, the only organ resembling, at least formally, an enforcement agency gave legitimation to a territorial situation resulting from an arguably grave breach of international law. Despite repeated protests against the intervention, Russia and China participated in the legitimation of the effective situation by not opposing the resolution. Even those international lawyers who had doubted the legality of the intervention in the first place simply recorded the fact that by passing Resolution 1244 under Chapter VII the SC restored its authority in the field of international peace and security and authorised the deployment of UNMIK and KFOR. Very similar features can be observed with regard to the Coalition's intervention in Iraq in 2003 and the attempt by the SC to 'normalise' the situation with *ex post facto* resolutions adopted under Chapter VII.[50]

Do the above examples show that effectiveness prevails over the principle *ex iniuria ius non oritur*, thus allowing the automatic recognition of the effects produced by a violation of international law? One may argue that this is a part of the reality of the international legal system, or to use David Kennedy's words, the 'dark side' of international law. The argument is that international law often cannot avoid the antinomy between effectiveness and validity and 'the catastrophic alternative between either denying the normative character of international law, or creating a fiction, incapable of serving even the minimum needs of international intercourse.'[51] This realist solution, albeit an attractive one in some situations, tends to oversimplify the phenomenon of violation and sanction in international law. It ends up reducing the question of 'normalisation' of unlawful situations to the sociological power of the *fait accompli* which is not vulnerable to any form of law enforcement and sanction. Another approach would be to adopt a 'normativist' argument, by putting aside the legality of the intervention *per se*, and considering the new territorial situation as legalised by the authority of the SC through Resolution 1244. This would appear a tenable position, and it would have the advantage of denying the automatic operation of effectiveness and safeguarding the principle *ex iniuria ius non oritur*. On the other hand, apart from presenting some flaws in the specific case of Kosovo from a strictly normative point of view as far as the endorsement of NATO's authority by the SC is concerned,[52] this latter approach only shifts the argument towards the procedure through which the effects of the violation are recognised. In other

---

[49] *Ibidem*, para. 7.
[50] See SC Res. 1483 (2003); SC Res. 1511 (2003); SC Res. 1546 (2004).
[51] Marek, *Identity and Continuity of States in Public International Law* (1968, 2nd ed.), 566.
[52] For a more detailed analysis of these issues concerning Kosovo see *infra* Ch. 6, section 4.

words, the factual situation created by the illegal intervention is indeed instantaneously recognised, with the aggravating factor that the organ allowing such recognition is the organ that, more than any other international actor, should uphold the rules of international law embodied in the Charter.

The present project is committed to both formal and substantive legality. From a formal perspective, it stresses the contradiction between the existence of a rule of law in the international society, and the fact that a violation of international law can produce *per se* legal effects only because of its sociological effectiveness. From a substantive perspective, it maintains the *ultra vires* character of those Chapter VII SC Resolutions attempting to instantaneously legalise the *status quo* produced by a grave breach of the Charter. At the same time, it is committed to a sound and helpful analysis of the role international law plays within the realities of international relations. Such analysis is not carried out departing from positive norms or modelling them on power politics, but trying to catch the relation between conduct and norm, and how an unlawful situation becomes 'normalised' because of its effectiveness. The present study tries to reconcile the inherent ambivalence of effectiveness as a juristic concept on the borderline between norm and social reality, by considering the concept of legitimacy, and how legitimacy may represent the key to reconciling an effectiveness that is in violation of international law and the creation of new law in illegal territorial occupations. We can preliminarily define legitimacy as the subjective perception that a certain rule, conduct or situation corresponds to the normative values of a certain society and therefore ought to be obeyed, justified or recognised.[53] The hypothesis of the present study is that while general recognition is the process through which unlawful territorial situations can gradually become lawful, the legitimacy of the underlying claim or the legitimacy conferred by an authoritative body is the discursive tool used by occupying powers to attract recognition of the unlawful territorial situation. The ambivalence of the concept of legitimacy and the fact that, while building on the fundamental principles of the international community, it goes beyond positive international legality show how legitimacy can be a very 'efficient' complement to effective power by providing, compared to legality, for less objective and less transparent criteria of power recognition in international law.

This latter assertion supplements the often stated binary relation between legality and legitimacy, where the former reinforces the latter, and *viceversa*. Legitimacy can work *beyond the positive norms* to allow a recognition of an originally unlawful situation by the legal system. The international community, in particular through its authoritative bodies such as the SC, recalls the 'unique' or 'exceptional' nature of specific situations – in particular those where the legal

---

[53] For a thorough analysis of the concept of legitimacy see *infra* Ch. 5, section 8.

norms cannot limit hegemony - and it uses broad and often vague principles, such as the 'maintenance of peace and security', 'the protection of human rights', 'the promotion of self-determination', in order to 'normalise' the illegality. [54] By evading the troublesome question of the relation between the violation of the applicable norms and the recognition of its effects, it paradoxically maintains the general validity of those norms, at the same time offering a practical solution to the normative force of (illegal) facts. In conclusion, the present work looks closely at those instances where effective power and legitimacy go hand in hand and sideline positive legality; and how the legal system reacts to such operation.[55]

While this book limits itself to analyse the specific issue of unlawful territorial situations, and the methodology adopted does not allow general conclusions on the current state of international law or on the broader relevance of the concept of effectiveness in contemporary international law, it is submitted that the reconciliation between effectiveness, legality and legitimacy may be possibly tested in other related areas of international law, such as the use of force, statehood and governmental recognition. Thus, the book not only offers a general study on unlawful territorial situations, but also offers an original theoretical perspective, which may shed some light and stimulate debate on how contemporary international law is conceived, and the function it plays in international relations. In other words, is international law a vehicle of international justice, or rather, does it represent a code of legitimation of the will and actions of the stronger? Alternatively, is it exactly by legitimising the will and actions of the stronger that international goes beyond the strict constructs of positive legality to promote international justice? Again, it is hoped that this book will contribute to the debate on these fundamental questions.[56]

Finally, one working assumption should be made clear at the very outset. It will be assumed that international law is defined as a system of objective and determinate legal norms created by states, and, for the most part, addressed to states primarily to regulate their behaviour. This is not a general epistemological choice, but it represents the best description of international law as it relates to

---

[54] On the tensions and the possibility of co-existence of sovereign equality and positivism, on the one hand, and hegemony, on the other, see Cosnard, 'Sovereign equality – "the *Wimbledon* sails on", in Byers, Nolte (eds.), *United States Hegemony and the Foundation of International Law* (2003), 117.

[55] This function of legitimacy *beyond* positive legality can be reconciled with Franck's concept of legitimacy as procedural fairness that responds to a community need for order. Indeed, the role of legitimacy as a factor promoting and boosting effectiveness in the context of unlawful territorial situations shows the priority given by the international community to order over justice. See Franck, *Fairness in International Law and Institutions* (1995), 25-46.

[56] A novel interest in the international legal literature for the impact of power relations on international law is signalled by Michael Byers' monograph, *Custom, Power, and the Power of Rules* (1999). Byers' study differs from the present book insofar as it focuses on the distinctive issue of customary rules' creation and modification.

issues of territorial sovereignty. This assumption is based on the recognition that, while states are not the only actors, they are the major actors in our analysis of unlawful territorial situations. In fact this book also takes account of the position of peoples, national liberation movements and international organisations in challenging or, alternatively, endorsing unlawful territorial occupations. Moreover, this choice does not detract from the important role played by individuals and collective human groups other than states in the broader legal process associated to unlawful territorial situations. For instance, individuals and civil society, through non-governmental organisations, can seek to enforce legal claims with regard to human rights violations carried out by the occupying power before regional tribunals, or, in some cases, even before the courts of the occupying power.[57] On the other hand, civil society may also play a distinctive role in contesting territorial occupations and putting pressure on occupying powers to make them comply with international humanitarian law or human rights law, or, alternatively, in supporting the effectiveness of the occupying power on the ground.[58] This legal dimension of unlawful territorial situations, involving the role of non-state actors and fundamental issues of human rights law and international humanitarian law, is not absent, but is dealt with only incidentally. Indeed, its analysis would require a full and extensive enquiry, which would be beyond the purpose and scope of the present work.

3. Book plan

The present book is structured in six chapters. Chapter 2 deals with the concept of effectiveness as a juristic concept. It addresses the conceptual meaning of effectiveness, its doctrinal elaboration within positivist jurisprudence, and the different functions it plays in the way international law affects international relations. In particular, it looks at the ambiguity of effectiveness as a concept that can be simultaneously located within positive law and outside positive law. Chapter 3 considers the impact of the concept of effectiveness on the law of territory. It shows how effectiveness is deeply entrenched in well-established ideas of statehood, and how those ideas have been transposed to the legal idea of territory and territorial sovereignty. It examines its function in the traditional modes of territorial acquisition and in the law of belligerent occupation. Chapter

---

[57] E.g., *Loizidou, supra* n. 13; *The General Security Service Torture Case*, Israeli Supreme Court (1999), in XI *Palestine Yearbook of International Law* (2000/2001), 261.

[58] E.g. Amnesty International, 'Israel and the Occupied Territories. The heavy price of Israeli incursions', Report of 12 April 2002, in <http://web.amnesty.org/library>. The Yesha Council: Council of Jewish communities in Judea, Samaria and Gaza District, in <http://www.moetzetyesha.co.il/archive_list.asp>.

4 focuses on the unlawfulness of territorial situations, in other words it spells out those principles and norms of substantive legality, which define when a territorial situation is unlawful and limit the action of effectiveness in that respect. The legal principles considered are the prohibition to use force to change territorial status, the principle of *uti possidetis*, the principle of self-determination and the principle of territorial integrity. Chapter 5 looks at the consequences of territorial unlawfulness as defined by the above principles. It analyses the limitations to the concept of territorial invalidity inherent in legality discourse as a result of the dualism between national and international spheres, thereby confirming the enduring strength of the concept of effectiveness in territorial issues. It assesses the impact of a definition of unlawfulness upon related areas of international law such as the *ius ad bellum*, statehood and the law of state responsibility. It also considers the importance played by legitimacy in the 'legalisation' of effective territorial occupations, showing the complexity of the relation between effectiveness, legality and legitimacy in the case of Iraq. Chapter 6 considers the territorial competencies of the UN, in particular of the SC, and how the exercise of such powers can produce or perpetuate an unlawful territorial situation. It spells out the criteria of effectiveness, legality and legitimacy to which such competencies are subject, and it considers the case of Kosovo as an example of unlawful territorial situation involving an *ultra vires* action by the SC, but also a reconciliation of effectiveness, legality and legitimacy in the longer run. Chapter 7 finally concludes recalling the main findings of the book concerning the possibility of reconciling the tensions between effectiveness, legality and legitimacy. It also reverses Jellinek's famous expression *die normative Kraft des Faktischen*, by considering *die faktische Kraft des Normativen*; it assesses the effectiveness of international law towards unlawful territorial situations, thereby showing the inherent ambivalence of the concept of effectiveness itself.

CHAPTER 2

THE CONCEPT OF EFFECTIVENESS IN INTERNATIONAL LAW

1. Introduction

The relationship between social reality and law is a basic problem of every legal order. Legal philosophers have debated this crucial question for centuries, without finding a conclusive argument supporting an ultimate causal relationship between the two. The arguments have tended to move back and forth between the two extremes of normativity and concreteness, to use Koskenniemi's words.[1] On the one hand, every norm having a legal nature must be referred to reality. A norm providing for the prohibition of mammoth hunting is valid in the eyes of the strictest of positivists, if it derives from a formal source of law. However, it would obviously represent a nonsense as a rule of conduct trying to regulate behaviour in a contemporary society. On the other hand, to reduce norms to reality, that is to give them only a descriptive substance of what is already in the world of facts, would be tantamount to the negation of the normative order itself. For instance, a norm simply stating 'you can commit murder under any circumstance when carrying a loaded gun' would certainly be a fair description of everyday reality. However, it would not a represent a rule of conduct, in the sense that it would simply record a physical and social phenomenon. In other words, the world of the 'is' and the world of the 'ought to be' cannot be exclusive in a legal order, unless we are ready to accept that the legal order may become a formalistic fiction.

Normativity and concreteness are continuously in dialectical tension within international legal discourse, yet they are both necessary but not sufficient conditions of the discourse itself. In the analysis of unlawful territorial situations in international law, the term effectiveness recalls the second of the two terms, the material part of a certain situation, whereas the term unlawful draws from the normativity and validity of international law. Effectiveness is one of the founding characteristics of classic international law in territorial matters. Demands for legal order and certainty in international relations surely exceeded demands for international justice in pre-1945 international law. Therefore, the adaptation of law to reality was a paramount element in international law, and therefore the material element played an important role in territorial situations. What the present research tries to explore is the contemporary relevance of effectiveness in

---

[1] Koskenniemi, *From Apology to Utopia: the Structure of the International Legal Argument* (1989).

respect to territorial matters, and, in particular, in relation to unlawful territorial situations. Despite arguments to the contrary, territory and sovereignty are still among the most sensitive issues of states' and peoples' international life. Testing the validity and efficacy of international law in respect to these issues is a task that can shed relevant light on the stage of development of international law today.

This chapter and the following one concentrate on the material element of territorial situations, whereas normativity is considered in the fourth and fifth chapters. This chapter considers the concept of effectiveness in international law using a broad theoretical perspective. Its main objective is to look into the theoretical and historical premises that sparked the doctrinal debate on effectiveness mostly in the 1950s and in the 1960s. This doctrinal debate is analysed, as well as more recent criticism from liberal international lawyers and critical legal studies representatives. The chapter draws some conclusions on the enduring ambiguities and questions surrounding the role of effectiveness in international law.

2. Effectiveness in international law: terminological and conceptual features

To what does the term effectiveness refer in international law and within the present project? *Effectiveness* is deployed here as a measure of the relationship and congruence between a rule or a legal situation and social reality. It mainly refers to the role of factual situations in respect to the application and creation of international law. Therefore, it corresponds to the material, factual element of law, to its concreteness. A state is recognised as such in international law because it is constituted by a stable and effective institutional machinery, an insurrectional movement is responsible under international law because it has effective control over a population and territory,[2] sovereignty over a territory is often conditional on an effective display of jurisdiction, the citizenship of an individual may be recognised in international law insofar as it entails an underlying effective

---

[2] The international legal personality of insurrectional movements, which gain independence and effective control in the course of a civil conflict, is accepted in modern and contemporary international law. See Article 10 (2), ILC Articles on State Responsibility. More controversial is the test of effectiveness in relation to the national liberation movements, where the claim to legal representation and the recognition of such claim by states and international organisations (in particular the UN) is sometimes detached from an effective control of a territorial basis. This was true for the PLO until the signature of the Oslo Accords in 1993, where the Palestinian Authority was granted a limited territorial jurisdictional in the Gaza Strip and East Jerusalem. On the question of the international legal personality of the PLO see also Italian Court of Cassation, Judgement n. 1981, 28 June 1985 in 69 *Rivista di diritto internazionale* (1986), 884.

relationship ('genuine link')[3] between the state and the individual, the membership to a minority or ethnic group may be determined under objective criteria of effective attachment.[4] In all these cases, effectiveness is in general a necessary, and often sufficient, element of a certain juridical situation. Unlawful territorial situations seemingly do not escape this strict logic, at the very least because they very often involve a situation where a certain state or potential entity is effectively displaying power over a certain territory despite the *prima facie* unlawfulness of the situation. A legal order which does not maintain itself into a relationship with social reality would be a useless abstract notion. Yet a problem arises where effectiveness allows the creation of law starting from an illegal act. Here, we encounter the concept of revolution, which has always been a critical point for lawyers, and it is particularly critical for the present study.

Some terminological qualifications may help in comprehending the concept we are analysing. *Effectiveness* has also been used interchangeably with the terms *compliance* and *efficacy*, however, the three terms should be distinguished for the purpose of the present project. Compliance is usually referred to as the conformity of states' actions to some legal prescriptions. Efficacy designates a broader concept. It is usually deployed in legal theory referring to the fulfilment of a certain social scope by a certain rule. For instance, if we consider alcohol-related legislation in Britain, we might measure its efficacy by the social results obtained in relation to the intentions of the legislature. Compliance, instead, refers to the conformity of British citizens to these behavioural regulations. The same could apply to an international treaty, for example, the Kyoto Protocol, which imposes some limitations on states' emission of greenhouse gases. Its efficacy will be measured on the objective to limit the greenhouse effect. Compliance will instead measure how many Western states have reduced the emission of greenhouse gases by a certain percentage within a certain time, as prescribed by the protocol. The sociological approach to international law has concentrated both on efficacy and compliance, and this may have some interesting implications for a study of the principle of effectiveness as a juristic concept; however, efficacy and compliance are not the object of this chapter.[5]

---

[3] *Nottebohm* case (Liechtenstein/Guatemala), ICJ Reports 1955, 23. See also Article 3 (2) ICJ Statute; *Mergé Claim*, 22 *ILR* (1955), 443. However, see *contra* the rejection by the ICJ of an effective control test for corporate entities in *Barcelona Traction* (Belgium/Spain), ICJ Reports 1970, 3, at 42.

[4] *Rights of Minorities in Upper Silesia*, 1926 PCIJ Series A, n. 12. But see also dissenting opinion from Judge Nyholm warning on the dangers of rigid objective criteria. More recently compare the jurisprudence of the *ad hoc* tribunal for Rwanda. In particular, *Prosecutor v. Akayesu*, ICTR, Case 96-4-T, in 37 *ILM* (1998), 1399 confirming effectiveness of attachment and *Prosecutor v. Kayshama and Ruzindana*, ICTR, Case 95-1-T, in <http://www.ictr.org/default.htm>, going towards a subjective definition of ethnic group.

[5] Why do efficacy and compliance have interesting implications for effectiveness? The consistent pattern in the lack of application of a certain norm led some writers (Touscoz, *Le principe d'effectivité*

They become useful tools, when the effectiveness of international law in respect to unlawful territorial situations is tested.

One last use of the term *effectiveness* is in respect of the efficacy of international tribunals and treaty instruments, in particular to those interpretative devices used to confer efficacy on the treaty provisions constituting international organisations.[6] As a measure of effectiveness of tribunals, it is usual to refer to those interpretations that look at the parties' intention, in order to make a treaty a living instrument according to changing reality. In a sense, this can be considered a wider application of the principle of effectiveness in its function of adaptation of law to reality. However, analysis on the effectiveness of tribunals has concentrated mostly on the implementation of social objectives sought within the spirit of the conventional instrument. That is why effectiveness in this context resembles the concept of efficacy of treaty instruments.[7]

In an attempt to provide a preliminary working definition, we may consider effectiveness as a *legal-normative* organising concept, which helps comprehend the transformation of effective realities into international law. It possibly represents the concept *par excellence* showing the concreteness and material nature of international law. However, its exact nature as a device situated on the borderline between law and social reality, or, alternatively, as a device situated within international legal norms has been disputed. From the latter approach, one derives that effectiveness should be kept conceptually separated from overlapping concept of 'socio-legal' effectiveness, efficacy or compliance. From the former, one may infer that these concepts may end up overlapping. The present chapter attempts to clarify these ambiguities that deeply inform the theoretical discussion over the concept of effectiveness.

---

dans l'ordre international (1964) and J. Stone, 'What Price Effectiveness' *Proceedings American Society of International Law* (1951), 199) to talk about *desuetude* of a certain rule and the loss of its normative value. In this case, the lack of compliance and efficacy of a certain norm touches upon its legal value, therefore *compliance, efficacy* and *effectiveness* overlap, however the three terms should be in principle kept distinct. Concerning this dual meaning of effectiveness see conclusions at Ch. 7.

[6] In particular Lauterpacht, *The Development of International Law by the International Court* (1958), 227.

[7] On the effectiveness of the ICJ, see Peck, Lee (eds.), *Increasing the Effectiveness of the International Court of Justice: Proceedings of the ICJ/UNITAR Colloquium to Celebrate the 50th Anniversary of the Court* (1997).

3. Effectiveness in the doctrinal debate

Jellinek is probably the first author to theorise a principle of effectiveness, even if in his work it was never referred to by name.[8] According to him, the relationship between fact and law in the creation of abstract norms either lies in the psychological attitude of people to consider as law what is customarily repeated in a given society; or the normative force of the fact lies in the fact itself, insofar as whatever exists in a stable way in the phenomenological reality has the tendency to transform itself into law. Thus, international law conceives the state as a social given, it accepts the *de facto* government as representative and with international capacity, and adverse prescription and occupation as titles to territory. Although some other contributions on the principle of effectiveness can be traced back to the inter-war period, the doctrinal debate is concentrated mostly in the three decades following the end of World War II.[9]

The existing law in those years was still exclusively based on the substantive and procedural framework of classic international law with the exception of the prohibition on the use of force as expressed in the UN Charter. The development of concepts like self-determination, *ius cogens* and *erga omnes* obligations at the end of the 1960s and the 1970s certainly represented a substantial limitation on the operation of the principle of effectiveness, and that may be why it is difficult to find many subsequent references to it. Yet it has been rightly pointed out that the

---

[8] Jellinek, *Allgemeine Staatslehre* (1922).

[9] Kelsen, 'Theorié generalé du droit international public' 42 *Recueil des Cours* (1932), 121; Kelsen, *Principles of International Law* (1952); Kelsen, *General Theory of Law and State* (1961); Ottolenghi, 'Il principio di effettività e la sua funzione nell'ordinamento internazionale' 15 *Rivista di diritto internazionale* (1936), 3, 151, 363; Sperduti, *L'individuo nel diritto internazionale: contributo all'interpretazione del diritto internazionale secondo il principio dell'effettività* (1950); Bellini, 'Il principio generale dell'effettività' 27 *Annuario di diritto internazionale comparato e di studi legislativi* (1951), 225; Tucker, 'The Principle of Effectiveness in International Law', in Lipsky (ed.), *Law and Politics in the World Community* (1953), 31; Bouchez, 'The concept of effectiveness as applied to territorial sovereignty over sea-areas, air space and outer space' 4 *Nederlands Tijdschrift voor Internationaal Recht* (1957), 151; Krüger, 'Das Prinzip der Effektivität, oder: Über die besondere Wirklichkeitsnähe des Völkerrecht', in *Festschrift fuer Jean Spiropulos* (1957), 265; Mjaja de la Muela, *El Principio de Effectividad en Derecho Internacional* (1958); Touscoz, *supra* n. 5; Jennings, 'Nullity and Effectiveness in International Law', in *Cambridge Essays in International Law* (1965), 64; De Visscher, *Les effectivité du droit international public* (1967); Balekjian, *Die Effektivität und die Stellung Nichtanerkannter Staaten im Völkerrecht* (1970); Chemillier-Gendreau, 'A propos de l'effectivité dans l'ordre international' 11 *Revue belge de droit international* (1975), 38; Wildeman, 'The Philosophical Background of Effectiveness' 24 *Netherlands International Law Journal* (1977), 335.

For more recent appraisals see Juste Ruiz, *Derecho Internacional Público* (1994); Miele, *La comunità internazionale* (2000, 3rd ed.); Cassese, *International Law* (2001); Di Stefano, *L'ordre international entre légalité et effectivité* (2002); Kreijen, *State Failure, Sovereignty and Effectiveness* (2004).

new principles of substantive legality build on the framework of existing international law, rather than replace it.[10]

3.1 Effectiveness and international law: continental affair?

The international legal literature relating to the principle of effectiveness in the aftermath of World War II was initially developed in continental Europe, and preliminarily appears to have received little interest from Anglo-American writers. Is there any particular reason behind this geographical characterisation of the doctrinal debate?

We must first look at the intellectual debate on international politics that took place in the Western world in the years after World War II, when there was a reaction against the idealistic political notions that had been shaped between the two World Wars. Concepts of self-determination, international organisation, and universal peace were blamed by many observers for having failed to observe reality and to control the expansion of aggressive and totalitarian powers. It was felt that people studying international society needed to go back to what really counts in inter-state life, that is the real power seen both in military and economic terms.[11] Any attempt to shape the world on new idealistic projects would lead to another risky misjudgement of the balance of power in the international community and to the inability to develop a sound policy of containment of hegemonic and aggressive powers. The criticism of political idealism as utopian was also extended to international law. Austin's philosophy defining international law as 'positive morality' became newly fashionable. How could a system of norms be compelling for states, if there did not exist any enforcement agency and compulsory jurisdiction? The answer was simple. States would follow rules of international law only as long as their self-interest was pursued. Every norm obliging them to do something contrary to their political interest would be ignored. The conclusion was that such a thing called 'international law' did not exist, and if a set of rules existed, they regulated only processes of secondary importance. An autonomous analysis of the reality of international society needed to be carried out. This could be an analysis on the powers involved in the international arena and should not be interested in the study of abstract norms.

This feeling was particularly strong in the US, which was for the first time the only Western super-power, also facing an enhanced threat from the Soviet Union. The 1950s and 1960s saw in the US both a separation of the two disciplines of international relations and international law,[12] and, at the same time, the development of McDougal's policy-oriented jurisprudence in Yale. This

---

[10] Cassese, *supra* n. 9, 31.
[11] See Boyle, *World Politics and International Law* (1985).
[12] E.g. Morgenthau, *Politics among Nations: the Struggle for Power and Peace* (1967).

latter approach, albeit not rejecting the idea of international law as such, conceived it as a process of authoritative decision-making, where rules and their interpretations played a role in this process, rather than being the true and objective 'essence' of international law. Power structures and authority would also play a fundamental role in this decision-making process, in other words, they would represent an endogenous element of international law.[13] In Western Europe, the memories of a collective tragedy were very fresh and the division in two opposing worlds was present in everyday life. If the project of a new realism in the analysis of international society had a strong appeal, the natural consequence of this was not considered to be a complete separation of the two disciplines and an implicit preference for international relations, or a new approach that would transform the idea of international law as a system of legal rules equally binding upon all members of the international society. This separation would lead to an apologist approach to the analysis of international society that in the European environment could not be accepted. International law would be useful, for example, in making clear that every intervention against the independence of states would not be admitted, and this principle linked both Marxist and conservative observers. International law was considered to be functional to a diminished role of Western European countries in the international arena.

Furthermore, the positivist tradition and the influence of Kelsen on international lawyers was strong. The Kelsenian idea that if there had to be an international legal system it had to be based on a set of positive norms, creating a self-sustaining structure independent from the social reality, shaped the whole jurisprudential debate in continental Europe. The debate was between those who supported Kelsen's 'pure' theory of law, and those who considered his theory another dangerous idealistic abstraction failing to record the disruptive influence of reality on norms (Marxist theorists and realist theorists reached about the same conclusion). However, the abandonment of an international legal system as a system of given and ascertainable legal norms was not an issue at all for Kelsen's critics, since this was considered destructive of the world order. Sociological jurisprudence deviated from Kelsen's pure theory of law, above all stressing differences of degree in the use of methodological instruments (empirical and inductive approach), but it maintained its main assumptions (objectivity and normativity of law). The call for a realist approach to the study of international society was not effected through a shift towards the creation of international relations theory or through new conceptions of international law, but through an incorporation of factual elements in the law-making and amending process,

---

[13] McDougal, 'International Law, Power and Policy: A Contemporary Conception' 82 *Recueil des Cours* (1953), 133.

which became the main function of the principle of effectiveness. Its progressive idea of the social reality could not but believe in a continuous shaping of the normative processes by factual situations. Therefore, a study on the principle of effectiveness was an absolute priority for those international lawyers.

Another issue which is relevant to the understanding of the doctrinal discussion on the principle of effectiveness in the 1950s, in the 1960s and in the first part of the 1970s is the codification of new areas of activity by states. The new technological means at states' disposal brought their interest to consider the benefits involved in the use of the Antarctica, the outer space, the high seas and the seabed. Multilateral regimes were negotiated as a consequence of rapid changes in social reality. The need to regulate them in a prompt manner led states to conclude multilateral treaties. In order to understand the incorporation into international law by states and international organisations of the historical and phenomenological order, international lawyers often used the principle of effectiveness as an additional analytical tool outside the customary process. This interpretation and applicative function of the principle was proposed by the French and Belgian sociological positivism, in particular by such authors as Touscoz,[14] De Visscher[15] and Chemillier-Gendreau.[16]

The question of the existence of a general principle of effectiveness was rarely dealt with in the Anglo-American literature. Tucker's contribution was the only systematic work and needs to be put in the context of the sceptical approach to international law which turned quickly to international relations theory.[17] In the English literature, for example, it is impossible to find a single systematic study on the principle of effectiveness. At most, effectiveness was considered in relation to specific issues like the application of foreign laws in domestic courts,[18] the recognition of governments,[19] territorial disputes,[20] the validity of a legal system[21] and the invalidity of international acts.[22]

In proposing his concept of *diritto spontaneo* ('spontaneous law'), Ago seems to give some suggestions on the place of effectiveness in the continental legal tradition as opposed to the Anglo-American one.[23] In Ago's view, legal norms are

---

[14] Touscoz, *supra* n. 5.

[15] De Visscher, *supra* n. 9.

[16] Chemillier-Gendreau, *supra* n. 9.

[17] Tucker, *supra* n. 9.

[18] Mann, 'Present Validity of Nazi Nationality Laws' 89 *Law Quarterly Review* (1973), 201.

[19] Lauterpacht, *Recognition in International Law* (1947).

[20] Jennings, *The Acquisition of Territory in International Law* (1963); Shaw, *Title to Territory in Africa* (1986); Brownlie, *Principles of International Law* (2003, 6th ed.).

[21] Hart, *The Concept of Law* (1994, 2nd ed.), 292.

[22] Jennings admits that 'it is a curious fact that relatively little has been written, at any rate in English' (*supra* n. 9, 64).

[23] Ago, *Scienza giuridica e diritto internazionale* (1950).

not exclusively the result of certain processes determined by the law (he talks about positive law in a narrow sense, because it is 'posited' by something external to it), but the social reality itself would be its source.[24] Ago maintained that this construction of reality as a source of law is normal among Anglo-American lawyers, as common law accepts the idea of a spontaneous creation of law through judicial policies.[25] Hart argued along the same anti-dogmatic lines as Ago and stated that the crucial problem of the fundamental norm cannot be solved but through a reference to law-creating facts (to be kept distinct from legal law-creating facts, that is formal sources). This would emerge very clearly in a system like the English one, where the sovereignty of parliament is not an abstract postulate embodied in a constitutional charter, but it is part of an historical process in which the existence and content of rules is also derived from courts, officials and private persons' practices.[26] Wildeman apparently supported Ago's idea, by saying that the emergence of legal principle from factual reality is a given in common law systems, since the judge is continuously legislating by departing from concrete cases.[27]

In opposition to Ago and Wildeman, Sereni argued that this was a misinterpretation of the rule of precedent in the common law tradition.[28] This tradition is based in Sereni's perspective on a natural law conception, where the law is not exclusively a creation of the state. The sovereign government itself is subordinated to the law, and the introduction of this idea in civil law countries through constitutions would be historically later than in the Anglo-American world. Furthermore, he argued that the idea itself of the doctrine of precedent was grounded on the impossibility that the pre-existent law can be modified by new factual situations. The same conclusion was reached by Mann who maintained that 'whatever legal philosophers may have to say about it, there is no evidence that English law accepts the legitimating characters of facts, that is to say, in Jellinek's famous phrase, the 'Normative Kraft des Faktischen', or the alleged principle of effectiveness, as a guide in the sense that facts or effectiveness create law and the absence of effectiveness involves the denial of a legal order.'[29]

It seems likely that the more pragmatic and case law oriented Anglo-American tradition led the doctrine to look at effectiveness in international law either in respect to specific issues or as a measure of efficacy of international tribunals and

---

[24] Ago, 'Positive Law and International Law' 51 *AJIL* (1957), 691.

[25] Ago, *supra* n. 23, 91-92.

[26] Hart, *supra* n. 21, 109-110.

[27] Wildeman, *supra* n. 9, 351. The author maintains that in the Anglo-American tradition there 'was a practical belief that "ius ex facto oritur", and it was the duty of the judge to find it.'

[28] Sereni, 'Dottrine italiane di diritto internazionale', in *Scritti di diritto internazionale in onore di Tommaso Perassi* (1950), Vol. 2, 281.

[29] Mann, *supra* n. 18, 203.

international law. However, to deny the law-making force of factual reality in the jurisprudence of common law countries is to deny the fact that, certainly more than in civil law countries, the law is not only the result of sovereign will expressed through legislation (and in this respect Sereni disputed Ago's arguments stating exactly the same), but it is also created through judicial policies and customary processes. The systematic theoretical approach taken in continental Europe in regard to the principle of effectiveness is probably due to the predominant influence played by the debate between Jellinek's, Schmitt's and Kelsen's jurisprudence, and its application in international legal theory. Furthermore, the influence of sociological positivism in France and the widespread criticism of Kelsen's theories developed in Italy in the post-War period represented a fertile ground for the elaboration of a general principle of effectiveness.[30] This, rather than an inherent abstract normativism of common law jurisprudence as opposed to a more 'material' approach to law in the European continent, would explain the continental focus on effectiveness in particular in the 1950s and the 1960s.

This is also confirmed by the fact that, despite a systematic treatment being initiated in the 1930s and developing in the post-War period, the legal roots of effectiveness can be dated back to the modern 19th century positivist theory of international personality and sources, which is fully shared by British and American jurisprudence of that age. We now turn briefly to this historical and jurisprudential enquiry.

3.2 The law of nations and effectiveness in the 19th century: peoples' sovereignty and the material element of custom

Despite being systematically theorised in a more recent age, a material notion of international law dates back hundreds of years, and a more or less explicit incorporation of a principle of effectiveness is inherent in the development of different legal institutions. Issues of personality and sources were the most debated points of positivist jurisprudence as it started to develop in the second half of the 18th century. The historical development of the concept of effectiveness in relation to issues of territorial sovereignty is dealt with in more depth in the next chapter.

As far as issues of international personality are concerned, it is important to look at the practice of recognition as it developed throughout the centuries. Throughout the 16th, the 17th and the first half of the 18th century recognition of foreign governments was not a preoccupation of European monarchies, unless

---

[30] E.g. Sperduti, *La fonte suprema dell'ordinamento internazionale* (1946); Giuliano, *La comunità internazionale* (1950).

there were rival succession claims and different pretenders. As Grewe points out, even 'the succession in electoral monarchies such as the Holy Roman Empire of the Germans or the Kingdom of Poland was regarded as an internal process which did not normally offer other powers a cause or justification for taking a position.'[31] When the separation of a part of the state occurred through dynastic succession, the practice of third states was to wait for recognition until the former sovereign had first given its own approval.[32] The first author to put forward the principle of effectiveness as opposed to a principle of legitimacy as a guiding principle for the recognition of new governments was Vattel, who preceded the actual development of this principle in states' practice.[33] The principle of effectiveness was embraced with great favour by the French monarchy and its foreign policy based on the rationalist principles of the *raison d'état*. France's attitude to the American revolution is the most clear expression of this approach. Shortly after the Declaration of Independence of 1776, France concluded a treaty of commerce and friendship and a military agreement of joint defence with the new government. On 14 March 1778, the French government informed London of these treaties and stated that the implicit recognition of the US was based on the effective independence of the colonies. Evidence of this was the application by the British government of the ordinary laws of war as they were recognised between sovereign states, that British forces had signed capitulation agreements with American forces and that the British government was dispatching commissioners with the purpose of peace negotiations with the Congress.[34] The British government responded that the situation was that of a mere rebellion, and stated that France had no right to intervene and support the unlawful activities of British citizens in North America. The French memorandum replied that it was not relevant whether independence had been obtained on a lawful basis and that neither the law of nations nor treaties, neither morality nor politics imposed a duty on France to preserve the loyalty of British colonies. It was sufficient that the American colonies had established themselves not only through a solemn declaration, but also factually, despite the British attempts to defeat them.[35]

Although the French revolution did not lead to the development of a new European public law, its ideals of self-determination and sovereignty of peoples can also be seen as having contributed to the decay of principles of legitimacy in

---

[31] Grewe, *The Epochs of International Law* (2000), 343.
[32] Frowein, 'Die Entwicklung der Anerkennung von Staaten und Regierungen in Völkerrecht' 11 *Der Staat* (1972), 145.
[33] The Swiss author wrote that '[p]our qu'une nation ait droit de figurer dans cette grand société, il suffit qu'elle soit véritablement souveraine et indépendante, c'est-à-dire qu'elle se gouverne elle-même, par sa propre autorité et par ses lois.' De Vattel, *Les droit des gens* (1758), Vol. 1, Ch. 1, 4.
[34] Grewe, *supra* n. 31, 348.
[35] Martens, *Causes célèbres du droit des gens* (1859, 2nd ed.), Vol. III, 140.

the recognition of governments.[36] This meant, in principle, a duty of non-intervention upon all European nations in respect of revolutionary events that would lead to a domestic constitutional upheaval. As a corollary of the idea of individual rights, revolutionary thought produced the idea of natural rights of sovereign states. In other words, the state was to be considered a natural person to which some inherent rights and duties would be attached. States would be sovereign and equal. Their legal existence would not be the result of a determination by rules of monarchic legitimacy, but would arise as a sociological expression of peoples' will. It goes without saying that this would go hand in hand with the application of a principle of effectiveness in the theory of international personality.[37]

Yet a discourse on the philosophical-theoretical basis of the concept of effectiveness cannot neglect to observe some profound contradictions that characterised this period. The practice of France from 1789 to the Congress of Vienna soon forgot these ideals and as Grewe has pointed out by the time 'the French armed expansion extended to the greater part of Europe the Revolution had come to an ideological standstill, its ideas began to fade away and its postulates had in large part been abandoned.'[38] The ideals of the Revolution needed to be exported and the duty of non-intervention in the internal affairs of other states as a result of their equality was soon replaced by revolutionary missionarism accompanied by a concept of just war.[39] In other words, France was more equal among equals, and often the ascertainment of peoples' will through plebiscite became a pure formality.[40] Furthermore, the non-universal nature of international law in the 19th century should be borne in mind. The acceptance of non-European nations within the family of nations still built on the idea of the standard of civilisation. The recognition of a quasi-sovereign status to African and Asian political communities was often conditioned on the very acceptance by these communities of unequal treaties and protectorate agreements that, rather

---

[36] Redslob, 'Völkerrechtlichen Ideen der Französischen Revolution', in *Festgabe für O. Mayer* (1916), 273.

[37] Frowein notes that these ideas of nation and peoples' sovereignty were linked after First World War to a notion of peoples' self-determination. Effectiveness as a rationalist criterion of recognition is linked by the US and Great Britain to the consensus of people (Frowein, *supra* n. 32, 228). See in this respect also Lauterpacht, *supra* n. 19, at 115, 172.

[38] *Ibidem*, 412.

[39] Schmitt, *Der Nomos der Erde im Völkerrecht des Ius Public Europaeum* (1950), 122.

[40] Disregard for peoples' will is indicated by the memoirs of General Dumuroiez about the plebiscite in Austrian Belgium in 1795 (Grewe, *supra* n. 31, 421), and it is also clear in regard to the 'sale' of Venice to Austria through the Treaty of Campoformio in 1797.

than celebrate their sovereignty, were an official seal for political dependence and ineffectiveness.[41]

Alexandrowicz provides us with a deep insight into the jurisprudential debate that the revolutionary events produced mostly in the German jurisprudence between the end of the 18th century and the beginning of the 19th. Both legitimist and de-factoist theories were to different degrees represented and this witnesses the disputes typical of the age of transition when these international lawyers lived.[42] Also, in the practice of states, the Holy Alliance reaffirmed in the 1820's century a principle of monarchic legitimacy through a system of collective security, which was rejected only by Great Britain, and led to the repression of republican insurgencies in Spain and Italy.[43] However, this seems to be the last episode and since then effectiveness became the main criterion of recognition in modern positivism and the law of nations of the 19th century.[44]

This conclusion is reinforced by the development throughout the 19th century in the American continent of what Alvarez calls the American public law based on the principles of republicanism, constitutionalism, democracy, liberalism, equality of nations and non-intervention.[45] Drawing from the Monroe Doctrine (1823), which formed the basis of a consistent refusal of the US to allow any further colonial enterprise by European powers, Latin American countries created a net of political and economic relations through a series of treaty instruments that would give a distinctive character to the international law of the American continent, which would go beyond the mere pronouncement of the Monroe doctrine mostly elaborated according to the US national interest. Such international law would be generally based on the rule of law in diplomatic relations and in particular on the principle of non-intervention, of self-determination of nations and of amicable settlement of disputes. Despite a series of hegemonic and unfriendly acts by the US like the Clayton-Bulwer Treaty (1850) and the proposal of its government to carry out a collective intervention

---

[41] Anghie, 'Finding the Peripheries: Sovereignty and Colonialism in Nineteenth-Century International Law' 39 *Harvard International Law Journal* (1999), 1. See also *infra* Ch. 3, section 3.2.

[42] Alexandrowickz, 'The Theory of Recognition *in Fieri*' 34 *BYIL* (1958), 176. See also Simpson, *Great Powers and Outlaw States* (2004), especially Ch. 4.

[43] Lauterpacht, *supra* n. 19, 103.

[44] The context is the law of nations defined as the European Public Law, that is international law governing among all European Christian states plus the United States and Latin American countries. Turkey was admitted as a full sovereign member of the 'family of nations' in 1856, and Japan in 1906. Outside this exclusive circle effectiveness did not apply, yet some states were often given partial recognition on condition of surrendering part of their competence to the colonial state. In other words, ineffectiveness was a condition of recognition. See *infra* Ch. 3, section 3.2 and Anghie, *supra* n. 41.

[45] See state practice in the American continent in Alvarez, *The Monroe Doctrine: Its Importance in the International Life of the States of the New World* (1924).

with European powers in order to defeat the Cuban insurrectional government (1875), the US stance towards recognition and external intervention is clear in the following passages, part of the message forwarded to the British government by the American ambassador in London Mr. Bayard on behalf of the government and the Senate and the House of Representatives (1895), in order to avoid a British military intervention to settle a boundary dispute over British Guyana and Venezuela:

'Our policy in regard to Europe, which was adopted at an early stage of the wars that have so long agitated that quarter of the globe, nevertheless remain the same, which is, not to interfere in the internal concerns of any of its powers; to consider the government *de facto* as the legitimate government for us; to cultivate friendly relations with it, and to preserve those relations by a frank, firm and manly policy, meeting, in all instances, the just claims of every power, submitting to injuries from none… We are now only concerned, therefore, only with that other practical application of the Monroe Doctrine the disregard of which by an European power is to be deemed an act of unfriendliness towards the United States. The precise scope and limitation of this rule cannot be too clearly apprehended. It does not establish any general protectorate by the United States over other American states. It does not relieve any American state from its obligations as fixed by international law nor prevent any European power directly interested from enforcing such obligations or inflicting merited punishment for the breach of them. It does not contemplate any interference in the internal affairs of any American state or in the relations between it and other American states. It does not justify any attempt on our part to change the established form of government of any American state or to prevent the people of such state from altering that form according to their own will and pleasure. The rule in question has but a single purpose and object. It is that no European power or combination of European powers shall forcibly deprive an American state of the right and power of self-government and of shaping of itself for its own political fortunes and destinies…'[46]

Bayard's statement shows a clear US sensitivity, in the 19th century, for a number of international law principles, including the effectiveness of legitimate governments, their international responsibility, non-intervention in their internal affairs.

A principle of effectiveness can also be tracked down in the modern theory of custom. Law does not exclusively develop through states' consent, but also from their consistent and repeated factual behaviour. Despite the fact that classic writers from Grotius to Bynkershoek elaborated a theory of custom which was deeply embedded in natural law principles and in a guiding factor of *recta ratio*, states' and tribunals' practice, in particular in judicial dispute settlement, reveals an almost exclusive reliance on the objective element of *vetustas* of a certain practice.[47] During the whole of the 19th century, American and British courts

---

[46] Quoted in *Ibidem*, 71-72.
[47] For a detailed account of the historical development of sources' theory see Guggenheim, 'Contribution a l'histoire des sources du droit des gens' 94 *Recueil des Cours* (1958), 5.

asserted the objective factor of usage as the only constitutive element of custom. Wheaton cites the exemplar judgement by Justice Marshall in the *Antelope* case (1825) where the President of the US Supreme Court declared illegal the capture by the US navy of Portuguese and Spanish vessels because they were trading in slaves. The argument put forward was that despite slavery being against the natural right of every human being to enjoy the fruits of their work, slave trade was rooted in a well-established and accepted usage of many of the civilised nations and therefore it could not be considered contrary to the law of nations.[48]

A concept of effectiveness was therefore present in the early positivist jurisprudence on sources. The norm is what the normal practice of states shows to be a common standard accepted as law. The abidance by principles of natural law was completely discarded in favour of a new rationalist approach. It is the repetition itself of certain behaviour that represents the main law-making factor. However, the doctrine soon proved not to be at ease with a purely objective concept of custom and therefore, starting from the German idealist thought with Puchta and Savigny, new subjective elements were put into play, no longer being expressed as divine or natural principles of just reason but as the common consciousness of a certain society, be it national or international. This develops in the modern theory of custom that sees the formation of a customary rule as subject to the existence of a certain usage plus the so-called *opinio iuris ac necessitatis*. This theory was recognised by the PCIJ in the *Lotus case* and later will be repeatedly adopted by the ICJ.[49]

---

[48] Cit. in Wheaton, *Histoire des progrés du droit des gens en Europe et en Amerique depuis la Paix de Westphalie jusqu'a nos jours* (1865, 4th ed.), Vol. II, 295.

[49] *Lotus Case*, 1927 PCIJ Series A, n. 10, at 28. E.g. *North Sea Continental Shelf* (Germany/Denmark and The Netherlands), ICJ Reports 1969, 3, at 43-45. Yet many distinguished authors, even recently, have disputed the necessary presence of a subjective element, and a careful analysis of states' and courts' practice seems to confirm the hypothesis that most of the times proof of a well-established practice is considered sufficient in order to identify a customary norm even nowadays. See Kopelmanas, 'Custom as a Means of the Creation of International Law' 18 *BYIL* (1937), 127; Kelsen, 'Theorie du droit coutumier' 1 *Revue international de la théorie du droit* (1939), 253; Guggenheim, 'Les deux élements de la coutume en droit international', in *La technique et les principes du droit public: Etudes en l'honneur de G. Scelle* (1950), Vol. I, 275; Lauterpacht, *supra* n. 6. More recently see Mendelson, 'Formation of Customary International Law' 272 *Recueil des Cours* (1998), 165, at 272. In Mendelson's view the *opinio iuris* is not generally considered a necessary element when international courts try to track down a certain customary rule. It can become important in specific cases, i.e. when certain usages could by their nature give rise to certain duties and rights, but they are prevented from a certain *opinio non iuris*; in cases of disclaimers; and when state practice is ambiguous like in the *Nuclear Weapons* case.

3.3 Effectiveness and its philosophical roots

Effectiveness as a distinctive feature of positivist jurisprudence in its more debated issues can be also interpreted from a philosophical perspective. Writing in 1977, Wildeman held that effectiveness was deeply rooted in the philosophical debate of the 19th century and the first part of the 20th century.[50] He distinguished three main philosophical inspirational factors that led to its development as a fundamental principle of modern positivism.

The first one is rationalism and empiricism as they developed in France. The adoption of the effectiveness criterion as the guiding principles for recognition of new governments by France can be seen as expression of rationalist principles in the conduct of foreign affairs. Furthermore, positivist sociology as developed by Comte became very influential in the jurisprudential debate and led jurists to leave aside abstract notions and go back to reality in its material sense. The eternal and immutable natural laws were radically rejected as utopian and the lawyers' role became to simply observe the law as it is in its technical sense. The lawyer as a sociologist or as an engineer was seen as pure technician. Criticism of the content of the law should not be his business. In other words, positivist jurisprudence developed a methodological analysis that was at the same time rigorous observation of the factual reality and legitimation of this latter. To reduce it to one of the two terms, as Wildeman did to its legitimation role, is in our contention historically inaccurate.

Secondly, an apparently contradictory theory like the Kantian, which is nowadays source of inspiration for cosmopolitan ideals and natural law theories,[51] triggered that distinction between *Sein* and *Sollen* that would fuel the jurisprudential debate in continental Europe for more than a century. A neat distinction between law and social reality was seen with scepticism in the age of empiricism. Apart from the Vienna School of law that systematically developed this distinction, the sociological approach looked for a *trait d'union* between a system like the legal one, which could not afford to lose its normativity, and the material reality whose features should be incorporated in the legal system itself. Jellinek's *normative Kraft des Faktischen*, Schmitt's idea of concrete order, Duguit's concept of social solidarity prepared the ground for what international lawyers would eventually call the principle of effectiveness.[52] Furthermore, the concept of effectiveness, as expressed in the formula of material constitution as opposed to a formal one, would become linked to a development of a state theory that would legitimise internally state power against counter-powers, such as religious

---

[50] Wildeman, *supra* n. 9.
[51] See Teson, 'The Kantian Theory of International Law' 92 *Columbia Law Review* (1992), 53.
[52] Wildeman, *supra* n. 9, 343.

institutions, in newly born states like Germany and Italy.[53] External legitimation of state power in the age of colonial imperialism happened by conferring a dominant role to effectiveness in international law as legal expression of the *fait accompli*.

Last but not least, another ideological root identified by Wildeman is Darwinian thought. This doctrine permeated all sciences by the beginning of the 20th century and would led in jurisprudence to the acceptance of might as a source of law. In other words, the law would be 'naturally' brought to accept the might of those in a given society that have been able to appropriate most of the resources. Different legal devices were elaborated by constitutional lawyers in order to explain the acceptance of this kind of law by the disadvantaged. According to Von Ihering, for example, the acceptance would derive from the fact that those layers of the society who do not benefit from most of the resources would be in relative terms better off, than if there was no law at all.[54] In Jellinek's view, the acceptance would build through a psychological process of adaptation of the minds of those who live in a society to what is historically given.[55] This recalls the idea of cultural hegemony developed by Gramsci some ten years later.[56] On the one hand, 'Darwinian' thought legitimised the power of elites in all European societies; on the other, it was also at the basis of racist doctrines that would be incorporated in domestic legislation first in Germany and later in Italy.

Wildeman's analysis is thought-provoking. It sheds more light on the proposition already explored according to which effectiveness would be inextricably linked to positivism, in particular sociological, in its theoretical elaboration and that it would be mainly a 'continental affair'. Finally, it indicates a crucial ideological link between national socialism in Germany and certain radical conceptions of effectiveness as a source of law, whose analysis reveals both the limits and 'dark sides' of this concept and its inherent criticism of modern liberal thought.[57]

---

[53] Seminal works on constitutional material theory in Germany and Italy were written by Jellinek (*Allgemeine Staatslehre, supra* n. 8*)* and Santi Romano (*L'ordinamento giuridico: studi sul concetto, le fonti e i caratteri del diritto* (1917)) respectively.

[54] Von Ihering, *Der Zweck im Recht* (1877), Vol. I.

[55] Jellinek, *supra* n. 8.

[56] See Gramsci, 'Culture, Hegemony, Ideology, Intellectuals' in Bennet (ed.), *Culture, Ideology and Social Process: a Reader* (1947), 192. And his recent re-interpretation in international relations by Halliday, 'Culture and International Relations: a new Reductionism', in Ebata, Neufeld, *Confronting the Political in International Relations* (2000), 47.

[57] On the question of effectiveness, Nazi international legal jurisprudence and its critique of liberal thought, see Carty, 'Carl Schmitt's Critique of Liberal International Legal Order Between 1933 and 1945' 14 *LJIL* (2001), 25. And reply to Carty's article in Gattini, 'Sense and Quasisense of Schmitt's *Großraum* Theory in International Law – A Rejoinder to Carty's "Carl Schmitt's Critique of Liberal International Legal Order"' 15 *LJIL* (2002), 53.

3.4 Overview of the literature on effectiveness

An overview of the main contributions to the study of effectiveness in international law reveals the complexity of its nature and the wide range of positions related to its definition in international law. However, it seems possible to conclude that the analysis of the principle of effectiveness was carried out within a wide range of positivist approaches that move between two ideal extremes. On the one hand, we have the approach of analytical positivism, also named pure or critical positivism. This stream of the positivist school argues that the legal nature of a certain norm lies in its conformity to a superior norm. The legal system is built on a hierarchical normative construction, with the constitution at its peak. But what does the constitution depend on? The ultimate rule is a juristic presupposition that the whole legal order is efficacious and valid. Being a hypothesis, it does not require any kind of validation. On the other hand, we have sociological positivism in which the validity of a norm does not rest on its source, but on its effectiveness. The legal order accepts only those rules and legal situations that are effective. A fictitious rule is not valid from the beginning, and a rule which does not find any correspondence in the sociological order loses its validity by desuetude. As a rule of custom acquires its validity from the practice of states, the same rule will lose its validity if states behave consistently contrary to it. In other words, sociological positivism postulates the principle of effectiveness as super-constitutional positive norm, that would dominate the whole legal system.

We may say that analytical positivism underlines fact as a condition for the operation of law, whereas sociological positivism considers it as a 'revolutionary' element, a juristic source itself. Some observations must be made on this theoretical differentiation. First, despite disguising profound divergence on the whole relationship between law and reality, it has as a presupposition only a different and opposite observational point of view. Let us consider a hypothetical example of how effectiveness operates. An example is a revolutionary event that leads to the creation of two new states (states B and C) from the ashes of an old one (state A). Setting aside the distinct issue of succession, we could argue that effectiveness, as a whole of historical and sociological changes, is itself the source of the new legal personality and identity. The sovereignty of state A is not protected anymore, it is states B's and C's distinct sovereignties which are protected. States B and C are now responsible for their own breaches of customary law due to the fact that they have become international persons. We could argue that here effectiveness operates as a fact-revolution. By contrast, if one wished to underline the normative nature of international law, he/she would stress fact as a condition for the operation of law, arguing that there is a rule of general international law that provides for the creation of a new state under the condition of effectiveness. As a corollary, there is a rule providing for the new state being bound by existing customary law and having those rights related to sovereignty. In this sense, fact would be a condition of the operation of existing law, not a source of the new law.

A number of authors have seen the principle of effectiveness as a general positive norm whose function is the adaptation of law to reality. Krüger, Kunz, Bellini, Touscoz and Stone have advanced the idea that the principle of effectiveness is the dominant principle of the international legal system since every rule's and subjective situation's validity would be determined by it.[58] The role that effectiveness plays in these authors' view resembles very closely a sociological form of positivism. This would be very clear in the institution of desuetude, the lack of value of verbal protest in stopping acquiescence, in the declaratory nature of recognition and the exclusively material nature of sovereignty. All these authors stress that the principle of effectiveness brings security and order to international relations through its adaptation of law to reality. According to Touscoz, the adoption of effectiveness as a measure of legal validity requires a close link between the study of international relations and of international law. In his opinion, the law is not the super-structure of the social and economic reality which determines it; it is not even a body of rules subordinated to a formal, abstract, *a priori* ideal. Legal sciences should never lose touch with reality in order to facilitate the process of adaptation of the two perspectives. Therefore, a separation and isolation of the two disciplines would give a very narrow perspective to the international lawyer.[59]

Strangely enough, Kelsen, who in his earlier work *Reinerechtslehre* theorised a purely independent legal system and is normally considered the leading exponent of analytical positivism, provides surprising insights on the role that the principle of effectiveness plays in international law in a later monograph on international law.[60] According to him the sphere of validity of a legal order is determined by the principle of effectiveness, which is a positive norm of international law. This norm operates when the state is effectively displaying a stable order. This is clear in territorial matters. States in international law are those organisations able to exercise an effective control of a certain territory and population. Their boundaries are determined according to the extent to which their legal orders are firmly established and obeyed, and acquisitions of territories can occur as a result

---

[58] Bellini, *supra* n. 9; Kunz, 'Revolutionary Creation of Norms of International Law' 41 *AJIL* (1947), 119; Touscoz, *supra* n. 5; Tucker, *supra* n. 9; Krüger, *supra* n. 9.

[59] Touscoz, *supra* n. 5.

[60] Kelsen, *Principles of International Law*, *supra* n. 9. There is an interesting ambiguity in role and nature of effectiveness in Kelsen's writings. See on this aspect, Kreijen, *supra* n. 9, 211. It is clear that Kelsen's opinions on the operation of a principle of effectiveness are moderated in the 2nd edition of *Principles of International Law* (1966, 2nd ed.). However, the editor Robert Tucker admittedly modified the part concerned with effectiveness, in order to keep in due account the changes occurred from 1952, the year of the first edition, to 1966. This is why for an original account of Kelsen's thought I have referred to the first edition and to *General Theory of Law and State*.

of an illegal act, as far they are effective. Yet international law as a horizontal system without any centralisation of powers always confers a right on the holder of effective power when deciding on a conflict with a nominal title. Validity of the legal order is dependant on the effective coercive power underlying its very existence.[61] On account of that, one cannot but conclude that Kelsen comes unexpectedly close to a formulation of sociological positivism, even if he never reached the conclusion that each norm of conduct is dependant on its efficacy.

On the other hand, Tucker's choice is somewhat less clear-cut and is half way between a sociological and 'purely' positivist stance. This is very well expressed by Tucker's analysis of the positive rule of effectiveness:

> 'The content of the positive rule of effectiveness in international law refers primarily to the conditions of validity of both those rules of a general character (general rules of conventional international law) and of an individual nature (individual norms creating concrete rights and duties for definite subjects). The positive rule of effectiveness does *not* have as part of its content the rights and duties specified by these rules themselves. Thus, the effective control of territory gives rise to specific rights and duties as a result of certain general rules of international law regarding territorial sovereignty. The rights and duties stipulated have nothing to do with the positive rule of effectiveness; but whether they apply in a given instance – let us say when the territory has been seized illegally – depends upon the interpretation states give to the content of this rule of effectiveness.'[62]

Tucker's view is that the positive rule of effectiveness applies only insofar as it is recognised by the states themselves. In other words, there are no self-evident facts or acts in law, but only facts and acts determined by a competent agency in a manner prescribed by the law. In a decentralised system like the international one, this competent agency is the states themselves, which can give validity to a certain rule or territorial situation. Therefore recognition or acquiescence (formal protest is not considered sufficient to stop the process of acquiescence) are constitutive of rights and duties and the facts themselves can never be taken as a source of law. This can also apply in cases of illegal unilateral acts. The principle *ex iniuria ius non oritur* would be qualified by the principle of effectiveness.[63] Furthermore, while agreeing with Kelsen that the validity of a legal system as a whole presupposes its effectiveness, he does not think that the principle of effectiveness in this respect represents a positive norm. It represents only 'a juristic presupposition or hypothesis', that is, a certain correspondence between normative prescriptions and reality which forms the basis for a normative interpretation of certain facts.[64]

---

[61] Kelsen, *Principles of International Law*, *supra* n. 9, 208.
[62] Tucker, *supra* n. 9, 44.
[63] *Ibidem*.
[64] *Ibidem*, 32.

A consistent group of authors represented by Balekjian, Verdross, Ottolenghi, Mjaja de la Muela, Sperduti, and Verzijil have taken a more critical position.[65] According to them, effectiveness constitutes a principle, but does not have any kind of normative value. Its content cannot be clearly delimited. It refers to situations which may be qualified as objective, like the status of widely recognised states, and to situations which constitute the object of conflict and legal disputes, like the status of new unrecognised states. Since the concept of effectiveness cannot be clearly defined, the general normative function of the corresponding principle cannot be ascertained clearly. However, such a function should be conceived as one subordinated to international law. The claim that effectiveness dominates international law is tantamount to the negation of the latter as a legal order. In other words, effectiveness does not impinge on validity, since the validity of a certain norm depends on its 'legitimacy' according to a superior one. The discourse advanced by these authors on the functional nature of the principle of effectiveness is important. In summary, these functions are: the promotion of peace and legal security; the mutual adaptation of legal norms and realities; its probative role in support of claims to international legal titles.

Ottolenghi, Balejikan, Verzijl, Mjaia de la Muela believe that the principle of effectiveness does not have any positive normative nature but is only a qualification of a certain fact. This qualification can entail a normative function insofar as it is 'recognised' either by an existing norm of positive law or by a new norm in the process of creation through states' willingness. Any departure from this idea of 'legitimate' effectiveness entails serious dangers, as a rule of effectiveness taken up as a source of law would mean a substitution of the law with the interpreter's and interested party's willingness. Its unlimited application would replace the rule of law in international relations with the rule of power.

3.5 Is effectiveness a general principle of international law?

According to Sperduti, the principle of effectiveness needs to be interpreted as an informing principle of international law (*principio informatore*).[66] Kelsen's mistake of giving normative value to the principle of effectiveness must be avoided, because this is not supported by state practice - for example, states do not only consider the customary process to be effected through actual behaviours, but also through the expression of an *opinio iuris* - . Secondly, that would lead to a reduction of the rule of law to the rule of power. Even one of the basic principles of international law, the mutual respect of territorial sovereignty, would lose its

---

[65] Balekjian, *supra* n. 9; Verdross, *Universelles Völkerrecht* (1984, 3rd ed.); Ottolenghi, *supra* n. 9; Mjaja de la Muela, *supra* n. 9; Sperduti, *supra* n. 9; Verzijl, *International Law in Historical Perspective* (1968).
[66] Sperduti, *supra* n. 9.

value since this constitutional principle of effectiveness would translate the mere fact of an armed aggression into a legal title.

However, what does 'informing' principle mean, according to Sperduti? He means a general character qualifying a consistent body of norms of international law, that allows the continuous modification and shaping of the international legal system towards historical and sociological reality. Its meaning and its general content can be reconstructed through the examination of the content of different norms with a process of induction and generalisation. Through this operation, it is possible to identify the main informing principles of international law, including the principle of effectiveness (another informing principle is the equality of states, which is one of the main principles on which classic international law is based, though embodied in a formal instrument like the UN Charter (Article 2 (1)). In other words, it is so frequent to find norms of the greatest importance for states whose application is subordinated to the realisation of an effective situation, that it is reasonable to talk of a principle of effectiveness shaping the international legal system, which is not the same as claiming that every norm is subordinated to the principle of effectiveness, and that, if a norm is not effectively applied, it loses its binding value. Just to consider some of the legal questions relating to the creation of states, their governmental organisation, their legal personality, their responsibility are all questions traditionally dealt with by international law through a careful observation of the historical-sociological reality. According to Sperduti, the principle of effectiveness would be the most evident sign of a realistic concept of international law. It gives expression to a dialectical tension between the sphere of the 'is' and the 'ought to be', a tension that through this principle is solved by a transformation of the legal reality and its adjustment to the phenomenological reality.

But if we employ the expression principle of effectiveness, what do we mean by principle? Is it a general principle of the civilised nations according to Article 38 (1) (c) of the ICJ Statute, or is it a fundamental principle of the international legal order as meant by Schwarzenberger? If we were to mean Article 38 principles as those drawn from the most developed domestic systems, we can certainly state that this is not the case, since the most developed domestic systems are normally associated with a limited role played by the principle of effectiveness. Fundamental principles of international law might mean what Sperduti thinks is an 'informing principle', as in both cases the principle is inducted from a process of generalisation of norms and judicial policies. Effectiveness seems to satisfy the three tests set out by Schwarzenberger.[67]

---

[67] According to Schwarzenberger, 'to decide whether any individual principle of international law may be regarded as fundamental' means applying the three following tests: '1) The principle must be especially significant for international law. Opinion on this matter is bound to be greatly

Further, judicial recognition has been given in a number of cases, to mention few, in *Island of Palmas*,[68] *Norwegian Fisheries*,[69] and *Nottebohm*.[70] One of the characteristics of a fundamental principle is the fact that there should be a presumption of supremacy in respect to other norms and principles in their application. This has been traditionally recognised if we consider it in respect to sovereignty, state responsibility, territorial disputes and nationality issues. We might say that if Sperduti's definition can be subsumed under Schwarzenberger's, then we can conclude that effectiveness can be defined as a fundamental principle of international law, being careful not to confuse it with Article 38 general principles.

Yet, if one asks which international law has among its fundamental principles that of effectiveness, we must agree that this is likely to be valid for modern international law until 1945. Post World War II rules on the use of force, on governmental legitimacy and on the principle of self-determination, and a shift towards a more limited acceptance of power as a 'source' of law suggest that effectiveness is no longer a fundamental principle, but must be taken in due consideration with other factors like principles of legality, recognition, acquiescence and protest. Certainly, as already stated, contemporary international law builds on classic international law, rather than replaces it. Yet, it would probably be even better to dispose of the whole notion of principle, since it can be misleading. Principle refers to a basic, primary notion, which generates logical application. Effectiveness for the international lawyer has a multiform qualitative meaning, relating to the impact of fact on the law, both in conserving it and modifying it. Its impact occurs on a variety of legal aspects: norms, subjective rights, legal titles. We cannot say that it determines them, but it certainly influences them. That is why De Visscher talks about *les effectivités*, underlying the fact that the concept of effectiveness cannot be subsumed to unity, but refers to a set of different legal situations[71]. It seems more appropriate to

---

influenced by anybody's pictures of international law in perspective; 2) The principle must stand out from others by covering a relatively wide range of rules of international law which appear to fall naturally under its heading; 3) The principle must be one which is either so typical of international law that it is an essential part of any known system of international law or so characteristic of existing international law that if it were ignored, we would be in danger of losing sight of an essential feature of modern international law.' 'The Fundamental Principles of International Law' 87 *Recueil des Cours* (1955), 191, at 204.

[68] *Island of Palmas* case (1928), RIAA (Vol. II), 829.
[69] *Norwegian Fisheries* (UK/Norway), ICJ Reports 1949, 116.
[70] *Nottebohm, supra* n. 3.
[71] De Visscher, *supra* n. 42.

define it a legal-normative criterion or, more generally, concept, and this is clear if we analyse its role in international law today. Hence, the use of the expression 'principle of effectiveness', commonly adopted in the literature, will be generally avoided.

To draw some conclusions from this analysis of the doctrinal debate, we can assert that the role played by effectiveness in international law is a symptom of the strongly realist nature of international law, which can afford legal fictions only to a limited extent. As a policy matter we have seen how it underlines security and order in international relations, rather than justice. Its impact on the law in its different manifestations can be summed up by three main functions: constitutive, modificative and adjudicative.

Through its constitutive function the concept allows the adaptation of law to the order established, to the *fait accompli*. It has in this respect a conservative function, because it 'freezes' a certain sociological situation and projects it into the legal sphere therefore legitimising it *erga omnes*. This function can be seen traditionally in several respects: the concept of state under international law that requires the effective power of a certain governmental organisation over a certain territory and population; the fact that a government is recognised as long as it wields effective power through habitual obedience/support by its population; the fact that a state is entitled to sovereignty over unoccupied territories when it exerts its actual authority; the fact that the laws of war are applicable not in virtue of a declaration of war, but in virtue of an effective state of armed conflict; and the fact that a blockade is admitted under international law when it is effective.

Effectiveness has a modificative function in the sense that it allows the modification of the law as a result of social change. It therefore possesses an amending role that allows an adaptation of the law to the new social situation. This is inherent in the concept of revolution, which through a social-factual process creates a new *Grundnorm* for the legal system.[72] For example, this role has been particularly strong in the aftermath of World War II as far as the new creation of states was carried out through national liberation movements has been concerned, and the new exigencies of regulation of the international society in respect of maritime delimitation and cosmic navigation. We could see this role of the concept of effectiveness as a progressive role. It is also the most problematic and relevant to the present book, as it is in this function that effectiveness may allow the creation of law from illegal situations.

A third function effected by the concept of effectiveness is adjudicative. It has indeed been used by international courts and arbitral tribunals as a principle of

---

[72] Kunz (*supra* n. 58) denies that an internal revolution may represent a revolution under international law, because the internal revolution is 'recognised' by the general principle of effectiveness.

solution of legal disputes involving competing claims. It is in this function applied to cases of conflicts of nationality both for individuals[73] and ships[74] and cases of territorial delimitation.[75]

To conclude, effectiveness is a critical concept for every international lawyer because it goes straight to the heart of the relationship between reality and norm and the validity of the latter. It has important functions in the international legal order, yet it is difficult to disagree with those jurists who have held that to consider the principle of effectiveness as dominant in international law is tantamount to the negation of international law. Effectiveness was a fundamental principle in modern international law before 1945, as the function of international law was often to 'co-ordinate' hegemonic behaviours and policies. This nature is what confers to effectiveness a sinister flavour in an era where international law, if not more egalitarian, has definitely become more value-oriented and justice-oriented. And this also explains why it has been subject to radical criticism in the doctrinal debate. Turning to this criticism, it is argued that while such critique rightly stresses the apologetic nature of any international legal project based on a sociological primacy of power, it also presents some important flaws in denying value to some of the functions effectiveness displays in international law.

3.6 Neo-liberal international lawyers: the quest for justice and democratic legitimacy

A systematic criticism of the concept of effectiveness is explicit in the neo-liberal approach to international law.[76] The theory of some of the representatives of this approach is that contemporary international law should be re-shaped according to justice and legitimacy rather than legality and effectiveness.[77] Justice would be represented by those values of international morality that are shared by the international community comprising a whole range of non-state actors (individuals, transnational corporations, NGOs), but that are not embodied in international instruments due to the formalist nature of international law that is still based on an outdated concept of state's sovereignty. Ultimately, international law would address the needs of individuals and that is why it would be useless and

---

[73] *Nottebohm*, *supra* n. 3.

[74] The *M/V Saiga (No. 2)* Case, 38 *ILM* (1999), 1323.

[75] E.g. arbitration between Yemen and Eritrea (S/1999/1265) and the commentary by Despeaux, 'Das Schiedsurteil *Jemen gegen Eritrea II* vom 17. Dezember 1999: Entscheidung über die Seeabgrenzung' 60 *ZaöRV* (2000), 447. *Infra* Ch. 3, section 3.3.

[76] I adopt here the expression 'neo-liberal'' referring to what Simpson also calls 'anti-pluralist' liberalism, which he rightly holds distinct from 'Charter' liberalism. Simpson, 'Two Liberalisms' 12 *EJIL* (2001), 537.

[77] Teson, *supra* n. 51; Slaughter, 'The Real New World Order' 76 *Foreign Affairs* (1997), 183.

dangerous to address two different levels of legitimacy: one at a national level embodying a concept of justice, one at an international level stressing order, stability and compliance. That is why according to these authors the form of government of a particular state should become one of the main priorities to be addressed by international law, according to a concept of justice that would not recognise non-democratic states.[78] Teson talks of the effectiveness criterion 'as the result of applying the political philosophy of Thomas Hobbes to the issue of international legitimacy. The notion of state sovereignty is Hobbesian because it underscores the citizens' obedience toward the sovereign, based on fear, as the only effective means of ending the internal state of nature.'[79] As a corollary of this revised concept of sovereignty, Teson and Reisman even propose a unilateral right of intervention.[80] The duty of non-intervention should be only directed to those states who are formally and genuinely committed to liberal democracy, the rule of law and human rights. The same conclusions on the point of governmental legitimacy are reached by Franck, who, however, bases his arguments in a positivist fashion and does not conceive of intervention outside the security framework provided by the UN.[81]

Teson's referral to the Hobbesian roots of the concept of effectiveness is correct, and, again, the present project does not want to turn away its eyes from the pathological role of effectiveness in international law, indeed it is committed to a full grasp of such role. However, the 'neo-liberals'' radical rejection of effectiveness is controversial, if not also self-interested. The point is not that an international law that embodies more and more shared constructions of justice is not desirable, indeed the contrary, but that the alternative offered by the authors presupposes a distinction between justice-based principles and order-based principles that does not take into account the justice dimension of these latter principles. In other words, the underlying values of sovereignty, legality and effectiveness are those of stability, order, peace and independence which represent principles of justice, in the sense that they can represent ideal aims to which individuals and peoples may strive and indeed, sometimes, prioritise, as compared to other values such as democracy and individual freedoms. Furthermore, if Teson's premises on a new Kantian international law were followed, that is international law addresses itself exclusively to individuals, and the state would appear like an agent of the individuals' will, one could simply dispense with the notion of the state. Even if a possible counter-argument would

---

[78] E.g. Slaughter, 'International Law in a World of Liberal States' 6 *EJIL* (1995), 503.

[79] Teson, *Humanitarian Intervention: an Inquiry into Law and Morality* (1988), 79.

[80] *Ibidem*; Reisman, 'Humanitarian Intervention and Fledgling Intervention' 18 *Fordham International Law Journal* (1995), 795.

[81] Franck, 'Legitimacy and the Democratic Entitlement', in Fox and Roth (eds.), *Democratic Governance and International Law* (2000), 25, at 46.

be that the state represents the most feasible solution to representation so far, and that it is not realistic to abandon it, then one should ask why, if democracy and justice are universal matters, there should not be a more democratic decision-making process at the international level, e.g. the transformation of the GA into a legislative body where each state has a proportional number of votes according to the population.[82] It is odd enough that, if democracy is a universal matter, it should only be addressed at a national level.

There is certainly strong support for the concept of popular sovereignty in contemporary international law. The problematic aspect of the process of translation of this concept into reality is that of the empirical determination of popular sovereignty and substantive democracy. The holding of periodic, free and fair elections generally constitutes a sound guarantee that the elected institutions represent a genuine expression of popular sovereignty. However, a privileged procedure should not turn away our attention from those cases where a sound procedure cannot compensate for the lack of substantive democracy. Elections can in some case become a periodical safe-conduct for oligarchic regimes, where two or three elites struggle for power.[83] The situation nowadays in some Asian and African countries confirms this danger. In other words, we cannot circumvent a substantive problem of definition of democracy by referring to a formal, procedural one. Moreover, apart from imposing a Lockean liberal concept of democracy in open contrast with the view held by the ICJ in the *Admissions* case and in *Nicaragua* and embodied in GA resolutions that seem to be expression of customary law,[84] stressing the liberal pluralism that underlies international law on this issue, the democratic entitlement theory does not consider other achievements reached by other political systems which have prioritised material equality and dignity over civil and political rights. In the advocates of a right to democratic governance, the discourse on human rights is indeed mostly centred on civil and political rights rather than economic and social rights, in accordance with Rawls' hierarchy between the two main principles of justice.[85] Furthermore, the unilateral intervention in other states' internal affairs in order to bring back democratic legitimacy, if not negotiated and decided within multilateral organisations, can become an easy way to enforce

---

[82] Onuma, 'The ICJ: An Emperor Without Clothes? International Conflict Resolution, Article 38 of the ICJ Statute and the Sources of International Law', in Ando *et al.* (eds.), *Liber Amicorum Judge Shigeru Oda* (2002), 191, at 207, note 37.

[83] Franck takes as indicator of democracy the domestic legal commitment to open and periodical elections. *Supra* n. 81, 27-28.

[84] GA Res. 45/150 (1990), 45/151 (1990) and 49/180 (1994).

[85] Rawls, *A Theory of Justice* (1999, 2nd ed.), 52. See on the point of self-interested human rights discourse Koskenniemi, 'Whose intolerance, which democracy?', in Fox and Roth (eds.), *supra* n. 81, 436.

national political agendas. The case of Iraq shows the dangers inherent in the unilateralistic formulations of the democratic entitlement theory.

As stated by Roth, due to the lack of empirical methods of determining popular sovereignty, effective control is still the most feasible way to determine governmental legitimacy.[86] An effective government and an effective political organisation within certain defined borders is also a pre-condition for democratic governance from the local to the central levels of state's governance. It is crucial for tackling matters of public policy that cannot be addressed from the outside. More specifically, it is crucial for the protection of human rights, whose primary responsibility lies with the sovereign government: the current situations in Somalia and Iraq are dramatic evidence of how the lack of an effective government leads to a situation of anarchy and general disrespect for the most fundamental of the human rights, such as the right to life. Moreover, in an age where the most fundamental economic choices have been transferred to a grey area of international governance where forms of legal accountability are still at a very infant stage, effectiveness still provides the minimal basis for crucial distributive choices at the local level and international legal responsibility of state and non-state actors. To simply do away with it in international law would not serve any cause for justice and democracy.

Of course, adopting effectiveness as a general criterion of governmental or state legitimacy does not mean that this criterion is without exceptions. Sovereignty has both a normative value and a functional nature. Fundamental rules of protection of human rights can be a guarantee for individuals. That is why the ICJ in giving its advisory opinion in the *Namibia* case held that denial of the right of self-determination and the South-African regime of apartheid created a situation of regime and territorial illegality that was opposable to both UN member and non-member states.[87] The same applies to the instalment of a government through illegal intervention, genocide, and mass deportation. Moreover, it is true then that the European experience of joint recognition of the new states from the former Yugoslavia seems to unveil a constitutive trend in the recognition policies of states, which stresses the respect for human and minority rights.[88] However, its relevance outside the European context could not be tested so far, which is why it is too soon to say whether it represents a setback for the

---

[86] Roth, *Governmental Illegitimacy in International Law* (1999), 137.

[87] *Legal Consequences for States of the Continued Presence of South Africa in Namibia notwithstanding Security Council Resolution 276* (1970), Advisory Opinion, ICJ Reports 1971, 6, at 56.

[88] EC Guidelines on the Recognition of New States in Eastern Europe and in the Soviet Union, in Harris, *Cases and Materials on International Law* (1998, 5th ed.), 147. See comment in Craven, 'The European Community Arbitration Commission on Yugoslavia' 66 *BYIL* (1995), 333, at 411, hinting at the constitutive nature of the collective process of recognition in the case of the Former Yugoslavia.

effectiveness criterion and a development towards a more universal substantive concept of state legitimacy. In conclusion, effectiveness is still a flexible criterion which can accommodate order and a relativist concept of justice in its general application and an universal concept of legitimacy in its exceptions.

3.7 Critical legal studies, deconstruction and language

The criticism advanced by the critical legal studies towards the concept of effectiveness concentrates on different issues. The first is epistemological. Effectiveness would be the product of the modernist attempt to divide between law on the one side and politics and morality on the other side. The positivist project after all is to discern objectively the rule of law as it is and to read reality as it is through normative provisions. The concept of effectiveness is clearly a realist one, a material device whose significance in shaping legal issues has been highlighted in the course of this chapter. A government is recognised as it is effective on a certain territory and population, an occupation of territory *nullius* gives a valid title to sovereignty since it is effective. This is objectively discernible, as it is possible to describe reality in an objective and scientific manner. The post-modern approach denies that such a description is possible without a commixture of personal moral beliefs and political views. The language itself is a result of moral and political beliefs, therefore objective knowledge is impossible and the quest for science is a sterile one. One should be aware of this intermingling of law and politics, and therefore should engage its personal values to interpret reality in a subjective way. The concept of effectiveness is dangerous because it can bring to apology and is unhelpful and indeterminate as a device of judicial policy.

It is submitted that the underlying philosophy of critical legal studies has inspired a much needed and stimulating systematic deconstruction of the language and the argumentative patterns and devices of international law. In the case of effectiveness, it has made explicit how a continuous reliance on the factual, material dimension of state sovereignty opens the door to extreme subjectivism and apologetic analysis.[89] However, it is submitted that the deconstruction of substantive arguments has always been, even if more implicitly, the normal task of every international lawyer and no scholar has ever engaged in a doctrinal debate without first analysing, in other words deconstructing, the literature on that debate. Furthermore, the systematic reduction of reality to language and the impossibility of studying the law and the reality as *they are* is not shared. It is not our intention to advocate a pure and dogmatic positivism, asserting a separation of the legal system from the surrounding world and giving to it a sort of logical-metaphysical nature. Yet putting the law into its historical

---

[89]Koskenniemi, *supra* n. 1; Kennedy, *International Legal Structures* (1987).

and social context can allow the adoption of one or more hypotheses, that is one or more observational standpoints; these hypotheses can be then verified, by looking at the role the law plays in the society. That is why the need of contextual analysis is shared here with critical legal studies, yet context analysis cannot be limited to language and discourse analysis, but must be able to look further in the world of facts. According to these premises, deconstruction becomes only the very first stage of the book, construction being its second necessary stage.

Aristodemou, for instance, disputes the claim that effectiveness can be a useful device for domestic courts in order to deal with acts of unrecognised regimes.[90] She develops her criticism in the following five points and questions. 1) Does effectiveness mean only habitual obedience or also popular support? 2) When does a government become effective? 3) If effectiveness implies popular support, what does this latter mean? 4) How is the consent of people to be ascertained? 5) Observational standpoints and contexts diverge and that is why the evaluation of the same facts can diverge. The author states that the practice of tribunals has not given an answer to these questions.

As a general reply to Aristodemou's criticism, it must be pointed out that effectiveness is taken as a general criterion or norm, because it enables courts to operate a contextual analysis of the situation without being forced in a straitjacket. Any legal criterion or norm has to be inevitably 'general', in order to apply to different concrete situations. Of course, the sociological level of effectiveness 'recognised' by the legal criterion or norm is a fluid concept, in the sense that different evaluations of effectiveness will operate as a result of the concept of effectiveness being applied in different contexts (recognition of governments, creation of states, international humanitarian law, or state responsibility) or by different people. As far as point 2) is concerned, despite there being no 'mathematical formula' to determine when a government should be considered effective, some useful indicators can be identified such as the level of obedience and popular support in the population, the level of resistance by competing factions claiming to become the 'official' government, the level of express or implicit international recognition. As far as the divide between habitual obedience and popular support is concerned (1 and 3), this is a theoretical dichotomy, which does not fit into reality. Most of the time, the situation is a mixture of both things even in most mature democracies. Because of the lack in general of empirical evidence of popular support, effectiveness still gives a presumption in its favour (4).

The second main criticism advanced by Aristodemou is of a political nature. According to her, effectiveness is inevitably linked with an unconditional

---

[90] Aristodemou, 'Choice and Evasion in Judicial Recognition of Governments: Lessons from Somalia' 5 *EJIL* (1994), 556.

acceptance of the *status quo*.[91] Its role would be conservative. Apart from a separate analysis that the political categories of 'conservative' and 'progressive' would require, this argument seems flawed from the analytic perspective that Aristodemou seems to consider. From the analysis made above of the concept of effectiveness, it is clear that it is a variable criterion, whose use can be both conservative and progressive. The recognition of a government because of its effectiveness in the long term, say, even if this government disregards basic human rights like the right to a fair trial or the right to minimal provision of food, involves a conservative role of effectiveness. However, the same will apply even if the government is fully devoted to democracy, substantial equality and the rule of law. In this case, effectiveness is conservative because it 'freezes' the situation and gives international legitimacy to that government. Yet, to define its influence on the development of the law of the sea in the last 50 years as a conservative role is misleading, since it has led to a considerable development in the regime of the continental shelf, which is seen by many as a very important achievement. Furthermore, inherent in the concept of effectiveness, and in the principle *ex factis ius oritur*, is the concept of revolution which is progressive *par excellence* in Hegelian analytic terms. Therefore, the qualification of effectiveness as conservative is a partial description of its function in international law and fails to record its progressive role in certain situations.

4. Some concluding reflections on the place of effectiveness in international law

As seen in the course of the present chapter, effectiveness has been elaborated as a conceptual device that captures the inter-relation between social reality and law and the influence of the former over the latter. The *Wirklichkeitsnähe* of international law, which according to many international lawyers is typical for a decentralised legal system, has been considered as one of the reasons why effectiveness is so fundamental to the understanding and functioning of the international legal system. The doctrinal debate on effectiveness has been mainly a positivist affair characterised by the dialectic between sociological and normativist approaches to the question of the relation between reality and legal norms. The other finding of the present chapter is that while international legal jurisprudence has developed since the 19th century along a strongly realist paradigm, where effectiveness implicitly held a privileged role and position, the systematic conceptualisation of effectiveness has been mainly a continental European doctrinal project situated within 20th century positivism. On the other

---

[91] *Ibidem.*

hand, the last thirty years have been characterised by a dramatic decrease in the attention that international lawyers have devoted to effectiveness. That has occurred as a result of the development of a number of principles of substantive legality, which are analysed in the following chapters, that have spread the feeling amongst international lawyers that the role of effectiveness was no more fundamental to the operation and understanding of their discipline.[92]

Interestingly, after many years of neglect, the concept has received renewed attention in a monograph published by Kreijen in 2004.[93] The author's thesis is that the responsibility for the phenomenon of state failure in sub-Shaharan Africa should be attributed to the choice of the international community to shift from a paradigm of statehood based on effectiveness, to a normative concept of statehood based on principles of legality, such as self-determination and *uti possidetis*. The gap between the internal reality of corrupt and inefficient regimes and the external idea of sovereignty protected by those principles of legality has assured a perpetuation of a grim, anarchic and violent *status quo* for those societies. The practical solution to the problem of state failure should lie with a policy of withdrawal of recognition by the international community and a revival of the UN Trusteeship Administration systems for those states which are unable to build or re-build by themselves the foundations of a functioning state. At a systemic level, the experience of state failure in Africa should caution against any departure from effectiveness as one of fundamental principles of international law should: it is in fact effectiveness the device that assures that unity between reality and ideas that is the pre-requisite for the functioning of any legal system.

Kreijen's book represents a very welcome contribution to a re-assessment of the role of effectiveness in contemporary international law. It is also of considerable merit for its impressive jurisprudential and philosophical enquiry in the inextricable link between the doctrines of sovereignty and effectiveness – a link that will be also explored in the next chapter of the present book. Kreijen's approach to effectiveness can be undoubtedly located within sociological positivism. Effectiveness is that legal device situated on the borderline between the norm and social reality that allows the mutual adaptation and unification. His positions on the validity of ineffective legal norms are somewhat nuanced, however it is clear that the author holds efficacy and effectiveness as measures of the validity of a specific legal norms.[94] It is not the purpose of the present section to debate Kreijen's sociological approach to effectiveness. The present author, however, holds a preference for a normativist approach to effectiveness that situates that concept within the realm of positive law. It is submitted that the task

---

[92] See in particular *infra* Ch. 4 and 5.
[93] Kreijen, *supra* n. 9.
[94] *Ibidem.*, 371-374.

of strictly separating the questions of validity and efficacy of the legal system is indeed an impossible one, and that the solution to the validity of the *Grundnorm* may ultimately depend on the overall efficacy of the legal system itself as shown in the next chapter. However, one should be wary of linking effectiveness and validity for other legal norms, as the concept of effectiveness is a fluid concept, hence to subject the validity of legal norms to their effectiveness would undermine the certainty of the law and the legitimate expectations of the addressees of legal norms.

What this book in fact explores is the 'outlaw' vocation of effectiveness, i.e. its capacity to create new law from situations created as a result of violations of international law. That is indeed the crux of matter in unlawful territorial situations, and it should be the crux of the matter for those international lawyers devoted to the normativity of law. The standard account of this issue, also espoused by Kreijen, is that the principle *ex factis ius oritur* often prevails - or indeed should prevail, according to the advocates of sociological positivism - over the principle *ex iniuria ius non oritur* in international law, because of the decentralised nature and the deficient system of enforcement and sanction of this latter.[95] That proposition, however true it may be, fails to answer some fundamental questions, which are at the heart of the relationship between effectiveness and legality. The most important are possibly the 'how often' and the 'how' question. In other words, can we really conclude that that is a characteristic of international law as compared to domestic law, i.e. of decentralised legal systems as compared to centralised legal systems? Can we identify a trend that tells us that the principle of *ex factis ius oritur* has most of the times prevailed over the principle *ex iniuria ius non oritur*? If yes, to what extent is that the case at present times, as compared to earlier historical contexts? Moreover, can we describe and analyse patterns in which effective situations prevail over principles of legality? If so, what are these patterns? This book's aim is to provide some answers to these questions in the context of unlawful territorial situations on the basis of an analysis of state practice. Providing these answers will contribute to eventually clarify the exact position of effectiveness in international law, whether within its positive norms or as a transforming device situated between reality and norms. As already anticipated, the concept of legitimacy

---

[95] *Ibidem.*, 174-178.

represents a crucial element in the construction of a theory of unlawful territorial situations, in particular for the understanding of the process of 'legalisation' of unlawful effectiveness.

CHAPTER 3

STATEHOOD AND TERRITORIAL SOVEREIGNTY: THE TRADITION OF CONCRETENESS AND REALISM

1. Introduction

The theoretical discussion surrounding the concept of effectiveness and its definition show how effectiveness lies at the core of the existential and foundational questions of international law. That is apparent if we consider one of the key legal concepts of international law, that of territorial sovereignty, whose understanding is crucial to a proper conceptualisation and analysis of unlawful territorial situations. Territorial sovereignty normally denotes a political and legal expression, which designates a relationship of power, supremacy or independence between an actor, the state, and an object, the territory. The qualitative expression of the relationship between state and territory, together constitute what is called territorial sovereignty. This chapter investigates the significance of effectiveness in the legal definition of statehood, and how the concept of state in international law is transposed to the relationship of sovereignty that the state may have with a certain territory. In other words, the implications of the concept of effectiveness for international law issues concerning the question of unlawful territorial situations will be considered, namely statehood, territorial sovereignty and military occupation.

Specifically, this chapter examines the material concept of state in its theoretical and jurisprudential elaboration, by looking at effectiveness in its internal and external dimensions. It assesses how effectiveness discourse has been transposed in the legal definition of territorial sovereignty. In particular, the chapter deals with the notion of territory and the classic modes of acquisition of territory, and how these aspects of international law have been affected by the concept of effectiveness. It is submitted that the material concept of territorial sovereignty defines itself in the colonial encounter, in particular in the institution of occupation of *terra nullius*. Despite the attempt of positivist jurisprudence to differentiate forms of legal encounter with the non-European world, the analysis highlights both the inconsistencies of such differentiations, and also how the standard of civilisation made in fact such world a *terra nullius*. The Cameroon-Nigeria ICJ litigation proves that effectiveness also played a legally dominant role in cases of agreements with local populations, and that the ICJ is still keen on recognising such role. Furthermore, the predominant role of a material or objective element in the institution of occupation of *terra nullius*, rather than a subjective requirement, according to the original scheme of the Roman law institute of *occupatio*, is described. Finally, the concept of military occupation is considered; effectiveness heavily impacts on its legal definition, and shows in a paradigmatic manner the ambiguity between the 'concrete' and the 'normative' in the nature of international law, as it relates to matters of territorial sovereignty. The legal determination of the powers of the occupants is often crucial to the understanding of the legal dimension of territorial situations, and it is often one of the most contentious issues in the underlying political dispute.

2. Statehood and effectiveness

By considering the role of effectiveness in determining legal issues related to statehood and sovereignty, we can fully appreciate its significance *vis-à-vis* the idea of positive legality. It is instructive to recall Martti Koskenniemi's analysis that the discourse on sovereignty in international law has been dominated by two contrasting positions on the nature of the state, the 'pure fact' approach, and the 'legal approach', which have created a spectrum within which every writer and tribunal have 'moved' their arguments.[1] The view, defined as 'Schmittian' by Koskenniemi, presupposes the sociological nature of the state to the legal one - like a person, its physical existence is *conditio sine qua non* to its legal existence -, whereas the view, defined as Kelsenian, sees the state as a legal order *tout court*, whose social and political elements must be distinct from its 'pure' legal form, and do not influence its legal existence. The question of governmental and territorial competencies does not escape this dualism, and therefore it is fundamental to examine those theories for a fuller understanding of the issue concerned.

Kelsen's normativist theory of the state inevitably walks a tightrope. Kelsen's principle of effectiveness, which represents the *Grundnorm* of the domestic legal system, is presented, on the one hand, like that degree of coercive power on which the validity of every norm is based, on the other hand, as a positive norm of international law from which every national constitution is based.[2] Kelsen begins by defining effectiveness in the former sense. However, in order to avoid a charge of presupposing a sociological axiom to a juristic one, he describes it as a 'general norm of the international legal order'.[3] At this stage, the author seems to maintain that the *Grundnorm* is a positive rule that because of its general character finds its foundation in the practice of states. But if state behaviour is a source of the *Grundnorm*, then it seems that either: a) the principle of effectiveness is not the

---

[1] Koskenniemi, *From Apology to Utopia: the Structure of the International Legal Argument* (1989).

[2] H. Kelsen, *General Theory of Law and State* (1961), 115-122.

[3] *Ibidem*, 121. Marek maintains that Kelsen's argument of facts acquiring normative force 'seems an intellectual *tour de force*, performed for the sake of logical perfection.' Marek, *Identity and Continuity of States in Public International Law* (1968, 2nd ed.), 47.

basic norm, rather the basic norm is the principle *consuetudo est servanda*; or: b) states do pre-exist the basic norm, so the sociological existence of a state is a presupposition of its normative existence. To avoid this counter-argument Kelsen admits that the principle of effectiveness is the basic norm of the national legal system, and *consuetudo est servanda* that of international law. Further, he argues that we do not need to presuppose the state to custom, since primitive social groups developed into states simultaneously with the development of international law. He argues by analogy with tribal law that develops in parallel with inter-tribal law.[4]

Kelsen's point is based on an historical observation. However, as a result, one can counter that socio-legal effectiveness plays a fundamental role in the break-up of Papal rule, and the development of new political and legal forms of national allegiance. It is important to understand the role that prescription and adverse possession played throughout medieval times and in the establishment of the Westphalia system. This was the basis of French and English claims to independent sovereignty; the argument was that sovereignty could not merely consist in the *ius alios excludendi*, but should be accompanied by legal authority and actual jurisdiction.[5] In the 14th century, observing the legal regime of the Italian communal states, Bartolus held in his *Commentaries in Infortatium*: 'You may observe that the Roman Emperor is the lord paramount of the world…This I think is true except in the case when prescription has been ruling for some considerable time.'[6] The instructions issued by the Sicilian King Robert to his ambassador at the Holy See in 1312 are also instructive: 'The Emperor may assert that they (*viz.* the Sicilians) are his subjects…according to the sequence of the above-mentioned scriptures…; but scripture has no force against a custom both contradictory and continued.'[7] There are other examples of this aspect of effectiveness and the usurpation of imperial power by new nation states. However, it is important to note that the two elements, on the one hand, the imperial law as embodied in the *corpus iuris* and the papal laws as embodied in the bible, and, on the other, the local statutes and the national laws, coexisted until 1648. Deference to the former was often a pure formality and to say that nation states developed only after Westphalia would be inaccurate. Yet, we cannot assert the opposite view and say that classic international law develops before Westphalia, since this would be reading history with modern eyes. What we face here is the action of facts towards the law in a very slow process of adaptation of the two elements. In

---

[4] Kelsen, *supra* n. 2, 370.
[5] Von der Heydte, 'Discovery, Symbolic Annexation and Virtual Effectiveness in International Law' 29 *AJIL* (1935), 448, at 449.
[6] Cit. in *Ibidem*.
[7] Cit. in *Ibidem*, 450.

conclusion, it can be argued that sovereignty is historically presupposed to international law.

Kelsen seems well aware of this argument, and therefore states that even if national legal systems developed before international law, we could say that at that stage effectiveness was not yet a positive norm of international law - since this latter did not exist -, but only a juristic presupposition.[8] Kelsen does not elaborate on this point, apart from saying that at a later stage, with the development of international law, effectiveness would become the basic norm and states would lose their sovereign status, thus becoming subordinated to international law.[9]

Crawford rejects the idea of a *Grundnorm* presupposing the state,[10] but argues that the nature of effectiveness in the creation of states is not sociological, which automatically and as such becomes accepted by international law, but is rather the result of a process of recognition by certain rules. He argues:

> 'The declaratory theory assumes that territorial entities can be – by virtue of their mere existence – readily classified as having the one particular legal status, and thus, in a way, confuses 'fact' with 'law'. For, accepting that effectiveness is the dominant principle in this area, it must none the less be a *legal* principle. A State is not a fact in the sense that a chair is a fact; it is a fact in the sense in which it may be said a treaty is a fact: that is, a legal status attaching to a certain state of affairs by virtue of certain rules. And the declaratist's equation of fact with law also obscures the possibility that the creation of State might be regulated by rules predicated on other fundamental principles – a possibility which, as we shall see, is borne out to some extent in modern practice.'[11]

In other words, Crawford agrees with Kelsen's idea that the principle of effectiveness is a positive customary rule, with the only difference that, writing twenty years later, he can observe the emergence of additional customary rules - such as the prohibition of aggression, the right of self-determination, the prohibition of apartheid - that condition the acceptance of territorial entities in the international community.

As a 'Schmittian' counter-argument, a series of judicial decisions, both international and national,[12] and state practice throughout the 20th century, seem

---

[8] Kelsen, *supra* n. 2, 369-370.

[9] *Ibidem*.

[10] Crawford states that 'one can only know the basic norm of a State when the State itself is identified as such. Like international responsibility, *the basic norm is a conclusion to the problems of existence, identity, and continuity, not the means of their solution* (italics added). Nor can there be such a thing as an "independent" basic norm; merely a basic norm of a State that is independent. Again, this is not to deny that the legal system of an entity is a part of its general system of government, and as such relevant to questions of existence, identity and continuity of statehood.' Crawford, *The Creation of States in International Law* (1976), 76.

[11] *Ibidem*, 4.

[12] E.g. Tribunal of Bolzano, *Kweton c. Ullman*, in 55 *Rivista di diritto internazionale* (1972), 12; Italian Court of Cassation, *Warenzeichenverband Regelungstechnik c. Ministero dell'industria, del commercio e*

to point to an opposite 'sociological' approach to effectiveness in the creation of states and their recognition.[13] In the *Aaland Islands* case (1920) one of the questions that the International Commission of Jurists needed to answer was at which stage did Finland become a state. The commission held that

'[i]t is, therefore, difficult to say at what exact date the Finnish Republic, in the legal sense of the term, actually became a definitely constituted sovereign State. This certainly *did not take place until a stable political organisation had been created, and until the public authorities had been strong enough to assert themselves throughout the territories of the State without the assistance of foreign troops*' (italics added).[14]

It is clear how the 'factual' approach to statehood prevailed. In 1921 the Polish-German arbitration tribunal in the case of *Deutsche Continental Gas Gesellschaft v. Poland* stated that

'according to the opinion rightly admitted by the great majority of writers on international law, the recognition of a State is not constitutive but merely declaratory. *The State exists by itself and the recognition is nothing else than a declaration of this existence*, recognised by the State from which it emanates' (italics added).[15]

The 1948 Bogotá Treaty creating the Organization of American States re-asserts the material nature of statehood and a declaratory view on recognition. Article 6 states that '[t]he right of each State depends not upon its power to ensure the exercise thereof, but upon the *mere fact* of its existence as a person *under international law*' (*italics added*). Despite its ambiguous drafting, the material nature of statehood becomes clear in Article 9, which endorses a declaratory theory of recognition:

'The political existence of the State is independent of recognition by other States. Even before being recognized, the State has the right to defend its integrity and independence, to provide for its preservation and prosperity, and consequently to organize itself as it sees fit, to legislate concerning its interests, to administer its services, and to determine the jurisdiction and competence of its courts […].'

---

dell'artigianato, Judgement n. 468, 7 February 1975, in 12 *Rivista di diritto internazionale privato e processuale* (1976), 354; House of Lords, *Carl Zeiss Stiftung v. Rainer and Keeler LTD* (no. 2) (1967) AC, 853.

[13] For a sociological approach to statehood see Verhoeven, *La Reconnaisance internationale dans la pratique contemporaine* (1975); Arangio-Ruiz, 'L'Etat dans le sens du Droit des Gens et la Notion du Droit international' 26 *Österreische Zeitschrift für öffentliches Recht* (1975-1976), 3, 265.

[14] *Aaland Islands Case* (1920), League of Nations Official Journal, Special Supplement, No. 3, 3.

[15] *Deutsche Continental Gas Gesellschaft v. Polish State* (1929), AD 11, at 13.

Article 10 goes further, asserting that '[r]ecognition implies that the State granting it *accepts* the personality of the new State.'[16] More recently the EC Arbitration Commission on Yugoslavia has held in its Opinion n. 1 that 'the existence or disappearance of the State is a question of fact' and that 'the effects of recognition are purely declaratory.'[17] In its Opinion n. 8 it added that

> 'the existence of a federal State, which is made up of a number of separate entities, is seriously compromised when a majority of these entities, embracing a greater part of the territory and population, constitute themselves as sovereign States with the result that federal authority may no longer be effectively exercised.'[18]

This judicial and state practice, which seems to point towards a sociological approach to statehood, could be reconciled with either Kelsen's or Crawford's view, if effectiveness is defined according to a general norm of international law. In other words, different points of view dictate different legitimate outcomes. It could be held that to name effectiveness a juristic presupposition or a positive norm is only a semantic and logical device used by lawyers in order to separate the sociological and juristic existence of the state. It is clear that its substantive, underlying value is a stable and organised political community, which is why the separation sounds overly fictitious.[19] International law would automatically recognise such existence. On the other hand, it could be also held that such recognition occurs through a general norm of effectiveness, which interacts with other norms in the acceptance of states by the international community. An important consideration in this respect is that, from the perspective of legal consistency, the latter view can be better reconciled with the existence of other norms regulating the creation of states, such as the right to self-determination and the *uti possidetis* rule.[20] The problem with the sociological approach is that if one conceives the state as a factual entity to which the system automatically attaches legal consequences (similarly to what happens for a natural person), it is difficult to see how its existence could be limited by rules of international law.

What is clear is that the underlying motive is a political-normative choice, and often, but not necessarily, a preference for either a dualist or monist conception of the relation between national law and international law. The sociological approach stresses the national community and its sovereignty as a source of

---

[16] Charter of the Organization of the American States, reprinted in 46 *AJIL (Documents)* (1952), 44.

[17] Arbitration Commission, EC Conference on Yugoslavia, Opinion n. 1 (29 November 1991), 92 *ILR* (1993), 162.

[18] Opinion n. 8 (4 July 1992), in *Ibidem*, 199. See comment in Craven, 'The European Community Arbitration Commission on Yugoslavia' 66 *BYIL* (1995), 333, at 357-375.

[19] On a similar criticism of Kelsen's *Grundnorm* see Hart, *The Concept of Law* (1994, 2nd ed.).

[20] Craven, *supra* n. 18, 359.

legitimacy for its action not only at a domestic level, but also in the international arena. It usually adopts a dualist conception. The normativist approach stresses the overarching structure and principles of international society as the main source of legitimacy for state behaviour in the international arena. It frequently adopts a monist conception with a primacy of international law over national law.[21] However, both approaches in the 20th century stress the crucial role of internal and 'material' effectiveness in the definition of state, regardless of whether such effectiveness is legalised by a superior norm, or whether its legalisation occurs automatically because of the *normative Kraft des Faktischen*.[22] To use Koskenniemi's categories, the former approach can also lead to an apology of state sovereignty and of its freedom in international relations, insofar as international law allows for effectiveness to display its fullest effects. Kelsen's radical conception of the principle of effectiveness is a reminder of that.

2.1 External effectiveness

In analysing the relevance of the principle of effectiveness for the purpose of studying *de facto* states, Balejikan maintains:

'The international legal personality of a state is, in the total absence of inter-state relations and international intercourse, a total abstraction, because the domestic effectiveness of an

---

[21] The primacy of international law over national law and a monistic conception are accepted by Malcom Shaw (*Title to Territory in Africa* (1986), 16). However, the author advances some reservations and states that 'this should not be understood so as to detract from the important social and psychological role played by the State in the life of a community. Sovereignty in international law reflects the need for security and stability, but it also constitutes, in Alvarez's words, "an institution, an international social function of a psychological character". Territorial sovereignty is the answer provided by international law as regards the needs for security, stability, and identity felt by a particular group within a certain area. It also constitutes the method by which a community may enter upon the international scene and by virtue of sovereign equality of States play a particular role in the development of the international system. It is submitted that, as regards these two functions, the concept of territory and sovereignty of States associated with it has been enthusiastically adopted by Third World States, although without foregoing the advantages of the global approach.' The question of whether this social and psychological nature of the States presupposes its normative existence or is a pre-condition of its legal constitution is not addressed.

[22] The role of effectiveness can be also seen in the law of state responsibility with regard to the issue of imputability of actions of non-state actors to the state. The ICJ in the *Nicaragua* case developed the effective control test to assess whether some of the actions of the *contras* in Nicaragua could be imputable to the US (*Military and Paramilitary Activities in Nicaragua* (Nicaragua/US), ICJ Reports 1986, 62, at 64-65). The criterion of effectiveness has been subsequently 'loosened' by international tribunals in the context of human rights law (*Loizidou v. Turkey (Merits)*, Judgement of 18 December 1996, ECHR Series A (1996-VI), 2219, at 2232-2236) and international criminal law (*Tadic* case, Appeal's Chamber Judgement (1999), 124 *ILR* (2003), 63, at 108-133). See ILC Commentary on Article 8 of the 2001 ILC Articles on State Responsibility in Crawford (ed.), *The International Law Commission's Articles on State Responsibility: Introduction, Text and Commentaries* (2002), 110.

entity as state is not *per se* identical with the effectiveness of the same as a subject of international law, and cannot *per se* induce, without the willingness of other states, the establishment of inter-state relations.'[23]

In fact, the author suggests an important argument on the issue of effectiveness in international law. As a linguistic matter, the term *effectiveness* recalls a situation producing effects. A government is effective if its power and control produces effects both of a legal and of a sociological nature. The link between nationality and a physical person is effective, if that person's attachment to a certain state produces effects of a moral, religious or juridical nature. The occupation of a certain territory is effective if it produces effects, e.g. the occupation is not disturbed, persons and objects are under the occupant's control. However, since the concept of state effectiveness is analysed here under the prospect of international law, it would seem paradoxical to envisage a state under international law that is effective only in internal matters, yet is completely ineffective at the international level.

In other words, for a state to be effective in its external relations, it must satisfy one of the traditional criteria of statehood laid down by the Montevideo Convention, that is 'the capacity to enter into relations with other states.' This criterion has been traditionally related to another criterion of statehood: independence. It has been submitted that an independent state *per se* has the capacity to enter into relations with other states. An entity *superiorem non recognoscens* is supposed to have no restriction on its capacity as an international person. External independence follows from internal independence, but the two sides of independence should not be confused. We may consider first the concept of independence.

In Anzilotti's famous dissenting opinion in the *Austro-German Customs Union* case, independence is presented in its formal sense:

'no more than the normal condition of States according to international law; it may also be described as *sovereignty (suprema potestas)*, or *external sovereignty* by which is meant that the State has over it no other authority than that of international law [...]. The idea of dependence therefore necessarily implies a relation between a superior State (suzerain, protector, etc.) and an inferior or subject State (vassal, *protégé, etc.)*; the relation between the State that can impose its will and the State which is legally compelled to submit to that will [...]. It follows that the legal conception of independence has nothing to do with a State's subordination to international law or with the numerous and constantly increasing states of *de facto* dependence which characterise the relation of one country to other countries.'[24]

---

[23] Balekjian, *Die Effektivität und die Stellung Nichtanerkannter Staaten im Völkerrecht* (1970), 206.
[24] *Customs Regime between Austria and Germany*, 1931 PCIJ Series A/B, n. 41, 77.

The formal nature of independence has been disputed,[25] and Crawford admitted that despite there being a presumption for lack of independence by so-called puppet regimes constituted under belligerent occupation or following an illegal intervention, it is also a question of fact whether a state is independent or not.[26] This is very clear from World War II cases, like Manchukuo, Slovakia and Albania, but also from more recent cases like the Republic of Srpska.[27] As a matter of fact, it is submitted that it is difficult to establish general criteria for determining whether a lack of factual independence affects statehood and an assessment will be needed in every case, since this determination is of the greatest importance for settling disputes on state succession and state responsibility.

The independence criterion is a complex intermingling of legal and factual elements. The purely positivist approach taken by Anzilotti fails to explain the situations of puppet states. A wide-ranging analysis of state practice reveals the fundamental importance of factual considerations in assessing independence. Traditionally, the internal situation of independence and effectiveness also made the state effective outside its borders. Yet, today, independence as a matter of fact and of law does not alone make a state effective at the international level, where there is widespread consensus that it lacks international legitimacy.[28] In other words, whereas a sociological notion of state underlines the sense of community and collective identity – regardless whether genuinely formed or artificially driven – and the ability of such community to carve up its *Lebensraum* as sources of international legitimacy, today the non-acceptance and non-compliance with fundamental principles of the international community leads to a lack of legitimacy on the international plane. This occurs where the creation of a state contravenes an international norm, possibly a peremptory one.[29]

Even then, widespread recognition from other states can legitimise the existence of that state despite its illegal origins. Recognition, strictly speaking, creates only rights and duties between the recognising and the recognised state. Yet recognition by many states is strong evidence of statehood and makes the state effective outside its own borders. Recognition of the fact becomes *the trait-d'union* between the positivist perspective and the sociological perspective. The effectiveness of a certain factual situation is incorporated as a juridical situation valid *erga omnes* due to the recognition of other members of the community. The

---

[25] Lauterpacht, *Recognition in International Law* (1948), 45; Marek, *supra* n. 3, 169; Kelsen, *Das Problem der Souveranität und die Theorie des Völkerrecht* (1920), 235.

[26] Crawford, *supra* n. 10, 64.

[27] *Tadic* case, Trial Chamber's Judgement (1997), 112 *ILR* (1999), 188; Appeals Chamber's Judgement (1997), *supra* n. 22.

[28] *Legal Consequences for States of the Continued Presence of South Africa in Namibia notwithstanding Security Council Resolution 276* (1970), Advisory Opinion, ICJ Reports 1971, 6.

[29] See Crawford, *supra* n. 10, 79.

material and normative character of international law is preserved because of a
notion of recognition that is both declaratory - it declares the existence of the
state as a matter of fact -, and constitutive - it gives legal 'dignity' to an originally
illegal situation -.[30] As international law stands today, such decision on
recognition of status must be qualified by some legal restraints, which have
developed within the law of state responsibility. According to Article 41 of the
ILC Articles on State Responsibility, when the creation of a state is pursued as a
result of a serious breach of peremptory norms - such as, for instance, when it is
effected in pursuance of racist policies, through denial of a right of self-
determination, or as a result of aggression -, states will have a general duty of
non-recognition, with a view to making the illegal state internationally ineffective.
Any state entering into international legal relations with this type of illegal state
will commit a wrongful act. [31]

3. Territorial sovereignty and effectiveness

Having considered the 'material nature' of the state in international law, we
now turn to the concepts of sovereignty and territory. The state is not a static
concept. As the legal expression of an organised and independent political
community, the state is a dynamic concept, like the political community it seeks
to regulate and like the life of international relations with the other political
communities in which it is involved. Its normal condition is referred to as
sovereign, which is often equated with supreme and independent authority within
a certain social and territorial framework. This is its condition in principle, but
since sovereignty comprises substantive internal and external rights, duties,
powers and competencies, it is also a dynamic concept and assumes different
quantitative meanings in different historical periods.[32] Both the quantitative
growth of international legal instruments as a result of the growing
interdependence and the development of human rights law and environmental
law, limiting the extent of reserved domain in domestic affairs, have produced a
transformation of its content. Nonetheless, the normative character of sovereignty
is still a fundamental character of international law, which is why an enquiry into

---

[30] De Visscher, *Les effectivités du droit international public* (1967), 39.
[31] See Article 41, 2001 ILC Articles on State Responsibility, *supra* n. 22; and *Namibia*, *supra* n. 28, 56.
See also *infra* Ch. 4, section 2; and Warbrick on the difference between non-recognition as part of
the law of state responsibility, and recognition of status ('States and Recognition in International
Law' in Evans (ed.), *International Law* (2003), 205, at 262).
[32] N. Schrijver, 'The Changing Nature of State Sovereignty' 70 *BYIL* (1999), 65.

that character is still necessary in a study dealing with unlawful territorial situations.[33]

As a leading case concerning the definition of territorial sovereignty, reference is usually made to the *Island of Palmas*. Indeed, Judge Huber's definition of sovereignty remains enlightening, in particular for the understanding of its material nature:

'Sovereignty in relations between States signifies independence. Independence in regard to a portion of the globe is the right to exercise therein, to the exclusion of any other State, the functions of a State. The development of the national organisation of States during the last few centuries and, as a corollary, the development of international law, have established this principle of the exclusive competence of the State in regard to its own territory in such a way as to make it the point of departure in settling most questions that concern international relations. ...If a dispute arises as to the sovereignty over a portion of territory, it is customary to examine which of the States claiming sovereignty possesses a title – cession, conquest, occupation, *etc.*- superior to that which the other State might be possibly bring forward against it. However, if the contestation is based on the fact that the other Party has actually displayed sovereignty, it cannot be sufficient to establish the title by which territorial sovereignty was validly acquired at a certain moment; it must also been shown that the territorial sovereignty has continued to exist and did exist at the moment which for the decision of the dispute must be considered as critical. This demonstration consists in the actual display of State activities, such as belongs only to the territorial sovereignty.

Titles of acquisition of territorial sovereignty in present-day international law are either based on an act of effective apprehension, such as occupation or conquest, or, like cession, presuppose that the ceding and the cessionary Powers or at least one of them, have the faculty of effectively disposing of the ceded territory. In the same way natural accretion can only be conceived of as an accretion to a portion of territory where there exists an actual sovereignty capable of extending to a spot which falls within its sphere of activity.'[34]

As is clear from Huber's description, the actual display of state activities is of paramount importance in determining the lawful sovereign over a territory. It is not a coincidence that international law has developed as a corollary of the growth of independent political communities. Its material conception of sovereignty derives from a material conception of the state. This is still a valuable starting point for understanding international legal matters concerning territorial situations.

The terms 'sovereignty', 'jurisdiction', and 'competence' designate the legal manifestations of the state with respect to territory and individuals. The whole of exclusive rights, duties, privileges, immunities, and liberties emanating from the state's legal order are usually designated in terms of 'sovereignty' or

---

[33] On a comprehensive discussion of the normative value of sovereignty and the dangers entailed in its abandonment in terms of inequality among states see Kingsbury, 'Sovereignty and Inequality' 9 *EJIL* (1998), 599.

[34] *Island of Palmas* case (1928), RIAA (Vol. II), 829, at 831.

'jurisdiction.'[35] These terms have been used interchangeably in international legal discourse, yet their use has not always reflected their precise meaning. According to Brownlie it is possible to find a certain regularity of meaning in the way these words have been used and to note a difference between the two terms:

> 'The normal complement of state rights, the typical case of legal competence, is described commonly as "sovereignty": particular rights, or accumulations of rights quantitatively less than the norm, are referred to as "jurisdiction". In brief, "sovereignty" is legal shorthand for legal personality of a certain kind, that of statehood; "jurisdiction" refers to particular aspects of the substance, especially rights (or claims), liberties and powers. Immunities are described as such. Of particular significance is the criterion of consent. State A may have considerable forces stationed within the frontiers of State B. State A may also have exclusive use of a certain area of State B, and exclusive jurisdiction over its own forces. If, however, these rights exist with the consent of the host state then State A has no sovereignty over any part of State B. In such case there has been a derogation from the sovereignty of State B, but State A does not gain sovereignty as a consequence.'[36]

From this differentiation between 'sovereignty' and 'jurisdiction', it is clear that the former refers to the normal condition of exclusiveness of the state's legal order because of its international personality, whereas the latter refers to the substantive legislative and enforcement faculties that are derived from that condition. Brownlie also shows that the two can be separated between two different legal persons in certain situations. The concept of territorial jurisdiction is instrumental for defining a territorial situation, whereas territorial sovereignty normally relates to the legal basis of that overall territorial jurisdiction; in other words, to its lawfulness or unlawfulness. Despite this theoretical differentiation, the derivation of the concept of territorial sovereignty from the concept of state, in particular from the independent exercise of its legal authority, shows that sovereignty and the exercise of territorial jurisdiction usually coexist, making the concept of effectiveness a protagonist in the international legal discourse concerning territory and territorial disputes. Turning to the legal definition of territory, different forms of territorial effectiveness and the role played by the concept of effectiveness in the colonial encounter are examined in the following sections.

3.1 The concept of territory in international law

Territory is the spatial sphere within which a state's sovereignty is normally manifested. Often the term sovereignty is used as a synonym of territorial

---

[35] The terms 'jurisdiction' and 'competence' have the same meaning. The former is mostly used in the Anglo-American tradition, the latter in civil law countries. See Miele, *La comunità internazionale* (2000, 3rd ed.), 107.
[36] Brownlie, *Principles of Public International Law* (2003, 6th ed.), 106.

sovereignty. The doctrinal debate has developed a number of theories in order to explain its meaning in international law, and authors have mixed elements from each, rather than radically espouse one. Therefore, this classification is explanatory and does not aim at a comprehensive description of the whole range of positions taken by the doctrine.

The importance of territory in classic international law derives from the fact that the application of Roman law sources in medieval, feudal Europe created the belief that the territory was the object of state's property. Like property, territorial sovereignty was exclusive and alienable. This was transposed in the belief of early writers who created a 'personification' of the concept of state, where the territory was the public *dominium* of the prince. The difference between *imperium* and *dominium*, the former referring to the supreme state's authority over a certain piece of territory, and the latter referring to individuals' and state organs' properties, was still unknown. This has been defined as the 'object theory',[37] 'theory of property', or *Eigenthumstheorie*,[38] and, despite the harsh criticism it has attracted,[39] it still plays an important role in the legal discourse on territorial sovereignty.[40]

Another theory which has found advocates mostly in Germany and which has been influenced by the organic Hegelian concept of state is the so-called *Eigenschaftstheorie*. According to that theory, the territory is an attribute of the state and not merely an object related to it. In other words, whereas in the 'object theory' the territory is not a constitutive part of the state, but only the object of its right of property - to use a private law analogy -, in the *Eigenschaftstheorie* the territory is the physical body of the state, a constitutive element of its personality. As a consequence, whereas a territorial modification does not affect the state's personality in the former case - it affects only its 'property' rights -, in the latter

---

[37] Lauterpacht, *International Law* (1970); and more recently Shaw, *supra* n. 21, 15.

[38] O'Connell, *State Succession in Municipal Law and International Law* (1967), Vol. I, 22; Donati, *Stato e Territorio* (1923). O'Connell states that the 'theory of property' is particularly strong in Anglo-American thinking, 'which is still dominated by the feudal conception of eminent domain, and which resists the disengagement of *imperium* and *dominium*.' An opposing view is given by Miele (*supra* n. 35, 107) who, in asserting a functional concept of territory which eventually ends up overlapping with the concept of jurisdiction, states that a formal concept of territory based on its objective nature is unknown in the Anglo-American tradition.

[39] The *Eigentumstheorie* has been much criticised as a) it fails to catch the public, political role of the state, which does not have a right to enjoy the territory, but regulates its enjoyment, and it confuses it with the feudal notion of patrimonial state (e.g. Westlake, *Principles of International Law* (1894); Cavaglieri, 'Règles générales du droit de la paix' 26 *Recueil des Cours* (1929), 315, at 385; Jennings, *The Acquisition of Territory in International Law* (1963), 3; b) a cession of a territory from one state to another does not affect in principle the private properties of citizens (Westlake, *supra*, 132); c) it fails to consider the importance of conquest as a traditional mode of acquisition of territory, which is still important today in case of intertemporal application of international law (Marek, *supra* n. 3, 19).

[40] This theory seems to underlie Brownlie's example cited above.

case, the state's personality is affected.[41] The theory has found little support due to its lack of adherence to state practice, which does not sustain the idea that a state's personality changes according to its territorial changes.

The theory of competence (*Kompetenztheorie*) has been developed within the Austrian school of pure theory of law.[42] According to this theory, the territory is neither object nor constitutive element of the state, but is only the spatial framework within which the national legal order is valid. A clear enunciation of this theory was given by France in its pleading before the PCIJ in the *Nationality Decrees in Tunis and Morocco* case. In that case M.A. de La Pradelle stated:

> '…territory is neither an object not a substance, it is a framework. What sort of framework? The framework within which the public power is exercised…territory as such must not be considered, it must be regarded as the external, ostensible sign of the sphere within which the public power of the state is exercised.'[43]

Following these premises, Kelsen talks about territory both in a narrower and in a wider sense. In the former sense, he refers to the spatial sphere where the state is exclusively entitled to exercise coercive powers - the space within state boundaries -, and in the latter he refers to those areas where the state does not hold exclusive sovereign rights, but it exercises them together with other states, - i.e. the High Seas, the state exercises jurisdiction over those ships flying its flag -. Whether it assumes the state's competence or jurisdiction as defined by the principle of effectiveness of general international law,[44] or by the state as an organised community of individuals,[45] the competence theory stresses the importance of the effective display of state power.[46] In other words, the territory of the state is a metaphysical essence, whose importance can be measured by reference to territorial (and personal, according to Verdross) competencies. The

---

[41] Fricker, *Vom Gebiet und Gebietshoheit* (1867); Jellinek, *Allgemeine Staatslehre* (1922). Jellinek, despite sharing the premises with Fricker's theory, does not draw the logical conclusion that a treaty of cession should change the state's personality.

[42] The doctrine was originally formulated by Radintsky in 1906 ('Die rechtliche Natur des Staatsgebiets' 20 *Archiv des öffentlichen Rechts* (1906), 313), and then systematised by Kelsen (*supra* n. 25) and Verdross (*Die Verfassung der Völkerrechtsgemeinschaft* (1926)). It then found support outside the Austrian context. See *inter alia* Schoenborn 'La nature juridique du territoire' 5 *Recueil des Cours* (1929), 85; Guggenheim, *Traité de droit international public* (1953), Vol. I, 369; Rousseau, *Droit international public* (1953), Vol. III, 8; Oppenheim and Lauterpacht (*International Law: a Treatise* (1947, 6th ed.), 408) seem to merge the object theory and the competence theory. In the same page, they declare the territory to be 'the public property of the State' and 'the space within which the State exercises its supreme authority.' Lauterpacht's and Oppenheim's opinion is later held by Shaw (*supra* n. 21, 15).

[43] *Nationality Decrees in Tunis and Morocco*, 1923 PCIJ Series B, n. 4.

[44] Kelsen, *Principles of International Law* (1966, 2nd ed.).

[45] Verdross, *supra* n. 42.

[46] Conforti, 'The theory of competence in Alfred Verdross' 6 *EJIL* (1995), 70.

operation of effectiveness as a material element of a certain territorial situation in Kelsen is radical. He states that a treaty of cession only confers a right to the cessionary state to take possession of the territory, but the actual transfer of sovereignty happens only with the actual possession of the territory.[47]

A fourth theory has been proposed by Quadri and later by Conforti.[48] The so-called functional theory expresses personal and territorial competencies as determined by the state function, which is considered worthy of protection by the international legal order. It defines competence as 'the independent title to exercise coercive powers recognized by international law.' Its starting point, in common with the *Kompetenztheorie*, is the rejection of a patrimonial notion of the state, which considers territory as an object of public property. Further, it considers competence as the central meaning of a legal notion of territory. Territorial sovereignty is nothing but 'the competence (or right) of the state to exercise jurisdiction within the framework of the territory.'[49] The cases of international administration, or belligerent occupation of parts of territory under nominal sovereignty by another state are nothing but cases of territorial sovereignty as exercised by the occupant state, 'albeit qualified by particular international obligations in relation both to the actual exercise and to withdrawal from the territory after a certain time.'[50] Therefore, territorial sovereignty cannot be divided from the actual exercise of territorial jurisdiction. Competencies outside the territorial framework are considered personal competencies and there is no need to discuss territory in a wider sense, because this gives rise to the overly artificial construction of territory as a movable object as advanced by the object theory and the competence theory (e.g. cases of jurisdiction on ships and aircraft explained with the metaphor of *territoire flottant*). The third distinctive category of competence is the functional one. This is related to the case in which a state's jurisdictional power is conferred by international law not in relation to a territorial or personal link, but in relation to a definite common or state's interest. This includes, for example, the right to arrest ships in the High Seas engaging in piracy, hijacking or major environmental pollution; and the powers of coastal states over the contiguous zone, the exclusive economic zone or the continental shelf. The functional theory stresses the role of effectiveness in territorial matters,

---

[47] However, his explanation of the relationship between ceding state and cessionary state, in case the former does not abide by the treaty, shows his point of view: 'If the ceding state, in violation of its treaty obligation, refuses to withdraw from the ceded territory, it commits an international delict, and the cessionary is authorised by general international law to take enforcement actions against the delinquent state; but the territory concerned remains the territory of the delinquent state, no territorial change taking place.' Kelsen, *Principles of International Law* (1952), 214.

[48] Quadri, 'Cours général de droit international public' 113 *Recueil des Cours* (1963), 245; Conforti, *supra* n. 46.

[49] *Ibidem*, at 75.

[50] *Ibidem*.

above all when competence is conceived as a state's subjective right rather than as an attribute recognised by international law.

The competence and the functional theory best represent the concept of territory under international law, by equating it to the legal competence and authority exercised in a defined spatial sphere. In other words, territory and territorial sovereignty assume the same legal meaning. The functional theory, however, has the merit of making a useful distinction between territorial sovereignty and sovereign powers outside state borders, which is not part of the competence theory. Therefore, the difference between the expression sovereignty and territorial sovereignty becomes clear. Moreover, it has the merit of envisaging the emergence of new competencies such as those related to the protection of the environment, which go beyond the strict divide between territorial and personal jurisdiction. Finally, it does away with the strict territorial approach to the theory of international legal personality, including national liberation movements and governments in exile at the stage where they do not have any permanent territorial basis.[51] However, the theory ought to be qualified when stating the identity territorial sovereignty-territorial jurisdiction, as sovereignty can be defined both in a formal and in a material sense.[52] Rather, the object theory still provides a valuable interpretative tool in cases of belligerent occupation and cases of international administration of territories, where territorial sovereignty and territorial jurisdiction become divorced. It also has the merit of underlining the difference between sovereign rights deriving from a title or a general norm and the effective exercise of power in territorial issues, so clearly spelled out by the Canadian Supreme Court in the *Quebec* case.[53]

---

[51] This approach enables us to understand the international legal personality of national liberation movements like the PLO, which despite not having a permanent territorial basis until the Oslo Accords, was considered having legal capacity and as representative of the Palestinian population living in the occupied territories. The same applies to governments in exile. See *Gdynia Ameryka Linie Zeglugowe Spolka Akcyjna v. Boguslawski* (1953) AC 11.

[52] This is also stated by Marek with regard to the question of identity and continuity of states. She states that adopting the principle of effectiveness as the exclusive criterion for deciding whether a state continues its existence or not can be deceiving. 'For there are cases in which customary international law temporarily dispenses with the principle of effectiveness as a condition for the continued existence of a State. The classical example is supplied by belligerent occupation which the occupied State survives even though its legal order may have become totally ineffective in the whole of its territory. There may be other cases of a State retaining only a *nudum ius* in its own territory, in which its legal order has yielded all effectiveness to the legal order of other States. Therefore, the absence of effectiveness does not necessarily mean the extinction of a State.' Marek, *supra* n. 3, 8.

[53] *Re Reference by the Governor in Council concerning Certain Questions Relating to the Secession of Quebec from Canada*, 115 ILR (1999), 535. See *infra* Ch. 4 section 5.

3.2 Effectiveness and territorial sovereignty in the colonial encounter

The material nature of the concept of state and the functional nature of territorial sovereignty can be traced back to the main legal institutions, which were utilised by the European powers in order to expand their influence over new territorial discoveries in the late 15th and 16th Centuries and during their colonial expansion of the 19th century. The legal devices developed mostly in the 19th century, - the age in which international law saw an attempt by the European international legal doctrine to systematise its contribution to the colonial expansion -, were the so-called occupation of *terra nullius*, and the transfer of sovereignty through agreement with the local populations. According to the status of the territory, if considered inhabited or uninhabited, European powers would proceed with their expansion through either an effective occupation, or through agreement with the local populations to the effect that the European powers would become sovereign over those territories.[54]

Such an apparently simple solution was complicated by two factors: a) the definition of *terra nullius* notwithstanding the long-established presence of local people; b) the real status of the local populations. In other words, did indigenous people have an international legal personality, thus being able to transfer their territorial sovereignty? The question is not merely of historical interest. As cogently argued by Anghie, 'no adequate account of sovereignty can be given without analyzing the constitutive effect of colonialism on sovereignty. Colonialism cannot be accounted for as an example of the application of sovereignty; rather, sovereignty was constituted and shaped through colonialism.'[55] This is evident when considering the material nature of state and territorial sovereignty. In fact, the institution of the occupation of *terra nullius* allowed the development of the concept of effectiveness in territorial disputes, as we know it today in territorial litigation. Furthermore, and despite a 'flavour' to the contrary provided by the ICJ in 1975 in the classic *Western Sahara*, the concept of effectiveness as a legal category also played an important role when European states entered into agreements with indigenous people.[56] This is due to the fact that despite the attempt to differentiate such acquisitions of territory from the occupation of *terra nullius*, those territories were and, indeed, still are retrospectively considered *terrae nullius*: literally, lands without any sovereign authority. This is exemplified by the recent dispute between Cameroon and

---

[54] New Zealand, for instance, unlike Australia, represents a case of title derived from an agreement with the local population. See Ehrmann, 'The Status and Rights of Indigenous People in New Zealand' 59 *ZaöRV* (1999), 463.

[55] Anghie, 'Finding the Peripheries: Sovereignty and Colonialism in Nineteenth-Century International Law' 39 *Harvard International Law Journal* (1999), 1, at 6.

[56] *Western Sahara*, Advisory Opinion, ICJ Reports 1975, 12.

Nigeria over the Bakassi peninsula, which also shows how colonial titles and different interpretations given to the concept of intertemporal law can affect outcomes in territorial disputes.

3.2.1 *The concept of terra nullius: struggling with history in court*

The term *terra nullius* is misleading, because the condition of territory was not necessarily the condition of an uninhabited and remote land, but was often characterised by the presence of indigenous populations. A unilateral assertion of territorial sovereignty over territories inhabited by indigenous people could not be considered conquest, as this implied a state of war between two equal international persons. As the PCIJ held in the *Eastern Greenland* case, it would be inappropriate to describe forcible subjugation of such territories as conquest, since 'conquest only operates as a cause of loss of sovereignty when there is war between two States and by reason of the defeat of one of them sovereignty passes from the loser to the victorious State.'[57] In other words, *terra nullius* was used as a device to justify control and jurisdiction of areas, which were very often populated by indigenous people, who were not considered equals. Much of the international law of those times was based on the idea of the standard of civilization, by which an entity could enter into the realm of international society.[58] Such standards were nearly exclusively European, and they did not allow the participation of any other form of social organisation.

---

[57] *Eastern Greenland*, 1933 PCIJ Series A/B, n. 53, 50.
[58] Crawford, *supra* n. 10, 176. Oppenheim in 1905 cited as members of the Family of Nations all European states including Turkey and Russia, all American states, Liberia, the Congo Free State and Japan (*International Law: a Treatise* (1905), 154-157). As Kingsbury stated 'the Eurocentric system excluded from its purview entities that powerful recognised states were not willing to treat as "states", whether because they wished to dominate or colonize these entities, or because these did not closely resemble "states" as the category had come to be understood, or because they showed little acceptance of the organizing ideas of the system or because they did not seem likely to uphold international legal obligations. While a weaker entity such as Abyssinia might be excluded on ground of difference, arguments that Meiji Japan was still too different were eclipsed by Japanese military victories, especially the 1904-1905 Russo-Japanese war. While power and interests were central to this system, they do not represent the whole explanation for the perpetuation of inequalities. The rejection of Japan's proposal for a racial equality clause in the League of Nations Covenant was evidence not just of the limited strength of Asian and African states in the Versailles diplomacy, but also of a deeper cognitive or identity-based resistance to racial equality as a global principle. This was connected not only with systematic racial discrimination in independent states, but also with colonial policy in territories where the maintenance of colonial rule had come increasingly to depend on the structuring of distinctions among ethnic groups.' *Supra* n. 33, 607. For a reconstruction of the historical development of territorial acquisitions stressing the importance of conquest rather than occupation see Korman, *The Right of Conquest: the Acquisition of Territory by Force in International Law and Practice* (1996).

This Euro-centric criterion adopted by international law in defining what could be appropriated as *terra nullius* and what could be appropriated through cession and conquest, therefore giving recognition to local political organisations, has been the object of much jurisprudential debate before Australian courts.[59] The primary legal point was whether pre-colonisation indigenous property rights could be considered valid. This was logically determined by the mode of acquisition of sovereignty over Australia by the British. If such sovereignty was acquired through occupation - or 'settlement' as defined by Australian courts - of *terra nullius*, those property rights were to be considered as replaced *in toto* by the new property rights of the British settlers. If it was acquired through conquest or cession, those property rights were to be considered as still existent, unless expressly repealed by British legislation. The issue revolved around the question of whether Australia could be considered *terra nullius* under international law. Drawing inspiration from Blackstone's Commentaries and despite admitting the presence of indigenous tribes, the Privy Council at the end of the 19th century in *Cooper v. Stuart* defined the land as unoccupied because of the lack of a legal system and a structured society.[60] Australian courts moved on in *Milirrpum v. Nabalco* to admit, according to updated historical and anthropological evidence, that Australian land was not factually *nullius*, because of the presence of settled societies and a legal system. However, as a matter of law, *stare decisis* should prevail.[61] And they finally reached the conclusion in *Coe v. Commonwealth* that social and legal local organisations did not satisfy the European standards of civilisation, and therefore should be considered as non-existent from a legal point of view.[62] Due to current moral and political imperatives and new international legal commitments and trends represented by the ICJ decision in *Western Sahara* a *corrigendum* was added in *Mabo*.[63] To consider Australia unoccupied land would be politically offensive and historically unjustified, therefore the whole application of the doctrine of *terra nullius* was discarded. However, the Court created a new category of acquisition, 'settlement in occupied land', which, despite recognising the legal existence of the indigenous communities as property holders, did not recognise any international legal standing to those communities. This would have led the Court to reach a determination to the effect that the British colonisation of Australia was the result of conquest, re-writing two hundred years of history and identity. However, a shift from occupation of *terra nullius* to 'settlement in

---

[59] See Simpson, '*Mabo*, International Law, *Terra Nullius* and the Stories of Settlement: an Unresolved Jurisprudence' 19 *Melbourne University Law Review* (1993), 195.
[60] *Cooper v. Stuart* (1889) AC 286.
[61] *Milirrpum v. Nabalco* 17 FLR (1970), 141.
[62] *Coe v. Commonwealth* 24 ALR (1979), 118.
[63] *Mabo v. Queensland* (1992), 112 *ILR* (1999), 458.

occupied land', while a substantial and welcome shift from the point of view of Australian law, hardly represented any shift under international law.[64]

In fact, despite drawing progressive inspiration from *Western Sahara*, it puts its rationale into a slightly sinister light.[65] *Western Sahara* was presented as the retrospective triumph of the right of self-determination, and the just recognition of the sovereign rights of the indigenous communities in the Sahara, and, more broadly, of pre-colonial non-European entities. However, as Cassese argues, the Court did not take any explicit position on the legal nature of colonial protectorates, and on the legality of the Spanish title to Western Sahara. In other words, the Court did not take a position in the dispute which characterised international legal doctrine at the turn of the 20th century as to whether or not local entities were able to enter into international treaties with the European powers.[66] The Australian court's conclusions seem to support the idea that occupation of *terra nullius*, settlement in occupied land, and transfer through agreement were only different devices adopted by the European powers *inter pares*, to justify their colonial expansion. The difference would be only of a constitutional rather than an international nature.[67] From an international law point of view, those lands were indeed considered *terrae nullius* and free for unilateral appropriation.

The suspicions raised by *Mabo* with regard to *Western Sahara*'s progress in recognising the international rights of indigenous populations have been confirmed by the *Case Concerning the Land and Maritime Boundary between Cameroon and Nigeria (Equatorial Guinea Intervening)* decided on 10 October 2002.[68] The case was brought in 1994 before the Court by Cameroon for the violation by Nigeria of its territorial sovereignty over Bakassi and with a view to delimiting the maritime boundary between the two countries.[69]

---

[64] Accordingly Judge J. Brennan, in *ibidem*, 492-494. And more recently *Western Australia v. Ward* (2002), 191 ALR 1, at 55-58; *Yorta Yorta v. Victoria* (2002), 194 ALR 538, at 550.

[65] On the relation between *Mabo* and *Western Sahara* see Scott, 'The Australian High Court's Use of the *Western Sahara* case in *Mabo*' 45 *ICLQ* (1996), 923.

[66] Cassese, 'The International Court of Justice and the right of peoples to self-determination', in Lowe, Fitzmaurice (eds.), *Fifty years of the International Court of Justice: Essays in honour of Sir Robert Jennings* (1996), 351, at 360-361.

[67] See Brierly, *The Law of Nations* (1955, 5th ed.), 158-159.

[68] *Case Concerning the Land and Maritime Boundary between Cameroon and Nigeria (Equatorial Guinea Intervening)*, in <http://www.icj-cij.org/icjwww/idocket/icn/icn_ijudgment_20021010.PDF>.

[69] *Ibidem*, Application Instituting Proceedings, ICJ Reports 1996, 5. In the course of the same year, Cameroon extended the scope of its application by requesting the Court to declare Cameroon's sovereignty over the area of Lake Chad, Nigeria's responsibility for the illegal occupation of Cameroon's territory and a series of border incidents, and to fix the whole of the boundary between the two countries from Lake Chad to Bakassi. *Ibidem*, 77. Nigeria subsequently raised eight preliminary objections. Seven were rejected by the Court and the eighth was considered not to have

The important issue for our purpose was the Nigerian claim to sovereignty over the Bakassi peninsula. Nigeria disputed the application requested by Cameroon of the *uti possidetis* principle on the basis that the 1913 Anglo-German Agreement through which Britain had transferred Bakassi to Germany was invalid in its relevant provisions.[70] This would be due to the fact that the title over Bakassi was vested at that time with the Kings and Chiefs of Old Calabar, not with Britain. Britain had indeed established its sphere of influence over the southern part of the border between Cameroon and Nigeria in a Treaty of Protection between Britain and the Kings and Chiefs of Old Calabar signed in 1884. However, Nigeria argued that the 1884 Treaty of Protection was merely a treaty by which Old Calabar sought British protection in exchange for a territorial limitation to German commercial ambitions beyond the Cameroons. Its legal content should be sought in the normal means of treaty interpretation, and the treaty text would not support Cameroon's argument that Old Calabar dissolved its international legal personality, and relinquished its territorial sovereignty over the Cross River delta area in favour of Britain.[71] In other words, Old Calabar retained its historical title over Bakassi, hence legally preventing Britain from unilaterally transferring title to Germany through the 1913 Anglo-German Agreement, according to the principle *nemo dat quod non habet*.

In response, Cameroon argued that there was insufficient and contradictory evidence presented by Nigeria with regard to the existence of an Old Calabar polity at any point in history.[72] Furthermore, Cameroon analysed the practice of colonial expansion in the second half of the 19th century, in particular at the time of the Berlin Conference of 1885, showing that the creation of colonial protectorates was only another method of annexing territory.[73] Such arrangements were often chosen by Britain to bypass the requirement of effective occupation that became embodied in the Final Act of Berlin in Article 35. The institution of a colonial protectorate was 'a cheap solution', instrumental to the British colonial model of indirect rule.[74] In the case of Calabar, there would be no doubt that territorial sovereignty was vested into Britain and that the reliance of

---

an exclusively preliminary character. *Preliminary Objections,* Judgment of 11 June 1998, ICJ Reports 1998, 274.

[70] *Ibidem*, Nigeria's Counter-Memorial (1999), 158-171.

[71] *Ibidem*.

[72] *Ibidem*, Cameroon's Reply (2000), 245-254.

[73] *Ibidem*, 260-275.

[74] *Ibidem*, 262-267.

British consuls and diplomats on the existing Efik federation was a way to enlarge the territorial scope of its area of influence *vis-à-vis* Germany.

The Court agreed with Cameroon's position in light of the legal nature of the 1884 Treaty of Protection:

'The Court calls attention to the fact that the international legal status of a "Treaty of Protection" entered into under the law obtaining at the time cannot be deduced from its title alone. Some treaties of protection were entered into with entities which retained thereunder a previously existing sovereignty under international law. This was the case whether the protected party was henceforth termed "*protectorat*" (as in the case of Morocco, Tunisia and Madagascar (1885; 1895) in their treaty relations with France) or "a protected State" (as in the case of Bahrain and Qatar in their treaty relations with Great Britain). In sub-Saharan Africa, however, treaties termed "treaties of protection" were entered into not with States, but rather with important indigenous rulers exercising local rule over identifiable areas of territory.'[75]

In support of this assertion the Court recalled a classic *dictum* of Judge Huber in the *Island of Palmas*, who stated that a treaty of protection

'is not an agreement between equals; it is rather a form of internal organisation of a colonial territory, on the basis of the autonomy of the natives…And thus suzerainty over the native States becomes the basis of territorial sovereignty as towards other members of the community of nations.' (*RIIA*, Vol. II, pp. 858-859)

The Court also recalled its previous decision in *Western Sahara*, in which it stated that agreements entered by Spain with local rulers having a social and political organisation amounted to 'derivative roots of title'. The annexation of territory was not effected through occupation of *terra nullius*. The difference between a treaty of cession and a treaty of protection was simply a matter of the internal organisation of the colonial power and did not affect its territorial sovereignty.

In arguing for the lack of international legal status of the 1884 Treaty of Protection, the Court recalled a number of treaties signed by Britain in Subsaharian Africa, and it disputed the international legal personality of Old Calabar. It doubted the existence of a central authority of the Kings and Chiefs of Old Calabar. It argued that Britain was not only 'protecting' Old Calabar, but was indeed administering the region of the Cross River delta. It hinted at the lack of evidence provided by Nigeria of the international relations of Old Calabar after 1884, with the exception of the delegation sent from Old Calabar to London to discuss matters of land tenure.[76] Furthermore, no evidence was

---

[75] *Ibidem*, Decision, para. 205.
[76] *Ibidem*, para. 207. The Court stated that: 'Nigeria itself has been unable to point to any role, in matters relevant to the present case, played by the Kings and Chiefs of Old Calabar after the

presented by Nigeria of any protest at the transfer of sovereignty over Bakassi to Germany in 1913 and at the accession to independence of Nigeria in 1960.[77] Hence the conclusion of the Court that Britain had the right to transfer Bakassi to Germany in 1913.

It is telling that the reasoning of the Court with regard to Nigeria's request for recognition of Old Calabar's historical title was opposed by a considerable number of judges from developing countries. Judges Koroma, Rezek, Al-Kashawneh and Abjiola disputed the Court's 'light' dismissal of the international relevance of the 1884 Treaty.[78] They held that the transfer of Bakassi to Germany was in breach of the principle *pacta sunt servanda* and the rights of Old Calabar under that treaty. In particular, they rejected the approach of the Court which was looking at reality on the grounds, and the fact that Britain was administering rather than merely protecting Old Calabar. They held that the task of the Court should have been to look at the intention of the parties according to the law of treaties, rather than looking at effective realities. According to the wording and the sense of Articles I and II, that intention was merely to ensure the protection of Old Calabar by Britain, and it was not to transfer territorial sovereignty to Britain. The judges also rejected the Court's differentiation between international and colonial protectorates, accepting instead the Nigerian thesis that the legal substance of protectorates should be assessed looking at the express terms of the treaty of protection, not to doubtful general categories.[79] They therefore concluded that Britain did not have a right to transfer the title to Bakassi to Germany in 1913.[80]

---

conclusion of the 1884 Treaty…The Court notes that a characteristic of international protectorate is that of ongoing meetings and discussions between the protecting Power and the Rulers of the Protectorate. In the case concerning *Maritime Delimitation and Territorial Questions between Qatar and Bahrain (Qatar v. Bahrain)* the Court was presented with substantial documentation of this character, in large part being old British State papers. In the present case the Court was informed that "Nigeria can neither say that no such meeting ever took place, or that they did take place…the records which would enable the question to be answered probably no longer exist" […]'

[77] *Ibidem*, para. 208.

[78] *Ibidem*, Judge Koroma Diss. Op., 5; Judge Rezek Diss. Op., 1; Judge Al-Kashawneh Sep. Op.; Judge *ad hoc* Abjiola Diss. Op., 29.

[79] *Ibidem*, Judge Koroma Diss. Op., 6; Judge Al Kashawneh Sep. Op., 3.

[80] Judge Al Kashawneh separate opinion is especially worth describing and quoting. He stated that 'the crucial factor is the agreement itself, and whilst it is entirely possible that such agreements vested sovereignty in the newcomers it is equally possible that they did not, in which case sovereignty was retained by the local ruler under an agreed scheme of protection or administration. These are questions of treaty interpretation and of the subsequent practice of the parties and cannot be circumvented by the invention of a fictitious sub-category of protectorates termed "colonial

3.2.2 Some comments on the reading of the colonial encounter in the above case law

The Court's approach in *Cameroon/Nigeria* to the effect that there exists no difference in international law between a treaty of cession and a treaty of protection with indigenous people suggests that the ICJ, like the Australian courts, is not ready to recognise a fully-fledged international status to pre-colonial independent social organisations. In other words, whereas in *Western Sahara* the ICJ avoided taking a position on the legal nature of colonial protectorates confining itself to deny that that territory was *terra nullius*, in *Cameroon/Nigeria* that position is taken, thereby limiting the impact of *Western Sahara*. In effect, to say that Bakassi, like Western Sahara, was not *terra nullius*, and then to argue that Britain acquired sovereignty over it, regardless of the content of the 1884 Treaty of Protection, is clearly contradictory. To argue the latter is tantamount to saying that under international law Bakassi was indeed a *terra nullius*. One should not underestimate the fact that, by denying the doctrine of *terra nullius* in *Western Sahara, Mabo* and *Cameroon/Nigeria*, at least the property rights of the indigenous populations are recognised. This may have an impact in the way domestic tribunals review the way colonial powers treated those rights. However, it is difficult to appreciate the impact that a revision of the *terra nullius* doctrine according to the allegedly identical 'rules of engagement' of the colonial powers

---

protectorates" where title is assumed to pass automatically and regardless of the terms of the terms of treaty protection to the protecting power, for that would be incompatible with the fundamental rule *pacta sunt servanda* and would lead to what has been termed "institutionalized treaty breach", a situation that no rule of intertemporal law has ever excused.' Furthermore, 'such an approach is clearly rooted in an Eurocentric conception of international law based on notions of otherness, as evidenced by the fact that there were at the time in Europe protected principalities without anyone seriously entertaining the idea that they had lost their sovereignty to the protecting Power and could be disposed of at its will. Intertemporal law is general in its application, its underlying rationale and unity of purpose being time *(tempore)* as its name implies, not geography, and cannot be divided into regional intertemporal law, all the more so when no State in the concerned region, be it sub-Saharan African or South East Asia, participated in its formation.' As for the latter concept of intertemporal law, he stated that despite Max Huber's seemingly straight-forward definition, its interpretation in practice is far from clear. In the case examined, he wondered why only the 'abusive' and 'deforming' practice of European powers should be considered as the law in force at that time. According to Al-Kashawneh, the lack of reference to intertemporal law in the VCLT would not be a coincidence, since neither the ILC nor the Vienna Conference were able to resolve the issue. On the basis of this critique, the Jordanian judge held that the 1913 Treaty could not possibly represent a valid basis for the transfer of title to Germany *per se*, but rather that the inaction and acquiescence of Old Calabar would have extinguished that title. The criticism of the concept of intertemporal law adopted by the Court was fully shared by Judge Ranjeva (Sep. Op., 3).

may have had on international law, if the European powers were free to disregard the explicit terms of those treaties. Cassese argues that the Court's *dictum* in *Western Sahara* may apply to future or present relations. He states that:

> 'Whenever there are territories inhabited by indigenous populations that are collectively organized (although not in such a manner as to constitute a state proper) and the state wielding sovereign authority over such territory decides to withdraw, it does not follow that the territories automatically become *terra nullius*, and hence open to appropriation by any state. Even if the indigenous populations may not come to be regarded as organized in the form of a state, they must be enabled freely to express their will as to the international status of the territory, i.e. whether they wish to associate or integrate into an existing sovereign state, or acquire some sort of international status gradually leading to independent statehood.'[81]

Cassese's position is problematic for a number of reasons. First, in his own admission, the Court dealt with the qualification of Western Sahara as inhabited land rather than *terra nullius* at the time of Spanish colonisation, not at the time in which Spain withdrew from the region. In fact, apart from not being asked to answer this question, there was little controversy over the fact that Western Sahara was an inhabited region, whose people enjoyed a right to freely choose their status regardless of their level of 'progress' in terms of political and social organisation. Second, even taking as decisive test the qualification of a certain territory at the time of colonisation, international instruments do not restrict the right of people to exercise their right of self-determination subject to the population being considered as based on inhabited land according to colonial criteria, but they also apply to those regions considered *terrae nullius* at the time of colonisation. Third, the case of Bakassi shows that the withdrawal of colonial powers from the region did not mean a right for the people of Old Calabar to choose independently their own future, as their territory had been incorporated into wider territorial units by the colonial powers.

To summarise, *Cameroon/Nigeria* limits the progressive message of *Western Sahara*, and it shows how the ICJ is keen to adopt the legal practice of European powers in colonial encounters with indigenous populations. This inevitably reflects a choice about the idea of international law in the 19th century that the ICJ assumes: whether, in Oppenheim's words, it is 'the name for the body of customary and conventional rules which are considered legally binding by civilised nations in their intercourse with each other',[82] or whether it is the law binding upon all collective organisations enjoying territorial sovereignty and entering into legal relations with other similar collective organisations. The former presupposes a narrow idea of intertemporal law, where the *interpretation* of

---

[81] Cassese, *supra* n. 66, 361.
[82] Oppenheim, *International Law* (1912, 2nd ed.), Vol. I, 3.

the law affecting those events is not affected by contemporary developments.[83] It is unsurprising that most of the judges from Africa, the Middle East and Latin America were uneasy with it. The assumption is an international law working unilaterally, rather than reciprocally, and a standard of civilisation based on a racial and cultural inferiority of those regions which settles a dispute between countries in those regions.[84]

To conclude, the concept of effectiveness also played an important role when the colonial encounter was 'legalised' through colonial protectorates and agreements with local populations. Rather than being the result of a process of the gradual establishment of state control and the exercise of state activities, the establishment of sovereignty was effected through a formal act. The substantive meaning did not change, as international law considered those acts only as legally relevant facts, whose unilateral nature could not be disposed of easily. This process shaped the concept of territorial sovereignty, leading the concept of effectiveness to play an important role in most modes of acquisition of territory.[85] Of course, the concept of effective control as a pre-requisite for title was developed with regard to the institution of occupation of *terra nullius*. The next section shall in fact deal with the issue of material possession as a pre-condition for territorial title.

3.3 Material possession and constitution of title

The concept of occupation was derived from Roman law. The analogy with private law institutions was effected by the first international lawyers who considered the principles inherited from the *corpus iuris* as just reason, in other words as principles of natural law. *Ius gentium* was the whole of these principles and states' practice and usages gave confirmation to these natural laws.[86] This

---

[83] When considering the concept of intertemporal law, one should separate the process of application of the law in force at the time of the events considered, and the process of interpretation of that law. See *Namibia*, *supra* n. 28, 16; *Aegean Sea Continental Shelf Case* (Turkey/Greece), Decision on Jurisdiction, 19 December 1978, ICJ Reports 1978, 4, at 35.

[84] Despite all that, the Court's decision appears correct in its conclusions rejecting Nigeria's claim based on Old Calabar's historic title. The lack of evidence presented by Nigeria in terms of protest or international commitments entered into by Old Calabar after 1884 and in the period between 1913 and 1960 supports a conclusion in favour of Cameroon, at least on the basis of acquisitive prescription and the consequent *uti possidetis*. However, it is agreed with Judge Al-Kashawneh that the Court should have reached this conclusion only on this basis, without supporting a very Eurocentric approach to intertemporal law.

[85] See *infra* section 3.4.

[86] Gentili, *De Iure Belli libri tres* (1598), Vol. I, c. 3, Holland (ed.), Oxford, 1877, 16: 'Ius etiam illis prescriptum libris Iustiniani non civitatis est tantum, sed et gentium et naturae…Ergo et principus stat, etsi est privatis conditum a Iustiniano.' E.g. Oppenheim, *supra* n. 82, 53; Westlake, *supra* n. 39, 30.

was particularly true for the issue of territorial acquisitions, where the analogy between sovereignty and private property provided a strong case for this operation.

Occupation was effected through two necessary elements: first, an intention to take possession of the land (*animus occupandi*), and, second, the effective display of activities over that piece of land, generally cultivating it (*corpus possessionis*). It is clear that possession, which in the very origin of Roman law was identified with property, became a just title to acquire property in the case of land belonging to nobody, and its theory was transposed to international territorial acquisitions. Possession stressed the role of effective occupation on a certain land. The material rather than the psychological element in the classic Roman doctrine emphasised its fundamental function, since the *animus*, the consciousness of a certain possessory relationship with the land was the natural consequence of a factual situation. Yet the re-elaboration of the original material by medieval lawyers brought a transformation by emphasising the psychological element and giving it complete autonomy and sometimes pre-eminence over the material element. Occupation of *terra nullius* became doctrine in 16th and 17th century Roman law, conceived as a pure psychological status opposable *erga omnes*. This historical context inevitably influenced the fathers of international law, who dealt at the same time with individual property and territorial sovereignty, often making no distinction between them.[87] Nevertheless, they were well aware of the distinctiveness of the *ius gentium* and of the novelty of the law governing independent and sovereign subjects, and therefore the requisite of possession was maintained as opposed to that of divine legitimacy as asserted by the Church. That is why, for example, in discussing the lawfulness of the Portuguese claims based on Alexander VI's Papal bull of 1493, that Grotius states in *Mare Liberum* (1608):

> 'to discover a thing is not only to seize it (*usurpare*) with the eyes but to take real possession of it. The grammarians accordingly use discover (*invenire*) and occupy (*occupare*) with the same meaning. Natural reason, the precise word of the law, and the interpretation of scholars all show clearly that discovery suffices to give a title to lordship only when it is accompanied by possession.'[88]

The same emphasis on the material element of occupation can be also found in Victoria, Gryphyander, Zouche, Bynkershoek and Vattel. In 1758 the latter asserts in *Le droit des Gens*: 'Le Droit des Gens ne reconnaîtra donc la propriété et la Souveraineté d'une Nation que sur les pays vides, qu'elle aura occupés

---

[87] E.g. Pufendorf, *Elementorum jurisprudentiae universalis libri duo*, cit. in Ago, *Il requisito dell'effettività dell'occupazione* (1934), 53.

[88] Grotius, *Mare Liberum*, c. 2, cit. in Goebel, *The Struggle for the Falkland Islands* (1927), 114.

réelment et de fait, dans lesquels elle aura formé un Etablissement, ou dont elle tirera un usage actuelle.'[89] In more ambiguous terms this is also asserted by Pufendorf and Titius, who however gave clear pre-eminence to the subjective rather than the objective element.[90] In general, it seems that according to 17th and 18th century doctrine, physical occupation could be represented initially by a formal or symbolic declaration of sovereignty, therefore losing at its initial stage its objective characteristic, but being only considered a manifestation of the *animus possidendi*. This manifestation had its own legal effects, which were differentiated from those produced by a material occupation. Nonetheless, full sovereignty over a certain territory was effected only through a complete display of state activities. This would serve to give legal significance to claims based on discovery. In these doctrines, the concept of *inchoate title*, which would later be advanced by Anglo-American writers, is already envisaged.[91]

It was often stated between the end of the 19th and the beginning of the 20th century that the criterion of effectiveness became of paramount importance to determine the lawful sovereign over a certain territory only at the beginning of the 19th century. Before that age discovery and those symbolic acts relating to it, like the planting of a flag or the construction of a fortress on the coast of the discovered territory, would give rise to a perfect title.[92] According to this doctrine there are three main periods characterising the law of acquisition of territory. The first period is between the 14th and 16th century, and is characterised by the conferral of sovereign rights through papal bulls. The second period is the period of discoveries, where title to territory would be conferred through acts of symbolic annexation. The third period is characterised by the requisite of effective occupation of the territory as embodied in the Final Act of the Berlin Conference of 1885.[93]

In reality, classical studies such as Goebel's and Ago's reveal that this doctrine is rather misleading.[94] The very beginning of the age of discoveries is dominated by the medieval conception of divine legitimacy, but the development of the

---

[89] De Vattel, *Les droit des Gens, ou Principles de la Loi Naturelle, appliqués a la conduit at aux affaires des Nations et des Souverains* (1758), 194.

[90] Titius, *Observationes* (1734), Vol. I, c. 12, 344, cit. in Ago, *supra* n. 87, 52; Pufendorf, *Elementorum jurisprudentiae universalis libri duo* (1913).

[91] Phillimore, *Commentaries upon International Law* (1857); Wheaton, *Elements of International Law* (1916); Oppenheim, *supra* n. 82.

[92] This theory was particularly strong in France and Germany. E.g. Nys, *Le droit international, les principes, les théorie, les faits* (1912); Jeze, *Etude theorique et pratique sur l'occupation comme mode d'acquérir les territoires en droit international* (1896); Bleiber, *Die Entdeckung im Völkerrecht: Eine Studie zum Problem der Okkupation* (1933); Verdross, *supra* n. 42. See also Judge Huber's decision in Island of Palmas, *supra* n. 34, 846.

[93] Ago, *supra* n. 87, 66-70.

[94] *Ibidem*; Goebel, *supra* n. 88.

modern state and the end of religious unity in Europe brought growing pressure to the exclusive claims advanced by Spain and Portugal on the oceans and the New World. The conception of acquisition of new lands as original from the end of the 16th century requires a legal basis which is consistent with the new historical developments. That is why the descriptions given by the first writers of the natural law principles concerning territorial sovereignty both influence and are influenced by states in their practice.

Yet, even before 1550, claims of papal and imperial legitimacy and claims based on discovery were mixed with claims based on effective possession.[95] The real and systematic challenge to doctrines of universal legitimacy and symbolic annexation came after 1550 from England, France and Holland, which in that period were trying to expand their influence in the Americas and to deny validity to Spanish and Portuguese claims based on those titles.[96] Despite their assertions to sovereignty based on effective occupation, the lack of means and resources needed to take effective possession of such vast territories and the need to reach a compromise between conflicting conceptions, often led states to use discovery as a legal criterion to settle claims.[97] In other words, in order to avoid permanent conflict, states took the view that acts of symbolic annexation produced their own legal effects that gave priority in claiming sovereignty over a certain territory. Nonetheless, perfect title was acquired by an effective occupation that needed to be brought about within a reasonable time. Accordingly, the Anglo-American doctrine developed the concept of *inchoate title* given by discovery, that only gave a right to occupy, but not a right to the territory itself.[98] This was also in accordance with the theory of the two elements of occupation, which considered the *animus possidendi* as the element producing legal effects in the first instance.[99]

---

[95] For a thorough analysis of this period see Von der Heydte, *supra* n. 5; Goebel, *supra* n. 94, 90; Wheaton, *supra* n. 91, 339.

[96] Von der Heydte, *supra* n. 5, 457-458.

[97] As Westlake states: 'In the application of this doctrine to particular cases, it is natural that the element of discovery which it contains should have been oftener appealed to by the Spaniards and the Portuguese, whose energies were so rapidly enfeebled that they failed to occupy the vast regions which they had been first to discover, and that the element of possession should have been oftener appealed to by the English and the other nations which entered on the field later. But there is no state which has not insisted in its turn on that part of the doctrine which best suited its convenience at the moment, or which has maintained a perfectly uniform attitude on the questions of detail into which the general doctrine revolves itself.' *Supra* n. 39, 158.

[98] The doctrine of inchoate title is developed by Anglo-American writers of the 19th and 20th Century (e.g. Phillimore, *supra* n. 91; Westlake, *supra* n. 39; Wheaton, *supra* n. 91; Oppenheim, *supra* n. 82). More recently, doubts about that doctrine have been expressed by Brownlie, who states that a title, 'which is in practice a question of the relative strength of state activity, is never "inchoate", though it may be "weak" in that it rests on a small amount of evidence of state activity.' Brownlie, *supra* n. 36, 140.

[99] Ago, *supra* n. 87, 56.

A significant development occurred in the course of the 19th century. Whereas during the age of discoveries it had not been feasible for states to effectively occupy all territories discovered, hence legal relevance had been given to symbolic annexations, by the 1830s and 1840s this effective occupation had eventually happened and titles to those territories had been perfected. Furthermore, new technical means allowed for effective exploitation of most of the earth, and colonial competition in unexplored continents such as Africa was at its peak. That is why effective possession became the only relevant criterion, and priority of discovery began to lose importance even as an inchoate title. For instance, Articles 34 and 35 of the General Final Act of the Berlin Conference of 1885 regulating the European colonial expansion in Africa gave a treaty basis to what had already been developed by international custom, further imposing a duty of notification to the other parties to the treaty and spelling out the functions of the principle of effectiveness.[100] The mediation effected by Pope Leon XIII in 1885 and the treaty concluded by Spain and Germany regarding the Caroline and Palos Islands is confirmation of how effective occupation had become as the primary criterion for dispute settlement.[101] A later systematic enunciation was then given by Judge Huber in *Island of Palmas*: '[I]nternational law, the structure of which is not based on any super-State organisation, cannot be presumed to reduce a right such as territorial sovereignty, with which almost all international relations are bound up, to the category of an abstract right, without concrete manifestations.'[102]

In sum, it was in the course of the 19th century that states finally revolved to effectiveness as the main criterion for the settlement of territorial disputes. Yet it is important not to simplify that historical pattern. State and judicial practice starting from that period and continuing in the 20th century until present days has shown how the criterion of effective occupation has been qualified in some important respects. Effective occupation as title to sovereignty has not meant that jurisdiction should be effectively exercised over every 'nook and corner' of the occupied territory, but it refers rather to the possibility of excluding others from

---

[100] Article 34 stated that '[t]he Power which henceforth shall take possession of a territory upon the coast of the African continent situated outside of its present possessions, or which, not having had such possessions hitherto, shall come to acquire them, and likewise, the Power which shall assume a protectorate there, shall accompany the respective act with a notification addressed to the other signatory Powers of the present Act, in order to put them in a condition to make available, if there be occasion for it, their reclamations.' Article 35 continued: 'The signatory Powers of the present Act recognize the obligation to assure, in the territories occupied by them, upon the coasts of the African Continent, the existence of an authority sufficient to cause acquired rights to be respected and, the case occurring, the liberty of commerce and of transit in the conditions upon which it may be stipulated.' Reprinted in 3 *AJIL (Documents)* (1909), 7, at 24.

[101] Cit. in Cavaglieri, *supra* n. 39, 410.

[102] *Island of Palmas, supra* n. 34, 831.

and to potentially extending jurisdiction over those parts of the territory which are not yet possessed. As long as there is a certain control and there is an intention to maintain it over the whole of the territory, effectiveness may become an ongoing process of 'progressive intensification of State control.'[103] Such state 'control' may not be necessarily 'material' possession, in the sense of establishing enforcement agencies in that territory. Exercise of legislative and administrative functions are equally considered forms of *effectivité*.[104] For instance, in the *Minquiers and Echreos* case, the ICJ considered as decisive in adjudicating the island of Echreos to the UK the initiation by the Royal Court of Jersey of criminal proceedings following events on that island.[105] In the more recent *Ligitan and Sipadan* case between Indonesia and Malaysia decided on 17 December 2002, the ICJ considered North Borneo's and Malaysia's regulations and licensing concerning the collection of turtle eggs as sufficient evidence of peaceful display of state authority.[106] Furthermore, as the arbitrators made clear in the *Clipperton Islands* and *Aves Island* cases pure symbolic effectiveness can be sufficient when considering uninhabited and remote islands.[107] In other words, effectiveness has become a variable criterion according to geographical, economic and strategic conditions. Finally, it has also been envisaged as a matter of competing claims as made clear by the PCIJ in the *Eastern Greenland* case (1932):

> 'It is impossible to read the records of the decisions in cases as to territorial sovereignty without observing that in many cases the tribunal has been satisfied with very little in the way of the actual exercise of sovereign rights, *provided that the other State could not make out a superior claim*. This is particularly true in the case of claims to sovereignty over areas in thinly populated or unsettled countries (italics added).'[108]

The same rationale was used some twenty years later by the ICJ in deciding the dispute between France and the UK on the small group of islands Echreos and Minquiers. In determining in favour of the UK, the Court looked at the

---

[103] *Ibidem*, 867.

[104] For a detailed and informative analysis of different forms of effectiveness considered by international tribunals see Kohen, *Possession contestée et souveraineté territoriale* (1997), 208.

[105] *The Minquiers and Echreos Case* (France/UK), ICJ Reports 1953, 47, at 64.

[106] *Case Concerning Sovereignty Over Pulau Ligitan and Pulau Sipadan*, in <http://www.icj-cij.org/icjwww/idocket/iinma/iinmajudgment/IINMA_judgment_20011023.PDF>, paras. 131-136.

[107] *Aves Island* (1865), in Lapradelle-Politis, *Recueil des Arbitrages Internationaux*, Vol. II (1924), 404. *Clipperton Island* Award (1931), in 26 *AJIL* (1932), 390. Even Judge Huber, despite his 'radical' approach to effectiveness in *Island of Palmas*, stated quite clearly: 'sovereignty cannot be exercised in fact at every moment on every point of a territory: The intermittence and discontinuity…necessarily differ according as inhabited or uninhabited regions are involved.' *Island of Palmas, supra* n. 34, 855.

[108] *Eastern Greenland, supra* n. 57, 46.

administrative and legislative functions exercised by the two states on the islands and found British evidence to be 'the nearest thing possible to the concept of effective occupation in terms of "possession" and "administration".'[109]

Another principle used by international tribunals and states in order to adjudicate and support claims lacking a thorough effective basis has been geographical contiguity. For instance, where a group of islands was occupied, or a certain coast was occupied, those islands belonging to the archipelago and those lying adjacent to the coast were considered part of the geographic unity of the territory even if not necessarily actually occupied. Again, this principle has found application in cases where a territory was uncharted or remote. It has stressed the functional nature of modern state sovereignty that was no more seen as settlement and exploitation but as a display of state activities.[110] In recognising its relevance in those cases, the PCIJ held in *Eastern Greenland* that the administrative and legislative acts enacted by Denmark on Greenland, despite having as direct addressees only the Western inhabited part of the island, referred to Greenland in its unitary geographical meaning and therefore should be considered as an intention to exercise sovereignty on the whole territory.[111]

We must agree with Brownlie that contiguity is a modern expression of effectiveness and bases its value on state activities, which may have a mere legislative and administrative value.[112] Its application by analogy is found in claims to the territorial sea and the continental shelf and in their regulation by the 1958 Geneva Convention and the 1982 Law of the Sea Convention. Thus, the terms effectiveness and contiguity should not be opposed. Nevertheless, the relevance of the principle should be limited to the particular geographical instances seen above, as the ICJ stated very clearly in the *Western Sahara* case,[113] and should be considered only under a clear manifestation of the willingness to rule over such uninhabited territories.

The *animus occupandi* can then qualify effectiveness in certain cases.[114] For example, it is instructive where it is not clear whether the first settlers in a certain territory acted as agent of a government, or where jurisdictional powers are

---

[109] *The Minquiers and Echreos Case, supra* n. 105, 239.
[110] Brownlie, *supra* n. 36, 142. Von der Heydte (*supra* n. 5, 463-464) found a series of arbitral awards where the principle of contiguity has been applied like the *Island of Aves*, the *Lobos Island* and the *Spitzbergen*.
[111] *Eastern Greenland, supra* n. 57, 46.
[112] Brownlie, *supra* n. 36, 142.
[113] *Western Sahara, supra* n. 56, 43.
[114] According to the decision of the PCIJ in *Eastern Greenland* 'a claim to sovereignty based not upon some particular act or title such as a treaty of cession but merely upon continuous display of authority, involves two elements each of which must be shown to exist: the intention and will to act as sovereign and some actual exercise or display of such authority.' *Supra* n. 57, 45-46. According to Brownlie this view does not always seem supported by practice (*supra* n. 36, 134).

conferred with the consent of the sovereign state through a treaty. Yet it is not always the case that courts have investigated its presence,[115] and a material display of state authority is normally considered the relevant test.

The different meaning given to the criterion of effectiveness according to the nature of territory and international standards applied in a certain historical context led Von der Heydte to talk about virtual effectiveness.[116] Sanchez Rodriguez has more recently talked about the *relativisation* of the peaceful and continuous exercise of state functions.[117] Both ideas explain that effectiveness develops as a relative concept under certain circumstances, and that it has to be understood in its functional nature. Therefore, during the discoveries period acts of symbolic annexation developed a sort of 'inchoate' effectiveness due to the fact that any counter-claim and intervention on territories discovered by another state would have been considered unfriendly acts, and would have spread continuous tensions among the European powers. The emphasis in the act of occupation was put on the exploitation and cultivation of the land. Once almost the entire globe was explored, the whole purpose of effective occupation became to guarantee stability, order and freedom of trade in certain areas, protection of foreign states and their nationals, and thus the effective state was the one which was able to accomplish these tasks and to exercise ordinary state functions.[118] Its application in the law of the sea has also had a functional nature, and it has aimed to guarantee optimal exploitation of resources and the freedom of navigation. Any current example of territorial litigation still shows the importance states attach to effectiveness as a way to prove a title to territory.[119] States party to a dispute normally go at great lengths to accumulate different forms of *effectivités* to show that their material possession amounts to title.[120]

From this analysis of the development of the institution of occupation in international law, it is clear that effectiveness developed according to the

---

[115] See Anzilotti Diss. Op. in *Eastern Greenland* case, *supra* n. 57, 83.

[116] Von der Heydte, *supra* n. 5.

[117] Sanchez Rodriguez, 'L'*uti possidetis* et les effectivités' 263 *Recueil des Cours* (1997), 161, at 259.

[118] *Island of Palmas*, *supra* n. 34, 846. According to Smedal (*Acquisition of sovereignty over polar area* (1931), 51) effectiveness is to be considered as 'the ability to secure respect for acquired rights, freedom of traffic and transit together with the maintenance of order.' Compare with Basdevant who argued that '[a] la base des droits du souverain territorial et spécialment de son droit à etre reconnu, il y a les devoirs qui lui incombent; les premiers sont les moyens mis à sa disposition par le droit international pour lui permette de remplir ses fonctions.' Basdevant, 'Règles générales du droit de la paix' 58 *Recueil des Cours* (1936), 475, at 617.

[119] E.g. *Case Concerning Kasikili/Sedudu Island* (Botswana/Namibia), ICJ Reports 1999, 1045; Eritrea-Ethiopia Boundary Commission, Decision of 12 April 2003, in <http://pca-cpa.org/PDF/EEBC/EEBC%20Decision-L.pdf>; *Cameroon/Nigeria*, *supra* n. 68, Decision.

[120] For an example of legal strategy in territorial litigation based on 'accumulation' of different forms of *effectivités* see Nigeria's strategy in *Ibidem*, Rejoinder of 2001, Vol. 1, Part 1, Ch. 2.

historical exigencies of international coordination. It was instrumental for an orderly and balanced territorial expansion of European powers, by reproducing in the law power relations among these states and *vis-à-vis* non-European entities. This has inevitably imposed a concept of territorial sovereignty, which is functional in its nature. In fact, the emphasis on effective possession in the original mode of acquisition of territory has been transposed onto other derivative modes of acquisition of sovereignty like prescriptive acquisition, conquest and cession. These modes of acquisition are examined in the following section.

3.4 Effectiveness in derivative modes of acquisition of territory

As with the emergence of the concept of sovereignty in medieval times, the institution of prescriptive acquisition is derived from the Roman law concept of *usucapio*. Long, undisputed and peaceful possession overrides a formal title to sovereignty. Sovereignty must display a function, in order for the legal system to afford it protection. Despite being sometimes impossible to distinguish between occupation of *terra nullius* and prescriptive acquisition, in theory, the distinction is in the first instance determined by the nature of the territory itself. In the former case, a territory belonging to no sovereign is involved, whereas, in the latter, there will be a sovereign title and an adverse possession by another international subject. Furthermore, the burden of proof of effectiveness is in principle higher in cases of prescription, rather than in cases of occupation of *terra nullius*, both in terms of the intensity of state activities and in terms of length of time. Finally, the element of acquiescence from the formal sovereign and other interested parties will be of paramount importance in prescriptive acquisition. In a wider concept of prescriptive acquisition we can also include the category of historical consolidation. This category was originally envisaged by the ICJ in *Norwegian Fisheries* with regard to the delimitation of maritime boundaries, and later transposed by the doctrine in land disputes.[121] However, more recently, in *Cameroon/Nigeria*, the ICJ seems to have declined any distinctive role concerning historical consolidation in adjudicating land boundaries as opposed to prescriptive acquisition.[122]

In state and judicial practice, the differentiation between the two categories has been blurred. As seen above, the distinction between *terra nullius* and inhabited land is not easily tenable if we consider colonial territories.[123] Often the

---

[121] *Norwegian Fisheries* case, ICJ Reports 1949, 233. And also Johnson, 'Consolidation as a Root of Title in International Law' 12 *Cambridge Law Journal* (1955), 215, at 220; De Visscher, *supra* n. 30, 107.

[122] *Cameroon/Nigeria*, *supra* n. 68, Decision, para. 62.

[123] *Supra* section 3.2.1.

issue has been a choice between competing claims based both on formal titles and on state activities.[124] The *Island of Palmas* case is an illustrative example, as it can be seen both as a case of occupation of *terra nullius* and of acquisitive prescription. Particular importance has always been given by international tribunals and states to the effective display of state activities.[125] What counts most is that in both cases the material element of state authority and the interests that it creates must be seen as worthy of protection by the legal system in order to create a perfect title.[126]

Another mode of acquisition of sovereignty where effectiveness plays an important role is conquest. Conquest has been outlawed under general international law at least since 1945.[127] Yet the application of principles of intertemporal law can still give to it some relevance. According to Oppenheim, conquest needs to be firmly established before it can give rise to a title through a formal treaty or declaration of annexation. Thus he says that 'the practice, which sometimes prevails, of annexing a conquered part of enemy territory during war cannot be approved.'[128] It goes without saying that the criterion of effective control plays a paramount role in disputes concerning conquest. Even in post-1945 international law the invalidity of such acts has been in very few instances tempered by the possibility of general acquiescence or recognition, despite a general duty of non-recognition of situations created by a serious breach of a peremptory norm. The international legitimacy of the factual situation produced by an act of conquest may, in this respect, play a paramount role in gradually transforming the illegal effective situation into a lawful territorial situation.[129]

Cession is the transfer of sovereignty through agreement between two or more states. The transfer of sovereignty is usually set out in detail, but problems may arise when the treaty is either ambiguous or silent on this point. Some authors have suggested that sovereignty is not transferred with the entry into force of the

---

[124] See criticism from Verzijl in *The Jurisprudence of the World Court: a Case by Case Commentary* (1966), 169; and Brownlie, *supra* n. 36, 147.

[125] Shaw argues that there is no real normative difference between occupation of *terra nullius* and acquisitive prescription, since 'although the time element has been seen as important for prescription, as distinct from occupation, it really is concerned with the effectiveness of such possession. Also in conquest effective and stable occupation is the most important requisite and its relevance is nowadays confirmed by international tribunals practice to use intertemporal law (see for example *Western Sahara* case).' Shaw, *supra* n. 21, 19.

[126] Sharma, *Territorial Acquisition, Disputes and International Law* (1997), 115.

[127] The doctrine agrees entirely on the unlawfulness of an act of conquest. Disagreement is instead on the possibility that an act of conquest may be recognised in the long run. See Korman, *supra* n. 58.

[128] Oppenheim, *supra* n. 82, 305.

[129] *Infra* Ch. 5, section 8.

treaty, but with the actual transfer of political powers.[130] Most, however, agree that sovereignty is transferred through the entry into force of the treaty, unless otherwise agreed, and, possibly apart from Judge Huber's award in *Island of Palmas* case, this has been confirmed by relevant judicial decisions.[131] Therefore, effectiveness does not have in principle a pivotal role in the acquisition of territory through cession. However, this role can and has been played in cases where one party is forced to the signature and ratification of the treaty. As stated earlier, during the 19th century treaties often provided for the legal justification of the colonial expansion of European Powers. Because of the coercion under which those treaties were concluded and because of the *ad hoc* recognition of a *quasi-sovereign* status that non-European political organisations were granted, those treaties have been named *unequal treaties*. Effective coercion was the main principle governing these legal relationships and the treaties produced legal effects only *vis-à-vis* third-party European states.[132] Nowadays, the 1969 Vienna Convention provides for the invalidity of such treaties.[133] Yet, as for conquest, acquiescence and recognition driven by the international legitimacy of a certain situation may give rise to a transfer of sovereignty despite the invalidity of the treaty itself.[134]

4. Military occupation and effectiveness

Another legal institution in which the concept of effectiveness plays a fundamental role is that of belligerent or military occupation. The very essence of military occupation is based on effective control and command over foreign territory. The law of occupation applies regardless of the legality of the military presence in a region. In other words, its legal effects are produced even in cases where such a presence is brought about by illegal means. In that sense, it is worth considering the law of military occupation, insofar as it represents one of the branches of international law where the concept of effectiveness plays a dominant

---

[130] Kelsen advanced the argument that also in cession the treaty only gives a legitimate title, but sovereignty is based on the actual apprehension of the territory concerned. His argument seems to recall the concept of inchoate title and was in line with the PCIJ decisions in *Certain German Interests in Polish Upper Silesia* (1926 PCIJ Series C, n. 11) and in the *Lighthouses in Crete and Samos* (1937 PCIJ Series C, n. 82). Kelsen, *supra* n. 47, 213-214; but also see Korman, *supra* n. 58, 17-18.

[131] See for example *Colombia v. Venezuela*, Swiss Federal Council, 24 March 1922, *AD* 1919-22, Case 54; the *Iloilo claims* case, British-American Tribunal, 19 November 1925, *AD* 1925-26, Case 254.

[132] See Anghie, *supra* n. 55.

[133] Vienna Convention on the Law of Treaties, Article 52.

[134] See case of Kosovo *infra* Ch. 6, section 4.

role. The law of belligerent occupation is often an important legal feature of unlawful territorial situations.[135]

4.1 The instruments regulating military occupation in international law

The term itself 'belligerent occupation' shows the original meaning taken by this institution at the beginning of the 20th century through the Regulations annexed to the 1907 Hague Convention. These regulations mostly dealt with the powers and duties of the occupying power as a governmental authority. In fact, the first definition of occupation was limited to cases of occupation of enemy territory in the context of war. Article 42 clearly showed the pre-condition of effectiveness applying to cases of belligerent occupation: 'Territory is considered occupied when it is actually placed under the authority of the hostile army. The occupation extends only to the territory where such authority has been established and can be exercised.'[136]

Occupation was not only limited by the exercise of effective military control and command over a certain area, but also by the existence of a state of war as formally defined by the practice of the 19th century. The Second World War saw a series of invasions and occupations in particular by Germany, which did not fit into a state of war or armed conflict. For instance, the occupation of Czechoslovakia was effected through coerced 'invitation' and no hostility broke out between the two countries. In the case of Denmark, despite the lack of any formal document paving the way for the German occupation, there was only sporadic military resistance which did not create a state of war or armed conflict.[137] This was the reason that led the Contracting Parties of the four 1949 Geneva Conventions to elaborate a common Article 2, which extended the concept of occupation to both situations of non-declared and non-recognised state of war and occupations meeting no armed resistance. The scope of application of the law of belligerent occupation was widened in 1977 to fill a gap with a category of conflicts related to decolonisation. A literal interpretation of

---

[135] For two useful commentaries on the law of military occupation see Roberts, 'What is a Military Occupation?' 55 *BYIL* (1984), 249; Gasser, 'Protection of the Civilian Population', in Fleck (ed.), *The Handbook of Humanitarian Law in Armed Conflicts* (1995), 209, at 240. More recently Kolb, 'Etude sur l'occupation et sur l'Article 47 de la IVeme Convention de Genève du 12 aout 1949 relative à la protection des personnes civiles en temps de guerre: le degreé de intangibilité de droits en territoire occupé' 10 *African Yearbook of International Law* (2002), 267. As for the relevance of the law of occupation to territorial disputes see Kohen, *supra* n. 104, 95.

[136] The text of the 1907 Hague Convention and the other relevant instruments analysed in this section can be found in Schindler, Toman (eds.), *The Laws of Armed Conflict: a Collection of Conventions, Resolutions and Other Documents* (1981).

[137] Roberts, *supra* n. 135, 252.

Article 2 of the 1949 Geneva Conventions as had been given by Israel with regard to its post-1967 occupation of Gaza, West Bank and East Jerusalem, left outside the scope of application of the Fourth Geneva Convention occupations related to territories whose international status was as yet undecided, or foreign occupations of territorial units having a right of self-determination.[138] This gap was filled by Article I, paragraphs 3 and 4 of the 1977 Additional Protocol I, which extended the application of the laws of occupation to

'armed conflicts in which peoples are fighting against colonial domination and alien occupation and against racist regimes in the exercise of their right of self-determination, as enshrined in the Charter of the United Nations and the Declaration on Principles of International Law concerning Friendly Relations and Co-operation among States in accordance with the Charter of the United Nations.'[139]

Thus, the function of this provision was to also include those cases where the occupying power was exercising jurisdiction over a territory under sovereignty of a non-Contracting Party, whose sovereign status is unsettled as in the cases of colonial non-self governing territories or territories under Mandate or Trusteeship Administration or, finally, in cases of racist regimes. The extension effected by the 1977 Additional Protocol I is of great importance, as it concerns the application of international humanitarian law to different categories of unlawful territorial situations. Furthermore, the adoption in 1977 of Protocol II extended the scope of application of international humanitarian law to internal armed conflicts. By adopting the additional instruments the drafters had in mind cases of attempted secession outside the colonial context, where the insurgent groups exercise effective control over a part of the territory of a state party 'as to enable them to carry out sustained and concerted military operations and to

---

[138] As of today the Israeli Government does not recognise the applicability of the 1907 Hague Convention and the Fourth Geneva Convention to the West Bank and Gaza, because those territories do not belong to any Contracting Party. Nevertheless, it agrees to a policy of *de facto* application of the principles concerning governance of the Hague Convention and the humanitarian provisions of the Fourth Geneva Convention. The position has been heavily criticised by international organisations such as the UN, the International Committee of the Red Cross and numerous scholars (see for instance two Isreali scholars' critiques in Dinstein, 'The International Law of Belligerent Occupation and Human Rights' 8 *Israeli Yearbook of Human Rights* (1978), 104; Benvenisti, *The International Law of Occupation* (1991), 107). See, however, the stance taken by the Israeli Supreme Court in *Affu v. Commander of the IDF Forces in the West Bank* (translated in 29 *ILM* (1990), 139), which has recognised the direct applicability of the Hague Regulations as customary law in Gaza; and, more importantly, the stance taken by the ICJ (*Legal Consequences of the Construction of a Wall in the Occupied Palestinian Territory*, Advisory Opinion (2004), in <http://www.icj-cij.org/icjwww/idocket/imwp/imwpframe.htm>, paras. 89-101), supporting the *de iure* applicability of both customary international law and the Fourth Geneva Convention to the occupied territories.
[139] Schindler, Toman, *supra* n. 136, 558.

implement this Protocol.'[140] Again the criterion of effectiveness becomes important as it triggers the application of international humanitarian law to the category of unlawful territorial situations, involving an attempt of secession through forcible means.[141]

The relation between these instruments is, formally, one of complementarity.[142] However, from a substantive point of view, Articles 42-56 of the Hague Regulations, which represented the classic formulation of the law of belligerent occupation, have been superseded by Articles 27-34 and 47-78 of the Fourth Geneva Convention. Whereas the approach of the Geneva Convention is much more focused on the protection of civilians, it inevitably addresses the powers and duties of the occupying power as a governmental authority.[143] However, the Hague Regulations still retain their importance as a separate source of law for specific issues such as the trigger of effective occupation for the application of the laws of war embodied in Article 42, and as a codification of customary law as stated at the Nuremberg Trials.[144]

Finally, it must be noted that the 1949 Geneva Conventions have been adhered to by 190 states, whereas the 1977 Additional Protocols by 161, excluding some important world and regional military powers such as the US, India, Indonesia, Iran, Israel, Morocco and Turkey.

4.2 Establishment and termination of military occupation

The establishment of a regime of military occupation is subject to the provision of Article 42 of the Regulations annexed to the 1907 Hague Convention. What is required is effective control over foreign territory and foreign population. The British Manual suggests a dual objective test in order to assess effective control: a) due to a foreign invasion, the national authorities are no longer able to exercise jurisdiction over their own territory and population; b) by contrast, the invading forces can now exercise and enforce their authority.[145] It follows that a simple incursion into foreign territory does not create a regime of occupation, despite being subject to the other provisions of international humanitarian law, in particular those dealing with the conduct of military operations and the protection of civilians. The Israeli Supreme Court has interpreted the Article 42 requirement in *Tsemel et al. v. Minister of Defence et al.* and in *Ansar Prison* concerning the 1982 invasion of Southern Lebanon as also

---

[140] 1977 Protocol II to the 1949 Geneva Conventions, Article 1(1).
[141] *Infra* Ch. 4, section 5.
[142] 1949 Geneva Convention IV, Article 154.
[143] See Pictet (ed.), *The Geneva Conventions of 12 August 1949, Commentary* (1958), Vol. IV, 614.
[144] *International Military Tribunal in Nuremberg, Trial of the Major War Criminals before the International Military Tribunal* (1947), 65.
[145] Para. 503 (cit. in Gasser, *supra* n. 135, 243).

potentially fulfilled in cases of temporally-, territorially- and purpose-limited occupations.[146] In the *Naletilic and Martinovic* case, the ICTY indicated some factors that may assist a tribunal in assessing the requirement of 'actual authority' established by Article 42: the occupying power must have substituted the authority exercised by the occupied state or entity with its own authority, and the occupied state must be unable to function publicly; the enemy's forces must have surrendered, withdrawn or been defeated, while sporadic, local resistance, even successful, does not affect the status of military occupation; the occupying force must be sufficiently present, or at least be in the position to send troops to restore control in a reasonable time; a temporary authority must have been established and the occupying power must be in the position to issue directives and regulations for the civilian population.[147]

A more troublesome aspect of the law of occupation is that of termination. As a corollary of Article 42, one would assume that the applicability of the law of occupation terminates when the occupying power no longer exercises effective authority over foreign territory. This is confirmed by Article 3 of the 1977 Geneva Protocol I which states that the 'application of the Conventions and this Protocol shall cease…in the case of occupied territories, on the termination of the occupation […].' However, Article 6 paragraph 3 of the 1949 Fourth Geneva Convention introduces a limitation to the full applicability of Section III concerning the law of belligerent occupation. This limitation applies after one year from the cessation of the military operations, and it concerns a series of provisions enumerated in Article 6 paragraph 3. This provision was introduced with the occupation of Germany and Japan by the Allies in mind.[148]

The one year time-limitation is mostly directed toward the possibility of the occupying power taking security measures, whose necessity is difficult to envisage months or years after the cessation of military activities.[149] In accordance with Article 6(3), most of the humanitarian provisions concerning the vital interests of the population are still applicable after one year. However, some are no longer applicable, including Articles 55 and 56, which provide for a duty of the occupying power to ensure the availability of food and medical supplies and medical and hospital establishments; and Articles 146 and 147 which provide for a 'grave breaches' regime associated with unlawful actions by the occupying forces, such as wilful killing, torture or inhumane treatment, deportation, wilful

---

[146] The two case are respectively quoted in Benvenisti, *supra* n. 138, 182 and Roberts, *supra* n. 135, 286.

[147] *The Prosecutor v. Naletilic and Martinovic*, Case No. IT-98-34-T, Trial Chamber's Judgement of 31 March 2003, para. 217, in <http://www.un.org/icty/naletilic/trialc/judgement/nal-tj030331-e.pdf>.

[148] Pictet, *supra* n. 143, 62.

[149] E.g. Article 78.

causing of great suffering, and extensive destruction and appropriation of property not justified by military necessity. Finally, whereas Article 6 paragraph 3 has been superseded by Article 3 of the 1977 Additional Protocol I, it is as such still binding on 30 states - including influential ones, as seen above. At any rate, the rationale for the 1949 provision is difficult to understand, even if it only minimally diminishes the humanitarian duties of the occupying power. If its purpose is to fight the idea that the law of occupation should apply indefinitely 'as an enduring safety net against the consequences of diplomatic immobilism',[150] it is hardly conceivable that this should be the ideal means to do it. If the underlying idea is that the law of occupation should be limited in time, a natural step further may have been to terminate it all together after an additional maximum period, say five years, to keep into account the prolonged nature of modern time occupations.

A powerful counter-argument is that a complete termination of the law of military occupation would leave those populations effectively at the mercy of the occupant's good will, or with the unfortunate choice of seeking protection of their human rights based on the extension of the occupant's legal system, hence annexation. The reality is that the whole concept of belligerent occupation is so entrenched in the idea of effective control that any departure from it is likely to do more harm to civilian populations than anything else. The formalistic and uncritical application by the ICJ of Article 6(3) to the Israeli occupation of the West Bank and Gaza in the *Legality of the Wall* advisory opinion shows the limits inherent in a provision that was not created with a view to regulating long term military occupations. Instead of focusing on the factual existence of a situation of military occupation and of a state of armed conflict at different stages - which can and should be reconciled with the wording, object and purpose of Article 6(3) -, the Court referred to the 'general close of military operations *leading to the occupation*' (emphasis added).[151] As rightly observed by Imseis, the Court's interpretation exempted from the full application of the Fourth Geneva Convention all military operations in which the Israeli Army has engaged since 1968, including the 1973 Arab-Israeli war of October 1973, Israel's *Operation Defensive Shield* in the West Bank in March 2002 and *Operation Rainbow* in the Gaza Strip in May 2004.[152] The Court would have done better by providing a treaty interpretation in full accordance with the object and purpose of the convention, which would have given full protection to the civilian population, and would have

---

[150] Roberts, *supra* n. 135, 272.

[151] *Legality of the Wall*, *supra* n. 138, para. 125. For criticism of the Court's findings see Imseis, 'Critical Reflections on the International Humanitarian Law Aspects of the ICJ *Wall* Advisory Opinion' 99 *AJIL* (2005), 102, at 106-107.

[152] *Ibidem*, 107-108.

shown the full applicability of the Fourth Geneva Convention to present time prolonged occupations.

Finally, and perhaps most importantly, a duty of termination of the military presence is imposed on the occupying power by norms of territorial unlawfulness and the use of force that will be addressed in the next chapter. The fact that some legal consequences stem from a military occupation, and that uncertainty and ambiguity may exist as to the temporal limitation of these consequences, does not do away with a duty of cessation of an internationally wrongful act, for instance in cases such as territorial aggressions or territorial annexations.[153] This is confirmed by the 1970 GA Declaration on Friendly Relations, which states that '[t]he territory of a State shall not be the object of military occupation resulting from the use of force in contravention of the provisions of the Charter.' It is doubtful whether even the SC is entitled to use its legal authority to recognise a *status quo* created by a military occupation resulting from a violation of peremptory rules.[154]

4.3 Effectiveness and formal territorial status in military occupations

The law of military occupation represents a limitation to a full impact of the principle of effectiveness in international law. In fact, as argued by Kohen, its *raison d'être* lies exactly in the possibility of distinguishing between a military *de facto* authority – temporally limited -, and the exercise of territorial sovereignty by the occupying power.[155] In other words, the law of belligerent occupation does not affect issues of formal territorial status, leaving no room for implicit or explicit recognition of a formal acquisition of territory. This was already inherent in the classic enunciation of Article 43 of the Hague Regulations, which bound the occupying forces to respect the laws in force in the occupied territory. It is reiterated in Article 47 of the Fourth Geneva Convention, which sets out the obligation of the occupying power not to deprive protected persons of the benefits granted under that convention following

'any change introduced, as the result of the occupation of a territory, into the institutions or the government of the said territory, nor by any agreement concluded between the authorities of the occupied territories and the Occupying Power, nor by any annexation by the latter of the whole or part of the occupied territory.'

---

[153] 2001 ILC Articles on State Responsibility, Article 30 (a).
[154] *Infra* Ch. 5, section 8.
[155] Kohen, *supra* n. 104, 102.

This latter provision is meant to protect the occupied territory and its inhabitants from any concessions granted by local authorities under duress or from an act of annexation.[156]

Despite that provision, the realistic nature of the institution of military occupation, and its link with the concept of effectiveness should not be underestimated. The striking element already analysed concerns the establishment and termination of a military occupation, which is conditional on the existence of an objective situation of effective territorial control. The legal consequence flowing from the establishment of such military control is the recognition by international law of certain legal powers and legal obligations, regardless of the legality of the use of force in the first place and the territorial status of the occupied territories – i.e. regardless of the legality of the established military presence.[157] This may appear to conflict with the affirmation of a series of principles of unlawfulness of territorial situations developed in the course of the 20th century, which are consider in the next chapter. In particular, it may be difficult to reconcile the duty of non-recognition of territorial situations established and maintained in serious violation of *ius cogens* principles, and the acceptance of certain legal powers and duties by the occupying power when its presence is blatantly illegal.[158] The solution and the rationale are likely to be found in the famous passage of the ICJ Advisory Opinion in *Namibia*, which exempted from the international duty of non-recognition those transactions and governmental acts 'the effects of which can be ignored only to the detriment of inhabitants of the Territory.'[159] The fact that the laws of Geneva are primarily focused on safeguarding human rights in territories under occupation makes their limitation to only those situations which are not *prima facie* unlawful out of tune with the aim and purpose of the laws of war and the consequences of territorial unlawfulness.

To conclude, the level of effectiveness 'tolerated' in the institution of military occupation responds to the overall humanitarian concern surrounding the laws of war. The real problem is not how to limit the role effectiveness plays in this respect, but rather to make humanitarian law applicable to occupying powers, which are often reluctant to consider themselves bound by it. In fact, claims of territorial sovereignty linked to formal acts of annexation make the application of

---

[156] Both categories are also likely to be found in violation of international law under other sets of norms such as treaty law, in particular Article 52 of the Vienna Convention on the Law of Treaties, and the law of territory.

[157] This position is widely accepted by international lawyers, even if it was occasionally disputed by Soviet writers with regard to the German occupation in World War II (e.g. Tunkin, *Theory of International Law* (1974), 411) and by the PLO in the past (see Roberts, *supra* n. 135, 293, note 168).

[158] See ILC Articles 40 and 41 and Commentary, *supra* n. 22, 288-289.

[159] *Namibia, supra* n. 28, 56.

the laws of military occupation and in particular Article 47 most often ignored. Where formal annexation does not occur, other 'legal' means may be adopted to circumvent the applicability of the laws of war, such as the extra-territorial application of civil legislation to occupied territories.[160]

5. Conclusions

This chapter has examined the role played by the concept of effectiveness with regard to the main legal institutions concerned with the law of territory. The chapter has considered how the theory of statehood was shaped around the concept of effectiveness, and how this notion of state was transposed into its main classic legal qualification: territorial sovereignty. The section concerning territorial sovereignty has also considered the legal notion of territory in international law, and how an eclectic model merging functional and object theory represents its best theoretical representation. The chapter has then looked at how the modern concept of territorial sovereignty has been shaped through the colonial encounter. Despite the jurisprudential elaboration behind this encounter and the different categories which have characterised colonial expansion, it has been shown how the distinction between *terra nullius* and inhabited land has been fictitious. The progressive message spread by *Western Sahara* in terms of recognition of pre-colonial political organisations has been scaled down by recent jurisprudence of national tribunals and the ICJ. Indeed, the chapter proves how the non-European world was considered as a *terra nullius* from the point of view of international law. This ensured that the law of territory would recognise a dominant role played by effectiveness, as a device ensuring co-ordination between equal European powers and the subordination of local communities. The analysis of the concept of material possession and effective control as it developed originally in the institution of occupation of *terra nullius* shows how these legal factors have also developed their substance and content in parallel with European colonial expansion and functionally to their political and historical ambitions. Furthermore, the role of effectiveness in other modes of acquisition of territory, namely acquisitive prescription, conquest and cession has been considered. This analysis of the role played by effectiveness in modes of acquisition of territory is all-the-more crucial, since unlawful territorial situations are frequently contested and often given rise to territorial disputes. Within territorial disputes, territorial claims may be articulated in terms of various forms of *effectivités* as independent titles to territory. Finally, effectiveness in military occupations has been considered, in particular the extent to which the laws of

---

[160] Benvenisti, *supra* n. 138, 132.

war with regard to military occupation represent a limitation of its full impact on the laws of territory, despite effectiveness being the main prerequisite for their operation. This is also important for the purpose of the book, since military occupations are often part and parcel of unlawful territorial situations.

Having considered the material and concrete nature of territorial sovereignty in international law, the focus now shifts to its normative side as a necessary complement to a comprehensive theory of unlawful territorial situations.

CHAPTER 4

DEFINING THE BOUNDARIES OF LEGALITY: UNLAWFULNESS OF TERRITORIAL SITUATIONS

1. Introduction

International law should not reduce itself to recording reality. If effectiveness, that is the adherence of the law to the world of facts, was the dominant principle of international law, we would have to question the normativity of the international legal system, and the capacity of international law to influence the behaviours of international actors. This would be particularly true of territorial situations, where the divide between lawful and unlawful would only rely on procedural restrictions on the 'legalisation' of effectiveness. The domination of concreteness over normativity was characteristic of pre-League of Nations international law, and, consequently, one of the main preoccupations of 19th century international lawyers was to prove the juridical nature of international law. Legality was at best defined in procedural terms.

The Covenant of the League of Nations represented a turning point in this sense. Despite its weakness and ineffectiveness, the League of Nations developed the first series of legal principles to limit war in international relations and the legal effects of waging war. Among other important changes, conquest as a mode of acquisition of territory began to be seen as unlawful. The principle of non-recognition of territorial aggrandisement by means of war was then confirmed in 1945 by the creation of the UN and by the entry into force of the UN Charter. In the following decades, in particular during the 1960s and the 1970s, two other substantive principles of unlawfulness of territorial situations developed as a result of political de-colonisation: on the one hand, the right of individuals to be ruled by a representative leadership, on the other hand, the right of the individuals as a group to freely determine their own political and territorial status without foreign or colonial interference.

This chapter outlines the way principles of substantive legality influence and determine territorial situations, completing a preliminary theoretical framework based on the dialectical tension between effectiveness and legality. The chapter defines the unlawfulness of territorial situations with respect to four legal principles and corresponding norms: a) the prohibition of the use of force as a mode of acquisition of territory or change of territorial status of a certain region; b) the principle of *uti possidetis*; c) the right to self-determination; d) the principle of territorial integrity. Despite arguing for the objectivity of the concept of legality, the chapter concludes by identifying some of the inconsistencies and difficulties that characterise legality discourse with respect to territorial situations.

2. Normative standards: the prohibition of the use of force as a means of modification of territorial status

The first principle of legality considered is that concerning the unlawfulness of a territorial situation established through the use of force. This question has been comprehensively dealt with in the legal literature.[1] Traditionally, the enunciation of this principle is traced back to the so-called Stimson doctrine of 1931, when the US Secretary of State Stimson, in two identical notes transmitted to China and Japan, declared the illegality of the Japanese occupation of Manchuria and the US willingness not to recognise any legal effect or instrument deriving from it.[2] However, restrictions on how the use of military force could modify the territorial formal status of a certain region are not a 20th century development in international law. The 18th and the 19th centuries saw the development of norms regulating the way sovereignty could be transferred through the use of force. For instance, the Treaty of Utrecht of 1713 represented a turning point in the history of the legal institution of conquest, by requiring that the transfer of sovereignty would be legitimised by a peace treaty and not only by military occupation or annexation.[3] These norms can be at best defined as procedural, but did not substantially impinge on the freedom of states to go to war in order to expand their own territory.

The principle of unlawfulness of territorial situations brought about through the use of force was developed first in Latin America, and it can be considered as the other side of the coin of another important principle of international law, that of *uti possidetis*. The principle prohibiting forcible annexations found expression in Article 11 of the Rio de Janeiro Treaty on Non-Aggression and Conciliation of 1933 and in Article 11 of the Montevideo Convention on Rights and Duties of

---

[1] E.g. Langer, *Seizure of Territory* (1945); Jennings, *The Acquisition of Territory in International Law* (1963); more recently see Korman, *The Right of Conquest: the Acquisition of Territory by Force in International Law and Practice* (1996).

[2] This is the text of the note: 'In view of the present situation and of its own rights and obligations therein, the American Government deems it to be its duty to notify both the Imperial Japanese Government and the Government of the Chinese Republic that it cannot admit the legality of any situation *de facto* nor does it intend to recognize any treaty or agreement entered into between those Governments, or agents thereof, which may impair the treaty rights of the United States or its citizens in China, including those which relate to the sovereignty, the independence, or the territorial or administrative integrity of the Republic of China, or to the international policy relative to China, common known as the open-door policy; and that it does not intend to recognize any situation, treaty, or agreement which may be brought about by means contrary to the covenants and obligations of the Pact of Paris of August 27, 1928, to which Treaty both China and Japan, as well the United States, are Parties.' Cit. in Langer, *supra* n. 1, 58. On the Stimson doctrine see also Meng, 'Stimson Doctrine', in Bernhardt (ed.), *EPIL* (1982) (Vol. IV), 690.

[3] Kohen, *Possession Contestée et Souveraineté Territoriale* (1997), 389.

States of the same year. These two conventions were regional conventions binding on American States.[4] Article 11 of the Covenant of the League of Nations represented the first universal treaty trying to limit the freedom of states to resort to war in order to enforce their claims; however, it was not until the Briand-Kellogg Pact of 1928 (also named Pact of Paris) that such renunciation became unconditional. The corollary of this would be that conquest became outlawed, yet express provisions to that effect were never drafted. A Committee of 11 Members was created with a view to modifying the League of Nations Pact in order to harmonise it with the Pact of Paris. It considered on 14 January 1930 a proposal by the Peruvian delegate, whereby peace treaties leading to a territorial change imposed through the use of force in violation of the Pact would be affected by nullity and could not be registered at the League Secretariat.[5] The amendment proposal was never brought into force. However, another important corollary of legality started to shape: the invalidity of peace treaties imposed through the use of force in violation of international law.[6]

The 1930s were an important turning point, as the League of Nations was faced for the first time with the chance to develop norms and policies with regard to the Japanese aggression of Manchuria in 1932, the Italian aggression of Ethiopia in 1935, and the German *Anschluss* of Austria and the Sudetenland in 1938. Apart from the consistent policy of American countries refusing any room for the seizure of territory through war - of which the Stimson Doctrine represents the most known, but neither the first, nor the most significant expression - the reaction of the League of Nations organs was a tangible sign of the contradictory imperatives of two different ways of conceiving international law at that time: one as value-oriented social contract willing to promote the equality of states and the common progress, the other as a system of co-ordination with a view to maximising the benefits deriving from political, economic and military power. The latter was soon to prevail.

On 16 February 1932, a few weeks after the Stimson Declaration was issued, the Members of the League Council directed a note to the Japanese government declaring that 'no infringement of the territorial integrity and no change in the political independence of any Member of the League brought about in disregard of this article ought to be recognised as valid and effectual by the Members of the League.'[7] The same principle was re-affirmed by the League Assembly on 11 March 1932.[8] As to the Italian annexation of Ethiopia, despite the initial imposition of sanctions on Italy, the principles of the League were sacrificed in

---

[4] See Bindschedler, 'Annexation', in Bernhardt (ed.), *EPIL* (2000) (Vol. I), 168, at 170.
[5] Ziccardi Capaldo, *Le situazioni territoriali illegittime nel diritto internazionale* (1977), 29-30.
[6] League of Nations Official Journal (1930), 78.
[7] Langer, *supra* n. 1, 62.
[8] *Ibidem*, 63.

order to appease Italy in its territorial claims in Europe and to prevent an alliance between Rome and Berlin (sic!).[9] By the end of 1938, apart from the Soviet Union, all European states had recognised the Italian sovereignty over Ethiopia and no explicit condemnation was ever expressed by any League organ of the Italian seizure. Even weaker, if not non-existent, was the reaction to the incorporation by Germany of Austria in early 1938 and of Sudetenland at the end of the same year. Also in these cases, the appeasement policy of the Western democracies was dominant over any claim of illegality or condemnation, and, through the Munich Agreement, the cession of Sudetenland was formally decided by France, Britain, Italy and Germany.[10] Spain and the USSR were isolated in condemning the inaction of the League.[11] The assessment one can make of this history is that, despite the existence of Article 11 and the inevitable conclusion that League Members were prohibited from annexing territory by the use of force, there existed a dramatic contradiction between conventional law as embodied in the Pact of Paris and a general acquiescence to the effects of the use of force as a means of territorial modification, both in the exercise of military annexation, and in the exercise of diplomatic coercion. One can conclude that such dramatic contradiction lay in the perceived legitimacy of resorting to force as a way to influence and settle the outcome of international disputes.[12]

The Post World War II system aimed at outlawing the phenomenon of war through a general prohibition on the resort to force included in Article 2(4) of the UN Charter. Article 2(4) explicitly refers to threat or use of force 'against the territorial integrity' of a state. However, no express provision was drafted to include the cases of illegal acquisition of territories. The attempt by the GA and the ILC to approve a Draft Declaration on the Rights and Duties of States, which included the express legal requirement of non-recognition of territorial changes brought about by the use of force in Article 11, was not successful, due to disagreement among members on the definition of aggression.[13] GA Resolution 2625 (1970) on Friendly Relations and Co-operation Among States, albeit non-binding per se, but widely considered a codification of customary international law, is the first UN written instrument declaring that '[t]he territory of a State shall not be the object of acquisition by another State resulting from the threat or

---

[9] See statements before the Council of the Polish representative, Mr Komarincki, and of the Chinese representative, Mr Wellington Koo of 12 May 1938, in *League of Nations Official Journal* (1938), 343.

[10] See note issued on 30 September 1938 by the Czechoslovak Government, in *Documents of International Affairs* (1938), Vol. II, 326.

[11] See statement of the Spanish Representative, Mr Del Vayo, 19 September 1938, in *League of Nations Official Journal* (1938), Special Supplement 183, 78; and statement of the USSR Representative, Mr Litvinov, 21 September 1938, in *ibidem*.

[12] See *infra* Ch. 5, section 8.

[13] Ziccardi Capaldo, *supra* n. 5, 44.

use of force. No territorial acquisition resulting from the threat or use of force shall be recognised as legal.'[14] The principle of non-recognition was reiterated in a later GA resolution of the same year.[15] Furthermore, GA Resolution 2625 also states that '[t]he territory of a State shall not be the object of military occupation resulting from the use of force in contravention of the provisions of the Charter.' Finally, in 1969, the VCLT had been adopted declaring the absolute nullity of treaties coerced over states through the unlawful use of force, thus also including treaties providing for the transfer or change of territorial status of territories.[16]

The existence of a rule of general international law providing for the unlawfulness of territorial situations, where the territorial status is modified through resort to the use of force, is further evidenced by the practice of the UN political organs and other international bodies, which did not suffer from the inconsistencies of their League's predecessors, at least, in the enunciation of the legal principle, if not in its enforcement. After the Six Day War in 1967, in which Israeli forces gained control over the West Bank of the river Jordan, the East Bank of the Suez Canal, East Jerusalem and the Syrian Golan Heights, the SC adopted under Chapter VI Resolution 242 reaffirming 'the inadmissibility of the acquisition of territory by war' and requiring the '[w]ithdrawal of Israeli armed forces from territories occupied in the recent conflict.'[17] The Israeli legislation extending civil jurisdiction over the occupied areas and the 1980 Israeli Basic Law, declaring 'Jerusalem, complete and united' capital of Israel, were declared to be null and void by both the GA and the SC.[18] In 1974, the occupation of the northern part of Cyprus was condemned by GA Resolution 3212, which urged 'all States to respect the sovereignty, independence, territorial integrity and non-

---

[14] GA Res. 2625 (XXV).

[15] GA Res. 2734 (XXV).

[16] 1969 Vienna Convention on the Law of Treaties, Article 52.

[17] SC Res. 242 (1967), Preamble and Para. 1(i). Compare, however, the ambiguity of the English version, that according to Israeli political leaders would leave room for an only partial withdrawal, and the French version, that is more in line with the principle of 'inadmissibility of the acquisition of territory by war.' For an interesting and critical discussion of the interpretation of Res. 242 see McHugo, 'Resolution 242: A Legal Reappraisal of the Right-Wing Israeli Interpretation of the Withdrawal Phrase with Reference to the Conflict between Israel and the Palestinians' 51 *ICLQ* (2002), 851.

[18] See SC Res. 298 (1971); GA Res. 3215 (XXXII); SC Res. 478 (1980); SC Res. 497 (1981). The legal position of Israel with respect to the occupied territories is the one of belligerent occupant, despite contradictory claims put forward by the Israeli government in the course of the years (see Playfair, 'Introduction', in Playfair (ed.), *International Law and the Administration of Occupied Territories: Two Decades of Israeli Occupation of the West Bank and Gaza Strip* (1992), 1). The extension of civil jurisdiction over those areas is a violation of this status, *a fortiori* the extension of sovereignty over East Jerusalem effected by the 1980 Basic Law. However, the Israeli Supreme Court has recognised the annexation of Jerusalem since 1967. *Hanzalis v. Greek Orthodox Patriarchate Court*, 48 *ILR* (1969), 93, at 98.

alignment of the Republic of Cyprus' and 'the speedily withdrawal of all foreign armed forces and foreign military presence';[19] such condemnation and demands were renewed by SC Resolution 367 (1975), which also condemned the attempts by Turkey to create a 'Turkish federated State' in the occupied part of the island.[20] More recently, following the 1990 Iraqi invasion of Kuwait, the SC declared the annexation null and void in its Resolution 662 adopted under Chapter VII.[21] During the Bosnian war the principle was clearly re-affirmed by the EC Arbitration Commission which stated that

> '[a]ccording to a well-established principle of international law the alteration of existing frontiers or boundaries by force is not capable of producing any legal effect. This principle is to be found, for instance, in the Declaration on Principles of International Law concerning Friendly Relations and Co-operation among States in accordance with the Charter of the United Nations (GA Resolution 2625 (XXV)) and in the Helsinki Final Act; it was cited by the Hague Conference on 7 September 1991 and is enshrined in the draft Convention of 4 November 1991 drawn up by the Conference on Yugoslavia.'[22]

The principle has been also confirmed by several SC resolutions concerning the conflict.[23]

This consistent state practice of non-recognition of unlawful territorial situations produced by the use of force seems to be contradicted by the cases of Israel's expansion in 1948, the Chinese incorporation of Tibet in 1951 and the Indian annexation of Goa in 1961. Rather than undermine the existence of the rule, these cases qualify it in two different ways. The first qualification refers to its interpretation from 1945 to 1960. In fact, the state-centric legal framework of the Charter, as it was conceived before the affirmation of the peoples' right of self-determination in 1960 through GA Resolution 1514, ensured that, where the status of the territory was contested and it was not generally considered as being placed under a state's sovereignty, the international community would be divided in taking a stance against such forcible annexations and extending the new principle of legality also to these situations. This was the case with the territorial aggrandisement of Israel in the 1948 war,[24] and the Chinese incorporation of Tibet in 1951.[25] Goa's annexation in 1961 was indeed condemned by a large

---

[19] GA Res. 3213 (XXIX).

[20] SC Res. 367 (1975).

[21] SC Res. 662 (1990).

[22] Opinion n. 3, 11 January 1992, Arbitration Commission EC Conference on Yugoslavia, 92 *ILR* (1993), 170.

[23] E.g. SC Res. 752 (1992) and SC Res. 757 (1992).

[24] On the 1948 Israeli-Arab conflict see Pelcovits, *The Long Armistice* (1993).

[25] On the case of Tibet see Crawford, *The Creation of States in International Law* (1979), 212-213; Van Walt van Prag, *The Status of Tibet: History, Rights, and Prospects in International Law* (1987); Berkin, *The Great Tibetan Stonewall of China: the Status of Tibet in International Law and International Policy* (2000).

majority of the SC members, however the adoption of a resolution was vetoed by the Soviet Union.[26] The subsequent recognition by the international community of India's sovereignty was due to the legitimacy, rather than the legality of its claim. This is the second qualification to the application of the principle, which refers to the role played by the concept of legitimacy in curing an originally unlawful territorial situation. This issue, with specific reference to Goa, is analysed more in detail at a later stage of the book.[27] Finally, the case of Latvia and Estonia is interesting, since it presents some elements of the League of Nations system and some of the post-1945 system. The two countries could revert to their original statehood, thus implicitly claiming the return to their pre-annexation boundaries; yet the *uti possidetis* principle applied required the acceptance of the Soviet administrative boundary, which was the solution adopted, thereby conceding room to a principle of effectiveness.[28]

The illegality of changes of territorial status through forcible actions is also qualified by the link between the norms of *ius ad bellum* and the law of territory. Actions in contravention of the basic principles of international law cannot produce any legal effect. However, stating this obvious conclusion should not prevent us from looking at the complexities of the issue. What if the use of force was lawful? What if sovereignty is acquired as a result of an act of individual or collective self-defence under Article 51 of the UN Charter? What if sovereignty is acquired as a result of a collective enforcement measure of the SC? The question of self-defence and the acquisition of sovereignty may be related to the 1967 Israeli occupation of the Sinai peninsula, the West Bank and Jerusalem. One of the claims put forward by the Israeli government was that it was acting in the exercise of its right to self-defence under Article 51 of the UN Charter. Some authors have linked this legality with the claim that the extension of sovereignty over parts of those areas was lawful.[29] However, as rightly argued by other authors, one should not consider the legality of the military action *per se* in the first place, and then derive from it the lawfulness of whatever action follows.[30] As confirmed by the ICJ in *Nicaragua*, the exercise of self-defence must always fulfil the criteria of necessity and proportionality. What really counts under

---

[26] S.C.O.R., 16th Year, 987th and 988th Meeting, 18 December 1961.

[27] *Infra* Ch. 5, para. 8.

[28] Mullerson, 'The Continuity and Succession of States by Reference to the Former USSR and Yugoslavia' 42 *ICLQ* (1993), 473, at 480-485.

[29] Blum, Yehuda, 'The Missing Reversioner: Reflections on the Status of Judea and Samaria' 3 *Israeli Law Review* (1968), 279; Levine, 'The Status of Sovereignty in East Jerusalem and the West Bank' 5 *New York University Journal of International Law and Politics* (1972), 485; Schwebel, 'What Weight to Conquest' 64 *AJIL* (1977), 344.

[30] Bowett, 'International Law Related to Occupied Territory' 87 *The Law Quarterly Review* (1971), 473; Jennings, *supra* n. 1, 55; Cassese, 'Legal Considerations on the International Status of East Jerusalem' 3 *Palestinian Yearbook of International Law* (1986), 13; Kohen, *supra* n. 3, 395.

international law is the aim and scope of the exercise of self-defence, to repeal the armed attack.[31] That must be strictly necessary and proportionate to the imminent threat represented by the attack and the means used by the aggressor state. It would be, at the very least, an odd law of armed conflicts that which would enable a state to expand its territorial sovereignty, in order to respond to an aggressive action. Indeed, SC Resolution 242 declares the 'inadmissibility of acquisition of territory by war', without drawing a distinction between a lawful or an unlawful war. As to an SC enforcement measure under Chapter VII, this would very much depend on the mandate given by the SC resolution. In turn, were the mandate given, the legality of the new territorial situation would depend on the legal limitations to which the SC is subject. These are analysed in Chapter 6.

3. Normative standards: the *uti possidetis* principle

The second important limitation of the role that effectiveness can play in determining territorial sovereignty is that of *uti possidetis*. As stated by Shaw '*uti possidetis* is not essentially a factual question, although dependant upon the same factual background, but a presumption of law concerning one aspect of the transmission of sovereignty from an existing state to a new state.'[32] As a corollary of the finding that the difference between territorial disputes and boundary disputes is only a difference of degree rather than of kind, the *uti possidetis*, meant as a legal presumption freezing the existing boundaries, belongs in principle to both kinds of disputes. It is true that it will play a larger role in cases where the boundary itself and the instruments identifying it are at the core of the legal dispute. However, nothing prevents the *uti possidetis* from playing an important role in conflicts of attribution. For instance, such role can be seen especially in conflicts over islands.[33]

A considerable amount of writing has been dedicated to the *uti possidetis juris* in the last decade, largely due to its revival in events such as the break-up of the Former Yugoslavia and the USSR.[34] The principle provides for the maintenance

---

[31] *Military and Paramilitary Activities in and against Nicaragua* (Nicaragua/USA), ICJ Reports 1986, 14, at 122.

[32] Shaw, 'Peoples, Territorialism and Boundaries' 8 *EJIL* (1997), 478, at 497.

[33] E.g. dispute between Venezuela and The Netherlands over the Aves Island, in La Pradelle and Politis (eds.), *Recueil des arbitrages internationaux*, Vol. II (1856-1872), (1957), 412; and dispute between El Salvador and Honduras over certain islands in the Gulf of Fonseca in *Land, Island and Maritime Dispute* (El Salvador/Honduras: Nicaragua intervening), ICJ Reports 1992, 351, at 558-559.

[34] See Craven, 'The European Community Arbitration Commission on Yugoslavia' 66 *BYIL* (1995), 333, at 385-390; Shaw, 'The Heritage of States: the Principle of *Uti Possidetis Juris* Today' 67 *BYIL* (1996), 75; Nesi, *L'Uti Possidetis Iuris nel diritto internazionale* (1996); Kohen, *supra* n. 3; Sanchez-

of pre-existing internal or international boundaries when a new state is created. It is antonymous to the principle of effectiveness, to the effect that an actual display of authority cannot in itself represent a better title to territory. It first developed in Latin America, where the creation of states as a result of the demise of the Spanish Empire was effected along the existing administrative boundaries. It played the function of claiming a duty of non-interference of the European powers in Latin American affairs based on the doctrine of *terra nullius*. It gained momentum once again during the de-colonisation period, with the creation of the newly independent states of Africa and Asia, and more recently during the demise of the Former Yugoslavia. In these contexts, the needs stressed in the application of the principle were that of stability of frontiers and the prohibition of the use of force as a way to settle territorial disputes. Its existence as a dispositive rule of general international law, which applies whenever states do not reach an agreement to the contrary, has been confirmed by the ICJ in *Burkina Faso v. Mali*, *El Salvador v. Honduras* and by the Badinter Commission, even if such assertion has been other times disputed by writers, and arguably some tribunals have hinted to its exclusively conventional nature.[35]

More often, the controversy over the exact nature of the principle of *uti possidetis* has revolved around its desirability rather than an analysis of international practice.[36] Firstly, one of the main policy objections is that its lack of flexibility works to the detriment of the bargaining power of some states in the process of dispute settlement. Similarly to maritime delimitation, equity should play an important role in deciding territorial disputes. Secondly, if the rationale is to prevent attempts of territorial aggrandisement by military force, one should not overlook the fact that there are other international rules addressing the issue. Thirdly and most importantly, the *uti possidetis* does not reflect the right of self-determination: it perpetuates and legitimises boundary lines drawn by the colonial powers irrespective of any ethnic distribution or will of inhabitants. In a

---

Rodriguez, 'L'*uti possidetis* et les effectivités dans les contentieux territoriaux et frontaliers' 263 *Recueil des Cours* (1997), 151.

[35] *Frontier Dispute* (Burkina Faso/Mali), ICJ Reports 1986, 554, at 558; *Land, Island and Maritime Dispute*, *supra* n. 33. See also *Rann of Kutch Case* (India/Pakistan), 7 *ILM* (1968), 633; *Beagle Channel Arbitration* (Argentina/Chile), 52 *ILR* (1979), 97; *Dubai/Sharjah Border Arbitration* (Dubai/Sharjah), 91 *ILR* (1993), 543; *Affaire de la Délimitation de la Frontiere Maritime entre la Guinée-Bissau et le Sénegal* (Guinea Bissau/Senegal), Decision of 31 July 1989, RIAA (Vol. XX), 119.

[36] For criticism of the principle on policy grounds see Ratner, 'Drawing a Better Line: *Uti Possidetis* and the Border of New States' 90 *AJIL* (1996), 590; Musgrave, *Self-Determination and National Minorities* (1997), 233; Salmon, in 'Débats', Corten (ed.), *Démembrements d'Etats et délimitations territoriales* (1999), 325-331; Kreijen, *State Failure, Sovereignty and Effectiveness* (2004).

sense, the *uti possidetis*, despite being envisioned to promote stability, would encourage further division and eventually, in extreme cases, genocide and mass-expulsion.

This debate will not be dealt with at great length, but for a few arguments which validly defend the function that the *uti possidetis* plays as a rule of customary law. The first argument is that the *uti possidetis* is a corollary of the principle of stability of frontiers. In other words, frontiers enjoy an objective status valid *erga omnes*, which is not dependent on the validity of a legal instrument.[37] They can be modified through a new agreement, which can create a new objective situation, but the situation inherited is always that existing before the territorial succession.[38] *Uti possidetis* is title to sovereignty in itself. To think that it does not do so, if not embodied in a conventional instrument, suggests that as long as an agreement is not reached two or more states may not have a frontier. Despite the existence of norms that address the prohibition of change of territorial status through forcible means, it is also true that military power and occupation will protract the territorial dispute, and eventually have an undeniable weight in reaching a final solution, the cases of Western Sahara and Palestine being two crystal clear examples in this sense.[39] Furthermore, the case of the Former Yugoslavia does not convincingly show that bloody conflict may have been avoided, if the principle of *uti possidetis* had not frozen unilateral territorial claims. Moreover, in the case of Africa, wars for the actual modification of borders have been relatively few when compared to civil wars for the control of government or internal control over natural resources, and one wonders what would have been the consequences in terms of further instability and conflicts had the African leaders not chosen the *uti possidetis* as a general principle.[40] As correctly argued by Shaw, scrapping the *uti possidetis* would result in more foreign interventions and armed conflicts which would be by definition not considered internal.[41] Finally, purely basing the principle of self-determination on ethnic, religious and linguistic commonalties is likely to create even more difficulties for the articulation of a principle, which has been object of much criticism based on its alleged inconsistency and indeterminacy. Even when the difficult task of defining a people by its inherent characteristics was accomplished, imbalances in political power may result in transfer of populations with a view to changing the boundary.

---

[37] See *Territorial Dispute* (Libya/Chad), ICJ Reports 1994, 6, at 37.
[38] Shaw, *supra* n. 32, 495.
[39] See *infra* Ch. 5, sections 6.2, 6.4.
[40] OAU Res. 16(I) (1964).
[41] Shaw, *supra* n. 34, 102.

3.1 The relation between *uti possidetis* and effectiveness

The conflict between *uti possidetis juris* and *uti possidetis de facto* in the Latin American continent, and in particular the reliance of the former Spanish colonies on the former and the reliance of Brazil on the latter, have been perceived to be one of the instances where legality and effectiveness collide in international law. The preference was eventually given to legality rather than effectiveness. In this sense, the present author has also taken the view that the *uti possidetis* principle represents one of the legal criteria that may define the unlawfulness of a certain territorial situation. In practice, however, the line between law and fact is not as neat as it may appear, exactly as the relation between legality and effectiveness in general is inherently ambiguous.

For instance, in the case of dissolution of federal states, the *ius* of *uti possidetis* often refers to juridical acts having validity with respect to domestic law.[42] Their normative value with respect to international law depends on the relation between international law and national law. If one takes a dualist position, a certain legislation drawing administrative boundaries will have the value of a juridical fact under international law, exactly as the actual exercise of jurisdiction. Therefore, the difference will be represented only by the form under which the two facts are presented, one being a title, the other being a set of behaviours. Thus, we are facing two forms of effectiveness, one legal and the other sociological.[43] This explains the assertion that the *uti possidetis* guarantees an objective situation *erga omnes*, the factual existence of a certain border, and not the legal validity of the underlying instrument.[44] International law gives priority to the latter, in order to ensure stability in international relations. However, that does not mean that material effectiveness does not play any role in determining a certain boundary.[45] It only means that it will play a subsidiary role, by interpreting the formal instrument. It is important in this respect to recall a very eloquent passage of the decision of the ICJ in *Burkina Faso/Mali* on the relation between *uti possidetis* and effectiveness:

---

[42] See, for example, the ICJ in *El Salvador v. Honduras* stating '[i]t should be recalled that when the principle of *uti possidetis iuris* is involved the *ius* referred to is not international law but the constitutional or administrative law of the pre-independence sovereign, in this case Spanish colonial law.' *Supra* n. 33, 559.

[43] *Frontier Dispute, supra* n. 35, 558.

[44] See Vienna Convention on Succession of States in Respect of Treaties, Article 11. This norm is also considered part of customary law. See Marquez-Carrasco, 'Succession d'Etats et questions territoriales', in Eismann and Koskenniemi (eds.), *State Succession: Codification Tested Against the Facts* (2000), 491.

[45] *Case Concerning Sovereignty over Frontier Land* (Belgium/The Netherlands), ICJ Reports 1959, 209, at 227-230.

'For this purpose, a distinction must be drawn among several eventualities. Where the act corresponds exactly to law, where effective administration is additional to the *uti possidetis juris*, the only role of *effectivité* is to confirm the exercise of the right derived from a legal title. Where the act does not correspond to the law, where the territory which is the subject of the dispute is effectively administered by a State other than the one possessing the legal title, preference should be given to the holder of the title. In the event that the *effectivité* does not co-exist with any legal title, it must invariably be taken into consideration. Finally, there are cases where the legal title is not capable of showing exactly the territorial expanse to which it relates. The *effectivités* can then play an essential role in showing how the title is interpreted in practice.'[46]

The Court was envisaging four different possible relationships between formal title and effectiveness. First, the actual display of authority may simply confirm the content of an international treaty or internal act delimiting a frontier. This is obviously a case of lawful territorial situations most of the time not giving rise to any territorial dispute. Second, effectiveness may be contrary to the formal title, in which case pre-eminence will be given to the latter and the exercise of jurisdiction will be considered mere usurpation.[47] This has been the way the ICJ, for example, interpreted the Libyan effectiveness contrary to a 1955 Treaty in the case between Libya and Chad in 1994.[48] Most recently, in the *Land and Maritime Boundary* dispute between Cameroon and Nigeria, the same Court ruled against Nigeria's claims of historical consolidation and display of state authority *à titre de souverain* over the Bakassi peninsula and the Lake Chad area, due to Cameroon's title on the basis of *uti possidetis*.[49] In the same decision, the Court has however left open the possibility that, despite the existence of a *uti possidetis juris*, long evidenced acquiescence can lead to a passing of title from one country to another.[50] In other words, the *uti possidetis* does not freeze a boundary forever, but it can be modified through formal agreement or acquiescence to effective control and display of sovereign authority. Third, when a formal title is missing, effectiveness will represent the factual territorial situation at a critical date and will represent a valid title to territory in itself. This was the case in the *Ligitan and Sipadan* dispute between Indonesia and Malaysia, where the ICJ, after having denied the existence of any treaty-based title in favour of either party, held in

---

[46] *Frontier Dispute, supra* n. 35, 37.

[47] However, see the arbitral award on the frontier dispute between Guatemala and Honduras of 1933 recognising effective control opposed to the line of *uti possidetis* as a title to sovereignty (*Honduras Borders* (Guatemala/Honduras) (1933), in RIAA (Vol. II), 1307. Note, however, that this possibility was already envisaged by the *compromis*.

[48] *Territorial Dispute, supra* n. 37.

[49] *Land and Maritime Boundary between Cameroon and Nigeria* (Cameroon/Nigeria, Equatorial Guinea intervening), Decision of 10 October 2002, para. 220, at <http://www.icj-cij.org/icjwww/idocket/icn/icn_ijudgment_20021010.PDF>.

[50] *Ibidem*, para. 67.

favour of Malaysia on the basis of British *effectivités* on the two islands in the period leading to the critical date, as confirmed by Malaysia's continuation of those state activities after its independence.[51] Fourth, when the formal title is unclear, effectiveness, defined as both physical control and acquiescence to a unilateral assertion of sovereignty, will be relevant to the understanding given by the parties to that particular instrument at the critical date. In *Guatemala v. Honduras*, the arbitral tribunal quite clearly stated that 'the concept of *uti possidetis iuris* of 1821…necessarily refers to an administrative control which rested on the will of the Spanish Crown' and that 'in ascertaining the necessary support for that administrative control in the will of the King of Spain, we are at liberty to resort to all manifestations of that will – to royal *cedulas*, or rescripts, to royal orders, laws and decrees, and also, in the absence of precise law or rescripts, to conduct indicating royal acquiescence in colonial assertion of administrative authority.'[52] This was the case for example in the *Taba* arbitration between Israel and Egypt, where physical demarcation carried out by the parties was taken as a definitive proof of the *uti possidetis* line between Palestine and Egypt established by a 1906 agreement between the Turkish Sultan and the Egyptian Kehdiv;[53] and also the thesis argued by Mali in its case against Burkina Faso at the ICJ, which was then confirmed by the Court in its decision.[54]

Following in particular the ICJ decision in *Burkina Faso v. Mali*, the interplay between effectiveness and *uti possidetis* has become one of the distinctive legal features of territorial disputes. As seen, the *uti possidetis* principle represents a limitation on the effective display of state authority as a way of acquiring and maintaining a territorial title. Yet its specific definition within state disputes over territorial titles has somewhat shadowed its function of protection of states' territorial sovereignty. In other words, does an adverse occupation contrary to the *uti possidetis* automatically result in an unlawful territorial situation? The answer may seem self-evidently affirmative. However, the refusal of the ICJ in the recent *Cameroon v. Nigeria* to consider Cameroon's claim for state responsibility related to the wrongful occupation of the Bakassi Peninsula and the Lake Chad area by Nigeria casts some doubts as to exactly how the *uti possidetis* protects a state territorial sovereignty from the adverse display of state authority.[55] The issue is

---

[51] *Case Concerning Sovereignty Over Pulau Ligitan and Pulau Sipadan*, in http://www.icj-cij.org/icjwww/idocket/iinma/iinmajudgment/IINMA_judgment_20011023.PDF>, paras. 126-136. See also *The Minquiers and Echreos Case* (France/UK), ICJ Reports 1953, 47.

[52] *Guatemala v. Honduras, supra* n. 47, 1324.

[53] *Taba Arbitration* (Egypt/Israel), 27 *ILM* (1988), 1501.

[54] *Frontier Dispute, supra* n. 35, at 586.

[55] *Land and Maritime Boundary, supra* n. 49, para. 319.

analysed in detail in the next chapter when dealing with question of state responsibility for wrongful occupations.[56]

4. Normative standards: the right of self-determination

The third limitation to the role of effectiveness in territorial situations is represented by the principle of self-determination. Despite having a long-standing pedigree as a political principle dating back to the idea of people sovereignty in the 18th century, it is only with the League of Nations and the UN system that the principle of self-determination became part of the legal discourse. However, even the UN Charter took a rather ambiguous stance towards the status of the principle, envisaging an asymmetric relationship between the UN member states and the people subject to their administration. This relationship was based on the undertaking of the former to promote human rights, well-being and self-government for the latter. Yet the provisions did not create any legal entitlement, nor was the principle elaborated as an ultimate right belonging to the people to decide the territorial status of the land where they were based.[57] In any event, even if not envisioning a 'territorial right', the Charter had the merit of focusing the right of self-determination on the colonial context, as divided in the two territorial macro-categories of Non-Self-Governing Territories (NSGT) and Trust Administrations. However, it is only with the development of the de-colonisation movement in the 1950s, the accession to independence of many of the Asian and African non-self-governing and trust territories, and the new internal balances within the institution, that the GA became the 'engine' of the right of self-determination. The most important breakthrough came in 1960, when the GA passed Resolution 1514 and Resolution 1541. Paragraph 1 of 1514 states the incompatibility between the UN Charter and any form of alien 'subjugation, domination and exploitation'; paragraph 2 declares that '[a]ll peoples have the right to self-determination; by virtue of that right they freely determine their political status and freely pursue their economic, social and cultural development.' Paragraph 5 draws the consequences of this statement of principle through a rather uncompromising language declaring that

> '[i]mmediate steps shall be taken, in Trust and Non-Self-Governing Territories (NSGT) or all other territories which have not yet attained independence, to transfer all powers to the peoples of those territories, without any conditions or reservations, in accordance with their freely express will and desire, without any distinction as to race, creed or colour, in order to enable them to enjoy complete independence and freedom.'

---

[56] *Infra* Ch. 5, section 7.
[57] UN Charter, Arts. 55-56, 73-76.

Resolution 1514 was adopted by a vote of 89-0-9 and it applies to both NSGT and Trust Territories.

Resolution 1541 is fundamental insofar as it spells out the territorial consequences of the right of self-determination for NSGTs, where colonial powers tended to retain control more tightly. Firstly, it defines a NSGT as 'a territory which is geographically separate and is distinct ethnically and/or culturally from the country administering it' and which is subject to 'administrative, political, juridical, economic, or historical' factors that 'arbitrarily place it in a position or status of subordination.'[58] Secondly, it spells out three ways according to which the right of self-determination can be exercised within NSGTs: 'a) Emergence as a sovereign independent State; b) Free association with an independent State; c) Integration with an independent State.'[59] It is important to note, that in the two latter cases the expression of popular will is linked to procedural requirements such as 'informed and democratic processes, impartially conducted and based on universal adult suffrage';[60] whereas no such requirement is attached to the option of independence. This is in accordance with what Roth sees as a legitimisation of national liberation movements rather than the one head- one vote model of the UN at that time.[61] Further, Resolution 1541 directly addresses the question of sovereignty, since NSGTs, unlike Trust Territories, were not only under the actual jurisdiction of the administering power but they were, according to the view of the colonial powers, also under their sovereignty.[62] Thus, the principle of self-determination had to operate at two different levels: that of transfer of a legal title claimed by those in effective control and that of transfer of effective control over these territories. The resolution was passed by a vote of 69-2-21.

It is interesting to note that the formulation of the principle of self-determination in the following decades by the UN political organs, and in particular by the GA, proposed the two-fold dimension that the principle has

---

[58] GA Res. 1541 (XV), Annex, Principles I, IV, V.

[59] *Ibidem*, Annex, Principles II, VI.

[60] *Ibidem*, Annex, Principle IX.

[61] Roth, *Governmental Illegitimacy in International Law* (1999), 234.

[62] This view was defended by the British representative at the GA in 1973 in a debate on the question of Guinea-Bissau, NSGT under Portuguese administration. According to the British view, Portugal 'was sovereign in international law' over Guinea-Bissau, thus could not 'be guilty of illegal occupation or acts of aggression.' *Ibidem*, 211, note 26. For the status of Trust/Mandate Territories see Judge McNair's separate opinion in *International Status of South West Africa*, Advisory Opinion, ICJ Reports 1950, 150 defining the question of sovereignty with respect to these territories as 'in abeyance; if and when the inhabitants of the territory obtain recognition as an independent state,…sovereignty will revive and vest in the new state.' This view has been generally accepted. See Roth, *supra* n. 61, 211, note 26.

assumed in the previous decade. On the one hand, the right to create an independent state and to become an integral part of the UN system; on the other, the right to freely choose the internal form of governance. In other words, the right assumed since its inception both an internal and an external aspect, one having a governmental dimension and the other one having a territorial dimension. In both senses, the principle of self-determination put a substantive limitation on the operation of the principle of effectiveness intended in its traditional sense as territorial control.[63] As to its relevance to the lawfulness of territorial situations, the external dimension is the one that should be principally explored, even if in some cases the governmental dimension has affected the reaction of the international community to questions of territorial status.[64]

The most contested occasions which were presented to the UN organs to develop the principle of self-determination both in its internal and external dimension are the cases of Namibia and Southern Rhodesia. Namibia, previously denominated South West Africa, was a former German colony placed under a Mandate after First World War. The Union of South Africa was to exercise full administrative and legislative powers over the Territory for the purpose of promoting the well-being and development of the inhabitants. However, ultimate authority was to be vested with the League of Nations according to Article 119 of the Versailles Treaty and Article 22 of the Covenant of the League of Nations. The mandate survived the succession between the League and the UN in 1945, and South Africa never made the decision to put Namibia under the Trusteeship system.[65] South Africa further claimed the extinction of the Mandate jointly with the extinction of the League of Nations and the right to rule over Namibia as legal sovereign with a view to blatantly perpetuating the domination of the 'white race'.[66] This started a long dispute between South Africa and the UN political organs, which reached its peak in the 1960s and the 1970s and would not be solved until Namibia's accession to independence in 1990.

In 1966, the GA determined through Resolution 2145 (XXI) that South Africa had disavowed the Mandate by creating a regime of *apartheid*, which

---

[63] If we take a political concept of effectiveness intended as capacity to gather a popular consensus around a fighting faction able to channel internally and externally a claim of self-determination, we will find an enhanced, rather than frustrated, principle of effectiveness. This is witnessed by the legal recognition of the category of national liberation movements, like the PLO for Palestine, POLISARIO for Western Sahara, and the PAIGC in Guinea-Bissau and the representation of the people by armed factions very often without an electoral mandate. The line of argument here follows the dialectic between territorial effectiveness and substantive international law, however the dimension of political effectiveness should not be overlooked as an element which goes beyond this bi-dimensional discourse.

[64] See *supra* Ch. 1, section 1.

[65] *International Status of South-West Africa*, *supra* n. 62, 128.

[66] See Roth, *supra* n. 61, 211, note 26. *Ibidem*, 243.

blatantly contradicted the thrust of the Mandate. The same resolution provided for the possibility of terminating the Mandate and of withdrawing the right of South Africa to rule over Namibia.[67] Through Resolution 2248 the GA appointed a governing body, the UN Council for Namibia, with the task of administering the Namibian situation until the accession to independence.[68] A whole series of sanctions and condemnations towards the continuing South African occupation followed in the years to come. The SC also adopted Resolution 276 that declared 'the continued presence of the South African authorities [...] illegal and that consequently all acts taken by the Government of South Africa on behalf of or concerning Namibia after the termination of the Mandate are illegal and invalid.'[69] This also sparked its request to the ICJ for an advisory opinion, which was rendered by the Court on 21 June 1971. In order to address the request's main question, that is the legal consequences for member states of Resolution 276, the Court also had to deal with the legal basis of Resolution 2145, which had declared the South African presence over Namibia illegal. The Court considered that the refusal of South Africa to submit itself to the political control of the UN and its disrespect for the right of self-determination of the Namibian people amounted to a material breach of the mandatory agreement.[70] This would enable the GA, the supervisory organ, to terminate unilaterally the right of South Africa to govern the Namibian territory.[71]

In general, whether or not the specific justification given by the Court for revoking the mandate is accepted, one can safely assume the general authority exercised by the GA over Trust Territories according to Article 85 and Article 87 of the UN Charter and the customary expansion of its powers under Chapter XI in the 1960s, as recognised by the ICJ in the case of *Northern Cameroons* of 1961.[72] Despite the lack of legal entitlement to govern over Namibia, the occupation of South Africa continued until 1990 when the first general free election was organised under UN auspices. Following the election, Namibia eventually gained its independence and statehood.

Another important case, which brought to the forefront the new legal entitlement related to the principle of self-determination, is the case of Southern Rhodesia. This is a clear instance where depriving the genuine right of self-

---

[67] The power of the GA to terminate a mandate or a trusteeship had already been recognised by the ICJ in the *Northern Cameroons Case* (Cameroon/UK), ICJ Reports 1963, 32.

[68] GA Res. 2248 (XXI).

[69] SC Res. 276 (1971), para. 2.

[70] *Legal Consequences for States of the Continued Presence of South-Africa in Namibia notwithstanding Security Council Resolution 276*, Advisory Opinion, ICJ Reports 1971, 6, at 29-30.

[71] *Ibidem*, 45-50.

[72] *Northern Cameroon* Case, *supra* n. 67.

governance in the internal affairs affected the legality of a certain territorial situation. Southern Rhodesia, formerly part of the federated state of Rhodesia, and nominally under British rule, had been effectively governed by an elite of white landowners since the beginning of the century. Due to increasing external pressure seeking to enhance the participation of the black majority in the political process, the ruling elite in 1961 decided to promulgate a new Constitution. According to the 1961 Constitution, a new electoral system was introduced which allowed a limited degree of political participation by the black majority. The system would ensure to the white minority an overwhelming majority in the parliament, and prevent the black 'majority' from enforcing any constitutional check on discriminatory legislation.[73] The GA responded by issuing a declaration that formally designated Southern Rhodesia as a NSGT and demanding that Britain, as administering power, promote a greater measure of self-government to the black majority.[74] Three years later the GA requested the British government to suspend the 1961 constitution, to declare null and void the elections and to call for a constitutional assembly for the purpose of granting the right of equal vote and representation to all members of the community.[75] The British government for its part pointed to the effective independence of the Southern Rhodesian institutions and the impossibility of intervening, notwithstanding simultaneously claiming formal sovereignty over the territory. Following further external pressures for including the black majority in a democratic political system, in 1965 the Southern Rhodesian government declared the independence of Southern-Rhodesia, despite the repeated invitations by the GA to refrain from such a action. As noted by Crawford in 1979, 'there can be no doubt that, if the traditional tests for independence of a seceding colony were applied, Rhodesia would be an independent State.'[76] However, the emergence of the right of self-determination, not only as a way to pursue territorial independence, but also as an international norm ensuring an effective participation in the political system, made sure that the traditional tests were set aside.

It is interesting to note that the response of the UN political organs was immediate, but was hardly directed against the state of Southern Rhodesia as such. The day following the declaration of independence, the SC condemned the declaration, defined the regime illegal and invited all states to deny recognition.[77] The following year, the Council toughened its stance by adopting Resolution 232 under Chapter VII, which for the first time determined an internal situation 'a threat to international peace and security' and demanded that member states

---

[73] Roth, *supra* n. 61, 237.
[74] GA Res. 1747 (XVI).
[75] GA Res. 2012 (XX).
[76] Crawford, *supra* n. 25, 103.
[77] SC Res. 216 (1965).

implement an economic embargo against the regime of Ian Smith. In 1970, the SC went further calling upon member states to take appropriate steps 'to ensure that any act performed by officials and institutions of the illegal regime in Southern Rhodesia shall not be accorded any recognition, official or otherwise, including judicial notice, by the competent organs of their State.'[78] Moreover, it demanded member states to sever all diplomatic, consular, military and trade relations with the illegal regime. As to the normative meaning of the SC's actions, Roth concludes:

> '[w]hereas the ordinary issue in self-determination is the legitimacy of a state's claim to encompass a territory – i.e, a question of whether the metropolitan state and the territory comprise one political community or two – the fundamental issue in the Rhodesian case was the legitimacy of a ruling apparatus. It was "the illegal regime in Southern Rhodesia", not the political community encompassing the inhabitants of the territory, that was problematic. That same political community was deemed deserving of statehood, but on the basis of the political arrangements then existing within it. Had "Zimbabwe" made a unilateral declaration of independence and established that it was effectively self-governing, it could lawfully have taken its place among the sovereign states; "Rhodesia" could not.'[79]

Roth identifies a possible division between a situation of governmental illegitimacy and one of territorial 'illegitimacy', defining Southern Rhodesia as a former situation. It is true that the actions of the GA and of the SC targeted the illegality of the regime, hence it is correct to characterise the case of Southern Rhodesia as paradigmatic in terms of government illegitimacy. However, if the legal definition of territorial sovereignty is both the *right* and the *competence* to exercise jurisdiction over a certain land, the way the *competence* is exercised may sometimes impinge on the *right* itself to exercise of jurisdiction.[80] In other words, the way the right of self-determination acted on the legal internal organisation of the political community prevented that political community - meant as people and their institutions - from gaining sovereignty. Thus, in Resolution 216, it was the statehood of Southern Rhodesia to be condemned in the first instance as the expression of an oppressive minority. The right of self-determination, through its internal rather than external dimension, affected the legality of the Rhodesian territorial situation. It continued to do so until 1979, when, after a series of attempts by the white minority to accommodate the requests of the international community to allow a limited degree of participation by black people in 'their' institutions, the leader of the national liberation movement Robert Mugabe found overwhelming support to rule the country under a UN supervised election.

---

[78] SC Res. 277 (1970).
[79] Roth, *supra* n. 61, 239-240.
[80] Compare with the definition of territory given in Ch. 3, section 3.1.

The final important case worth noting for the impact it had on the development of the principle of self-determination is the case of the Portuguese colonies in Asia and Africa, comprising Goa, East Timor, Guinea-Bissau, Mozambique and Angola. These were regarded as internal provinces under the Portuguese constitution, and the continued assertion of Portuguese sovereignty over those provinces received implied support for the ICJ in the *Right of Passage* case.[81] The GA had been prompt in declaring them NSGT in 1960 and requiring Portugal to submit itself to the 'information transmission' provision of Article 73(e) of the Charter.[82] Because of the refusal of Portugal to comply with this request the SC passed in 1963 Resolution 180

'urgently call(ing) upon Portugal to implement the following:
The immediate recognition of the right of the peoples of the Territories under its administration to self-determination and independence [...];
The immediate cessation of all acts of repression and the withdrawal of all military and other forces at present employed for that purpose;
Negotiations, on the basis of the recognition of the right to self-determination, with the authorized representatives of the political parties within and outside the Territories with a view to the transfer of power to political institutions freely elected and representative of the peoples, in accordance with resolution 1514 (XV);
The granting of independence immediately thereafter to all the Territories under its administration in accordance with the aspirations of the peoples.'

Moreover, the SC adopted a series of sanctions against Portugal, requesting member states to refrain from trading in military equipment with Portugal where used 'to continue its repression of the peoples of the Territories.' In 1972, there was a fully-fledged arms embargo against Portugal.[83] The debate at the GA over the specific continuation of the Portuguese administration over Guinea-Bissau once again showed the profound division between a strong majority of those states adhering to the Non-Aligned Movement and the Soviet Block, and the remaining colonial powers concerning the question of sovereignty over NSGTs. In 1973, the British representative to the GA asserted that Portugal was 'sovereign in international law' over its African territories, and therefore could not 'be guilty of illegal occupation or acts of aggression'. In GA Resolution 3061 the British view was voted down 93-7-30. The question was eventually resolved with the return to democracy in Portugal the following year and the renunciation to all overseas possessions, even if such renunciation opened a new chapter of civil wars and foreign interventions which lasted until recently for some of these colonies.

---

[81] *Right of Passage Case* (Portugal/India), ICJ Reports 1960, 39.
[82] GA Res. 1542 (XV).
[83] SC Res. 312 (1972).

The question of sovereignty over NSGTs and the possibility of the principle of self-determination to determine the illegality of a certain territorial situation is not free from difficulty in the way the ICJ considered the matter. In a sense the Charter was also ambiguous on this matter: Article 73 concerned 'responsibility for the administration of territories' that would arise directly from having effective control over those communities, but not necessarily possessing the full sovereign title. As already noted, even in 1961 the Court in the *Right of Passage* case took as implicit the existence of Portuguese sovereignty over its Indian possessions.[84] In *Western Sahara*, the Court deliberately avoided rendering any opinion on the type of legal title vested upon Spain during the colonisation of Western Sahara.[85] Only Judge De Castro in his Separate Opinion stated a view on the matter, by arguing for the impossibility of a legal dispute between Spain and Morocco over Western Sahara:

> 'Even if Spain had accepted Morocco's proposal to bring before the Court by way of contentious proceedings the two questions raised in the letter of 23 September 1974, the case would not have been viable. Spain did not have at that time, and does not have today, capacity to be party to a dispute with Morocco, or with any other State, as to the present or past titles to sovereignty concerning a territory which has the status of a non-self-governing territory, and of which it is administering Power.'[86]

Interesting in the *Guinea-Bissau v. Senegal* case was the elaboration by the arbitral tribunal with regard to the competence of the administering powers to conclude treaties affecting the exploitation of natural resources within those territories.[87] Guinea Bissau argued for the invalidity of a 1960 agreement between France and Portugal on the delimitation of maritime sectors, because it was in violation of a norm of *ius cogens*, thus for the impossibility of Guinea-Bissau and Senegal to succeed to that agreement. The decision of 31 July 1989 concluded that such treaties were within the competence of the colonial power until the local national liberation movement acquired international relevance (*portée internationale*).[88] Surprisingly, the Tribunal tested such international relevance by looking at the employment of exceptional measures by the administering power in order to restore order and control.[89] In other words, the Tribunal referred to a test of internal effectiveness to establish the external

---

[84] *Right of Passage Case, supra* n. 81.
[85] 'The Court finds that the request for an opinion does not call for adjudication upon existing territorial rights or sovereignty over territory.' *Western Sahara*, Advisory Opinion, ICJ Reports 1975, 12, at 28.
[86] *Ibidem*, Sep. Op. De Castro, 145.
[87] *Guinea Bissau v. Senegal, supra* n. 35.
[88] *Ibidem*, 138.
[89] *Ibidem*, 139.

effectiveness of the national liberation movement. It is unclear whether the reasoning of the Court hints to a change of territorial status as determined by the effectiveness of the national liberation movement. However, it reduces the limiting function of self-determination on effectiveness, by reinforcing the value of effectiveness in the way the right of self-determination impacts on other norms of international law, such as those related to natural resources and succession of treaties.

Finally, in the *East Timor* case, the Court, although developing in principle the normative significance of the principle of self-determination by declaring it as having an *erga omnes* character,[90] adopted a very cautious approach which represents a serious setback for its enforcement. The Court was called by Portugal, the former administering power, to adjudge the legality of a treaty concluded by Australia and Indonesia in 1989, the occupying power at that time. The ICJ refused jurisdiction on the matter because of the legal position of a third state, Indonesia, which was not party to the dispute, and whose legal situation would be inevitably affected by a decision of the Court. It is interesting to observe that the Court, apart from avoiding any engagement with the question of the legality of the Indonesian presence in East Timor *ergo* with the validity of the 1989 East Timor Gap Treaty, refrained from pronouncing upon the status of East Timor as a NSGT. It limited itself to concluding with the sibylline sentence that it 'has taken note in the present Judgement (paragraph 31) that, for the two Parties, the Territory of East Timor remains a non-self-governing-territory and its people has the right to self-determination.'[91]

In conclusion, the principle of self-determination has represented an important limitation upon the primacy of effectiveness in territorial situations. This has been clearly enunciated by the GA in its Resolution 2625 (XXV):

> 'The territory of a colony or other non-self-governing territory has, under the Charter, a status separate and distinct from the territory of the State administering it; and such separate and distinct status under the Charter shall exist until the people of the colony or non-self-governing territory have exercised their right of self-determination in accordance with the Charter, and in particular its purposes and principles.'[92]

---

[90] *East Timor Case* (Portugal v. Australia), ICJ Reports 1995, 90, at 102. The *erga omnes* character of the right to self-determination has been confirmed by the ICJ in its 2004 Advisory Opinion *Legality of Wall in Palestine*, where the Court found the construction of security wall by the Israeli Defence Forces to be in violation of a number of rules of international law, including the right of the Palestinian people to self-determination. See *Legal Consequences of the Construction of a Wall in the Occupied Palestinian Territory*, Advisory Opinion (2004), at <http://www.icj-cij.org/icjwww/idocket/imwp/imwpframe.htm>, para. 155; and Judge Higgins' dissenting opinion on this latter point in her Separate Opinion, paras. 30-31.

[91] *East Timor, supra* n. 90, 106.

[92] GA Res. 2625 (XXV), Declaration on Principles of International Law concerning Friendly Relations and Co-operation among States in accordance with the Charter of the United Nations.

No doubt it is exactly to the change of territorial status that the self-determination addresses its impact, making sure that any claim of sovereignty by the metropolitan state is considered unlawful, where not backed by the genuine consent of the people under its administration. Furthermore, the right of self-determination impacts upon the legality of any claim and/or implementation of effective statehood which does not take into account a genuine expression of popular will, but is openly discriminatory towards the majority of the population. Its essential role in the context of de-colonisation can hardly be overestimated, as it represented the rhetorical, political and legal point of reference for the political emancipation of millions of people.

However, its enforcement as a legal entitlement has not been free from difficulty, on account of the disadvantaged procedural position in international law of the peoples as right-holders. The *East Timor* case - with the ICJ's solemn declaration of its *erga omnes* character, together with the impossibility of the East Timorese to have their right recognised through a legal process - witnesses a profound contradiction, characterising a legal system expanding *uti universi ratione personae*, but at the same time maintaining a privileged role of states in the process of determination and enforcement of the law. The lack of judicial enforcement by the right-holders has also led to a degree of ambiguity on the relation between the right to self-determination, and the protection of the peoples' territorial sovereignty. In other words, international law has not been able to provide a precise answer as to *when* the occupying or administering power becomes wrongful occupant, thereby leading to confusion as to *how* it can act with regard to the occupied territory. Whereas Namibia and Southern Rhodesia have represented two straightforward cases of denial of self-determination leading to an unlawful territorial situation, in other cases, such as that shown in the arbitration *Guinea Bissau v. Senegal*, the line between self-determination and unlawful territorial situation has been much more blurred. This answer is of the outmost importance for a precise definition of unlawful territorial situation, and it is further considered within the context of state responsibility for wrongful occupations.[93]

5. Normative standards: the principle of territorial integrity

A problematic aspect of the right of self-determination is its current significance in a period where many of the NSGTs have reached independence (15 still remaining as of today) and the last Trust Territory reached independence

---

[93] *Infra* Ch. 5, section 7.2.

in 1992. This question has been revived by the dramatic events of the 1990s in Eastern Europe, where several secessionist movements have tried, some successfully, to detach parts of territories from large multi-ethnic states and create new states along the lines of ethnical identity. Secessionist movements have gained momentum not only in unstable regions, but also in politically stable countries, such as Canada, Italy and Spain. Political movements in these countries have called for the secession of territorial units within a state with a view to implementing their 'inalienable right to self-determination'.

The creation of states has traditionally been considered a question of fact either automatically accepted by international law or recognised as such by a general norm.[94] Either way, the principle of effectiveness played an unchallenged role in determining the acceptance of new states as international legal persons.[95] However, the fact that international law accepted the consequences of factual situations, does not equate to vesting a *right* in those groups seeking to create a new state. This was made clear by the Commission of Jurists appointed by the League of Nations in the *Aaland Islands* case.[96]

Crawford demonstrates how little in the practice of states indicates the development of this right after 80 years since that decision.[97] It is true that one can find at least twenty cases of creation of new states in the post-1945 practice outside the colonial context, however, in some cases, the situation was one of dissolution rather than secession, in other cases, the agreement of the relevant authorities intervened. In cases of dissolution, the process is by definition factual, and effectiveness determines the disappearance of the old state and the creation of new ones on the same territory.[98] Reciprocal consent may be also essential in determining a new set of legal relations.[99] In only one case, that of Bangladesh, the forcible separation of East Pakistan was recognised by the international community, however no explicit mention was made in the recognition of any positive right of self-determination giving entitlement to secession. Rather, effectiveness and the final acceptance by the Pakistani government were decisive in leading the GA and the SC to recognise Bangladesh.[100] Even more eloquent is the practice of attempted unilateral secession. When the central government refuses to grant independence to the seceding entity, the latter has not obtained

---

[94] See, however, the seminal study of Crawford highlighting the limitations to the role of effectiveness in the creation of states. Crawford, *supra* n. 25.

[95] *Supra* Ch. 2.

[96] *League of Nations Official Journal*, Special Supplement 3 (1920), 5.

[97] Crawford, 'State Practice and International Law in Relation to Secession' 69 *BYIL* (1998), 85.

[98] See Opinion n. 1 Badinter Commission, *supra* n. 22.

[99] E.g. Minsk Agreement Establishing the Commonwealth of Independent States, 8 December 1991, 31 *ILM* (1992), 143.

[100] Crawford, *supra* n. 97, 95-96.

recognition by the international community, even when achieving a large degree of effectiveness. This observation begs the question of what is a state in international law, what role effectiveness plays and what role recognition plays. However, it clearly indicates that unilateral attempts to secede cannot be framed in terms of an international legal right.

By contrast, the opposite principle, the one of territorial integrity, finds overwhelming support in international practice. For example the Friendly Relations Declaration in elaborating the normative content of the right of self-determination states that:

> 'Nothing in the foregoing paragraphs shall be construed as authorizing or encouraging any action which would dismember or impair, totally or in part, the territorial integrity or political unity of sovereign and independent States conducting themselves in compliance with the principle of equal rights and self-determination of peoples as described above and thus possessed of a government representing the whole people belonging to the territory without distinction as to race, creed or colour.'[101]

The same principle, notwithstanding a slightly different formulation, is affirmed by the 1993 Vienna Declaration issued at the conclusion of the UN World Conference on Human Rights.[102] The principle of territorial integrity has been re-affirmed, at least nominally, even in cases where international intervention was considered necessary due to the repression of national minorities, as was the case of Iraq with Kurdistan and the Federal Republic of Yugoslavia with Kosovo. The international reaction to these internal crises sought a degree of substantial autonomy and internal self-determination, rather than the creation of new states.[103] Furthermore, even a high degree of effectiveness in the cases of Biafra, Somaliland, Republic of Srpska and Chechnya has not led to the recognition of those states by the international community, and, in all of these cases apart from Somaliland, central authorities have been able to re-gain, at least in part, control over those areas by forcible actions.

In this respect the decision of 20 August 1998 of the Supreme Court of Canada in the case referred to it by the Governor in Council relating to the secession of Quebec from Canada should be recalled.[104] Of the three questions referred by the Governor in Council the relevant one for the present discussion is the second:

---

[101] 1970 GA Declaration on Friendly Relations, *supra* n. 92.
[102] UN World Conference on Human Rights, Vienna Declaration and Programme of Action, 25 June 1993, 32 *ILM* (1996), 1661, at 1665.
[103] See SC Res. 686 (1991); SC Res. 687 (1991); SC Res. 1244 (1999).
[104] *Re Reference by the Governor in Council concerning Certain Questions Relating to the Secession of Quebec from Canada*, 115 *ILR* (1999), 535.

'Does international law give the National Assembly, Legislature or Government of Quebec the right to effect the secession of Quebec from Canada unilaterally? In this regard, is there a right to self-determination under international law that would give the National Assembly, Legislature or Government of Quebec the right to effect the secession of Quebec from Canada unilaterally?'[105]

The Supreme Court's analysis is interesting, since it argues along two main possible justifications for a right of secession: A) the argument of self-determination; B) the argument of 'effectivity'. As to the first argument, the Court indicates three specific situations, where the right of self-determination may affect the title to territory over a certain region: 1) in cases of colonial occupation; 2) in cases of foreign occupation; 3) in cases of systematic denial of civil and political rights by the central government. As to 1) and 2) the analysis of the Court is correct and is based on the legal justifications presented in the precedent section. As to 3) the Court submits one important *caveat* stating that 'it remains unclear whether this third proposition actually reflects an established international law standard.'[106] In fact, the assertion of such a right is problematic because of the lack of pertinent international practice. It appears that despite the increasing importance of human rights, the focus on territorial integrity is not less important at present. Even where grave violations of the human rights of minorities are alleged, the response of the international community has been to impose a series of sanctions on the central governments and promote the right to substantial autonomy, rather than disrupt territorial unity.[107]

Very interesting is then the treatment by the Court of the principle of effectiveness. The argument advanced by Quebec was that, even in the absence of a positive right to secede, the effective creation of an independent state would validate a claim to secession. The Court firstly draws a powerful distinction between *power* and *right* to act in relation to a purported declaration of independence by the Quebec National Assembly:

'A distinction must be drawn between the right of a people to act, and their power to do so. They are not identical. A right is recognized in law: mere physical ability is not necessarily given status as a right. The fact that an individual or group can act in a certain way says nothing at all about the legal status or consequences of that act. A power may be exercised even in the absence of a right to do so, but if it is, then it is exercised without legal foundation.'[108]

---

[105] *Ibidem*, 537.

[106] *Ibidem*, 587.

[107] See Ringelheim, 'Considerations on the international reaction to the 1999 Kosovo crisis' 32 (1999) *Revue belge de droit international*, 475; and Bennoune, 'Sovereignty v. Suffering'? Re-Examining Sovereignty and Human Rights through the Lens of Iraq' 13 *EJIL* (2002), 243.

[108] *Secession of Quebec*, *supra* n. 104, 577.

It then provides a crystal clear analysis of the role played by the principle of effectiveness in respect of secessionist claims:

'Arguments were also advanced to the effect that, regardless of the existence or non-existence of a positive right to unilateral secession, international law will in the end recognize effective political realities – including the emergence of a new state – as facts. [...] [I]t should first be noted that the existence of a positive legal entitlement is quite different from a prediction that the law will respond after the fact to a then existing political reality. These two concepts examine different points in time. The questions posed to the Court address legal rights in advance of a unilateral act of purported secession. While we touch below on the practice governing the international recognition of emerging states, the Court is as wary of entertaining speculation about the possible future conduct of sovereign states [...].' [109]

The Court continues at a later point of its decision:

'[The principle of effectiveness] proclaims that an illegal act may eventually acquire legal status if, as a matter of empirical fact, it is recognised on the international plane. Our law has long recognised that through a combination of acquiescence and prescription, an illegal act may at some later point be accorded some form of legal status. In the law of property, for example, it is well known that a squatter on land may ultimately become the owner if the true owner sleeps on his or her right to repossess the law. In this way a change in the factual circumstances may subsequently be reflected in a change in legal status. It is, however, quite another matter to suggest that a subsequent condonation of an initially illegal act retroactively creates a legal right to engage in the act in the first place. The broader contention is not supported by the international principle of effectivity or otherwise and must be rejected.' [110]

These Court's passages are important because they discuss two often misunderstood points of international law with respect to the creation of new states. The first is the assumed neutrality of international law concerning the secession of new states. International law, as it is said, would neither prohibit nor allow the secession of regions, but it only takes into account an effective situation which would be consequently validated. The Court rejects this notion. There is no positive right of an internal entity to secede and the principle of territorial integrity speaks against this right. If as a matter of *power* to do so (and not of *right*) an entity manages to secede, establish an effective situation and find international support, recognition and acquiescence may validate the effective situation. However, recognition of the legal effects of a *de facto* situation and its subsequent validation are not tantamount to legalisation of the original act, creating a right *a posteriori*. This idea is further elaborated in the following chapter, however suffice it to say that effectiveness does not create any right of self-determination and

---

[109] *Ibidem.*
[110] *Ibidem*, 591.

secession *ex post facto*, exactly as the squatter cannot claim the lawfulness of his initial conduct in occupying land.

In conclusion, it is here argued that a right to secession outside the colonial context does not exist under current international law. The principle of territorial integrity enjoys priority and, in fact, it represents the fourth limitation upon effectiveness in territorial situations. This may be the consequence of the dominant role played by states in the law-making process which have a vested interest in protecting their own integrity. However, recognition and acquiescence can make effective situations legally valid. The extent of recognition will most likely depend on the international legitimacy of the underlying claim - for example, where at the origin of a secessionary movement there is a widespread violation of the rights of a minority- and/or the conferral of legitimacy to the new state by an authoritative body such as the GA or the SC.[111]

6. Conclusions: problems with the definition of unlawfulness of territorial situations

According to the legal norms analysed above, territorial situations could be defined as lawful or unlawful. Effectiveness does not amount to lawfulness where contrary to the prohibition of territorial change by force, the principle of *uti possidetis*, the principle of self-determination of people under colonial or foreign occupation or the principle of territorial integrity. These principles arguably present a well discernible legal core. Their strength lies in their ability to accommodate both a need for stability and a need for justice and change. Their impact on the law of territory represents one of the main features of international law as it is presently conceived. The lawful/unlawful divide ought to be neat and objective. In principle, *tertium non datur*.

Whereas these criteria of legality are fundamental to defining the unlawfulness of territorial situations, they 'suffer' in two important respects. The first is the precise normative content of these criteria *vis-à-vis* the sovereignty of states or peoples they intend to protect. Whereas territorial situations established and maintained in defiance of the above criteria should not be considered lawful, in the sense that international law does not vest a competence to administer the territory in question with the occupier, international law does not necessarily translate an adverse occupation into an unlawful territorial situation, in the sense that it considers such occupation wrongful. That is because the same principles of legality play two different and not necessarily overlapping functions: one vesting title in a state or people, and the other protecting the exercise of territorial

---

[111] *Infra* Ch. 5, section 8.

sovereignty resulting from such a title. This fundamental issue is explained in the following chapter when dealing with the question of state responsibility for wrongful territorial occupations in defiance of the principle of *uti possidetis* and the principle of self-determination: it is, however, important to already bear in mind the double function that these principles play, as that adds an additional problem of determination of the divide lawfulness/unlawfulness in territorial situations.

Secondly, the other fundamental problem related to the definition of a certain territorial situation as unlawful is that such 'objective' status must be defined by an authoritative body, either judicial or political, or by an international legal instrument, in order to gain international 'non-recognition'. The lack of a comprehensive system of compulsory jurisdiction often renders such definition problematic, as much as the difficulty to agree on legal determinations in political bodies such as the GA or the SC, which were not orginially envisaged to exercise quasi-judicial functions. The case of East Timor is illustrative in this respect. This tiny portion of territory in the Indonesian archipelago had been administered by Portugal until 1975 as a NSGT which, according to international law, was entitled to self-determination. In 1975, after the last Portuguese troops left East Timor, Indonesia invaded and declared its annexation. Indonesia asserted that the annexation of East Timor as its 27th province had been carried out in accordance with the wishes of the population as expressed by the vote of the 'Regional Popular Assembly'. This assembly had not been elected but had been established by pro-Indonesian parties.[112] The East Timorese people, represented by FRETILIN, their national liberation movement, claimed together with their former administering power their status as a NSGT and their entitlement to exercise freely their right to self-determination. However, there could not be any judicial decision directly concerned with question of legality/illegality, since national liberation movements do not enjoy *locus standi* before international tribunals and tribunals did not have the chance to pronounce. This was made clear in the *East Timor* case, where the issue of the lawfulness of the territorial status of East Timor was brought to a judicial body by the former colonial power. The structure of the international legal system was such that Portugal, comparable to a trustee for the East Timorese people, claimed on their behalf rights related to their sovereignty over natural resources. The Court refused to adjudicate upon the dispute because of the lack of participation in the proceedings of the occupying power, Indonesia. The 'objective' formal status of East Timor as a NSGT and, as a consequence, the right of self-determination of the East Timorese people was recalled briefly as 'contractualised' by the two parties to the dispute, Portugal and Australia.[113]

---

[112] Cassese, *Self-Determination of Peoples: a Legal Reappraisal* (1995), 224.
[113] *East Timor Case, supra* n. 90, 105-106.

However, the Court did not go so far as to assume an objective unlawful status as evidenced by SC resolutions. Indeed, the SC through Resolution 384 (1975) and Resolution 389 (1976) had only requested respect for the territorial integrity of East Timor and the speedy withdrawal of Indonesian military forces, but never passed judgement on the unlawfulness of the Indonesian annexation, nor on the obligation of member states to refrain from recognising such annexation. In contrast, one can consider SC Resolution 276 (1970) with regard to Namibia a binding determination of unlawfulness, as evidenced by the ICJ approach in *Namibia*.[114]

This comparison discloses not only the inconsistencies in the way normative criteria are applied by UN political bodies, but also the fundamental role these institutions play in either upholding and enforcing those principles, or sacrificing them in the interest of 'diplomacy'. It also shows some of the controversial issues related to the nature of the powers exercised by UN political bodies,[115] in particular, with regard to the possibility for such bodies to adopt a legal determination of a certain situation, similarly to the function exercised by a judicial body. In the present author's opinion, the Council may use its Chapter VII inherent powers to determine the legal rights and duties of states, when that is necessary for its action to maintain international peace and security, and when procedural guarantees and equality between the parties involved are ensured.[116] Of course, there is nothing conclusive or definitive in a legal determination by the Council, and such a determination should not aim at interfering with the exercise of the judicial function, especially that of the ICJ. Moreover, even when the illegal status is defined by a judicial body, perhaps as a result of a request of an advisory opinion to the ICJ by a UN organ, or the application of a 'protecting' state in contentious proceedings, the judicial body may not be in a position to fully assess the claim of one of the parties to the political dispute, since such claim may not be exactly matching the interest that the 'protecting' power is attempting to protect.[117] Finally, even an objective assessment of unlawfulness ought not remain a mere statement of principle if international law is to have any role in

---

[114] *Namibia, supra* n. 70, 53.

[115] See *infra* Ch. 6, section 2.2.

[116] Frowein, Krisch, 'Article 41', in Simma (ed.), *The Charter of the United Nations: a Commentary* (2002), Vol. I, at 742.

[117] *East Timor Case, supra* n. 90, Sep. Op. Vereshchetin, 135.

regulating inter-state relations. The following chapter therefore intends to explore what are the consequences at a normative level, both in terms of elaborating of a general theory of invalidity of unlawful territorial situations, and in terms of their impact upon other areas of international law.

CHAPTER 5

CONSEQUENCES OF UNLAWFULNESS

1. Introduction

The present chapter considers the normative impact of a definition of unlawfulness of a certain territorial situation. Firstly, it looks at the meaning of 'unlawful' in terms of general theory of invalidity. It tries to spell out the difficulties involving a satisfactory and comprehensive theory of 'invalidity' of territorial situations, with particular reference to the legal consequences of such invalidity. As relevant cases highlighting the limits inherent in the concept of invalidity of territorial situations, the jurisprudence of the ICJ with respect to Namibia and of the ECHR with respect to the Turkish Republic of Northern Cyprus will be considered. Secondly, the analysis reviews the way a determination of unlawfulness can influence the application of other relevant norms regulating the underlying political disputes, in particular the norms concerning the use of force, the law of belligerent occupation, the creation of states. Thirdly, the chapter examines another important legal consequence of a situation of territorial unlawfulness, the question of international responsibility, which helps us define the exact borders of the primary norms protecting states' and peoples' territorial sovereignty considered in the previous chapters. Finally, it considers the concept of legitimacy and its crucial relevance to the legal description of unlawful territorial situations, in particular its relevance for the 'legalisation' of effectiveness.

2. Consequences of unlawfulness: the 'invalidity' of unlawful territorial situations

Even overcoming the difficulties in ascertaining the unlawfulness of a territorial status thanks to uncontroversial political and judicial decisions, there remains the problem of conceptualising the consequences of such unlawfulness from a legal perspective. The first fundamental legal consequence is that of invalidity. If a certain juridical act is vitiated, that is, one of its elements does not satisfy a certain set of criteria spelled out by the legal system, normally this will attach a series of legal consequences intrinsically linked to that act, which can be summed up under the concept of invalidity. This area has been relatively under-investigated by the international doctrine, probably due to the fact, as correctly argued by Sir Robert Jennings some decades ago, that a coherent system of invalidity requires a centralised system of judicial enforcement that can ascertain the unlawfulness of a certain act, and decide on the consequences of that invalidity.[1] Further, the issue has found conventional regulation only in the area of treaty law, namely through the 1969 VCLT, which has also allowed the elaboration of a differentiation between relative and absolute nullity.[2] Yet, treaties are not the only juridical acts which can be vitiated. Very often in the unlawful territorial situations the kind of act whose validity is at stake is an unilateral act, such as an act of annexation or act of secession. The rules of invalidity of these acts must be sought in customary international law.

A preliminary point relates to the exact meaning of the concept of invalidity as it relates to unlawful territorial situations. The concept of validity or invalidity can only concern legal acts, and we cannot relate it to an unlawful territorial situation as such, as the latter only designates a factual *status quo* which is found to be in violation of applicable international law. However, the relevance of invalidity with regard to unlawful territorial situations can be appreciated with regard to those juridical acts which are associated to a territorial regime, e.g. an act of secession, an act of annexation, a treaty concerning the occupied territory, a legislation enacted by the unlawful occupant. In respect of these latter, we can indeed apply the concept of invalidity.

Guggenheim, in one of the few studies on the concept of nullity in international law, explains the traditional differentiation between wrongful act and invalid act.[3] In the latter case the act lacks some fundamental elements provided by the legal system, thus the same legal system attaches to it some consequences as to the production of its legal effects. Such elements would be a competent party, a proper object, free consent and valid form. For instance, in the traditional laws of war a case of null act is the ineffective blockade or a declaration of independence of a political entity missing the minimum criteria of statehood. The differentiation between invalid and wrongful act is proposed by Judge Anzilotti in his dissenting opinion in the *Eastern Greenland* case. The occupation of *terra nullius* by Norway was considered by the PCIJ as non-existent and invalid, since Greenland was already occupied by Denmark, thus depriving it of its purported character of uninhabited land. Anzilotti contested this finding on

---

[1] Jennings, 'Nullity and Effectiveness in International Law', in *Cambridge Essays in International Law: Essays in Honour of Lord McNair* (1957), 64.

[2] 1969 Vienna Convention on the Law of Treaties. The theory of invalidity of treaties has been effected through a 'transfer' of domestic principles on the invalidity of contracts to international law. Thus the validity of a certain conventional rule can be affected because of defects related to the object of the treaty (i.e. object contrary to *ius cogens*) and defects related to the formation and manifestation of a certain will (i.e. treaty concluded because of error or fraud). See, however, the difference between concepts of relative and absolute nullity in municipal law and international law. Rozakis, 'The Law on Invalidity of Treaties' 16 *Archiv des Völkerrechts* (1973), 150.

[3] Guggenheim, 'La validité e la nullité des actes juridiques internationaux' 74 *Recueil des Cours* (1949), 195.

the basis that, while Eastern Greenland was indeed uninhabited, it was not free for appropriation due to a binding undertaking entered into by Norway *vis-à-vis* Denmark. In other words, the act should have been considered wrongful rather than invalid.[4] The wrongful act (*acte illicite*) may in fact normally produce its own effects, which can be voided or non-recognised. For example, a domestic legislation which is in breach of international law may be a wrongful act, but be valid at the same time: it produces its own legal effects, but it gives rise to the state responsibility and a corresponding duty of reparation. In fact, the production of legal effects is the result of reception of a given act by a certain system. If such an act is considered as producing legal effects *per se*, we can define it as a juridical act. This will mean that the legal system attaches to it some legal consequences. Invalidity of that act will be a consequence of that act being vitiated under that system, so that the system prevents it from producing legal effects. Else this will be considered a legally relevant fact whose legal consequences limit themselves to state responsibility.

For example, if we had a legislation in breach of a customary rule protecting fundamental human rights, its execution will breach international law and give rise to state responsibility, yet its validity will not be put into question as its legal effects are produced by the domestic system where it has been enacted. Of course, this explanation assumes that the domestic system and the international system are two separated and autonomous legal systems, albeit with capacity to 'exchange information'. By contrast, if we adopt a monist view on the relationship between the two systems, we may submit that the issue of validity is also regulated under international law, and therefore the result will be an absolute nullity of the act concerned.

There is always a danger inherent in trying to analyse the reality of state practice in international affairs through the lenses of legal principles or theoretical constructions. In 1987, John Dugard, in opening his study on the practice of non-recognition in the UN, rightly affirmed that '[a]ny writer who attempts to examine the mysteries of State practice on recognition with the intention of providing a coherent explanation of the behaviour and expectations of States within a framework of legal principle and theory exposes himself to certain

---

[4] '[…] the Court could not have declared the occupation invalid, if the term "invalid" signifies "null and void". A legal act is only non-existent if it lacks certain elements which are essential to its existence. Such would be the occupation of territory belonging to another State, because the status of a *terra nullius* is an essential factor to enable the occupation to serve as a means of acquiring territorial sovereignty. But this does not hold good in the case of the occupation of a *terra nullius* by a sovereign State in conformity with international law, merely because the occupying State had undertaken not to occupy it. Accordingly, it would have been for the Norwegian Government to revoke the occupation unlawfully carried out, without prejudice to the Danish Government's right to apply to the Court, as reparation for the unlawful act, to place this obligation on record.' *Eastern Greenland Case* (Denmark/Norway), PCIJ Series A/B, n. 53, at 95.

ridicule and vituperation.'[5] The same awareness of being exposed to 'ridicule and vituperation' should also accompany any attempt to consider the question of invalidity of acts related to unlawful territorial situations, indeed a topic strictly interlinked with the concept of non-recognition. On the other hand, the present project is devoted to 'providing a coherent explanation of the behaviour and expectations of States within a framework of legal principle and theory', which is why it will not shy away from providing a logical, structured and realistic reading of how unlawful territorial can be defined in terms of invalidity and recognition.

It is submitted as an hypothesis that the dualist scheme still best explains the concept of unlawful territorial situation. Suffice at this stage to say that like an internal legislation contravening international human rights law, an act of secession purported through a declaration of independence of a part of territory is for the international legal system a legally relevant act, and a fact at same time which violates international law. However, the fact may produce legal effects internally if the new entity is effective. As observed by Marek, 'the illegal act in question combines in itself supreme illegality with supreme law-creating force, thus exposing the basic problem of international law in all its vulnerability.'[6] The same could be said of an act of annexation, which will be unlawful on the international plane if contrary to the legal criteria seen in the previous chapter, but it may still create legal effects at the domestic level.[7] Far from being of a purely theoretical relevance, this point is important in understanding some of the common misconceptions related to unlawful territorial situations. In particular, it is important since under customary international law there exists no duty for a court to withhold recognition of a wrongful act and of its internal legal effects. However, there might be a resolution of the SC adopted under Chapter VII demanding member states to refrain from any act of recognition of the unlawful occupant as in the case of Southern Rhodesia or Namibia.[8] In that case, even an act of judicial recognition would be contrary to an obligation deriving from a sanctioning measure adopted by the SC.

2.1 The chain of invalidity and the duty of non-recognition

Given these premises, it becomes clear how the criteria of legality spelled out in the first part of this chapter operate at an important, yet somewhat unsophisticated level. They only declare a certain territorial situation unlawful, and they prevent the acquisition of legal title to the territory. However, effective control assures the exercise of all functions normally exercised by a state, and

---

[5] Dugard, *Recognition and the United Nations* (1987), 5.
[6] Marek, *Identity and Continuity of States in Public International Law* (1968, 2nd ed.), 554.
[7] Cfr. SC Res. 478 (1980); and *Hanzalis v. Greek Orthodox Patriarchate Court* 48 *ILR* (1969), 93, at 98.
[8] SC Res. 216 (1965); SC Res. 276 (1971).

often they can lead to the creation of a *de facto* state of affairs. Far from living in a sort of limbo, *de facto* entities, both institutionally and at the level of individuals, entertain relations with other international actors. Inevitably, the 'unlawful' legal system 'exchanges' information with the international and other national legal systems. How do these systems react? Do they consider those data as a legal nullity? Or is there a reciprocal recognition? Is there a chain of invalidity that re-conducts the validity of a certain act to a sort of invalid *Grundnorm*? The ICJ Advisory Opinion on Namibia and two decisions of the ECHR in relation to the TRNC cast some light on the issues anticipated above, and on a possible general operational code on how to deal with unlawful territorial situations from a perspective of legal policy.

2.1.1 The classic case: the ICJ Advisory Opinion on Namibia

The historical events which led to the dispute between South Africa and the UN political organs over Namibia have already been illustrated.[9] SC Resolution 276 (1970) had declared the South African occupation illegal and, consequently, that all acts taken by the Government of South-Africa on behalf of or concerning Namibia after the termination of the Mandate were illegal and invalid. SC Resolution 284 (1970) requested the ICJ to render an advisory opinion on 'the legal consequences for States, of the continued presence of South Africa in Namibia notwithstanding Security Council resolution 276 (1970).'

In its reply, the Court affirmed the duty of UN member states to carry out their obligations according to Article 25 of the Charter, thus to abide by SC resolutions on the regime of sanctions to be imposed upon South Africa. Importantly, it stated the pre-eminently political nature of sanctions, that

> '[t]he precise determination of the acts permitted or allowed – what measures are available and practicable, which of them should be selected, what scope they should be given and by whom they should be applied – is a matter which lies within the competence of the appropriate political organs of the United Nations acting within their authority.'[10]

However, the Court in responding to the SC's question, went one step further and gave

> 'advice on those dealings with the Government of South Africa which, under the Charter of the United Nations and general international law, should be considered as inconsistent with the declaration of illegality and invalidity made in paragraph 2 of resolution 276

---

[9] *Supra* Ch. 4, section 4.
[10] *Legal Consequences for States of the Continued Presence of South-Africa in Namibia notwithstanding Security Council Resolution 276*, Advisory Opinion, ICJ Reports 1971, 6, at 55.

(1970), because they may imply a recognition that South Africa's presence in Namibia is legal.'[11]

It analysed a series of acts, such as entering into treaty relations, invoking and applying already existing treaties, exchanging diplomatic or consular missions, and entering into economic relations, which member states should consider incompatible with the illegality of South Africa's presence in Namibia. However, the Court made an important exception to the policy of non-recognition, stating that

'the non-recognition of South Africa's administration of the Territory should not result in depriving the people of Namibia of any advantages derived from international co-operation. In particular, while official acts performed by the Government of South Africa after the termination of the Mandate are illegal and invalid, this invalidity cannot be extended to those acts, such as, for instance, the registration of births, deaths and marriages, the effects of which can be ignored only to the detriment of the inhabitants of the Territory.'[12]

In the elaboration of this differentiation the Court avoided expressing a general principle of invalidity, and its differentiation was only the divide benefit/detriment of the individuals. This divide is not endogenous to a legal act *per se*, but it is part of the political decision-making. In other words, envisaging such differentiation is giving policy advice on a question of sanctions and non-recognition, rather than providing a criterion of validity. The differentiation is indeed based on an extra-legal appreciation, an appreciation of the international legitimacy of the act involved. This seems to be consistent with the argument presented at the outset of the opinion and with the detailed analysis of possible actions presented by Judge Ammoun in his separate opinion.[13] The idea was made explicit by Judge Petren in his separate opinion:

'The wording of paragraph 2 [of resolution 276] gives the impression that the non-validity of all acts taken by South Africa concerning Namibia is considered to be an automatic effect of the illegality of its continued presence in that Territory. The sense of paragraph 5 therefore seems to be that States must not recognize such acts as valid. However, having regard to the foregoing, the duty incumbent on States not to recognize South Africa's right to continue to administer Namibia does not entail the obligation to deny all legal character to acts or decisions taken by the South-African authorities concerning Namibia or its inhabitants. In this regard, the notion of non-recognition leaves to States, as I have said, a wide measure of discretion.'[14]

---

[11] *Ibidem.*
[12] *Ibidem*, 56.
[13] *Ibidem*, Sep. Op. Judge Ammoun, 67.
[14] *Ibidem*, Sep. Op. Judge Petren, 135.

Moreover, according to the French judge, if the criterion on which to base recognition was the benefit of the Namibian people, it was unhelpful for the Court to make such a neat division between international and domestic acts. Some international agreements as well, for instance on postal or railway matters, can be considered internationally legitimate due to practical or humanitarian considerations.[15]

The reasoning of the Court went further, and it analysed the consequences upon non-member states of the declaration of invalidity of the SC. In other words, the Court relied on norms of general international law, rather than Article 25 of the Charter. It is important to recall this passage of the Court's decision:

> 'In view of the Court, the termination of the Mandate and the declaration of the illegality of South- Africa's presence in Namibia are opposable to all States in the sense of barring *erga omnes* the legality of a situation which is maintained in violation of international law: in particular, no State which enters into relations with South-Africa concerning Namibia may expect the United Nations or its Members to recognize the validity or effects of such relationship, or of the consequences thereof.'[16]

The unlawfulness of the Namibian territorial situation was objective and opposable *erga omnes*, and it was not up to the single state to decide whether to give recognition to the legal acts and effects produced by the dealings between any state and the illegal occupant. This seems to depart from the previous approach, but, in fact, it only complements it. Whereas previously the Court seemed to derive the duty of member states to refrain from entering into relations with South Africa on the basis of Article 25 of the Charter to abide by sanctions imposed by the SC, but not from a general question of invalidity of those acts, in this passage it made explicit reference to the issue of validity. How can we reconcile the two approaches of the Court? It seems that the relationship between UN law and general international law is only hinted at in the reasoning of the Court and in some of the separate opinions, but never made explicit.

Despite the little and contradictory practice available in this area, and the complex relationship between the law of invalidity and the law of state responsibility, a logical solution can be possibly identified. General international law provides that the illegality of a certain territorial situation displays its effects in terms of 'invalidity', in the sense that the occupying power is in violation of another state's or people's territorial sovereignty; thus, it does not have a legal competence to create rights and obligations concerning that territory. Consequently, all international legal acts, such as treaties entered into by the occupying power, agreements or unilateral behaviours having international legal

---

[15] *Ibidem.*
[16] *Ibidem*, Decision, 56.

relevance are deprived of their legal effects. We can talk about invalidity in the classic sense that one of the essential elements of the international transaction is missing – a proper object -, hence the treaty is a nullity. In some cases, the occupying power, by entering into international commitments with regard to the territory will violate norms of *ius cogens* – e.g. the right of self-determination -, thus rendering those agreements a nullity under Article 53 of the VCLT. For example, a treaty entered into by South Africa with a neighbouring state on the exploitation of the continental shelf on the Namibian coast would have been both illegal - contrary to an international law norm - and invalid - it would not have produced any legal effect. To mention an actual case, the same could be argued for the many agreements concluded since the 1970s between Morocco and Spain and later between Morocco and the EC concerning fishing in the waters facing the coast of Western Sahara, despite the disclaimers concerning the recognition of Morocco's sovereignty over Western Sahara both by Spain and the EC, and the different formulas used in these agreements only recognising the jurisdiction of Morocco over the waters south of Cape Noun.[17] The same can be held for the hypothetical case where a third State entered into an agreement with Turkey concerning the opening of airports in Northern Cyprus to private flights from and to that third State without Cyprus' consent.[18]

The corollary of this invalidity is that third states automatically have a duty of non-recognition as affirmed by the ICJ in *Namibia*. It is interesting to note that the Court refers to a duty of non-recognition regarding acts related to unlawful territorial situations in general, not only those related to territorial situations established as a result of serious violations of peremptory norms as Article 41(2) of the ILC Articles on State Responsibility claims.[19] The ILC Commentary to Article 41 is slightly misleading when referring to *Namibia*, as it suggests that the *erga omnes* invalidity of the territorial situation can be derived only from the seriousness of the original or continuing violation of peremptory norms.[20] Such *erga omnes* invalidity is rather derived from the objective character of unlawful territorial situations, whose acts' invalidity can be opposed *erga omnes* because of its territorial nature. Further confusion to this controversial issue has been added by the ICJ in its 2004 Advisory Opinion *Legality of the Wall*, in which it has

---

[17] For an analysis of these different agreements see Soroeta Liceras, *El Conflicto del Sahara Occidental, reflejo de las contradicciones y carencias del Derecho Internacional* (2001), 227. See also Lahlou, *Le Maroc et le droit des pêches maritime* (1990), 173.

[18] For a very interesting account of the problematic issues involved in the opening of Northern Cyprus' airports to international traffic see Talmon, 'Luftverkehr mit nicht anerkannten Staates: Der Fall Nordzypern' 43 *Archiv des Völkerrechts* (2005), 39.

[19] Article 41, 2001 ILC Articles on State Responsibility, in Crawford (ed.), *The International Law Commission's Articles on State Responsibility: Introduction, Text and Commentaries* (2002).

[20] *Ibidem*, Commentary, 251.

determined that states have a duty of non-recognition of the unlawful situation created by the construction of the Israeli security wall on the basis of the *erga omnes* character of the norms breached, such as the right to self-determination.[21] Judge Higgins has rightly pointed out in her Separate Opinion that '[t]hat an illegal situation is not to be recognized or assisted by third parties is self-evident, requiring no invocation of the uncertain concept of *"erga omnes."*[22]

As to the internal acts of the administering powers, these are received by the international legal system as mere facts. They may be illegal, thus giving rise to state responsibility, yet international law will not control the production of their legal effects, since this is controlled by national law. In this sense, it will be up to each state to decide whether to recognise or not to recognise the legal effects produced by such acts at the domestic level. For example, a concession by South Africa within the same treaty framework mentioned above for the exploitation of natural resources by a company incorporated in a neighbouring country would represent an internationally wrongful act, but it would not be invalid *per se*.[23] It is

---

[21] *Legal Consequences of the Construction of a Wall in the Occupied Palestinian Territory*, Advisory Opinion (2004), at <http://www.icj-cij.org/icjwww/idocket/imwp/imwpframe.htm>, para. 159.

[22] *Ibidem*, Separate Opinion of Judge Higgins, para. 38. On the question of non-recognition of unlawful territorial situations, the present author begs to differ with the authoritative view expressed by Dugard in his book, *Recognition and the United Nations (supra* n. 5), that the duty of non-recognition applies only to situations deriving from violations of *jus cogens*. For a more recent expression of the same view see Raic, *Statehood and the Law of Self-Determination* (2002). *A fortiori*, the present study's view on the duty of non-recognition with regard to unlawful territorial situations is at variance with that expressed by the ILC in Article 41 of the 2001 Articles on State Responsibility that restricts the duty of non-recognition to situations resulting from *serious* violations of peremptory norms. The difference of approach may be explained as follows. Both the ILC approach and Dugard's and Raic' approaches are more in line with state practice, as an 'objective' determination of illegality of a territorial situation by UN organ and a practice of collective non-recognition is often limited to those situations produced by the most serious violations of peremptory norms, hence the perception that the duty of non-recognition applies only to those instances. When such authoritative determination lacks, uncertainty over the legality of the situation will most of the times prevail among states, giving rise to different views and policies of dealing or non-recognising. However, in theory, if we depart from an assumption of illegality of a territorial situation, there is little to support the idea that states may be legally entitled to enter into international legal relations with illegal states, say, resulting from an act of unilateral secession. In practice, the difference is relatively minor, at least as compared to Dugard's view, as most of unlawful territorial situations as defined in the present book derive from violations of *ius cogens* norms.

[23] It is in this respect interesting to consider the legal opinion rendered by the UN Legal Counsel in 2002 on the compatibility of agreements entered into by Moroccan authorities with oil corporations regarding the exploitation of natural resources in the continental shelf off the coast of Western Sahara. The counsel approached the issue as a problem of legality, rather than validity, and he concluded for the 'legality' of the concession agreements between Morocco and Kerr McGee and TotalFinaElf on the basis that they provided the exploration, not the exploitation, of natural resources in the area. Letter dated 29 January 2002 from the Under-Secretary-General for Legal Affairs, the Legal Counsel, addressed to the President of the Security Council (S/2002/161).

in this particular respect that the law of state responsibility for serious violations of peremptory norms plays a distinctive role, as in those cases states will be under an obligation not to render any aid or assistance to the occupier, thus arguably also imposing an obligation not to give effect to internal acts.[24] Furthermore, the SC, by imposing a regime of sanctions, can create new obligations not to recognise internal acts and reinforce already existing obligations not to recognise international acts. This possibility is also provided by Article 41(1) of the ILC Articles on State Responsibility, which spells out a positive duty upon states to cooperate through appropriate bodies in order to bring to an end any serious violation of peremptory norms.

2.1.2 Cases involving the TRNC before the ECHR: background of the decisions

The issue of invalidity can be also highlighted by considering the jurisprudence of the European Court of Human Rights (ECHR) on the Cyprus issue. Before analysing the way the ECHR has dealt with the question of validity of the TRNC legal system, the background of Cyprus' continuing unlawful territorial situation must be explained. Cyprus, formerly a British colony, had been granted independence and provided with a constitution in 1960. The constitutional framework was backed by a complex system of international guarantees, including a Treaty of Guarantee concluded by Britain, Turkey and Greece that would ensure an external supervision over the proper functioning of the new constitution. This constitution would ensure a fair representation of the two main communities of the island, the Greek and the Turkish, in its institutions. In the face of continuing deadlocks and difficulties in successfully implementing the constitutional framework and the ensuing tensions between the two communities, a *coup d'etat* was organised on 15 July 1974 by the Greek military junta which led to the deposition of President Makarios and the substitution of a new government with support from the Greek military. After five days, Turkey, claiming a right under Article IV of the Treaty of Guarantee,

---

However, see Written Statement of the Secretary-General in *Namibia* (Pleadings, Vol. 1, 109) claiming that 'since all titles, grants, concessions, charters, incorporations, and other rights in Namibia purportedly granted, transferred or vested by the Government of South-Africa after the termination of the Mandate are void and without effect, no such rights or acts should be acknowledged or upheld in the jurisdiction of any state.'

[24] Article 41(2), 2001 ILC Articles, *supra* n. 19.

intervened militarily and occupied the north-eastern part of the island.[25] Despite the withdrawal of Greek forces from Cyprus, the return to the previous civil administration after only 3 days, and the demand of the SC for 'an immediate end to foreign military intervention in the Republic of Cyprus',[26] the occupation by Turkish forces continued over the years resulting first in the creation of a Turkish Federated State of Cyprus, with a view to developing a new federal framework for the whole of Cyprus, and, after years of unsuccessful negotiations, to the declaration of independence of 15 November 1983 of the Turkish Republic of Northern Cyprus. Three days later, the SC in Resolution 541 deplored the declaration of independence and qualified it as 'legally invalid'.

As of today, the TRNC has been recognised only by Turkey, but the *status quo* in the status of the island continues. Despite the accession of Cyprus to the European Union in 2004, the attempts to reach a diplomatic solution that would preserve the formal unity and territorial integrity of the island and recognise a state with no international legal personality for the Turkish Cypriot community were thwarted on 24 April 2004, when the UN sponsored Peace Plan for Cyprus was rejected by the Greek Cypriots in a referendum.[27]

2.1.3 Linking illegality of TRNC to the invalidity of its internal provisions

A. Loizidou v. Turkey

In the case *Loizidou v. Turkey (Merits)* the ECHR had to deal with the claim brought by Mrs. Titina Loizidou against Turkey, for having denied her access to her properties in an area occupied by Turkish forces. Turkey argued that the property had been expropriated for a public necessity according to Article 159 of the TRNC constitution. The Court, considering the applicability of Article 159 of the TRNC constitution, claimed the invalidity of that provision, thus reaching the conclusion that the claimant never lost her title to property. Thus Turkey should be held responsible for denying access to property under the European Convention of Human Rights Protocol I. Its conclusion derived from the reaction

---

[25] 'In the event of a breach of the provisions of the present Treaty, Greece, Turkey and the United Kingdom undertake to consult together with respect to the representations or measures necessary to ensure observance of those provisions. In so far as common or concerted action may not prove possible, each of the three guaranteeing Powers reserves the right to take action with the sole aim of re-establishing the state of affairs created by the present Treaty.' 1960 Cyprus Treaty of Guarantee, 16 August 1960, UKTS (1961), No. 5.

[26] SC Res. 353 (1974).

[27] See UN Peace Plan for Cyprus, 26 February 2003, in <http://www.cyprus-un-plan.org>. The plan was endorsed by the SC in Res. 1475 (2003). The most prominent reasons behind the rejection of the plan by the Greek Cypriots were the constitutional federal structure that provided for very few central powers, the restrictions on the access by Greek Cypriots to properties in the northern part of the island and the maintenance of a strong Turkish military presence until 2011.

of the international community, which, apart from Turkey, never recognised the existence of a separate legal entity:

> 'In this respect it is evident from international practice an the various, strongly worded resolutions referred to […] that the international community does not regard 'TRNC' as a State under international law and that the Republic of Cyprus has remained the sole legitimate Government of Cyprus […]. Against this background the Court cannot attribute legal validity for purposes of the Convention to such provisions as Article 159 of the fundamental law on which the Turkish Government rely.'[28]

In other words, the Court took an approach of constitutive recognition to the question of TRNC statehood. However, the Court did not engage in a discussion of what was the legal basis of this policy of non-recognition. This is in contradiction with the heavy reliance put on this original illegality to explain the chain of invalidity.

Furthermore, it avoided spelling out a general principle of interpretation on the relationship between the validity of international norms and national norms. It stated that it 'does not consider it desirable, let alone necessary, in the present context to elaborate a general theory concerning the lawfulness of legislative administrative acts of the TRNC.'[29] It then concluded by recalling the ICJ Advisory Opinion in the *Namibia* case, where the ICJ asserted the validity of certain administrative acts of unlawful *de-facto* entities, for instance as regards the registration of births, deaths and marriages, 'the efficacy of which can be ignored only to the detriment of the inhabitants of the territory.'[30] Despite the claim of the Court to the effect that no general theory of invalidity is developed, the underlying assumption of the Court's reasoning seems to be that the unlawfulness of a certain *de facto* entity affects the validity of its acts, with the exception of those administrative acts whose non-applicability would be detrimental to individual interests. This interpretation would assume a 'relative invalidity' of the unlawful territorial situation, with some legal effects still being produced and recognised in the international sphere due to its 'remote' link with the original unlawfulness.[31]

---

[28] *Loizidou v. Turkey (Merits)*, Judgement of 18 December 1996, ECHR Series A (1996-VI), 2219, at 2231.

[29] *Ibidem.*

[30] The theory can be found already in the Resolution of the Institut de Droit International of 1936 where it was stated that '[c]es effets extra-territoriaux ne dépendent pas cependant de l'acte formel de reconnaisance du gouvernement nouveau. Même à défaut de reconnaisance, ils doivent être admis par les jurisdiction et administrations compétentes lorsque, considerant notamment le caractère réel du pouvoir exercé par le gouvernement nouveau, ces effets sont conformes aux intérêts d'une bonne justice et à l'interêt des particuliers.' 39 II *Annuaire de l'Institut de Droit International* (1936), 304.

[31] Jennings, *The Acquisition of Territory in International Law* (1963), 75.

This approach would support a monist relationship between the international legal system and the domestic legal system.

It is submitted that the Court in reality adopts, perhaps unwillingly, a dualist approach disguised as a monist one. Rather than considering a chain of invalidity and effecting a test of remoteness, it considers the internal acts of TRNC as mere facts that can be applied by an international court according to their compliance with an international rule. It is interesting to note that the conclusion of the Court is that it 'cannot attribute legal validity *for purposes of the Convention to such provision as Article 159*' (emphasis added).[32] In other words, the internal act will not be tested on its validity *per se*, since it is not a legal act, but only a legally relevant fact. It will be tested against the background of an international instrument, in this context, the ECHR. As it is found in breach of that instrument, it gives rise to Turkey's international responsibility and the duty to remedy that situation. It is not then a coincidence that the Court, in declaring the 'invalidity' of the TRNC constitution, heavily relies on the reaction of the international community, rather than testing on legal criteria the supposed 'invalidity' of the territorial situation. In fact, such 'invalidity' can be only construed as a sanction, and it is rather the non-recognition of certain legal effects, which arises as an obligation due to authoritative decisions of UN organs, that can substantiate a claim of unlawfulness. The acts themselves are legally valid under the domestic TRNC system, but they represent wrongful acts under international law giving rise to state responsibility. In fact, Judge Pettiti in his dissenting opinion criticised the finding of the Court on the issue of validity by maintaining that 'the Court accepted the validity of measures adopted by the TRNC authorities in the fields of civil law, private law and the registration of births, deaths and marriages, without specifying what reasons for distinguishing between these branches of the law and the law governing the use of property justified its decision.'[33] The reliance on the concept of invalidity is indeed misleading.

B. *Cyprus v. Turkey*

Another important decision in this respect is the one delivered on 10 May 2001 by the ECHR in an inter-state dispute between Cyprus and Turkey.[34] The case was referred to the Court by the government of Cyprus on 30 August 1999 and by the European Commission of Human Rights on 11 September 1999 in accordance with the provisions applicable prior to the entry into force of Protocol 11. The case had originated in an application against the Republic of Turkey brought before the Commission under former Article 24 of the Convention by

---

[32] *Loizidou, supra* n. 28, 2231.

[33] *Ibidem*, Diss. Op. of Judge Petitti, 2252-2253.

[34] *Case of Cyprus v. Turkey (Merits)*, Judgement of 10 May 2001, ECHR Series A (2001-IV), 5.

the applicant government on 22 November 1994. The applicant government claimed that Turkey had continued to violate the Convention, in particular Articles 1 to 11 and 13, as well as 14, 17 and 18, read in conjunction with the aforementioned provisions, and Articles 1, 2, 3 of Protocol 1 with reference to the following subject-matters: Greek-Cypriot missing persons; home and property of displaced persons; the right of displaced Greek–Cypriots to hold free elections; the living conditions of Greek-Cypriots in Northern Cyprus; and the situation of Turkish Cypriots and the Gypsy community living in Northern Cyprus.

As pointed out by one of the judges, Judge Loucaides, in a commentary over the case, the extent of the finding of the Court in regard to 'continuing violations of so many rights affecting such a large number of persons over such a long period of time' is unprecedented.[35] However, it is not our intention to look at the substantive findings of the Court in respect to Turkish human rights violations. Rather, operative paragraph 5 is here considered, where, by ten votes to seven, the Court held that

'for the purposes of former Article 26 (current Article 35 (1)) of the Convention, remedies available in the "TRNC" may be regarded as "domestic remedies" of the respondent State and that the question of the effectiveness of these remedies is to be considered in the specific circumstances where it arises (paragraph 102).'

In other words, the Court spelled out almost a presumption in favour of the effectiveness of judicial remedies in the TRNC. This seems in contradiction with the view taken in the admissibility stage, where the Court recalled its findings in *Loizidou* and rejected the objection to its jurisdiction advanced by Turkey, on the ground that the alleged violations should not be attributed to Turkey but to the TRNC. However, following its previous reasoning in *Loizidou*, the Court concluded that the Republic of Cyprus remains the sole legitimate government in Cyprus by looking at international recognition, and that the TRNC should be considered as a puppet-state under Turkish effective control.[36]

In the inter-state case *Cyprus v. Turkey* the Commission's report stated that, in order to consider the applicant Government's claims, the limitation of Article 26 of the old Convention should be addressed, that is whether effective domestic remedies had been exhausted. Whether the remedies provided by the TRNC were to be considered effective should be evaluated on a case-by-case basis. The Commission concluded that, for the purposes of former Article 26 of the Convention, remedies available in Northern Cyprus were to be regarded as 'domestic remedies' of the Turkish state. The Commission avoided making any

---

[35] Loucaides, 'The Judgment of the European Court of Human Rights in the *Case of Cyprus v. Turkey*" 15 *LJIL* (2002), 225, at 226.
[36] *Cyprus v. Turkey, supra* n. 34, 28-29.

statement on the validity of internal acts of the TRNC like the Court did in *Loizidou*. However, by recalling *Namibia*, it stated that 'where it can be shown that remedies exist to the advantage of individuals and offer them reasonable prospects of success in preventing violations of the Convention, use should be made of such remedies.'[37] In its judgement the Court makes clear that 'life goes on in territory concerned for its inhabitants' and these would be unfairly punished if they had to live in a legal vacuum where they were not recognised any legal status outside their borders.[38] The Court follows the approach of the Commission based on *Namibia*, and it tries to look for a 'pragmatic' approach that may ensure the protection of the inhabitants' individual rights. As argued by the dissenting judges, it is controversial whether recognising those remedies as in principle effective would work in favour or to the inhabitants' detriment, considering the distrust of the Greek Cypriot community towards TRNC's institutions.[39] In any case, and more importantly for the issue of validity, the Court recalls *Loizidou* and it spells out explicitly the consequences of a dualist approach. The Court endorses first the findings of the Commission that 'avoided making general statements on the validity of the acts of the "TRNC" authorities from the standpoint of international law, and confined its considerations to the Convention-specific issue of the application of the exhaustion requirement contained in former Article 26 of the Convention in the context of the 'constitutional' and 'legal' system established within the "TRNC".'[40] Moreover, it recalls the fact that the 'invalidity' of Article 159 in *Loizidou* was pronounced with respect to the Convention, but it did not imply a general statement of invalidity.[41] Further, the Court explicitly broadens the scope of the public/private act divide proposed by Judge De Castro in his separate opinion in *Namibia*, by admitting that recognition may also include 'acts related to public-law situations, for example by granting sovereign immunity to *de facto* entities or by refusing to challenge takings of property by the organs of such entities.'[42] Finally, it is interesting to read the conclusion of the Court that '*for the purposes of former Article 26 (current Article 35) of the Convention*, remedies available in the "TRNC" may be regarded as "domestic remedies" of the respondent State' (*emphasis added*).[43] In other words, the particular domestic act is tested against an international legal instrument: rather than its validity, the Court finds on its legality. The underlying

---

[37] *Namibia*, *supra* n. 10, 56.

[38] *Cyprus v. Turkey*, *supra* n. 34, 30-31.

[39] *Ibidem*, Partly Diss. Op. of Judge Palm joined by Judges Jungwiert, Levits, Pantiru, Kovler and Marcus-Helmons, 107, at 110-111.

[40] *Ibidem*, Decision, 28.

[41] *Ibidem*.

[42] *Ibidem*, 31.

[43] *Ibidem*, 32.

assumption is a dualist approach to the relationship between domestic and international law.[44]

The Court's decision on this point, however, found the opposition of numerous judges. The reservations on the question of nullity is clear in the Partly Dissenting Opinion of Judge Palm joined by Judges Jungwiert, Levits, Pantiru, Kovler and Marcus-Helmon. The dissenting opinion recalls *Loizidou* on the issue of nullity of Article 159 of the Constitution. Yet, unlike the majority decision, it only endorses the pronouncement of invalidity, without stressing the relation of that invalidity to the specific violation of the ECHR. It recalls the wish of the Court not to elaborate any general theory on the validity of acts of *de facto* regimes. It asks for a policy of judicial restraint on the grounds of three main considerations:

- any consideration of effective remedies under the TRNC courts' system has to cope with the fact that this judicial system finds its legal basis in a constitutional provision 'whose validity the Court cannot recognise – for the same reason it could not recognise Article 159 in the *Loizidou* case – without conferring a degree of legitimacy of an entity from which the international community has withheld recognition';[45]

- the Court is considering the TRNC judicial system as impartial and above all 'established by law', if it assumes its effectiveness, which should not be done according to the invalidity pronouncements of the international community;[46]

- finally, according to Judge Marcus-Helmons, the recognition of the Court's decision is at odds with the practice of non-recognition of the international community as witnessed by important domestic judicial decisions.[47]

---

[44] This approach to the 'invalidity' for the purpose of the Convention of the legal system created by an illegal regime was confirmed by the ECHR in a later decision, the *Ilascu v. Moldova and Russia* judgment of 8 July 2004. The Court, in assessing the Article 5(1) application to the situation of the secessionist Moldavian Republic of Transdniestria, specifically stated that while '[i]n certain circumstances a court belonging to the judicial system of an entity not recognised under international law may be regarded as a tribunal "established by law" provided that it forms part of a judicial system operating on a "constitutional and legal basis" reflecting a judicial tradition compatible to the Convention, in order to enable individuals to enjoy the Convention guarantees … [t]he requirement of lawfulness laid down by Article 5 § 1 (a) ("lawful detention" ordered "in accordance with a procedure prescribed by law") is not satisfied merely by compliance with the relevant domestic law; domestic law must itself be in conformity with the Convention, including the general principles expressed or implied in it, particularly the principle of the rule of law, which is expressly mentioned in the Preamble to the Convention.' *Case of Ilascu and Others v. Moldova and Russia*, Application n. 48787/59, Judgment of 8 July 2004, paras. 460-461, in <http://cmiskp.echr.coe.int/tkp197/view.asp?item=1&portal=hbkm&action=html&highlight=ilascu&sessionid=4358038&skin=hudoc-en>.

[45] *Ibidem*, Partly Diss. Op., *supra* n. 39, 118.

[46] *Ibidem*.

[47] *Ibidem*, Partly Diss. Op. Judge Marcus-Helmons, 125, 127.

Despite the dissenting judges' demand to refrain from elaborating on a general theory of invalidity, it seems clear that the six judges are taking a monist view, with a general chain of invalidity deriving from the unlawful establishment of the TRNC. The same approach was taken by the ECJ with respect to sanitary certificates issued by the TRNC for import into EU countries in the case *Anastasiou I*, which were considered invalid as they had not been issued by Cyprus official authorities.[48] That decision has received critical comments in case reviews, as confusing a matter of political discretion to be left to the decisions of competent bodies with matters of legal invalidity.[49] For instance, Talmon's conclusion is that 'the Court of Justice misjudged the scope and consequences of the principle of non-recognition in international law. It went far beyond that principle and, in fact, applied economic sanctions, a measure that should be reserved for political bodies responsible for the conduct of the Community's foreign relations.'[50] Interestingly, the ECJ decision is not recalled in the dissenting opinion of *Cyprus v. Turkey*.

In his separate opinion Judge Marcus-Helmons recalls the practice of foreign courts in relation to the question of validity of domestic acts of unrecognised states. He recalls *Adams v. Adams* as a 'recent case' where 'the English Court categorically refused to recognise any effect for the acts of the secessionist government concerned (the former Rhodesian government following the adoption of a unilateral declaration of independence).'[51] A careful reading of that judgement reveals that the judicial review of internal acts by the secessionist South Rhodesian government was still part and parcel with the practice of English courts to follow the recognition policy of the Foreign Office, in order to avoid a situation where the state appears to be speaking 'with two voices.' The reform in recognition policies by the FCO in 1980 and the 1991 Foreign Corporations Act providing that UK courts are now bound to accept the corporate responsibility of a company incorporated in an unrecognised state (with the only condition that the 'State' is established in identifiable territory and it has a judicial system) clearly indicate that courts are now free to give effect to internal acts of *de facto* governments as long as they are effective.[52] More recent case law applies new principles and make the judiciary independent from the FCO in its

---

[48] Case C-432/92 *Anastasiou I* [1994] ECR I-3087.
[49] Greenwood, Lowe, 'Unrecognised States and the European Court' 54 *The Cambridge Law Journal* (1995), 4; Talmon, 'The Cyprus Question before the European Court of Justice' 12 *EJIL* (2001), 727.
[50] *Ibidem*, 750.
[51] *Cyprus v. Turkey, supra* n. 34, Partly Diss. Op. Judge Marcus-Helmons, 127.
[52] See Talmon, 'Recognition of Governments: an Analysis of the New British Policy and Practice' 63 *BYIL* (1992), 231.

decisions.[53] Also the reference advanced by Marcus-Helmons to US Supreme Court case law during the Civil War seems misleading. It is true that US tribunals have consistently followed the executive in matters of recognition, but the practice of the US courts applies quite consistently a neat public/private, domestic/external distinction and recognises those acts whose non-application would be detrimental to the protection of individuals' rights.[54] For example, in the case *Kadic v. Karadzic* (1995), the Second Circuit Court of Appeal reversed the findings of the District Court that held that the Republika Srpska could not be considered a state under international law because of the lack of recognition.[55] It recalled the *Restatement (Third) of the Foreign Relations Law* that provides that 'under international law, a state is an entity that has a defined territory and a permanent population, under the control of its own government, and that engages in, or has the capacity to engage in, formal relations with other such entities.'[56] According to the Court of Appeal recognition would not be a pre-condition of statehood that would be accorded by the US government for political reasons. It is probably true, as Balejikan stated 35 years ago, that it is not possible to track down a dominant function of recognition and effectiveness if we analyse the last 200 years, but it is also arguable that there has been a growing tendency to give effect to the acts of *de facto* states and render the judiciary more and more independent from the executive in these matters, including in states like the US and Britain where traditionally recognition played a paramount role.[57] This seems to indicate that a legal situation arising out of a breach of international law cannot *per se* be invalidated, but that reasons of public policy and protection of individual interests are to be considered at least as important.

2.2 Final remarks on invalidity

The bottom line gives confirmation to the initial hypothesis. The term 'invalidity' is used sometimes as synonymous with 'illegality', but, in order not to raise confusion, the two terms and the two categories should be kept distinct. Rather than having a purely academic significance, this differentiation serves to clarify a confusion, which has a practical impact in the way international actors deal with unlawful territorial situations. Firstly, we should not talk of invalidity of a territorial situations as such, but only of specific legal acts related to it. Secondly, policies of non-recognition of internal acts of *de facto* entities or

---

[53] *Republic of Somalia v. Woodehouse Drake*, (1993) All ER 371.
[54] *United States v. Rice*, 4 Wheat. 246, 254 (1819); *MacLeod v. United States*, 229 US 416, 33 S.Ct. 955 (1913); *Russian Socialist Federated Soviet Republic v. Cibario*, 139 NE 259, 235 NY 255 (1923).
[55] *Kadic v. Karadzic*, 70 F. 3d 232, 2nd Cir. (1995), in 34 *ILM* (1995), 1592.
[56] *Ibidem*, 1606.
[57] Balekjian, *Die Effektivität und die Stellung Nichtanerkannter Staaten im Völkerrecht* (1970), 210.

situations should be construed as sanctions, rather than as an invalidation of those acts *per se*. The internal act will be recognised or sanctioned on the basis of its international legitimacy, i.e. on the basis of the appreciation of its function in ensuring the day-to-day administration of order and justice in favour of the civilian population, or, alternatively, in consolidating and perpetuating the unlawful occupation. Invalidity based on international norms only relates to international legal acts, such as international treaties creating territorial obligations between the occupying state and a third state: the duty of non-recognition upon third states shall automatically derive from their intrinsic invalidity.

A monist theory of invalidity supporting the invalidity of all legal acts adopted in the context of an unlawful territorial situation hardly captures the practice of states and international tribunals. It is at odds with a flexible administration of the dealings with the unlawful occupant's authority, which should allow the recognition of those acts that bring about a benefit for the individuals subject to the occupation. It is also difficult to reconcile with the limited powers that the unlawful occupant may derive from the application of international humanitarian law, in particular the Hague Regulations and the Fourth Geneva Convention. Furthermore, the fact that a dualist framework can be derived from judicial decisions shows international tribunals' awareness that the responsibility of non-recognition is better placed with international political actors. This conclusion, rather than unveiling a general 'impotence' of international law towards unlawful territorial situations, vests enhanced responsibilities upon states both in their individual dealing with such situations and in their collective dealing through international organisations. Finally, in terms of internal dynamics and in addition to developing a comprehensive system of invalidity of unlawful territorial situation, the definition of 'unlawfulness' given to certain territorial situations by international law may potentially produce a remarkable impact on related areas of international law, such as the law on the use of force or the law of statehood. This impact is analysed in the following sections.

3. Consequences of unlawfulness: protection of *status quo* and *ius ad bellum*

The first area of international law where the impact of a definition of unlawfulness is likely to be felt is the international law on the use of force. The prohibition of Article 2(4) of the UN Charter shows clearly how the law on the use of force and the law of territory are closely intertwined. Indeed, according to that provision, states shall refrain from the threat or use of force 'against the territorial integrity' of any other state. What the drafters of the Charter had in mind were the attempts of territorial aggrandisement through forcible annexation, which had so dramatically characterised the Interwar period and Second World War. This norm is spelled out in greater detail in the 1970 GA Declaration on Friendly Relations which states that '[e]very State has the duty to refrain from the threat or use of force to violate the existing international boundaries of another State or as a means of solving international disputes, including territorial disputes and problems concerning frontiers of States.'[58]

Despite some ambiguity in these formulations,[59] the content of these two norms and the emphasis in the Charter on the peaceful settlement of disputes – for instance Article 2(3) and Article 33 – seem to exclude a modification of an unlawful *status quo* through the use of armed force. In other words, a definition of unlawfulness of a territorial situation does not affect the duty of an interested state to refrain from using force in order to establish or re-establish a state of legality.[60] This principle has been illustrated by the practice of the SC during the Falkland/Malvinas conflict. On 2 April 1982, the Argentine army initiated a major military operation taking control of the Falkland/Malvinas Islands, which had been since the 19th century under British administration. The military operation was presented by Argentina as enforcement action to re-gain control over its own territory and as an action in self-defence in response to British aggression.[61] The day after the start of the military operations the SC adopted Resolution 502, which condemned the Argentine military action, called for an immediate cessation of hostilities, demanded the immediate withdrawal of Argentine forces from the islands and called on both governments to seek a diplomatic solution to the dispute.[62] A few days later the British government launched a major military response, which led to the full re-taking of the island by mid June of the same year.

The invasion by Argentina of the Falkland/Malvinas islands is indeed a *locus classicus* of the principle that the lawfulness of a territorial claim does not do away

---

[58] GA Res. 2625 (XXV), Declaration on Principles of International Law concerning Friendly Relations and Co-operation among States in accordance with the Charter of the United Nations.

[59] Schachter pointed out that 'it would be useful to make it clear in authoritative instruments that the expression "territorial integrity" in Article 2(4) refers to the State which actually exercises authority over the territory, irrespective of disputes as to the legality of that authority.' Schachter, 'International Law in Theory and Practice. General Course in Public International Law' 178 *Recueil des Cours* (1982), 143.

[60] See in this sense Kohen, *Possession Contestée et Souveraineté Territoriale* (1997).

[61] It was never exactly specified by the Argentine government what the act of aggression had been. As argued by Harris, it is likely that by that it was meant either the British taking of the Island in 1833 or a series of minor incidents occurred in March 1982 between the British army and Argentine nationals on South Georgia. Harris, *Cases and Materials on International Law* (1998, 5th ed.), 903, note 52.

[62] SC Res. 502 (1982), adopted with 10 votes in favour, 1 against (Panama) and 4 four abstaining (China, Poland, USSR, Spain). See debate in S/PV.2345, S/PV.2346.

from the duty to refrain from the use of force. The debate at the SC supported quite unconditionally that principle.[63] However, it did not address the question of whether the protection of possession by international law is unlimited. If that was the case, the formula would represent the triumph of immobility in international relations.[64] It may be also concluded that the British military action to re-take the islands and the subsequent re-occupation were unlawful. Such reading would be in accordance with the request by the Council to the Parties in Resolution 502 to settle the dispute peacefully, and with the dominant view in the Council seeking an immediate cease-fire.[65] To a further extent, Iraq's possession of Kuwait in 1990-1991 would be protected. This radical reading of the concept of *status quo* is obviously untenable. The solution is to be found in the linkage between the *ius ad bellum* and the law of territory. The Charter framework on the use of force defines the rules protecting an originally unlawful possession. In other words, when the re-taking of a territory is part and parcel of a lawful military action, the original *status quo* will not be protected. Of course, the mandate given by the SC or the proportionality of the self-defence exercised will be the major factors on which to assess the legality of the (re)occupation. For instance, in 1991, the Coalition's liberation of Kuwait had been explicitly authorised by the SC, therefore international law did not protect the Iraqi *status quo*.[66] As to the British re-taking of the Falkland/Malvinas, despite some reasonable arguments to the contrary, in particular concerning a level of contradiction between an action of self-defence and Resolution 502, it seems that overall the action was founded on Article 51, and it satisfied the criteria of necessity and proportionality. Therefore, Argentina's possession was not protected.

4. Consequences of unlawfulness: denial of self-determination and *ius ad bellum*

Another important point to be made is that the use of force in a situation defined as unlawful according to the criteria spelled out in the previous chapter can never be considered as having exclusively domestic relevance, thus being

---

[63] *Ibidem*.
[64] See Grewe stating: 'But as protection of possession is not the last word in civil law, the international legal order should also provide ways and means to examine and to correct situations of unlawful possession. It should avoid becoming a rigid order of immobility which may lead to violent explosions. In this respect there is much unfinished business to be accomplished.' Grewe, 'Status Quo', in Bernhardt (ed.), *EPIL*, (2000) (Vol. IV), 687, at 690.
[65] S/PV.2373. A draft resolution to that effect was supported by nine members and vetoed by Britain and the United States.
[66] SC Res. 678 (1990).

within the reserved domain of the administering state. This is a corollary of the fact that the definition of unlawfulness itself shows the relevance of international law to those situations. It can be clearly seen in cases of denial of a right of self-determination by the administering power. The first consequence of a definition of unlawfulness for the administering power is the fact that any forcible action against the people under subjugation will be considered unlawful. The principle is clearly asserted in GA Resolution 1514 and the 1970 Declaration on Friendly Relations among States.[67] As correctly argued by Cassese, in cases of foreign occupation the principle reinforces and restates the general ban on the use of force in international relations established in Article 2(4), therefore it does not represent in itself a new development.[68] However, it represents a subsequent development of customary law in respect to one more specific issue: the denial of the right of self-determination of peoples or racial groups within a certain community through unilateral coercive measures and repressive means.[69] The second consequence is that foreign supplies of arms and logistical assistance to the colonial or occupying power are unlawful. This was one of the first corollaries to be developed by the GA and the SC in the 1960s.[70] One of the main problems with this principle is that, when not defined within a general policy of arms embargo by the SC, it still leaves wide room for sale of military equipment apparently for diverse reasons, the same equipment being finally re-directed towards repression.[71]

More problematic is the question of the legality of the use of force by the oppressed people living on a territory which has not yet acquired statehood. Such use of force has taken shape in the form of the creation of national liberation movements that would represent all the efforts to gain independence through a mix of military and political initiatives. Very often the military successes at the national level were the pre-condition for their political recognition at the international level. Despite the perceived legitimacy of their armed struggle, and the effort of Socialist and Non-Aligned Countries to transform this legitimacy into a legal entitlement, the right to enforce the right of self-determination through military means was opposed by Western states as inconsistent with the UN

---

[67] 'Every State has the duty to refrain from any forcible action which deprives peoples referred to above in the elaboration of the present principle of their right to self-determination and freedom and independence.' 1970 Declaration on Friendly Relations, *supra* n. 58.

[68] Cassese, *Self-Determination of Peoples: a Legal Reappraisal* (1995), 96.

[69] E.g. GA Res. 172 (LIV).

[70] E.g. SC Res. 180 (1963) 'requesting' states to refrain from the sale of military equipment and arms to the Portuguese Government for the use in colonial repression.

[71] See in the *Namibia* case (*supra* n. 10), the separate opinion of Judge Ammoun, which spells out in detail the obligation for states not to provide assistance to Namibia (at 94).

principles of peaceful settlement of disputes.[72] The 1970 Declaration on Friendly Relations begged the question of foreign military assistance for national liberation movements when it stated that they 'are entitled to seek and receive support in accordance with the purposes and principles of the Charter of the United Nations.' A focus either on peaceful means of settling - supported by Western states - or on the right of people to respond to an external aggressive policy so long as the SC did not take action - supported by the majority of the countries - would dramatically change the reading to be given to the 'purposes and principles of the Charter'. Whatever the reading given, it seems that the limitation of the principle of territorial integrity would not apply for struggles against foreign or colonial domination. Therefore, the best that could be said is that, on the one hand, national liberation movements could not avail themselves of the pledge of self-defence according to Article 51. On the other hand, they could count on the *neutrality* of international law towards their claim to resort to a military struggle.[73] Never has a struggle for self-determination *per se*, even if conducted by military means, been declared illegal.

A different question is whether a struggle for self-determination may become illegitimate, because of the means employed such as forms of terrorism against the civilian population of the occupying power. Despite the risk that struggles for self-determination or against foreign occupations may be perceived as illegitimate when pursued and carried out through illegal means, such as in the case of terrorism, it appears that the international community has even recently maintained the distinction between the legitimacy of the aim and the legitimacy of the means.[74]

The conclusion is different as far as the right to invite foreign troops in support of their military effort is concerned. Despite a general view that peoples under continuing foreign domination were the object of a form of aggression and the widespread practice of states in the 1960s and in the 1970s in giving support to national liberation movements, the claim of self-defence by national liberation movements has not been accepted.[75] Notwithstanding the lack of a legal entitlement, it is correct to observe with Roth that

'[g]iven the prevalence of the state practice of rendering military assistance to liberation movements, the GA's pronouncements favouring it and the utter lack of collective *opinio juris* opposing it, one can only conclude that such assistance does not constitute "use of force

---

[72] See, for example, GA Res. 3013 (XXVIII) defining anti-colonial armed struggle 'in full accordance with the principles of international law', which was met with the opposition of 13 votes cast by the Western states.

[73] See Cassese, *supra* n. 68, 153.

[74] Cfr. more recent GA resolutions concerning Palestine A/RES/ES-10/13 and A/RES/57/198.

[75] See *Namibia*, *supra* n. 10, Sep. Op. Ammoun, 89-90.

against the territorial integrity or political independence of any state, or in any other manner inconsistent with the Purposes of the United Nations" under Article 2(4).'[76]

This is in line with the fact that those territories are not under the sovereignty of the state, thus the military actions cannot be possibly considered against the territorial integrity or political independence of the occupying state. Further, the legitimacy of the armed struggle of peoples under foreign domination makes sure that such violations were generally and widely tolerated.

5. Consequences of unlawfulness on the *ius in bello*

As far as the *ius in bello* applicable to conflicts related to unlawful territorial situations is concerned, the 1977 Protocol I to the Geneva Conventions applies not only to the transboundary use of military force, but also to 'armed conflicts in which peoples are fighting against colonial domination and alien occupation and against racist regimes in the exercise of their right to self-determination' by virtue of Article 1(4). In other words, these conflicts are considered by all means international armed conflicts under the First Protocol. The provision has so extended the application of the law of belligerent occupation to certain categories of unlawful territorial situations, which were not covered by the 1907 Hague Regulations and the 1949 Geneva Conventions.[77] The specific provision was adopted with a vote of 84 states in favour, 11 abstaining and 1 against.[78] The only vote cast against is particularly significant, because it came from Israel, an occupying power which, as of today, has not become party to the First Protocol and still claims the application of the relevant conventions on belligerent occupation on a *de facto* basis. Also among the abstaining countries – which as of today are still not parties to the First Protocol – we find countries, such as Morocco and Indonesia, which are or have been until recently occupying powers under the terms of Article 1(4).

Article 1(4) also confirms that the unlawfulness of a territorial situation should not impinge on the application of the laws of military occupation. The real problem however lies in the fact that in most unlawful territorial situations the occupying power does not see itself as such, thus it does not feel the need to limit its powers according to the Fourth Geneva Convention and the 1977 First Protocol. The application of the laws of military occupation would run counter to the recurrent claim that the military presence is established either due to the request of the local government, for instance in East Timor or Northern Cyprus,

---

[76] Roth, *Governmental Illegitimacy in International Law* (1999), 215.
[77] *Supra* Ch. 3, section 4.1.
[78] Cassese, *supra* n. 73, 201.

or due to the fact that the territory is indeed under the occupying power's sovereignty, for instance in Western Sahara or Bakassi. As of today, the only occupying powers recognising the applicability of a regime of military occupation to their presence in Palestine and Iraq are Israel and the US and some of the Coalition states, respectively, even if, at least in the case of Israel, such application is limited to a full application of the customary laws of the Hague Regulations and the *de facto* application of the humanitarian provisions of the Fourth Geneva Convention.[79] Regardless of the subjective recognition by the occupying power of the applicability of international humanitarian law to their occupation, it appears likely that an international body or domestic court will recognise the need to assess the actions of the occupying power on the basis of international humanitarian law as a separate basis for a review of validity of the occupant's acts typical of unlawful territorial situations.[80] Indeed, a determination of unlawfulness will not affect the application of international humanitarian law, which will apply equally and regardless of the validity of the legal basis for the territorial occupation. Generally, any measure or legislation instrumental to the maintenance of order and safety in the occupied territory shall be considered within the legal powers of the occupant.[81] This confirms the primacy of effectiveness as a legal criterion for the application of international humanitarian law, and the very limited impact that criteria of territorial unlawfulness can play in this respect.[82] On the other hand, the unlawful occupant will remain under an

---

[79] See CPA/Reg/16 May 2003/01. For a commentary on the regime of occupation in Iraq see e.g. Roberts, 'The End of Occupation: Iraq 2004', 54 *ICLQ* (2005), 27. *Supra* Ch.3, section 4.

[80] *Supra* section 2. A review of legality of the occupant's power on the basis of international humanitarian law was carried out by the ICJ in the Advisory Opinion, *Legal Consequences of the Construction of a Wall in the Occupied Palestinian Territory*, in <http://www.icj-cij.org/icjwww/idocket/imwp/imwpframe.htm>. The request by the GA (GA Res. A/ES-10/L.16 of 3 December 2003) sought an evaluation of 'the legal consequences arising from the construction of the wall being built by Israel, the occupying Power, in the Occupied Palestinian Territory, including in and around East Jerusalem, as described in the Report of the Secretary-General considering the rules and principles of international law, including the Fourth Geneva Convention of 1949, and relevant SC and GA resolutions [...].' Possibly the most important finding of the Court with regard to the application of international humanitarian law to Gaza and the West Bank is the *de iure* applicability of the Fourth Geneva Convention, despite the limitation on the full extension of the regime of belligerent occupation resulting from the strict interpretation given by the Court to Article 6(3) (paras. 89-101) . See *supra* Ch. 3, section 4. See also Report of the Special Rapporteur of the Commission on Human Rights, Mr John Dugard, on the situation of human rights in the Palestinian territories occupied by Israel since 1967, 6 March 2002, E/CN.4/2002/32.

[81] For a thorough review of domestic courts' decisions on this issue see Kaikobad, 'Problems of Belligerent Occupation: The Scope of Powers exercised by the Coalition Provisional Authority in Iraq, April/May 2003 – June 2004', 54 *ICLQ* (2005), 253, at 256-260.

[82] For the rationale behind the primacy of effectiveness in international humanitarian law, see *supra* Ch. 3, section 6. The conclusion does not aim at underestimating the role that the new principles of

obligation to withdraw as a result of the application of the criteria of territorial illegality spelled out in the previous chapter.[83]

6. Consequences of unlawfulness: access to statehood and referendum-setting

Potential room for making international law effective with respect to unlawful territorial situations may be found in the relationship between a situation of territorial unlawfulness and issues of state creation, continuation and extinction. The present section investigates how a determination of illegality of a given territorial situation can enhance the possibility for statehood of those subjects who are victims of this violation. Four cases are reviewed, Guinea-Bissau, Palestine, Bosnia-Herzegovina and Western Sahara, to see whether the balance effectiveness/legality has shifted with respect to statehood in a parallel move to that of the territorial status in general.

6.1 Guinea-Bissau

In 1972 the UN Special Committee on Decolonization dispatched a Special Mission to 'liberated' zones in Guinea-Bissau. Guinea-Bissau was an African NSGT under Portuguese administration, which had not yet gained independence, because of the Portuguese policy of opposition to a free exercise of self-determination. The Special Mission was composed of five people, who visited a comparatively small portion of territory in a period of roughly a week.[84] The conclusions reached were rather categorical in terms of the situation observed on the ground, and they claimed that the African Party for the Independence of Guinea and Cape Verde (PAIGC) was in control of about two-thirds of the territory of Guinea-Bissau. The basis for this conclusion was the information gathered from the PAIGC itself, and the verification of foreign journalists and observers. The following year the PAIGC declared the independence and creation of Guinea-Bissau, obtaining unilateral recognition by 65 states. These

---

territorial unlawfulness played in leading to the development of international humanitarian law and the extension of its scope of application to new types of conflicts.

[83] On the relation between criteria of territorial unlawfulness and state responsibility see *infra* section 7.

[84] Note, 'The United Nations, 28th Session: Recognition of Guinea-Bissau', 15 *Harvard Journal of International Law* (1974), 482, at 488, cit. in Roth, *supra* n. 76, 219.

states then sought an act of collective recognition by the GA, by presenting a draft resolution.

The ensuing debate was very interesting, as it highlighted the controversy that the new principle of self-determination sparked on the vision of statehood supported by states. As observed by Roth, '[w]hereas supporters of the resolution stressed the equities of the situation – the right to self-determination, the prolonged and harsh Portuguese recalcitrance, the heroism and accomplishments of the liberation struggle – opponents focused on legal doctrine.'[85] Quite surprisingly, the debate rather than weakening the case for effectiveness in matters of statehood, seemed to reinforce it. Firstly, the conclusions of the UN Special Mission were opposed by Portugal, France and the US, which had on their side the fact that the capital, Bissau, and other densely populated areas were under Portuguese control.[86] Chile, Greece and Canada on their side highlighted the difficulty to fit the case of Guinea-Bissau into the international legal notion of statehood, because of the lack of overwhelming effective control over the territory, and the rejection of a constitutive notion of statehood. Even more interestingly, the proponents never advanced the thesis of a progressive development in the legal doctrine.[87] Finally, Resolution 3061 (XXVIII) was adopted by a majority of 93-7-30, which showed a considerable measure of division on the issue. The largest Western states all voted against the resolution. The deadlock was to find a solution one year later with the leftist *coup* and the renunciation of Portugal to all its colonial possessions, which may have led to the impression, contrary to the above analysis, that the case of Guinea-Bissau showed a triumphant right of self-determination over effectiveness. On the contrary, the debate on statehood of Guinea-Bissau before the GA, and the outcome itself with the voluntary relinquishment of Portugal's claims, seem to show how effectiveness was still at the heart of the general legal understanding of statehood, despite the consensus over the illegality of the continued Portuguese colonial occupation.

6.2 Palestine

Even more adamant in this respect is the case of Palestine. Palestine, formerly a British Mandate, had been divided in 1947 into two territorial units, one Arab and one Jewish, according to a controversial UN partition plan passed through a GA resolution adopted with a majority of 33-13-10.[88] The resolution envisaged the division of the Mandate Territory in six separate zones, three to be assigned to the prospective Arab State and three to the prospective Jewish State, each

---

[85] Roth, *supra* n. 76, 220.
[86] GA Official Records, 2163rd meeting, 130.
[87] Roth, *supra* n. 76, 221.
[88] GA Res. 181 (II).

connected by few crossing points. Bethlehem and Jerusalem were to be internationalised under the supervision of the UN Trusteeship Council. On 15 May 1948, the day after the mandatory power, Britain, had withdrawn its presence from Palestine and terminated the Mandate notwithstanding its refusal to give implementation to the partition plan, a coalition of Arab states including Egypt, Transjordan, Lebanon, Syria and Iraq intervened militarily. These neighbouring states had opposed explicitly the UN partition plan and with their intervention sought to maintain the unity of what they argued was the newly born state of Palestine. No declaration of independence of a Palestinian state was ever effected, because that would have implied acceptance of the GA partition plan. They claimed that they were ensuring respect of the will of the majority of the population, and that they were acting under the invitation of the Palestinian leadership. Israel, which had proclaimed itself as an independent and sovereign state on 14 May 1948 in the territory assigned by GA Resolution 181, claimed its right of self-defence against the Arab aggression. What ensued was an armed conflict that continued until January 1949 and which was followed by a series of armistices between Israel and the Arab countries. These armistice lines were to be observed and maintained by a UN Truce Supervision Organisation (UNTSO). The control over Palestine was carved up among Israel, Egypt and Jordan, filling at a jurisdictional level the sovereignty *vacuum* which had followed the termination of the mandate. The territory belonging to the former Mandate was put under the military administration of these three countries. The Six Day War of 1967 led to a shift in the balance of effective powers in Palestine, as the West Bank and the Gaza Strip were occupied by Israel. Following the breakout of a rebellion against Israeli military rule over Palestine in 1987, on 15 November 1988, the Palestine National Council Meeting in Algiers declared the independence of the State of Palestine, having as a territorial basis the West Bank, the Gaza Strip and East Jerusalem. The declaration enjoyed alternate fortunes for the question of Palestine's statehood. Palestinian statehood was recognised by over 100 states and on 15 December 1988 the GA adopted Resolution 43/177, essentially recognising the new state of Palestine. However, the further attempts by the PLO leadership to see Palestinian statehood recognised at a more substantive level failed.[89]

In fact, the renunciation by Jordan to any territorial claim over the West Bank, the official acceptance by the PLO Chairman Arafat of the right to existence of an Israeli state within the limits spelled out in SC Resolutions 242 and 338, and the PLO commitment to the renunciation of terrorism all enabled the beginning of a series of negotiations for an overall solution of the Palestinian problem. These negotiations culminated in the signature in Washington on 13

---

[89] See Van De Craen, 'Palestine (1996 Addendum)', in Bernhardt (ed.), *EPIL* (1997) (Vol. III), 865.

September 1993 by the Israeli Prime Minister Rabin and PLO Chairman Arafat of the Declaration of Principles on Interim Self-Government Arrangements.[90] The declaration was a fully-fledged international agreement, which had the objective to implement a right of internal self-determination of the Palestinian people by creating a Palestinian civil administration (Palestinian Authority) for the West Bank and Gaza substituting the Israeli military administration. It represented the legal framework within which the Erez Checkpoint/Gaza Agreement of 29 August 1994 was concluded, which provided for the assumption of Palestinian jurisdiction in the spheres of education, culture, health, social welfare, tourism, direct taxation and value added tax on local production.[91] More importantly, despite the recalling of Resolutions 242 and 381, the Oslo Agreements did not address the question of Palestinian sovereignty and statehood, and the Israeli claim to sovereignty over East Jerusalem. They did not envisage any substantive objective for the solution of the permanent status of Palestine and its statehood, the complete withdrawal of Israeli troops and the question of Jewish settlements, even if a commitment to a general solution of these issues was recalled in Article V. Furthermore, the internal effectiveness of the Palestinian Authority was reduced by the residual but substantial jurisdictional powers of Israeli forces over settlements in the West Bank and Gaza, and the maintenance of an Israeli substantial military presence along the main ways of communication.

Despite initial encouraging steps towards the gradual establishment of the Palestinian autonomy, the process has come to a dramatic standstill since the outbreak of the second *Intifada* in 2000, which has resulted in a re-occupation by Israeli forces of the Palestinian territory and a strong policy of creation of new settlements and new physical barriers between Jewish and Arab communities. The Road Map for a Permanent Two-State Solution, published on 30 April 2003 under the auspices of the US, EU, UN and Russia, has spelled out clearly the final aim of an independent, viable and sovereign State of Palestine with permanent borders to be reached by 2005.[92] Despite setting a final and conclusive solution to the Middle East conflict based on a precise timetable, the Road Map has hardly addressed any of the most contentious issues concerning Palestinian statehood, such as the physical re-drawing of the West Bank border by the construction of a wall, the dismantlement of Israeli settlements, Israeli military outposts within the West Bank and Gaza and the question of East

---

[90] 1993 Declaration of Principles on Interim Self-Government Arrangements, in 32 *ILM* (1993), 1525.
[91] 1994 Agreement on Preparatory Powers and Responsibilities, in 34 *ILM* (1994), 455.
[92] A Performance Based Road Map to a Permanent Two-State Solution to the Israeli-Palestinian Conflict, 30 April 2003, in <http://www.un.org/News/dh/mideast/roadmap120002.pdf>.

Jerusalem. Little surprise that the objective of a Palestinian state by the end of 2005 appears out of question at the time of writing.

The aim of the UN Partition Resolution was to ensure the exercise of a right to self-determination within two new territorial entities, which would allow the co-existence between Jewish and Arab communities. However, it is clear that Israel could become a state since its very declaration of independence and be admitted to the UN as a fully-fledged member thanks to its effectiveness. Likewise, it is clear that Palestine has not been a state under the traditional Montevideo criteria, because of the lack of an effective governmental authority. Even under the 1993 Oslo Agreement with the establishment of a general governmental authority over Gaza and the West Bank, the level of effectiveness of the Palestinian Authority was limited to certain cities and areas. Further, such effectiveness was legally weakened by the very singular provision of Article 3(b), Annex 2 that did not extend the jurisdiction of the Palestinian Authority over Israeli peoples and illegal settlements. The Road Map has surely represented a step forward in the sense that it has spelled out in detail crucial requirements for the democratic and efficient reform of the Palestinian institutions. That process has been revitalised by the change of Palestinian leadership in 2004. Whether it can also lead to the creation of a 'viable Palestine' 'with maximum territorial contiguity' and with permanent borders according to Resolution 242 and Resolution 338 is again the most difficult challenge ahead. Whereas the decision of the Israeli government to withdraw from Gaza in summer 2005 has represented a positive step towards that goal, the interpretation given by the Israeli government to the requirement contained in the Road Map of removal in the first phase of illegal settlements built since 2001 is not re-assuring, as it is not re-assuring the lack of objection to that interpretation by the US, the main guarantor as far as the document's implementation is concerned. In his statement of 4 June 2003 after the Aqaba Summit meeting, Prime Minister Ariel Sharon claimed: 'In regard to the unauthorized outposts, I want to reiterate that Israel is a society governed by the rule of law. Thus, we will immediately begin to remove unauthorized outposts.'[93] It is clear that the reference is to Israeli law, rather than

---

[93] Statement by Prime Minister Ariel Sharon after the Aqaba Summit meeting, 4 June 2003, in <http://www.israel-mfa.gov.il/mfa/go.asp?MFAHO0nfv0>. See also the Letter sent by US President George W Bush to Prime Minister Ariel Sharon of 14 April 2004 (at <http://www.whitehouse.gov/news/releases/2004/4/20040414-2.html>), in which the President wrote that '[A]s part of final peace settlement, Israel must have secure and recognized borders, which should emerge from negotiations between the parties in accordance with UNSC Resolutions 242 and 338. In light of new realities on the ground, including already existing major Israeli populations centres, it is unrealistic to expect that the outcome of final status negotiations will be a full and complete return to the armistice lines of 1949, and all previous efforts to negotiate a two-state solution have reached the same conclusion. It is realistic to expect that any final status agreement will only be achieved on the basis of mutually agreed changes that reflect these realities.'

international law, and also the substitution of the expression 'illegal settlements' with the expression 'unauthorized outposts' is telling. Furthermore, the so-called process of 'natural growth' of existing settlements in the West Bank has continued since 2002 with the construction of new houses and new bypass roads, including a 50- to 75- metres buffer zone on each side of the road in which no building is permitted.[94]

Another disturbing development for the implementation of the Road Map has been the construction of a security fence, in some points in the form of a concrete wall, running parallel to the border between Israel and the West Bank, but located within the West Bank itself.[95] The security fence was initially declared by the GA 'in contradiction with relevant provisions of international law';[96] the GA subsequently referred the matter to the ICJ for a determination of the legal implications of the construction of the fence.[97] In the advisory opinion rendered on 9 July 2004, the Court confirmed that the construction of the wall and its associated regime are contrary to international law; and it determined the legal consequences of such violation, such as the duty of cessation of the wrongful actions, the duty to make reparation for the damage caused, the obligation for third states not to recognise the illegal situation and not to render assistance or aid in maintaining the situation and, for states parties to the Fourth 1949 Geneva Convention, the duty to ensure compliance by Israel with its obligations under that convention.[98]

Leaving aside the question of security and the merits of the Israeli decision to address such problems through these means - a question whose treatment by Court was indeed far from satisfactory, especially with regard to the application of international humanitarian law - ,[99] the construction of the security fence has raised and continues to raise two troublesome questions with regard to Palestinian statehood. The first one is the creeping annexation of Palestinian territory through the construction of a physical border that may well become accepted as a *fait accompli* in the final status negotiations. This was acknowledged

---

The position of the Bush administration on settlements in the West Bank has come very close to the unconditional support for the Sharon government's position.

[94] Report of the Human Rights Commission's Special Rapporteur for Palestine, *supra* n. 80, 12.

[95] See Brubacher, 'Le mur de la honte', November 2002, *Le Monde Diplomatique*, 20. See also *Legality of Wall in Palestine*, *supra* n. 80.

[96] GA Res. ES-10/13, 27 October 2003.

[97] GA Res. A/ES-10/L.16, 3 December 2003.

[98] *Legality of the Wall*, *supra* n. 80, *dispositif*.

[99] *Ibidem*, Declaration of Judge Buergenthal.

by the Court when it stated that it 'considers that the construction of the wall and its associated regime create a "fait accompli" on the ground that could well become permanent, in which case, and notwithstanding the formal characterization of the wall by Israel, it would be tantamount to *de facto* annexation.'[100] The second one is the legality under international law of a disarmed, 'democratic' and 'self-determined' statelet. In other words, the creation of a Palestinian state under those circumstances and conditions would most likely make its status under international law controversial and, possibly, would continue the situation of territorial unlawfulness, as was the case with the South African *bantustans* during the 1980s. Whereas in this latter case the illegality derived from the coerced exercise of self-determination imposed upon the black majority of South Africa and the policy of systematic racial discrimination, in the case of Palestine, the illegality of a prospective Palestinian state may derive from the lack of factual independence and the lack of effective jurisdiction, as a result of the Israeli military coercion, over basic state functions, such as custom and border controls, air traffic regulations, roads and coastline controls, defence policy.

In conclusion, if the right of self-determination had been worked out as a criterion of statehood, it should have worked *a fortiori* in the case of Palestine as opposed to Guinea-Bissau. Like in the case of Guinea-Bissau, state entities were claiming sovereignty over parts of the Palestinian territory, for example, the claims of Israel to sovereignty related to Jerusalem and the claims of Jordan to the West Bank.[101] Like in the case of Guinea-Bissau, the PLO was meeting a test of political allegiance in the Palestinian population. However, whereas Guinea-Bissau involved the question of a colonial power unwilling to relinquish its grip over its overseas territories, Palestine had been the object of external aggressive policies both from Israel and Arab countries. The two criteria of illegality, the prohibition of forcible territorial change and the principle of self-determination, should have re-enforced each other and promoted the case of Palestinian statehood even more than in the case of Guinea-Bissau. However, the criteria of illegality have only determined the unlawfulness of the territorial situation, without attaching to it full-scale legal consequences. In other words, self-determination and the prohibition of forcible territorial change have limited the criterion of effectiveness at the level of Palestine's territorial formal status, but they have not ousted it in the more general question of Palestine's statehood. In a system largely based on the centrality of the state, the timid role played by legality

---

[100] *Ibidem*, Advisory Opinion, para. 121.
[101] Malanczuk, 'Israel: Status, Territory and Occupied Territories', in Bernhardt (ed.), *EPIL* (1999) (Vol. II), 1468, at 1489-1494.

in dictating questions of statehood is unfortunate for the credibility of international law as an effective tool to restore justice in these territories.

6.3 Bosnia and Herzegovina

The importance of statehood to the solution of disputes related to unlawful territorial situations can be hardly overestimated. Statehood means equality of status with the occupying power not only in bilateral negotiations, but also and more importantly at those multilateral political bodies such as the GA and the SC which are entrusted with the solution of these issues. Statehood also means access to legal means of adjudication in the international arena. Statehood means, in principle, unconditional legal protection of territorial integrity and political independence. The case of Bosnia and Herzegovina stands out in this respect in stark contrast to that of Palestine, since the usual terms of the relation between territorial unlawfulness and access to statehood were radically reversed.

Whereas in the cases of Guinea-Bissau and Palestine territorial unlawfulness was presupposed to the entitlement to statehood, in the case of Bosnia the access to statehood promoted by the international community defined the unlawfulness of a series of territorial situations. These territorial situations were the Yugoslav Federal Army intervention from March to at least May 1992,[102] the creation of the Republika Srpska as an independent state from December 1991 to December 1995, and the creation of the Croat Republic of Herzegovina-Bosnia from November 1992 to March 1994. The outcome was that territorial re-adjustments became a non-negotiable issue at Dayton, hence the statehood and territorial integrity of Bosnia and Herzegovina in its 'internationally recognised boundaries' was part of the non-negotiable principles.[103] The immediate recognition of statehood also allowed a largely ineffective government which from 1992 to 1995 retained control over only 30% of its territory, to participate in the works of the SC as a fully fledged member of the UN, to start judicial proceedings at the ICJ against a neighbouring country for its alleged involvement in the policies of genocide carried out by the Bosnian Serb leadership, to have full protection by the UN Charter in its territorial preservation.[104] To be noticed is the fact that the Bosnian people were not exercising a right of self-determination according to Resolution 1514, and that the external intervention of the FRY was considered terminated after May 1992. Even after the recognition by the FRY of the Bosnian statehood in the Dayton agreements, the system of state governance has

---

[102] *Tadic v. Prosecutor*, ICTY Trial Chambers (1997), in 112 *ILR* (1999), 1, at 49-51.

[103] Holbrooke, *To End a War* (1999).

[104] SC Res. 755 (1992); SC Res. 770 (1992); *Application of the Convention on the Prevention and Punishment of the Crime of Genocide*, Application of the Republic of Bosnia and Herzegovina of 20 March 1993, in <http://www.icj-cij.org/icjwww/idocket/ibhy/ibhyframe.htm>.

been largely ineffective and is slowly being implemented thanks to a considerable international effort. What matters most, however, for our discussion is that for once effectiveness was put aside, favouring principles of substantive legality, in particular territorial integrity and *uti possidetis*.

It is submitted that the case of Bosnia-Herzegovina is important not so much because it creates a general model for creation of states in international law, but because it shows the potential for unlawful territorial situations of a substantial shift in the way statehood is seen under international law. Fully displaying the effects of principles of territorial legality also in the field of statehood enhances the possibilities of those who are subject to unlawful territorial situations to acquire their sovereignty. Further, it considerably diminishes the room of the occupying state for manoeuvre and its bargaining power in the 'peace process'.[105] That would hardly mean a drastic change in the way positive statehood is seen. It would only apply in case of unlawful territorial status, where principles of legality have already played an important role and they have often played an important role in denying statehood - consider for example the cases of Transkei or Southern-Rhodesia. Instead of an active policy of non-recognition, it would imply an active policy of recognition. Widespread international recognition of statehood would also mean *external effectiveness* and the possibility of an enhanced internal one. Of course, to support internally ineffective statehood would require a commitment by the international community to its principles of legality through competent bodies, which should result in a system of effective sanctions against those who do not abide by those principles and the possibility to decisively intervene through the establishment of direct or mandated elements of territorial administration. History has proven that such commitment is often successful in the long term. However, lack of commitment has always proven its dramatic failures. The history of Western Sahara is a reminder of that.

6.4 Western Sahara

A one-step approach automatically linking statehood to the unlawfulness of a territorial situation, instead of the commonly adopted two-step approach, would also address some of the most important problems related to the process of moving to sovereignty and statehood in cases of denied self-determination. One of these is the so-called question of referendum-setting. A mandatory requirement that the right of external self-determination envisioned by Resolution 1541 should be implemented through a popular consultation has never existed. This

---

[105] See the critical remarks by Catriona Drew on the fashionable language and substance of peace processes as a renunciation to legal entitlements in favour of pragmatic approaches. Drew, 'The East Timor Story: International Law on Trial' 12 *EJIL* (2001), 651, at 681.

has only applied to cases of integration or association of former colonies.[106] As the ICJ made clear in Western Sahara:

'The validity of the principle of self-determination, defined as the need to pay regard to the freely expressed will of the peoples, is not affected by the fact that in certain cases the General Assembly has dispensed with the requirement of consulting the inhabitants of a given territory. These instances were based either on the consideration that a certain population did not constitute a "people" entitled to self-determination or on the conviction that a consultation was totally unnecessary, in view of special circumstances.'[107]

In his separate opinion, Judge Ammoun stressed the fact that such special circumstances included the struggle of national liberation movements against foreign domination. He stated that '[n]othing could show more clearly the will for emancipation that the struggle undertaken in common, with the risks and immense sacrifices it entails. That struggle is more decisive than a referendum, being absolutely sincere and authentic.'[108]

However, practically, when the international community has started considering the possibility of integration or association, the referendum-setting process has become unavoidable. In other words, as argued by Catriona Drew, the standard approach to self-determination has implied a conceptual shift from its substantive territorial meaning to its electoral procedural meaning. This has also meant coming to terms with a substantial recognition of often forced processes of population transfer, illegal settlements and refusals to grant an unlimited right of return to refugees by the occupying power. With regard to Palestine, Drew argues that,

'[o]nce the right of self-determination has been stripped of its core entitlements to territory and resources, it becomes possible – for states, institutions and commentators alike – to assert both the *inalienable, jus cogens* character of the Palestinian right to self-determination, *and* declare the future of Israeli settlements as a matter for political negotiation; to affirm the primacy of the right of self-determination, including the option of a state, *and* envisage a future for Israeli settlements on the West Bank.'[109]

Furthermore, it has perpetuated the continuation of unlawful territorial situations, while the parties have engaged in long negotiations over the organisation of referenda, in particular voting entitlements, language of the ballot question and environmental and security conditions under which the choice should be exercised.[110]

---

[106] *Northern Cameroons Case*, ICJ Reports 1963, 15, at 32.
[107] *Western Sahara*, Advisory Opinion, ICJ Reports 1975, 12, at 33.
[108] *Ibidem*, Sep. Op. Judge De Ammoun, 83, at 100.
[109] Drew, *supra* n. 105, 666-667.
[110] *Ibidem*, 671.

The case of Western Sahara represents possibly the most dramatic failure of UN involvement in favouring the organisation of a referendum leading to either the independence and full statehood of Western Sahara or its integration with Morocco. In fact, 34 years have lapsed since the ICJ unambiguously stated the right of the people of Western Sahara to self-determination and Morocco occupied the region, and 20 years have lapsed since the Settlement Plan for the referendum on the final status of Western Sahara was published by the UN Secretary-General.[111] The biggest impediment to the implementation of the Settlement Plan proved to be from the very outset the identification of those people entitled to vote in the referendum. According to the plan, those entitled to vote would be all Saharans aged 18 years or over counted in the 1974 Spanish census. The Identification Commission, the body entrusted with the task of providing a final list of qualified voters, was mandated by the settlement plan to update the 1974 census on the basis of a calculation of births and deaths and the movements of the Saharawi population.[112] One of the most problematic issues turned out to be the identification of the thousands Shaharawi refugees in the neighbouring countries and other countries to be identified by the UNHCR. Even more problematic was the unwillingness by POLISARIO to accept the promotion by Morocco of thousands of applications with respect to certain tribal groups and in particular with respect to some specific subfractions of these tribal groups, as the number of members of these groups had been expanded in the years of occupation through Morocco's demographic policy. With regard to these contested groupings, another point of friction was the admission of written documentation in place of the oral testimony by one of the *sheiks* appointed by POLISARIO to overcome the refusal by POLISARIO to participate in the identification process. This led to an impasse in the process from 1995 to 1997.

In 1997, the Settlement Plan was re-vitalised by the appointment of James Baker, formerly US Secretary of State, as Personal Envoy of the Secretary General for Western Sahara. The first tangible result was a series of direct talks between the parties in Lisbon, London and Houston which led in September to the Houston accords.[113] The agreements vested the Special Representative with the final and exclusive authority for the organisation and celebration of the

---

[111] SC Res. 658 (1990); SC Res. 690 (1991); S/21360; S/22464. Possibly the most comprehensive monograph on the history of the unaccomplished decolonisation of Western Sahara from the point of view of international law is the recent work by Juan Soroeta Liceras, *supra* n. 17. See also Franck, 'The Stealing of the Sahara' 70 *AJIL* (1976), 694; Zoubir, 'The Western Sahara Conflict: a Case Study in Failure of Prenegotiation and Prolongation of Conflict' 26 *California Western International Law Journal* (1996), 173.

[112] Ramcharan, 'Recourse to the Law in the Settlement of International Disputes: Western Sahara' 6 *African Yearbook of International Law* (1998), 205, at 216.

[113] S/1997/742.

referendum, committed Morocco to stop any policy of new settlements,[114] and POLISARIO to accept applicants from contested subfractions at the condition of these applicants not being solicited by Morocco. The implementation of the Settlement Plan provided by the framework of the Houston accords seemed to work smoothly at the initial identification stage. In January 2000, the Secretary General published the complete voters list. Of the 198469 applicants, 86386 were held eligible to vote.

The Moroccan reaction was to doubt the impartiality of the UN in completing this list and to solicit the appeal of about 79000 applicants. A new controversy between Morocco and POLISARIO arose as to which applicants were entitled to appeal the UN decision. This led to a second situation of impasse in the identification process, aggravated by the Secretary General's new and unexpected policy of stressing the lack of enforcement mechanisms dealing with the post-referendum transitional period.[115] After a series of inconclusive negotiations in the summer of 2000, the action of the Secretary General and his representative James Baker saw a U-turn with the attempt to reach a 'political solution' to the dispute. The Settlement Plan would not be abandoned, but merely 'put on hold'.[116] A new Draft Framework Agreement provided for the creation of a Western Saharan Executive authority and an Assembly with a substantial degree of self-government and autonomy, recognising for Morocco the exclusive competence for foreign relations, national security and external defence.[117] A referendum would be held within five years from its entry into force, and those eligible to vote would be all full residents of Western Sahara for the preceding year.[118]

The change of policy was dramatic as the procedural barriers to an internationally recognised and fully-fledged core entitlement to territory were overcome by apparently only shifting procedural mechanisms, but in substance reducing the impact of substantive entitlements to territory and resources and of the definition of territorial unlawfulness on the final solution. Firstly, the Draft Framework Agreement represented the first formal UN *de facto* recognition of

---

[114] The policy of settlement of civilians in Western Sahara had continued uninterrupted for over 20 years, which has led some commentators to talk about the Second Green March. For instance, the population of the capital Laayoune increased from 30000 inhabitants in 1975 to 130000 in 1992, a large part of this population being composed of Moroccan public officials and their families. Berrada Gouzi, Godeau, 'Laayoun, plus fort que le désert', in 'Que font les Marocains au Sahara?', 34 *Jeune Afrique* 1994, 74, cit. in Soroeta Liceras, *supra* n. 17, 305, note 1105. Of course, the Settlement Plan, by taking as exclusive point of reference the groups and tribes censed by Spain in 1975, nullifies the effects of such policy on the number of eligible voters.

[115] SG Report of 13 February 2000, S/2000/131.

[116] SG Report of 20 June 2001, S/2001/613.

[117] S/2001/613, Annex 1.

[118] *Ibidem*, para. 5.

Morocco as administrative power, since foreign relations, national security and external defence were vested with Rabat.[119] Also 'symbolic' issues like Morocco's flag, currency, postal and telecommunications were formally extended to the whole of Western Sahara.[120] The Agreement ambiguously also referred to the 'preservation of the territorial integrity against secessionist attempts whether from within or without the territory' among Morocco's prerogatives.[121] Secondly, the agreement did away with the main thread of the identification process since the elaboration of the Settlement Plan – and confirmed by the Houston accords – which was to declare eligible to vote in the referendum only those individuals which had a real attachment to the groups and tribes defined in the 1974 census. By allowing to vote residents in Western Sahara for the year preceding the referendum, the agreement would have allowed access to the polls for thousands of new Moroccan settlers. It is not surprising that POLISARIO condemned the new Baker plan as 'in reality pav[ing] the way for a programmed annexation of Western Sahara by the Kingdom of Morocco.'[122] Also Algeria rejected the plan on the basis that it represented a radical departure from the Settlement Plan, and it proposed the establishment, by action of the SC under Chapter VII, of a civil and military mission to implement the Settlement Plan following the models of Kosovo and East Timor.[123] Morocco, on its part, welcomed the new plan, while refusing to consider the new proposals by POLISARIO to overcome the stalemate in the Settlement Plan.

This led the Secretary General in his Report of 19 February 2002 to reject the Algerian proposal in vague terms and state in unusually plain language that '[w]e are currently faced with a rather bleak situation with regard to the future of the peace process in Western Sahara.'[124] The Secretary General proposed to the SC to consider one of the following options: 1) to move on to consider the 130000 appeals and continue with the Settlement Plan without requiring the concurrence of the parties before action could be taken; 2) to allow a revision of the Draft Agreement by the Personal Envoy taking into account the concerns expressed by

---

[119] *Ibidem*, para. 2.

[120] *Ibidem*.

[121] *Ibidem*.

[122] Memorandum from the Frente Popular para la Liberacion de Saguia el-Hamra y Rio de Oro (Frente POLISARIO), in S/2002/41, Annex 1.

[123] Memorandum by the Government of Algeria on the Draft Status Agreement for Western Sahara, in S/2001/613, Annex 2.

[124] The reason for the rejection of the Algerian proposal was quite laconic: '[My Personal Envoy] is also of the view, which I share, that the proposals submitted by Algeria in lieu of the draft framework agreement, by which the United Nations would assume sovereignty over Western Sahara in order to implement provisions that appear identical to those of the settlement plan, has no more chance than the settlement plan of bringing about an early, durable and agreed resolution of the conflict over Western Sahara.' S/2002/178.

the parties, however without agreement from the parties if necessary to reach a solution and with an endorsement by the SC; 3) to negotiate with the party a possible division of the territory, and, in case of lack of agreement, to formulate the division himself, present it to the SC, which then would endorse it and submit it to the parties on a non-negotiable basis; 4) to terminate MINURSO and to recognise the impossibility of reaching a solution.[125] The SC did not agree to adopt any of these courses of action, but insisted on the effort to reach a 'political solution', despite at the same time underlying the continuing validity of the Settlement Plan.[126]

The latest proposal drafted by the Personal Envoy was informally submitted to the parties in January 2003 and circulated in May of the same year as an annex to a Report of the Secretary General.[127] The 'Peace Plan for self-determination of the people of Western Sahara' is fundamentally an amendment of the Draft Framework Agreement with new elements added to meet some of the concerns of POLISARIO and Algeria. The most important feature is possibly the addition of a third option as agreed by Morocco and the new Western Sahara Authority (WSA) in the referendum to be held no earlier than four years after its entry into force and no later than five. As admitted by the Secretary General, the envisaged option is that of substantial autonomy of the Western Sahara within the framework of Morocco's sovereignty. The main features of such substantial autonomy is already envisaged in the Peace Plan, as the executive, legislative and judiciary of the WSA enjoy a fully-fledged autonomy apart from a number of areas left within the competence of Morocco. These areas are the same as in the Draft Status Agreement, but for the prohibition of Morocco to 'prevent, suppress, or stifle peaceful public debate, discourse or campaign activity, particularly during any election or referendum period' aiming at promoting the independence of Western Sahara.[128] Furthermore, the foreign relations concerning Western Sahara will be exercised by Morocco 'in consultation with the Western Sahara Authority on matters that directly affect the interests of Western Sahara.'[129] In other words, the Peace Plan would also represent the first UN *de facto* recognition of Morocco as administrative power in Western Sahara. The other important element is the new shift in policy towards eligibility for the referendum. Whereas the Chief Executive and the Legislative Assembly shall be elected by following the criteria of the Settlement – that is, 1999 provisional voter list plus UNHCR list – among those entitled to vote for the referendum, the Peace Plan also includes those who have resided continuously in Western Sahara

---

[125] *Ibidem.*
[126] SC Res. 1429 (2002).
[127] S/2003/565, Annex 2.
[128] *Ibidem*, para. 8(b).
[129] *Ibidem*, para. 9.

since 30 December 1999.[130] The extension envisaged by the Draft Status Agreement is confirmed even if making the requirement of residence stricter. The question of identity of the 'people' of Western Sahara is still re-opened by the Peace Plan and risks affecting substantially the process and outcome of self-determination.

The reaction of the parties shows that their positions are still distant and leave little room for a successful negotiation. Morocco's main criticism concerns the relative departure from the approach of the Draft Status Agreement, and, more specifically, with the principle of subsidiarity applied to the *interim* institutional arrangement in favour of the WSA and with the power conferred to the Secretary General to issue binding interpretations in case of disagreement between the parties.[131] Most importantly, as far as the final status is concerned, Morocco has reiterated its refusal of any solution leading to full independence and statehood of Western Sahara.[132] POLISARIO has recalled the need to abide by the terms of the Settlement Plan in order to reach a just and lasting solution. Once again, according to POLISARIO, the Peace Plan would recognise the policy of annexation and transfer of population effected by Morocco for more than 20 years.[133] Algeria's reaction has been open to the new proposal of departure from the UN voters' list, but it has stressed the need for the UN to have a stronger role in supervising the fairness of the electoral process and implementing the results of the referendum. Furthermore, Algeria has stressed the need for the UN to put into practice a series of mechanisms to ensure a safe return of the refugees listed in the UNHCR list, and to avoid new transfers of population in the areas occupied by Morocco.[134]

In conclusion, the effective control by Morocco of large areas of Western Sahara for more than 30 years has left tangible signs not only in the landscape of the region with the longest man-made wall ever built since the Chinese wall (over 2000 kms.), but also in the way the process of self-determination has been developed. The new language of the 'peace process' and 'political solution' is perhaps the most pragmatic approach in a situation where the SC fails to fully discharge its primary responsibility in the field of international peace and security in accordance with international law, and the occupying power fails to

---

[130] *Ibidem*, para. 5.

[131] Observations of the Kingdom of Morocco on the proposal of James Baker entitled 'Peace plan for self-determination of the people of Western Sahara', in *ibidem*.

[132] S/2004/325, Annex 1; S/2004/760.

[133] Letter dated 8 March 2003 from the Secretary-General of the Frente POLISARIO to the Secretary-General of the United Nations, in *ibidem*.

[134] Memorandum from Algeria concerning the proposal from the Personal Envoy of the Secretary-General of the United Nations entitled 'Peace plan for self-determination of the people of Western Sahara', in *ibidem*.

acknowledge a fully fledged right of self-determination for the people of Western Sahara. However, it contributes to put under a sinister light from the point of view of international law what is possibly the last process of decolonisation. The reference to Morocco's 'territorial integrity', 'national security', 'determination of borders – maritime, aerial and terrestrial – and their protection by all appropriate means'[135] not only puts the process of self-determination and possible transition to statehood of Western Sahara in an odd framework of *de facto* recognition of its annexation, but also recognises the lawfulness of the territorial situation as such. Rather than moving away from effectiveness and shift the focus on the entitlement to self-determination and statehood, the Peace Plan, by legally recognising Morocco's occupation of the region, risks undermining the essence of self-determination as a legal principle which limits the impact of effectiveness on territorial situations, and consequently empowers peoples with the right to choose an appropriate form of self-rule. Its precedential value may reinforce the case for effectiveness and occupation as a bargaining strategy, and provide an incentive for the continuation of unlawful territorial situations all over the world. Instead of a decisive one step forward, Western Sahara risks remaining on historical and international law records as a case of two steps backwards.

7. State responsibility in unlawful territorial situations: re-assessing the boundaries of legality

Another important consequence of an unlawful territorial situation is that of the international responsibility incurred by the occupying state. This follows straight from the fact that '[e]very internationally wrongful act of a State entails the international responsibility of that State.'[136] A territorial situation established in violation of the principles and norms considered in the previous chapters shall inevitably entail the international responsibility of the occupying state. In fact, the ILC in its Commentary on the 2001 Articles on State Responsibility provides among the examples of continuing wrongful acts 'the unlawful occupation of part of the territory of another State or stationing armed forces in another State without its consent'.[137] The 2001 Articles spell out the secondary obligations deriving from a determination of state responsibility, namely a duty of cessation of the wrongful conduct and reparation for the moral or material injury caused in the form of restitution, compensation or satisfaction in order of priority.[138] The obligation to respect another state's territorial sovereignty being an obligation to

---

[135] Peace Plan for Western Sahara, *supra* n. 127, para. 8(a).
[136] 2001 ILC Articles, Art. 1, *supra* n. 19.
[137] *Ibidem*, Commentary, 136.
[138] *Ibidem*, Arts. 30-37.

abstain and being the violation a continuing one, the secondary obligation to cease the wrongful conduct overlaps with the continued duty of performance of the obligation breached. In other words, the typical remedy is withdrawal from the occupied territory, which is both resulting from the continued duty of performance of the primary obligation and from the secondary obligation to cease the wrongful conduct. Withdrawal is also part of the secondary obligation of restitution, which in some cases will provide a full reparation. In other cases, however, reparation may involve restitution of property – for instance cultural property – removed from the territory, and above all monetary compensation for the destruction of public and private property, the use of natural resources and the depletion of the environment. It is notable that this type of duty of reparation may result from the violation of other international obligations such as those deriving from international humanitarian law and international environmental law.[139]

However, the controversial point is the exact interpretation and understanding of the primary norm, the duty to respect the territorial integrity of another state. The controversy is particularly relevant to those unlawful territorial situations which crystallise in border or territorial disputes.[140] Does an adverse territorial occupation represent a violation of territorial sovereignty? Does it automatically follow a judicial decision concerning a territorial dispute that the occupying state which is found to have no legal title over a certain territory must be considered internationally responsible? The following section addresses these questions by looking at the very few territorial disputes dealt with by the ICJ, in which a state submitted a claim of state responsibility for illegal occupation. Providing an answer to these questions also helps us to make more precise the exact content of the criteria of legality analysed in the previous chapter.

---

[139] The book does not examine the issue of state responsibility of the occupier for violations of other sets of norms such as international humanitarian law, human rights law, international environmental law and the law of natural resources, which under certain circumstances can provide for more effective remedies, as compared to the law of territory. See e.g. *Legality of the Wall, supra* n. 80; Report of the Special Rapporteur for Palestine of the Commission on Human Rights, Mr John Dugard, *supra* n. 80. This aspect also raises the issue of double responsibility of the occupier (e.g. UNCC Governing Council's Decision 9, para. 12, S/AC.26/1992/9) and the issue of directness of damage (e.g., *Ibidem*, S/AC.26/1991/1; S/AC. 26/1991/7/Rev. 1; S/AC.26/1/1992/15), which have been addressed by the UNCC with regard to the Iraqi occupation of Kuwait.

[140] As said above (Ch. 1, note 24), the difference between territorial disputes and border disputes is not a difference in kind, but it is only a quantitative difference in terms of the disputed territory.

7.1 Unlawful territorial situations, territorial disputes and the ICJ

The leading case to be considered is the recent *Case Concerning the Land and Maritime Boundary between Cameroon and Nigeria (Equatorial Guinea Intervening)*.[141] In the course of the litigation before the ICJ, Cameroon advanced a series of requests with regard to Nigeria's international responsibility, including those concerning the continuing occupation of the Bakassi peninsula and the Lake Chad area by Nigeria. Cameroon stressed the violations of Article 2(4) of the UN Charter, of the duty of non-intervention in Cameroon's internal affairs, of the *uti possidetis* principle, and, more in general, of Cameroon's territorial sovereignty and integrity caused by the forcible setting up of a civil and military administration in those areas in the course of the 1980s and 1990s.[142]

Cameroon first asked the Court to declare Nigeria's duty to withdraw its civilian and military presence from the peninsula and from the Lake Chad area, to cease the exploitation of natural resources in those areas, and to stop its actions aiming at the settlement of Nigerian nationals.[143] Secondly, Nigeria ought to stop its *aggression juridique* such as the administrative arrangements designated to incorporate Bakassi in the Nigerian federal structures, in particular the creation of the Council of Bakassi in October 1996 and the circulation of maps supporting Nigeria's claim to the peninsula.[144] These duties would derive from the duty to cease the unlawful conduct inherent in the compliance with the primary norm of respect for Cameroon's territorial integrity. Furthermore, Cameroon asked the Court to declare Nigeria's international responsibility and a secondary duty of reparation for material and non-material damage in a form determined by the Court, including restitution and compensation to be assessed at a subsequent stage of the proceedings.[145] As for restitution, Cameroon demanded the return of all properties confiscated, and the return or re-building of all equipment and infrastructure used or destroyed during the occupation.[146] A claim for restitution in territorial disputes would have an important precedent in the *Temple of Vihear* case, in which Cambodia successfully claimed the return by Thailand of pieces of cultural property taken during the occupation of the area.[147] With respect to compensation, this should cover the military equipment destroyed during the

---

[141] *Case Concerning the Land and Maritime Boundary between Cameroon and Nigeria (Equatorial Guinea Intervening)*, ICJ Decision of 10 October 2002, in <http://www.icj-cij.org/icjwww/idocket/icn/icn_ijudgment_20021010.PDF>.

[142] Cameroon's Memorial (1995), 609-613.

[143] *Ibidem*, 630-636.

[144] Oral Pleadings of Cameroon, Tomuschat, CR 2002/16, 64-68.

[145] Cameroon's Reply (2000), 473-475.

[146] Cameroon's Memorial (1995), 638.

[147] *Temple of Vihear* (Cambodia/Thailand), ICJ Reports 1962, 6, at 11 and 37. See Cameroon's Reply (2000), 473-475.

Nigerian military actions, the damage suffered by the civilian infrastructures such as roads, the losses of physical property and profits due to the abandonment of economic activities related to oil and fisheries exploitation, and the damage caused in general to Cameroon's potential economic development due to the downfall in economic activities and the military effort required.[148] Compensation shall be also provided for the moral injury caused to Cameroon.[149] Finally, Cameroon demanded a commitment by Nigeria not to violate Cameroon's territorial sovereignty in the future and not to question its internationally recognised boundary.[150]

The Nigerian response is of particular interest, as it spells out some of the difficulties associated with a claim for state responsibility in a territorial dispute. It was built on two lines of defence. The first line of defence argued that Nigeria was not in breach of an international obligation *vis-à-vis* Cameroon. Firstly, Nigeria had indeed sovereignty over Bakassi and the Lake Chad area, therefore no issue of state responsibility could possibly arise. The sending of a substantial military presence to those areas since 1987 would only reinforce an already well established security presence in those areas, with a view to controlling a situation of civil unrest and the increasing incursions by Cameroon's army and police forces.[151] In case the Court would decide to adjudicate Bakassi and the Lake Chad area to Cameroon, Nigeria was claiming and exercising control over them in good faith. What in fact international law protects from the use of force directed against a state is not so much formal sovereignty but a *status quo*, whatever solution a tribunal may reach at the end of a process of territorial litigation.[152] Such a *status quo* is not protected only when it contradicts an internationally recognised boundary, and when it has been obtained through resort to force. Both conditions would not apply to the present dispute, since the boundary is obviously contested and Nigeria has not used force to acquire control over regions it has controlled over a long period of time.[153] Furthermore, a claim for state responsibility was unprecedented in territorial litigation.[154] The case of *Temple of Vihear* would not support any doctrine of state responsibility concerning territorial disputes, since a claim of state responsibility as such was not raised by Cambodia, but it was limited to the return of specific items as an ancillary of Thailand's withdrawal.[155]

---

[148] Cameroon's Memorial (1995), 640-641.
[149] *Ibidem.*
[150] *Ibidem.*
[151] Oral Pleadings of Nigeria, Abi-Saab, CR 2002/20, 21.
[152] *Ibidem*, 19-20.
[153] *Ibidem*, 22.
[154] Oral Pleadings of Nigeria, Watts, CR 2002/20, 26.
[155] Nigeria's Rejoinder (2001), para. 15.57.

As a second line of defence and argument in the alternative, Nigeria claimed that, should the Court have reached the conclusion that a wrongful act of forcible occupation had been committed, the following defences exempting Nigeria's responsibility would apply: reasonable mistake or honest belief, and self-defence.[156] As to the ground of reasonable mistake or honest belief, Nigeria argued that the defences listed in the ILC Articles on State Responsibility, despite not including these concepts, would not be exhaustive, and the possibility to use such defences would particularly characterise territorial litigation. Moreover, one should also consider the content of the primary obligation, whether it would entail a threshold of objective or fault liability.[157] Nigeria could not be held responsible for actions it had undertaken in the genuine, reasonable and honest belief of being the lawful sovereign over Bakassi. As to the ground of self-defence, Nigeria claimed that it was exactly exercising that right when responding to a series of incursions and military operations by Cameroon's military forces. Whether these acts amounted to an armed attack under Article 51 was something to be left to the Court for consideration, but the level of force involved made at least a *prima facie* case for Nigeria, so giving rise to its right to respond militarily.[158]

The Court's decision is condensed in paragraph 319 of the judgement. It obviously begs many of the questions raised by the parties in their written memorials and oral pleadings:

'In the circumstances of the case, the Court considers moreover that, by the very fact of the present Judgment and of the evacuation of the Cameroonian territory occupied by Nigeria, the injury suffered by Cameroon by reason of the occupation of its territory will in all events have been sufficiently addressed. The Court will not therefore seek to ascertain *whether and to what extent* Nigeria's responsibility to Cameroon has been engaged as a result of that occupation.' (*emphasis added*)

The Court concedes that an injury was suffered by Cameroon due to the Nigerian occupation, however, it refuses to determine whether this injury was the result of an unlawful conduct entailing Nigeria's international responsibility. The Court stresses clearly that ordering the withdrawal from the disputed territory shall provide a sufficient and effective remedy for Cameroon, as it had been the case in *Temple of Vihear* and *Libya/Chad*.[159] It further stresses that

---

[156] Watts, *supra* n. 154, 30.

[157] *Ibidem*, 31-32.

[158] *Ibidem*, 32-33.

[159] Decision, *supra* n. 141, paras. 312-317. An injury or damage can also result from an act which is not prohibited under international law or that it is even permitted, insofar entailing a diminished level of reparation. See ILC Commentary, *supra* n. 136, 74-75, 2001 ILC Draft Articles on Prevention of Transboundary Harm from Hazardous Activities and Commentary, in <http://www.un.org/law/ilc/texts/prevention/preventionfra.htm>.

'the implementation of the present Judgment will afford the Parties a beneficial opportunity to co-operate in the interests of the population concerned, in order notably to enable it to continue to have access to educational and health services comparable to those it currently enjoys. Such co-operation will be especially helpful, with a view to the maintenance of security, during the withdrawal of the Nigerian administration and military and police forces.'[160]

This approach, possibly wise from the point of view of a practical solution to the complex dispute between the two countries and of the preservation of the interests of the local communities affected by it, begs some of the important questions with regard to state responsibility as they relate to unlawful territorial situations. Is a claim of state responsibility for unlawful occupation of territories incompatible with a territorial or border dispute settled by judicial means as argued by Nigeria? What is the exact content and meaning of the primary norm protecting a state's territorial sovereignty? Can the defences of honest belief and reasonable mistake advanced by Nigeria be applied in order to preclude the wrongfulness of an otherwise illegal occupation? Finally, is the Court possibly implying a form of strict liability upon Nigeria for acts not prohibited under international law such as the maintenance of a territorial *status quo*? These four questions are now considered.

As far as the first question is concerned, it is fair to say that the claim for state responsibility and reparation for an illegal occupation of territory was almost unprecedented in inter-state litigation. This can be imputed to the fact that nearly all territorial disputes considered by the ICJ and other judicial bodies have been referred to these bodies by *ad hoc* agreements, which did not refer to the court any issue of state responsibility, but only asked for a final delimitation of the boundary. The present case was almost unique because it was brought unilaterally by Cameroon under Article 36(2).[161] In fact, the only two territorial litigations which involved *prima facie* issues of state responsibility were cases brought unilaterally by one of the parties to the dispute.

In 1932, in the case between Denmark and Norway on the *Legal Status of the South-Eastern Territory of Greenland*, Denmark in its application reserved the right to ask the Court for reparation due to the Norwegian violation of the existing legal status of South-Eastern Greenland.[162] The proceedings were discontinued the year after due to Denmark's withdrawal of its application.[163] In the *Temple of Vihear* case, Cambodia successfully claimed the return by Thailand of pieces of

---

[160] Decision, *supra* n. 141, para. 316.

[161] *Land and Maritime Boundary Between Cameroon and Nigeria*, Application Instituting Proceedings, 29 March 1994, in <http://www.icj-cij.org/icjwww/idocket/icn/icnframe.htm>.

[162] *Legal Status of the South-Eastern Territory of Greenland*, Application Instituting Proceedings from the Danish Government, 18 July 1932, 1933 PCIJ Series C, n. 69, 12.

[163] *Ibidem*, Order of 11 May 1933, 1933 PCIJ Series A/B, n. 55.

cultural property taken during the occupation of the temple's area.[164] However, as argued by Nigeria, it is true that in that case Cambodia did not raise a claim of state responsibility as such, but it claimed the return of specific items as an ancillary of Thailand's withdrawal.[165] In the pending case *Territorial and Maritime Dispute* brought by Nicaragua against Colombia under Article 36(2) and the Pact of Bogotà, Nicaragua has reserved 'the right to claim compensation for elements of unjust enrichment consequent upon Colombian possession of the Islands of San Andres and Providencia as well as the keys and maritime spaces up to the 82 meridian, in the absence of lawful title.'[166] In conclusion, the judicial practice of states is very scanty in this respect. However, the three mentioned cases prove that the demands inherent in a claim for state responsibility are not incompatible with a territorial litigation, and, in fact, they characterise most of the territorial disputes brought unilaterally before the ICJ.[167]

What, however, both *Cameroon/Nigeria* and *Temple of Vihear* do not answer is the second question as to the exact content and meaning of the primary duty to respect another state's territorial sovereignty. Such determination is of the greatest importance, since the violation of the counter-part sovereign rights is one of the two pre-conditions for the existence of an internationally wrongful act (the other being attribution). A precise understanding of the primary norms is also necessary to re-assess the principles of legality that define the 'unlawfulness' of territorial situations. Sir Arthur Watts' reference to a threshold of objective or, alternatively, of fault liability in Nigerian oral pleadings is particularly apt to catch this problem.[168]

A certain degree of fault may be required in territorial disputes, since there can be situations where one state reasonably and in good faith believes to have sovereignty over a certain area it occupies. This can apply for example where the parties to the dispute agree on the instrument drawing their boundary, but not on the exact interpretation of that instrument. Or, for instance, where a peaceful display of effective authority has not been contested by the other party for a long time. In this case, the reasonable mistake can apply to the significance to be

---

[164] *Temple of Vihear, supra* n. 147, 11 and 37.

[165] Nigeria's Rejoinder (2001), para. 15.57.

[166] *Territorial and Maritime Dispute* (Nicaragua/Colombia), Application of 6 December 2001, in <http://www.icj-cij.org/icjwww/idocket/inicol/inicolorder/inicol_iapplication_20011206.html>.

[167] One may ask why states which agree to delimit their boundary by judicial means do not also want the tribunal to consider the issue of responsibility and possibly claims for reparation. The answer may probably lie in two joint factors. First, most of the territorial disputes are about the exact drawing of the boundary and the re-attribution of land is often minimal and/or the dispute does not entail any steady pattern of adverse occupation. Second, a risk and cost-benefit analysis of choosing judicial litigation may discourage both sides from jointly submitting issues of state responsibility.

[168] Watts, *supra* n. 156, 31-32.

accorded to that acquiescence. In *Cameroon/Nigeria* it is difficult to think that Nigeria's occupation of Bakassi originated from a reasonable mistake or honest belief. It should have been manifest to Nigeria that Bakassi had been considered part of the Cameroons during the British Mandate and Trusteeship Administration. Furthermore, Nigeria had recognised the *uti possidetis* according to the 1913 Treaty in 1961, and it continued to negotiate its maritime boundary with Cameroon under that assumption until 1975. These negotiations even resulted in the signing of a formal instrument, the 1975 Maroua Declaration. After 1975, Nigeria's actions and its presence in Bakassi were the object of a limited but significant number of protests and actions by Cameroon. Even if it doubted the validity of certain provisions of the 1913 Treaty because of the encroachment on Old Calabar's rights - this being a reasonable doubt -, it should have been evident to Nigeria that because of Old Calabar's inaction until 1961 and its inaction until 1975, Cameroon had title to Bakassi. Furthermore, the qualification of 'honest belief', even if established, should apply only for the areas under established peaceful control, and not for the areas of the peninsula acquired in 1993-1994 through military action. As argued by Nigeria itself, a peaceful *status quo* is protected against forcible measures when not itself resulting from military action.[169] Such definition of peaceful *status quo* certainly did not apply to some of Cameroon's towns occupied *ex novo* by Nigeria in 1993-1994. Finally, choosing a threshold of fault liability also excludes the possibility to use the same concepts of 'honest belief' and 'reasonable mistake' as defences available precluding the wrongfulness of an act of occupation as done by Nigeria in its Counter-memorial and Rejoinder.[170] This is in tune with the Commentary to the 2001 ILC Articles, which does not list the two concepts among the defences available, and suggests that the set of circumstances precluding wrongfulness is exhaustive.[171]

The final question posed is whether the remedy imposed by the Court upon Nigeria implies what international lawyers have defined as 'liability for acts not prohibited under international law'. It must be said at the outset that the elaboration of the concept of liability for lawful acts has been elaborated by the ILC with regard to state liability for transboundary harm arising out of hazardous activities, which seems to rule out its application to the question of territorial disputes. The category has also attracted considerable criticism, notably from Brownlie, who, back in 1983, claimed that '[t]he search for principles governing 'liability' for 'lawful activities' seems to fly in the face of all existing legal

---

[169] Abi-Saab, *supra* n. 151, 19-20.
[170] *Ibidem*.
[171] ILC Arts. 20-27. Commentary, *supra* n. 136, 162.

experience.'[172] Yet, there appears to be two features of the laconic decision of the Court, which apparently fit into the category of liability for non-prohibited acts. The first feature, as stated above, is the diminished level of reparation envisaged by the Court as a remedy, which differs from the full reparation that state responsibility requires.[173] In fact, the withdrawal requested of Nigeria by the Court certainly represents a form of territorial 'restitution' insofar entailing a diminished level of reparation, which does not include the compensation and the undertaking of non-repetition asked by Cameroon. Such a feature is also present in *Temple of Vihear*, as Cambodia did ask for the withdrawal of Thailand and the restitution of archaeological items, without raising a claim for state responsibility jointly with a claim for full reparation. Most importantly, a declaratory judgment in itself and, in some cases, an explicit request of withdrawal from the territory have represented the typical form of remedy envisaged by international tribunals in the adjudication of territorial disputes not involving a claim for state responsibility.[174] The second feature is a form of strict or risk liability regarding territorial situations which are found to be contrary to the exact determination of territorial sovereignty effected by the international tribunal. In fact, all judicial decisions concerning territorial disputes involving an adverse possession normally require the 'restitution' of the occupied territory and the compliance with the tribunal's determinations. This is a form of reparation provided for by the primary norm despite the *bona fide* claim of the losing party to the dispute. In other words, the very fact of the occupation of a disputed territory potentially affects the legal interest of the other party, and it is thus subject to a form of risk liability when such occupation is found to be adverse to the determination of the Court.

---

[172] Brownlie, *System of the Law of Nations: State Responsibility (Part I)* (1983), 50.

[173] The commonly quoted passage of the *Chorzow Factory* case (*Factory at Chorzow*, 1928, P.C.I.J., Series A, No. 17, 47) states that 'reparation must, so far as possible, wipe out all the consequences of the illegal act and reestablish the situation which would, in all probability, have existed if that act had not been committed. Restitution in kind, or, if this is not possible, payment of a sum corresponding to the value which a restitution in kind would bear; the award, if need be, of damages for loss sustained which would not be covered by restitution in kind or payment in place of it –such are the principles which should serve to determine the amount of compensation due for an act contrary to international law'. See also Article 31, 2001 ILC Articles. As for the differences regarding reparation between responsibility for wrongful acts and liability for acts not prohibited under international law see Barboza, 'International Liability for the Injurious Consequences of Acts not Prohibited by International Law and Protection of the Environment' 247 *Recueil des Cours* (1994), 291, at 313-314.

[174] E.g. *Sovereignty over Frontier Land* (Belgium/The Netherlands), ICJ Reports 1959, 209; *Case Concerning the Frontier Dispute* (Burkina Faso/Mali), ICJ Reports 1986, 554; *Case Concerning the Land, Island and Maritime Frontier Dispute* (El Salvador/Honduras, Nicaragua intervening), ICJ Reports 1992, 351; *Territorial Dispute* (Libya/Tchad), ICJ Reports 1994, 6.

If we adopt by analogy the concept of liability for non-prohibited acts in order to explain the decisions of the Court with regard to territorial occupations and state responsibility, we can reach diverging interpretations. One is that Thailand's occupation of the Temple of Preah Vihear area, and Nigeria's occupation of the Bakassi peninsula and the Lake Chad area did not represent unlawful acts, *ergo* they did not infringe upon the counterpart's rights. This conclusion is warranted if the Court considered both occupations as not entailing a degree of fault, in which case the analysis given of the primary norm is tenable, however different may be the evaluation of the Nigerian conduct, or, alternatively, that the analysis of the primary norm has to be adjusted. The argument here bounces back to the question of fault, as defined above by the concepts of good faith, reasonable mistake and honest belief. It has been argued that Nigeria's occupation of Bakassi could not possibly originate after 1975 from an honest belief or reasonable mistake. It is difficult to say whether the Court is implying a higher threshold of burden of proof regarding the fault by requiring evidence of *dolus* or malicious conduct, or whether it simply was convinced that Nigeria's claim originated from an honest belief or reasonable mistake. The silence of the Court on this point and the little jurisprudence available do not assist in answering this question. Some useful indications to make sense of this uncharted area may be found instead in state practice and judicial decisions related to unlawful territorial situations resulting from serious breaches of international law and not involving judicial litigation.

7.2 Unlawful territorial situations resulting from serious breaches of international law

Some useful elements can be drawn from state practice with regard to state responsibility arising out of an attempt of territorial aggrandisement by force, or of the forcible denial of the right of self-determination of peoples leading to the establishment of unlawful territorial situations. In accordance with Article 40 of the ILC Articles, these cases are often considered to be serious breaches of peremptory international norms, defined as 'a gross or systematic failure by the responsible State to fulfil the obligation.' The ILC Commentary suggests that one of the elements involved, apart from the magnitude of the violation, is the intent to carry out such acts in defiance of fundamental norms.[175] Thus these violations already entail a substantial degree of fault, thereby excluding the possibility to claim a reasonable mistake or honest belief.

International practice does not leave any doubt as to whether territorial situations in violation of peremptory norms entail the responsibility of the

---

[175] ILC Commentary, *supra* n. 136, 247.

occupying state. Firstly, the nature of these violations also characterises them as threats to international peace and security, which is why in some instances the SC has decided to take action in their respect. In the case of the Iraqi invasion of Kuwait in 1990, this has also involved a determination of state responsibility. SC Resolution 687, which put an end to the First Gulf War, affirmed Iraq's liability under international law 'for any direct loss, damage, including environmental damage and the depletion of natural resources, or injury to foreign governments, nationals and corporations, as a result of Iraq's unlawful invasion and occupation of Kuwait.'[176] On that occasion, the SC also set up a claims settlement mechanism, by creating the UN Compensation Commission, which has dealt, and in fact is still dealing, with claims from individuals, corporations, governments and international organisations.[177] With regard to South Africa's occupation of Namibia, the UN Secretary General affirmed in his written pleadings submitted to the ICJ the international responsibility of South Africa deriving from its breaches of *ius cogens* norms.[178] The same position was adopted by the Organization of African Unity, India and Finland.[179] The Court, despite being requested by the SC to deal with the legal consequences for third parties, also affirmed South Africa's international responsibility for its continuing occupation.[180]

After twenty years of work and discussions, the ILC finally managed to reach a consensus on a normative framework that would give expression to the particular stigma that the international community attaches to the most serious violations of international law, and would specify the enhanced consequences deriving from such wrongful acts. With all its half-hearted endorsements and its compromises, the end result was in the words of Gattini 'the most reasonable and feasible product of a codification effort that is possible in the turbulent and confused state of development in which international law finds itself at present, torn as it is between the ideal aspirations of '*communitarisme*' and the frustrating realities of bilateralism.'[181] An apparently peculiar element of these violations was finally spelled out in Article 41(2) of the 2001 ILC Articles, which states that '[n]o State shall recognize as lawful a situation created by a serious violation within the

---

[176] SC Res. 687 (1991), para. 16.

[177] SC Res. 692 (1991). See Gattini, 'The UN Compensation Commission: Old Rules, New Procedures on War Reparation', 13 *EJIL* (2002), 161; Caron, Morris, 'The UN Compensation Commission: Practical Justice not Retribution', in *Ibidem*, 183.

[178] *Namibia*, *supra* n. 10, Written Statements and Oral Pleadings, Vol. 1, 102.

[179] *Ibidem*, Oral Statement OAU, Vol. 2, 101; Written Statement of India, Vol. 2, 117; Written Statement of Finland, Vol 1, 373. Finland also demanded compensation for damages.

[180] *Ibidem*, Decision, 54.

[181] Gattini, 'A Return Ticket to '*Communitarisme*', Please' 13 *EJIL* (2002), 1181, at 1199.

meaning of article 40, nor render aid or assistance in maintaining that situation.' The two parts of the provisions must be analysed separately.

The first part of the provision must be reconciled with the theory of invalidity of acts related to unlawful territorial situations developed by the Court in the *Namibia* case, including the 'humanitarian' exception. The ILC Commentary confirms such need.[182] However, it cannot go unnoticed the fact that the ICJ in *Namibia* did not limit the duty of non-recognition to territorial situations established as a direct result of 'serious violations of peremptory norms', but to all unlawful territorial situations because of the objective, *erga omnes* character of their illegality.[183] Given the choice of the Court in *Legality of the Wall* to deal with the legal consequences for third states deriving from the construction of the security barrier in the West Bank and around Jerusalem, one would have hoped in a clarification on the difference of approach between *Namibia* and the ILC, thus on the exact applicability of the duty of non-recognition. Instead, the Court cast further confusion to a sufficiently complicated issue, by relating the duty of non-recognition to the *erga omnes* character of the obligations breached through the construction of the wall.[184] It is impossible to disagree with Judge Higgins, when in her Separate Opinion she held that the use by the Court of the concept of *erga omnes* obligations was misleading. The concept in fact only refers to the legal interest all states have in the protection of certain rights, and not to the obligation not to recognise situations established and maintained in violation of those rights.[185] It is instructive to fully quote para. 38 of the Judge's Separate Opinion:

'That an illegal situation is not to be recognized or assisted by third parties is self-evident, requiring no invocation of the uncertain concept of *"erga omnes"*. It follows from a finding of an unlawful situation by the Security Council, in accordance with Articles 24 and 25 of the Charter entails "decisions [that] are consequently binding on all States Members of the United Nations, which are thus under obligation to accept and carry them out" (*Legal Consequences for States of the Continued Presence of South Africa in Namibia (South West Africa) notwithstanding Security Council Resolution 276 (1970), Advisory Opinion, I.C.J. Reports 1971*, p. 53, para. 115). The obligation upon United Nations Members not to recognize South Africa's illegal presence in Namibia, and not to lend support or assistance, relied in no way whatever on *"erga omnes"*. Rather, the Court emphasized that "A binding determination made by a competent organ of the United Nations to the effect that a situation is illegal cannot remain without consequence." (*Ibid.*, para. 117.) [...] Although in the present case it is the Court, rather than a United Nations organ acting under Articles 24 and 25, that has found the illegality; and although it is found in the context of an advisory opinion rather than in a contentious case, the Court's position as the principal judicial organ of the United Nations suggests that the legal consequence for a finding that an act or situation is illegal is

---

[182] ILC Commentary, *supra* n. 136, 251-252. *Namibia*, *supra* n. 10, 54-56.
[183] *Ibidem*, p. 56.
[184] *Legality of the Wall*, *supra* n. 80, para. 155.
[185] *Ibidem*, Separate Opinion Judge Higgins, para. 37.

the same. The obligation upon United Nations Members of non-recognition and non-assistance does not rest on the notion of *erga omnes*'.[186]

Whereas Higgins' convincing analysis seems to remain within the scope of UN law, the ICJ in *Namibia* extended its reasoning to the consequences under general international law for non-member states, and it found the illegality of the Namibian territorial situation to be opposable 'to all States in the sense of barring *erga omnes* the legality of a situation which is maintained in violation of international law'.[187] In conclusion, the duty of non-recognition upon third states simply derives from the objective illegality of the situation and from the duty of states not to give legal *validity* to acts related to an illegal situation, rather than from the nature of the violation or, even less persuasively, from the *erga omnes* character of the obligations breached.

If we accept the emergence of a duty of non-recognition, by definition its breach will entail the international responsibility of the violating state. In the *East Timor* case, for instance, Portugal in its application asked the Court 'to adjudge and declare that, by the breaches indicated [...], Australia has incurred international responsibility and it has caused damage, for which it owes reparation to the people of East Timor and to Portugal, in such form and manner as may be indicated by the Court.'[188] Among the alleged breaches related to Australia entering into a treaty of continental shelf delimitation and exploitation with the occupying power Indonesia, Portugal also claimed the breach of 'the right of the people of East Timor to self-determination, to territorial integrity and unity and its permanent sovereignty over its natural wealth and resources.'[189] In its written pleadings Portugal argued that reparation may take the form of Australia's cessation of its unlawful activities, a commitment to non-repetition, and finally compensation for the material damage caused to the East Timorese people, possibly by financing a common fund for the promotion of East Timor's independence to be put under UN administration.[190] The case did not proceed to the merits stage due to the Court's finding that it lacked jurisdiction.[191]

The second part of Article 41(2) instead sets forth the separate duty for states not to 'render aid or assistance' in maintaining the unlawful situation. This duty has to be read in conjunction with Article 41(1), which provides that 'States shall cooperate to bring to an end through lawful means any serious breach within the meaning of Article 40'. Whereas this latter paragraph refers to a positive duty for

---

[186] *Ibidem*, para. 38.
[187] *Namibia, supra* n. 10, 56.
[188] *East Timor Case* (Portugal/Australia), ICJ Reports 1995, 90. Application Instituting Proceedings, 22 February 1991, 19.
[189] *Ibidem*.
[190] *Ibidem*, Written Pleadings of Portugal, 231-234.
[191] *Ibidem*, Decision.

third states to co-operate and work in particular through competent international bodies to bring the unlawful situation to an end, the second part of para. 2 refers to a duty to abstain from providing economic, financial and military aid to the occupier. Again Higgins' analysis comes to help when explaining the content of the duty, as well as Judge Kooijmans' Separate Opinion in the same case, when it hints at the need to exclude from the scope of application of Article 41(2) any humanitarian assistance that states should provide to the victims of the illegal situation.[192] However, in contrast to the duty of non-recognition which is the result of the intrinsic *illegality* of the situation and the *invalidity* of related acts, the ILC's limitation of the scope of this part of Article 41(2) as well as Article 41(1) to situations deriving from serious violations of peremptory norms seems to be appropriate, and it is fully supported by the practice of states within the UN system, in particular at the SC and the GA.[193]

The important point to highlight is that the difference between wrongful occupations typically dealt with before an international tribunal, and wrongful occupations resulting from the serious breach of peremptory norms, relates both to the gravity of the violation and to a difference of approach in the way the international community treats these unlawful territorial situations, rather than the result of the application of different legal principles to the two categories. In fact, also unlawful territorial situations resulting from serious breaches of peremptory norms can often be the result of or crystallise into territorial disputes, and they are also concerned with violations of the law of territory. For instance, both Iraq with regard to Kuwait and South Africa with regard to Namibia articulated their claim in terms of territorial entitlement, and the two issues can be without any doubt classified as being also territorial disputes.[194] The question of fault or bad faith *a fortiori* also applies to these cases, and the seriousness of the breach is mostly due to the level of open and deliberate disregard of fundamental international obligations, rather than the *erga omnes* character as such of these obligations. That is also why the enhanced regime provided by Articles 40 and 41 of the ILC Articles applies *only* to 'gross and systematic failure to fulfil the

---

[192] *Legality of the Wall, supra* n. 21, Separate Opinion of Judge Koojmans, para. 45. See also Imseis, 'Critical Reflections on the International Humanitarian Law Aspects of the ICJ *Wall* Advisory Opinion' 99 *AJIL* (2005), 102, at 116-117.

[193] ILC Commentary, *supra* n. 19, 249-252.

[194] As to South Africa's claim to Namibia based on conquest and acquisitive prescription see Oral Statement of the UN Secretary General's Representative, in *Namibia, supra* n. 178, Oral Statements and Correspondance, Vol. II, 57-58. The Iraqi claim to the total incorporation of Kuwait was based on an historical title deriving from the inclusion of Kuwait in the province of Basra during the Ottoman Empire and the Iraqi succession to that territorial title. See in particular the Statement of Iraq before the Security Council of 2 August 1990, in S/PV.2932. For analysis and criticism of the Iraqi claim see Mendelson, Hulton, 'La revendication par l'Iraq de la souveraineté sur le Koweit' 36 *Annuaire Française de Droit Internationale* (1990), 195.

obligation' (with the qualifications on the duty of non-recognition explained above).[195]

As an analogy to the two cases just mentioned, we can take the Nigerian occupation of Bakassi and the Israeli occupation of Gaza and the West Bank. These latter cases involve an attempt of forcible territorial aggrandisement, the case of Israel involves a denial of self-determination as well. What, however, may differ is the magnitude of the alleged violation and the level of malicious conduct involved in breaching international law. In fact, Nigeria's claim does not involve a claim of total annexation of Cameroon, but it is limited to boundary areas. This is a common feature when states agree to refer their territorial dispute to an international tribunal for boundary delimitation or demarcation. As for Israel's occupation of Gaza and the West Bank, a legal assessment of the faulty conduct of Israel in occupying those areas and in preventing the exercise of self-determination by the Palestinian people is necessarily more controversial, as more controversial are the political issues underlying the territorial dispute as compared to the territorial disputes normally brought before the ICJ. Israel's occupation has been justified since 1967 earlier on the basis of a war of self-defence (rather than a war of aggression), and, after the 1993 Oslo Agreements, on security grounds to tackle terrorist activities, rather than a general disregard for the right of self-determination of the Palestinian people. In addition, the territorial adjustments to the 1949 Armistice line claimed by Israel are relatively minor, and they are sought within the framework of final status negotiations between the two parties in the conflict.[196] These elements seem to indicate that the occupation does not represent a serious breach of the right of self-determination of the Palestinian people. This proposition appears to supported by the policy of many states that does not fit into the picture of enhanced consequences for state responsibility envisaged by Article 41 of the ILC Articles. Western states in particular have provided throughout the years and still provide military and economic aid to Israel, which necessarily ends up supporting its military effort in the occupation of Palestine; also, despite not recognising the

---

[195] ILC Commentary, *supra* n. 19, 247-248.

[196] As far as the final negotiations are concerned, a problematic issue with regard to the continuing Israeli occupation could be the duress under which the Palestinian side would negotiate the final territorial settlement. On this aspect see McHugo, 'Resolution 242: A Legal Reappraisal of the Right-Wing Israeli Interpretation of the Withdrawal Phrase with reference to the conflict between Israel and the Palestinians', 51 *ICLQ* (2002), 851, at 861. It should be noticed however that the nullity of treaties procured through military coercion provided in Article 52 of the Vienna Convention on the Law of Treaties requires the establishment of a causal link between the military coercion and the conclusion of an international agreement, and a mere situation of general duress may not suffice to prove such causation (on this aspect see Milano, 'Security Council's Action in the Balkans: Reviewing Kosovo's Territorial Status, 14 *EJIL* (2003), 999).

legality of the occupation and of the measures undertaken by Israel in that context, they have not actively cooperated to bring to an end that situation.

One conclusion that can be drawn from the practice analysed above is that, where the occupation is the result of a gross or systematic violation of a peremptory norm, international responsibility will be undoubtedly entailed together with a series of legal consequences for third states. The problem, however, still remains for those acts which do not present the same level of magnitude or *dolus*, like for instance the two mentioned examples of Bakassi and Palestine. The differentiation between serious violations of peremptory norms and 'non-serious' violations of these norms concedes to the argument that there exists a series of cases where these norms can be violated without entailing the same level of magnitude or *dolus*. Unfortunately, the ILC is silent as to which instances it is referring to. Obviously, determinations by authoritative organs like the SC most of the time define the seriousness of the breach, but, due to political nature of these organs, these legal determinations inevitably entail a degree of inconsistency. However, a judicial body assessing a territorial dispute should be in the position to independently decide the matter by looking at the level of malicious conduct involved and the magnitude of the alleged violation. It is submitted that the concepts of honest belief, good faith, reasonable mistake and peaceful *status quo* tested against the pattern of the adverse occupation and the legal claims underlying it should help to define the threshold of fault leaving for the tribunal a wide enough margin of appreciation. To envisage a too high threshold of malicious conduct means to render difficult the distinction between standard violations of a state's territorial sovereignty and serious violations, at the same time making the rules of territorial sovereignty particularly loose and weak in terms of remedies available. That is inconsistent with the enormous legal, political and symbolic importance states attach to territorial sovereignty.

By analogy, it is possibly to refer to the *Corfu Channel* case, insofar as the Court, in that case, was engaged in determining the content of due diligence obligations and the responsibility incurred by states for the breach of such obligations.[197] Particularly significant is the passage where the Court stated that 'it cannot be concluded from the mere fact of the control exercised by a State over its territory and waters that the State necessarily knew, or ought to have known, of any unlawful act perpetuated therein [...]. This fact, by itself and apart from other circumstances, neither involves *prima facie* responsibility nor shifts the burden of proof.'[198] In other words, inasmuch as Albania's responsibility for mine-laying was not triggered as a result of its exercise of jurisdiction over those waters, the mere adverse occupation or control over a territory does not *per se* entail the

---

[197] *The Corfu Channel Case* (UK/Albania), ICJ Reports 1949, 4.
[198] *Ibidem*, 18.

responsibility of the occupying state. Yet, inasmuch as Albania responsibility was determined by the Court on the basis of its lack of due diligence in preventing unlawful activities, by analogy, in a case such as *Cameroon/Nigeria*, we might expect that the threshold of international responsibility is reached when the occupying state must have known, or reasonably should have known, that it was occupying territory beyond the *uti possidetis* line and that the other state was contesting it. *Corfu Channel* also shows how evidence of the state's fault might be found not only in direct evidence of its 'mental belief' such as a clear statement by the executive, but also in indirect evidence that indicates that the state should reasonably have known that the rights of another state were affected.

This confirms the validity of the analysis made above concerning the occupation of Bakassi by Nigeria, and, because of the direct and indirect evidence presented by Cameroon with regard to Nigeria's awareness of the *uti possidetis* line, it also puts into question the choice made by the Court not to consider Cameroon's claim of State responsibility exactly. As for the case of the West Bank and, until recently, of Gaza, the prohibition to change a peaceful *status quo* by force, the stance adopted by the SC and the GA in various occasions demanding the withdrawal of Israel,[199] the settlement of hundred thousands Israeli citizens throughout the years, the promotion, approval and security support by the Israeli authorities of these settlements even during the years of the Oslo peace process, all seem to point to a lack of due diligence in ensuring a smooth and peaceful process of self-determination of the Palestinian people. More importantly, the ICJ in its recent Advisory Opinion on the *Legality of the Wall* has characterised the construction of the wall, along with the policy of settlement, as a breach of Israel's obligation to respect the right of self-determination. *A fortiori* that determination can apply to the occupation *per se*, even if the Court has carefully avoided dealing with the legality of the occupation itself. All these factors warrant the conclusion that the occupation is illegal *per se*, thereby entailing the international responsibility of Israel, although it is not necessarily a serious violation of a peremptory norm for the reasons outlined above.

In conclusion, the law of state responsibility as it applies to the law of territory helps us define the exact content of the primary norms protecting states' and peoples' territorial sovereignty. Whereas the principles of legality analysed in the previous chapter by their automatic application may with certainty define the entitlement to territory, the way these principles also protect the exercise of territorial sovereignty has revealed itself to be less clear-cut. Cases involving a change of territorial status through the use of force and/or the secession from a state will *ipso facto* lead to the creation of an unlawful territorial situation, unless

---

[199] See in particular SC Res. 242 (1967); SC Res. 338 (1973); SC Res. 478 (1980); more recently GA Res. A/ES-10/11.

the forcible change can be construed within a legal use of force and the act of secession is legal (obtained through consent and/or in implementation of the right of self-determination). In other words, the analysis formulated in previous sections is sufficient to define the lawful/unlawful divide. However, in territorial disputes where the principles of *uti possidetis* and/or the principle of self-determination are at stake, an adverse occupation resulting from a reasonable mistake, good faith conduct and an honest belief – in other words in situations where bad faith, malicious conduct, and magnitude of the alleged violation are not proven – will not be considered *ipso facto* unlawful. They will entail a form of objective liability for acts not prohibited by international law. That makes a definition of unlawfulness of a territorial situation more problematic than suspected, and it may explain the reason why international judicial and political bodies are often reluctant to expressly make such determination. Rather than providing a justification for the lack of engagement by authoritative bodies with this important legal issue, such explanation highlights the need, especially for judicial bodies, to map a surprisingly unexplored area of international law.

8. Legitimacy, recognition and legitimation of unlawful territorial situations

A final important aspect to analyse is that of legitimacy, as this concept also impacts on the definition of the legal consequences of unlawful territorial situations. My main proposition in this section is that while recognition is the process through which states and international organisations recognise the legal effects produced by an unlawful territorial situation, in some cases gradually transforming the original unlawfulness into lawfulness, legitimacy provides the conceptual element to explain why in some cases such recognition is widespread, while in some others it is only isolated. In other words, legitimacy is the key concept in reconciling a violating effectiveness and the principles of territorial unlawfulness.

The concept of legitimacy has attracted much attention in the fields of law, political theory and international relations in the course of the 20th century.[200] Focusing on the international arena, it is interesting to analyse the debate in international relations and international law.[201] For instance, Ian Hurd, an

---

[200] For an analysis of the concept of legitimacy from a legal and philosophical perspective see Roth, *supra* n. 76, 17-35.

[201] For some interesting accounts of the way legitimacy is conceived in international relations theory see Barnett, 'Bringing in the New World Order: Liberalism, Legitimacy, and the United Nations' 49 *World Politics* (1997), 526; Hurd, 'Legitimacy and Authority in International Politics' 53 *International Organization* (1999), 379.

international relations theorist, defines legitimacy as 'the normative belief by an actor that a rule or institution ought to be obeyed'.[202] Hurd, despite continuously referring to 'norms' and 'rules', hardly mentions the expression 'international law'. It may be argued that the concepts of 'normative belief' and 'rule' in international relations are broader than the way the same concepts are seen by an international lawyer. Yet the 'case-study' used by Hurd to test his approach to compliance and legitimacy deals with the principle of non-intervention, one of the basic principles of international law.

On the other hand, much work on the concept of legitimacy in international law has been carried out by Thomas Franck, whose concern has been mostly to define which inherent characteristics a positive rule must have to be considered legitimate in the international society and therefore complied with.[203] These inherent characteristics are, according to Franck, determinacy, symbolic validation and coherence.[204] Their existence would ensure what Franck calls the 'pull towards compliance' by international actors, so fundamental for a legal system without a developed mechanism of centralised enforcement. In other words, it seems that Hurd is approaching legitimacy in the same way as Franck, only with a different language. Yet a closer analysis unveils some important differences, which apply by and large to the approach shared by international lawyers regarding the concept of legitimacy. International lawyers have tended to focus on the legitimacy of positive rules and the decisions of authoritative decision-making bodies in the international arena. Whereas Franck provided the most original contribution on legitimacy in positive rules, Georgiev addressed the question of reconciling potentially contradicting legal principles and norms through legitimate decision-making. While he refers to the legitimacy of rules or behaviours in the following passage, it is clear that he is also referring to the legitimacy of specific decisions within a certain positive legal framework. He states:

> 'Answering the question about the legitimacy of a rule or of behavior will involve…making choices and constructing solutions which have to conform with contradicting and indeterminate principles. Therefore, these choices and solutions could be called 'political'. Even so, this would be politics *within law*, politics which would *not* be sheer unrestrained arbitrary power. It would not be 'subjective' politics destroying the 'objectivity' of international law but a process of 'politicisation' of law (*and* perhaps of 'legalisation' of

---

[202] *Ibidem*, 381.
[203] Franck, 'Legitimacy in the International System' 82 *AJIL* (1988), 705.
[204] Franck, *The Power of Legitimacy among Nations* (1990).

politics) which aims at solving the contradictions within international law and enhancing its pertinence for an international rule of law.'[205]

Goergiev's argument is that the broad scope of certain rules, like for instance self-determination and the prohibition to use force, makes their application potentially contradictory, thus legitimacy discourse becomes important in this respect. When a certain factual background is exactly and uncontroversially matched by a positive norm definition, legality discourse will provide all we need to analyse the divide lawfulness/unlawfulness. However, when the legal assessment of a certain factual situation requires examination and application of different and perhaps opposing broad principles, then it will be exactly legitimacy discourse, which will justify one choice rather than another. This level of legitimacy analysis is particularly useful to assess the action of the SC within its broad powers under Chapter VII of the Charter with regard to territorial issues. In fact, a more specific analysis of 'legitimate decision-making' in international law has been concerned with the legitimacy of SC's actions, as a way to enhance its credibility and effectiveness as a major actor in the field of international peace and security.[206]

Another important level where legitimacy acts is the 'accommodation' of the legal order to certain actions that, despite representing violations of an international norm, produce effects or situations which are perceived as legitimate by a part of the international community, or the international community as a whole, and therefore are acquiesced to or more or less reluctantly accepted. This does not mean that that particular act does not represent a violation of international law, it only means that the system 'tolerates' and 'recognises' the effects of the factual situation produced by that violation. This function of legitimacy is particularly important in some unlawful territorial situations. Typically, international lawyers have focused on recognition as a key to reconciling an unlawful territorial effectiveness and its long run accommodation by states or the international community as a whole. A useful differentiation has also been made with regard to recognition of status - a discretionary power -, and the decision to enter or non-enter into relations -

---

[205] Georgiev, 'Politics or Rule of Law: Deconstruction and Legitimacy in International Law' 4 *EJIL* (1993), 1, at 13-14. A similar point is made by Brad Roth, who talks about 'legal legitimacy' (*supra* n. 76, 33).

[206] Caron, 'The Legitimacy of the Collective Authority of the Security Council' 87 *AJIL* (1993), 552, at 557; Fassbender, 'Uncertain Steps into a Post-Cold War World: the Role and Functioning of the UN Security Council after a Decade of Measures against Iraq' 13 *EJIL* (2002), 273, at 292; White, 'The Will and Authority of the Security Council after Iraq' 17 *LJIL* (2004), 645. See also *infra* Ch. 6, section 4.

which belongs to the law of state responsibility.[207] Yet it is submitted that a step further should be made by explaining *why* in some cases unlawful territorial situations become legalised, whereas in others they do not. Explaining the reasons behind this process helps us define exactly the process by which that happens, which does not consist of a 'supernatural' power of states to transform illegality into legality, only by issuing different unilateral declarations of recognition, or other types of acts implying recognition of a lawful status. It also points to legitimacy as *trait d'union* and process through which effectiveness and legality are reconciled. Some examples clarify this point.

One example is the 1997 Canadian Supreme Court's decision in the *Quebec* case.[208] In that case the Court made clear that the right to secede and the possibility that a certain secession, once factually established, creates legal effects at the international level were two different matters from a legal point of view. The 'legalisation' of the effective situation would not change the violating nature of the unilateral secession. However, the concept of legitimacy would represent the link between those two gaps between violation and legality. If the purported secession of Quebec was declared in defiance of the Canadian constitutional principles - democratic principle, federal principle, rule of law - and the fundamental principles of the international community - respect of human rights, peaceful settlement of disputes, etc.- the process would most likely be seen as illegitimate and gain only limited if any recognition in the international community.[209] The action of effectiveness would be more easily limited. If by contrast effectiveness is accompanied by a legitimate claim, its role is boosted. In other words, the role of effectiveness as power is enhanced by the legitimacy of the claim and the legitimacy of the process through which such a claim is articulated.[210] To be noted is the fact that the legitimacy is not a concept foreign to the law, but it builds on the basic legal principles of a certain community, be it national or international. The Supreme Court goes so far as to state that 'one of the legal norms which may be recognized by States in granting or withholding recognition of emergent States is the legitimacy by which the *de facto* secession is, or was, being pursued.'[211]

Despite arguing for the neutrality of international law towards secession, Buchheit similarly explains the recognition or non-recognition of attempted

---

[207] Warbrick, 'States and Recognition in International Law', in Evans (ed.), *International Law* (2003), 205, at 241-242.
[208] *Re Reference by the Governor in Council concerning Certain Questions Relating to the Secession of Quebec from Canada*, 115 ILR (1999), 535. See *supra* Ch. 4, section 5.
[209] *Ibidem*, 576.
[210] On legitimacy as a procedural factor underlying a broader notion of fairness see Franck, *Fairness in International Law and Institutions* (1995).
[211] *Quebec* case, *supra* n. 208, 589-590.

secessions through the lenses of legitimacy.[212] In particular, Buchheit defines legitimacy through two criteria, the 'internal merits of the claim' and 'the disruption factor'.[213] The 'internal merits of the claim' refer to criteria of effectiveness of the self-determining unit such as the ethnic and social cohesiveness, the occupation of a distinct territorial basis and the economic viability of a future state. On the other hand, 'the disruption factor' refers to the end result of the secession in terms of maintenance of regional and international peace and security, the existence of minorities in the self-governing unity and the willingness to respect those groups' linguistic and cultural rights, and the compliance in general with fundamental human rights. In other words, 'the disruption factor' refers to the potential threat of the secession for regional and international peace and security, and its compliance with fundamental international norms. In conclusion, Buchheit too seems to envisage a legitimacy built within an international legal framework as being pre-conditional to the legalisation of an effective secession.

Another case highlighting the relevance of legitimacy to unlawful territorial situations, and, in particular, the way such unlawfulness can be cured by its legitimacy, is the case of Indian occupation of Goa. On 17-18 December 1961, Indian military forces invaded the Portuguese territories of Goa, Danao and Diu on the Indian sub-continent. On 18 December, Portugal asked the SC 'to put a stop to the condemnable act of aggression of the Indian Union, ordering an immediate cease-fire and the withdrawal forthwith from Portuguese territories of Goa, Danao and Diu of all the invading forces of the Indian Union.'[214] A resolution along these lines was discussed but not adopted by the Council because of the veto put by the USSR. A draft resolution rejecting the Portuguese complaint was voted down by seven votes to five.[215] The discussion that ensued at the SC is interesting because whereas Western states underlined the violation of the international norms on the use of force by India and the refusal to accept any unilateral change through the use of force, India and those countries supporting its territorial claims claimed along the lines of the existence of a right of self-determination of those people under colonial domination to have international support in their struggle for liberation. The case of Goa is from a legal point of view analogous to the one of East-Timor. A territory under Portuguese administration having the status of NSGT; a territorial contiguity of the annexing state; a claim by the annexing state to enforce the right of the people to free themselves from colonial domination; the lack of democratic expression towards

---

[212] Buchheit, *Secession* (1978).
[213] *Ibidem*, 228-238.
[214] S/5030, 18 December 1961.
[215] SCOR, 987th Meeting (1961).

the acceptance of the annexation. Yet the invasion of Goa was not condemned by the UN political organs, and Portugal recognised Indian sovereignty in 1974 followed by the whole international community. The significance of this general recognition is not so much of importance because it suddenly transforms an illegal act - the invasion and the annexation in the first place - into a legal act; it is important because it witnesses the legalisation of the status deriving from the illegal act and, in particular, the annexation from a certain point in time onwards because of the legitimacy of the claims behind it.[216] Unlike in East Timor, in the case of Goa there was support in the population for the incorporation with India. Unlike in East Timor, there was no national liberation movement struggling for the option of independence. The claim of India acquired legitimacy at the international level because of its conformity with the fundamental principles of the international community, in particular that of self-determination, and so did its effectiveness on the former Portuguese territories.[217] The legal paradox behind this idea of legalisation of status through legitimacy is that the recognition of status and the dealings with the illegal occupier may be in breach of the duty of non-recognition owed to the lawful sovereign, as long as the cumulative effect of different acts of recognition does not change the situation from unlawful to lawful. This is a similar case to what happens with the modification of customary international law, where state practice leading to the articulation of a new rule may be in breach of the existing customary international law that it is aiming to change.

Whereas the above examples rely more on the *compliance* with other fundamental principles of international law to justify the legitimisation of a territorial situation produced by an original violation of the norms protecting states' territorial sovereignty, the case of Iraq relies more on the *authority* of the body conferring legitimacy to an originally unlawful territorial situation, namely

---

[216] Crawford similarly argues that '[t]he significance of self-determination in this context is not so much that it cures illegality as that it may allow illegality to be more readily accommodated through the processes of recognition and prescription, whereas in other circumstances aggression partakes of the nature of a breach of *jus cogens* and is not, or not readily, curable by prescription, lapse of time or acquiescence.' Crawford, *The Creation of States in International Law* (1979), 113. See also Dugard, *supra* n. 5, 115.

[217] This appears to be also the grounds on which The Independent International Commission on Kosovo based its conclusion that NATO military intervention in Kosovo was illegal but legitimate. According to the Commission, *Operation Allied Force* was in breach of positive *ius ad bellum*, but its aims, the protection of ethnic Albanians' human rights and their right to self-government, and means, an aerial campaign which complied with rules of international humanitarian law 'better than any air war in history', showed a general compliance with the 'spirit' of the UN Charter and of international law, thereby making it legitimate. Following the Commission's argument, we may add that, as in the case of Goa, also in the case of Kosovo, a Russia-sponsored SC resolution condemning the action was defeated (S/1999/328). The Independent International Commission on Kosovo, *The Kosovo Report* (2000), 163-198.

the UN, and, only to a limited extent, to the subsequent compliance with international law of the occupying states. In fact, the concept of authority in legitimacy analysis has been neglected by international lawyers,[218] who have mostly focused on how authoritative decision-making bodies can change international rules and legal situations, or can make their actions more effective by fulfilling internal criteria of substantive and procedural legitimacy. International lawyers have looked at legitimacy as a way to make an international body more authoritative, in other words, they have considered the internal dimension of authority.[219] On the other hand, international relations writers have borrowed from political science to focus on the concept of authority. For instance, Blau states that 'we speak of authority, therefore, if the willing unconditional compliance of a group of people rests upon their shared beliefs that it is legitimate for the superior…to impose his will upon them and that it is illegitimate for them to refuse obedience.'[220] If we export this idea to the international arena, authority becomes the external vehicle to confer legitimacy upon international norms or situations.[221] This is very important in unlawful territorial situations, as the conferral of legitimacy by an authoritative decision-making body, like the SC or the GA, upon an unlawful territorial situation is one of the ways a violating effectiveness becomes legalised.

8.1 Legitimating the illegal: the case of Iraq

The recent history of Iraq is an interesting example, as it shows how a carefully planned process of gradual international legitimation can substantially make good for what was arguably a gross violation of international law. On 20 March 2003, the US and the UK with the support of some coalition partners started a massive military operation against Iraq (*Operation Iraqi Freedom*) with the aim of invading the country, overthrowing the regime of Saddam Hussein and getting rid of its weapons of mass destruction. The legal claim shared by the US and the UK was the authority conferred by a joint reading of SC Resolutions

---

[218] With possibly the only exception of policy-oriented jurisprudence, which sees authority as a necessary element of its notion of law as a process of communication of authoritative decisions. E.g. McDougal, Reisman, 'The Prescribing Function in World Constitutive Process: How International Law is Made' 6 *Yale Studies in World Public Order* (1980), 249; Reisman, 'International Lawmaking: A Process of Communication: The Harold D. Lasswell Memorial Lecture' 75 *ASIL Proceedings* (1981), 101.

[219] *Supra* n. 206.

[220] Blau, 'Critical Remarks on Weber's Theory of Authority' 57 *American Political Science Review* (1963), 305, at 307.

[221] Hurd, *supra* n. 201, 399.

678, 687 and 1441.[222] The military operation was a success for the Coalition forces. By mid April, Saddam was no longer in power. On 8 May 2003, the US and the UK informed the SC of the creation of the Coalition Provisional Authority (CPA) 'to exercise powers of government temporarily, and, as necessary, to provide security, to allow the delivery of humanitarian aid, and to eliminate weapons of mass destruction.'[223] On 22 May 2003, the SC adopted Resolution 1483, which, despite 'reaffirming the sovereignty and territorial integrity of Iraq', 'recogniz[ed] the specific authorities, responsibilities, and obligations under applicable international law of these states [i.e. the US and the UK] as occupying powers under unified command (the "Authority").'[224] It also

'call[ed] upon the Authority, consistent with the Charter of the United Nations and other relevant international law to promote the welfare of the Iraqi people through the effective administration of the territory, including in particular working towards the restoration of conditions of security and stability and the creation of conditions in which the Iraqi people can freely determine their own political future.'[225]

Was the territorial situation in Iraq after SC Resolution 1483 lawful or unlawful using the normative framework elaborated above? The first issue relating to the *ius ad bellum* is whether *Operation Iraqi Freedom* was lawful, thereby justifying the ensuing occupation of Iraq. The legality of the use of force in Iraq sparked a very lively debate among international lawyers.[226] It is here dwelled upon only briefly, as the focus is primarily on the legality of the occupation, rather than the use of force as such. It is contended that the military action in Iraq was unlawful, as its legal justification was based on an authorisation to use force which dated back to 1990, granted in order to deal with the different situation of the Iraqi invasion of Kuwait. Resolution 1441 put into motion a process of enhanced regime of UN inspection with a view to conceding a last opportunity to Iraq to comply with previous UN resolutions. The process was based on the authority of the SC to deal with the situation on the basis of the UN Chief Inspector's reports.[227] In his last report the Chief Inspector welcomed some positive steps undertaken by the Iraqi authorities and asked for more months to

---

[222] The legal case for war can be found in the UK Attorney General Statement of 17 March 2003, <http://www.guardian.co.uk/Iraq/story/0,2763,916078,00.html>. The same legal grounds were claimed by the US and Australia.

[223] S/2003/538.

[224] SC Res. 1483 (2003), Preamble.

[225] *Ibidem*, para. 4.

[226] See *inter alia* Meyer, White, 'Editorial: The Use of Force Against Iraq' 8 *Journal of Conflict and Security Law* (2003), 1; Crawford *et al.*, 'War would be illegal', *The Guardian*, 7 March 2003; Greenwood, 'International Law and the Pre-emptive Use of Force' 4 *San Diego International Law Journal* (2003), 7; Taft *et al.*, 'Agora: Future Implications of the Iraq Conflict' 97 *AJIL* (2003), 553.

[227] SC Res. 1441, in particular para. 11.

give a conclusive assessment to the SC.[228] It is clear that the US and the UK, which had prepared the military operation for months, were not ready to wait for such a long period of time.[229] It is also clear that the US, the UK and Spain, despite the strong diplomatic pressure put on many of the members of the SC, were not able to gather a majority behind a new resolution authorising military action.[230] It is submitted that *Operation Iraqi Freedom*, rather than being based on the authority of the SC and being an enforcement of previous resolutions, was exactly the contrary, a military action pursued in defiance of the authority of the SC, therefore contrary to international law.

The determination of illegality of the military action is crucial, as the unlawfulness of the UK and US presence from April at least until the 22nd of May, when the SC adopted Resolution 1483, derives from it.[231] Next it must be asked what is the effect of the SC recognition of the US and UK occupation embodied in Resolution 1483. One may argue that the wording of the preamble referring to the recognition of the 'specific authorities, responsibilities and obligations under applicable international law of these states as occupying powers' may entail only a recognition of the *de facto* situation of belligerent occupation. In that sense, SC Resolution 1483 would not *per se* affect the unlawfulness of the territorial situation. However, it is clear that the recognition of the 'Authority' entailed in Resolution 1483 is broader, as its powers extend to the 'effective administration of the territory', the formation of an Iraqi interim administration,[232] and the management of the Development Fund for Iraq for the 'humanitarian needs of the Iraqi people, for the economic reconstruction and repair of Iraq's infrastructure, for the continued disarmament of Iraq, and for the costs of Iraqi civil administration, and for other purposes benefiting the people of Iraq.'[233] The Coalition Provisional Authority (CPA), on 13 July 2003, in fact appointed the Governing Council of Iraq, an interim governing body composed of 15 members, with the aim of running the Iraqi ministries and making decisions

---

[228] S/2003/232; S/PV.4714, Statement of UNMOVIC 7.

[229] *Ibidem*, Statement of US 14; Statement of UK 25.

[230] 'Draft resolution on Iraq: text', in <http://news.bbc.co.uk/2/hi/europe/2795747.htm>.

[231] See Dyer, 'Occupation of Iraq illegal, Blair told', *The Guardian*, 22 May 2003. The author reported on leaked parts of the legal advice given by the British Attorney General Lord Goldsmith to Prime Minister Tony Blair on 26 March 2003, warning the government on the lack of legal basis for a long term occupation working towards the de-baathication of the Iraqi society without a new SC resolution. One quote by the Attorney General is particularly interesting: 'The government has concluded that the removal of the current Iraqi regime from power is necessary for disarmament, but the longer the occupation of Iraq continues, and the more the tasks undertaken by an interim administration depart from the main objective, the more difficult it will be to justify the lawfulness of the occupation.'

[232] SC Res. 1483 (2003), para. 9.

[233] *Ibidem*, paras. 12-14.

in the civil sphere in co-operation with the CPA.[234] Resolution 1500 adopted on 14 August 2003 'welcom[ed] the establishment of the broadly representative Governing Council of Iraq on 13 July 2003, as an important step towards the formation by the people of Iraq of an internationally recognized, representative government that will exercise the sovereignty of Iraq.'[235] Most interestingly, Resolution 1511 adopted on 16 October 2003 'authoriz[ed] a multinational force under unified command to take all necessary measures to contribute to the maintenance of security and stability in Iraq.'[236] Such command was to be vested with the US military.[237]

Resolutions 1483, 1500 and 1511 obviously went beyond the mere recognition of the powers of the 'Authority' as belligerent occupant under the 1907 Regulations annexed to the Hague Convention IV and the 1949 Geneva Convention IV. The SC was using its powers under Chapter VII to derogate from strict application of law of belligerent occupation, and to confer legality to a previously unlawful territorial situation. The following question is whether the SC can under international law use its powers under Chapter VII to confer legality to a territorial situation produced by an illegal military action. The answer to this question presupposes an analysis of the relation between SC powers under Chapter VII and international law, which is provided in the next chapter. My hypothesis at this stage is that the answer is negative, as such endorsement is against the principles and purposes of the UN Charter, and, possibly, it recognises the effects of a violation of a norm of *ius cogens*.[238] In other words, it is submitted that the SC was acting *ultra vires* when adopting certain parts of Resolutions 1483, 1500 and 1511, thus it did not affect the original unlawfulness of the Coalition's occupation of Iraq.

The next phase of the complex Iraqi post-war territorial situation has been inaugurated by the adoption of SC Resolution 1546 on 8 June 2004.[239] The very outset of the preamble of 1546 is telling as the SC 'welcom[es] the beginning of a new phase in Iraq's transition to a democratically elected government, and *look*[s] *forward* to the end of the occupation and the assumption of full responsibility and authority by a fully sovereign and independent Interim Government of Iraq by 30 June 2004'. Indeed, the Interim Government had been appointed a few days before by the Governing Council, thanks to the mediation of the UN envoy Brahimi. The CPA dissolved on 28 June and, the same day, the Interim

---

[234] 'The new men, and women, in charge', *The Economist*, 19 July 2003, 20.

[235] SC Res. 1500 (2003), para. 1.

[236] SC Res. 1511 (2003), para. 13.

[237] S/PV. 4844, Statement of the United States 10.

[238] The hypothesis will be developed in the next chapter, when dealing with the competence of the SC to regulate territorial issues.

[239] SC Res. 1546 (2004).

Government headed by Dr Iyad Allawi took office. As stated in the first sentence of the preamble, the Interim Government was to exercise full sovereignty over Iraq. It had full powers and responsibilities in the civil sphere for the lead-up period to the democratic elections, to be held by 31 January 2005.[240] As for the military affairs, 1546 contains both an *invitation* by the then prospective Interim Government to the continuation of the multinational force under US command, and it reaffirms the *authorisation* embodied in Resolution 1511.[241] The invitation, together with the express power of the Interim Government to terminate the mandate of the multinational force earlier than 31 December 2005,[242] was meant to symbolise the return of Iraq to its full internal sovereignty and the end of the occupation of the country; on the other hand, as argued elsewhere, the Interim Government had not yet taken office at the time of the letter of invitation (or even SC Res. 1546 for that matter), thus did not have the sovereign power to express consent to the presence of the multinational force.[243] Even if we consider valid consent to have been expressed once it actually took power through various statements and pieces of legislation providing for co-operation in the military field with the multinational force, there still remains the fact that the Interim Government was elected by a political body specifically set by the 'illegally' occupying power, thus its consent hardly represented an exercise in self-determination of the Iraqi people.[244] At the same time, the extension of the authorisation first provided by Resolution 1511 may not add anything to the *ultra vires* nature of a Chapter VII SC resolution aimed at recognising the effects of a territorial situation established in defiance of norms of *ius cogens*, thus it still does not affect *per se* the original unlawfulness of the military presence in Iraq.[245]

On the other hand, a simple determination of unlawfulness does not render the whole complexity of the role played by international law and international institutions with regard to the Coalition's occupation of Iraq. The role played by

---

[240] *Ibidem*, para. 4(c).

[241] *Ibidem*, Annex, Text of Letters from the Prime Minister of the Interim Government of Iraq Dr. Ayad Allawi and United States Secretary of State Colin L. Powell to the President of the Council, 5 June 2004; SC Res. 1546, paras. 9-10.

[242] *Ibidem*, para. 12.

[243] Le Mon, 'Legality of a Request by the Interim Iraqi Government for the Continued Presence of United States Military Forces', *ASIL Insights*, June 2004, Addendum, in <http://www.asil.org/insights/insigh135.htm>.

[244] In the present author's opinion, nothing short of a constitutionally elected and representative government could represent a sovereign authority established in accordance with international law, and could give a valid consent for the presence of an international security presence under US command. 31 December 2005 is the date by which the political process leading to the approval of a constitution and the election of a 'constitutional' government of the country should be completed, according to para. 4(c) of SC Res. 1546.

[245] See *infra* Ch. 6, sections 2.2 and 4.

the SC through Resolutions 1483, 1500, 1511 and 1546 does not only consist in the attempt to transform overnight an unlawful territorial situation in a territorial situation valid *erga omnes*: the legal non-recognition of the US appointed new Governing Council by Arab League Members and by Mexico in the aftermath of resolution 1500 witnesses that this attempt was, at least in part, unsuccesful.[246] It is also and foremost aimed at providing an increasing level of international legitimacy to a whole operation of regime change in Iraq, which had until recently been looked at with suspicion, if not open opposition, by the largest part of the international community. The role of such a legitimacy seal provided by the SC is exactly to boost the effective power of the US, the UK and their partners in Iraq, by facilitating a gradual process of recognition by the international community of the legal effects in the military and civil sphere produced by the situation on the ground. The conferral of legitimacy upon an unlawful territorial situation is, in this case, effected mostly thanks to the international authority of the UN collective body responsible for international peace and security, and, at the same time, to the perception that the UN co-operation with the multinational force is aiming at an early devolution of powers to a democratically and constitutionally elected government; in other words, that it aims at a full transfer of sovereignty to the Iraqi people through a democratically legitimate political process.[247] In the run-up to the adoption of resolution 1546, this process of UN legitimation is witnessed by the strong involvement of the UN envoy Lakhdar Brahimi in the negotiations for the formation of the new Iraqi Interim Government. This process leads in the long run to a general recognition of the legality of the civil authority and the international military presence, therefore transforming the originally unlawful territorial situation in a lawful *status quo*. Whether this is already the case at the time of writing is not an easy question to answer. However, the holding of democratic elections in January 2005, the likely approval of the new constitution through the referendum held in October 2005, the full acceptance and blessing of the Iraqi Interim Government as the legitimate representative and sovereign government of Iraq at the United Nations and at regional organisations, such as

---

[246] E.g. Nasrawi, 'Arab Nations Won't Recognize Iraq Council', *Associated Press News* 5 August 2003; S/PV.4808, Statement of Syria. See also the statement of the Mexican representative to the effect that 'we associate ourselves with the Security Council consensus on welcoming the establishment of the provisional Governing Council as a first logical step towards establishing a genuinely representative government that exercises the sovereignty of the Iraqi people. That welcome does not constitute legal recognition. Nor should it be interpreted as endorsement. It is not because the Governing Council is still under the authority of the occupying Power.' *Ibidem*.

[247] The conferral of legitimacy by the SC upon an unlawful territorial situation can be also seen with regard to SC Res. 1244 concerning the post-war regime for Kosovo. In that case, the legitimacy was arguably reinforced to a greater extent as compared with Iraq by the aims and means of *Operation Allied Force*. See *supra* n. 217.

the League of Arab Nations, the increasing co-operation of international donors and the increasing contributions by many countries to the maintenance of stability in the country are elements that seem to point in the direction of an accomplished process of 'legality of status' through legitimacy.

In conclusion, the principles of legality determining a situation of territorial unlawfulness may not be able to dictate the legal consequences of such unlawfulness, when the violating effectiveness is accompanied by a legitimate claim and legitimate process and/or is legitimated by an authoritative body. This may even lead to a transformation of the original illegality of the territorial situation in a subsequent legality. Effectiveness can still play an important role in dictating legal outcomes to territorial situations, but it is no more the mere acceptance of the *fait accompli* typical of an era when effectiveness was a fundamental principle of international law. It is linked to the internal legitimacy of its underlying claim and/or to its external legitimation. It is undeniable that legitimacy, compared to legality, provides for looser, less transparent and less objective devices of power acceptance. It is also undeniable that legitimacy discourse can be easily manipulated, and it is one of the most sophisticated forms of 'soft power' exercised by the hegemon, in the sense that it can perfectly complement the 'hard power' of effectiveness. However, it is at least built starting from a general normative framework provided by the fundamental norms of the international society, and by the institutions mandated to uphold and enforce these fundamental norms. Moreover, explaining the process of recognition of unlawful territorial situations through legitimacy helps us to maintain the integrity of the international rule of law, by denying the possibility that an illegal act produces *per se* legal effects considered in accordance with international law in contradiction to the principle *ex iniuria ius non oritur* or, that *a fortiori*, such effects may be lawfully endorsed by authoritative bodies like the SC. Finally, one must concede the process of recognition of status through legitimacy does not provide a satisfactory answer to some difficult questions of invalidity, state responsibility and non-recognition that situations like that of Iraq arise. How do we reconcile the duty of non-recognition with the process of gradual legitimation of the unlawful territorial situation through Chapter VII resolutions? Is the third state entering into legal relations with the illegal occupier still violating the obligation of non-recognition despite the legitimation by the SC? An answer to these questions presupposes an analysis of the Council's powers under international law, and it is therefore provided in the next chapter.[248]

---

[248] See *infra* Ch. 6, section 2.2.

9. Conclusions

In conclusion, the normative impact of a definition of unlawfulness of a certain territorial situation is manifold. In terms of invalidity of the territorial situation, the system still shows an inherent dualism between the domestic and the international plane. Such dualism witnesses both the strong role played by the concept of effectiveness, and the inability of international law to pervasively regulate the effects of a *de facto* unlawful situation, if not backed by an institutional policy of sanction and non-recognition. At the level of impact on other norms of international law, the law of territory and the *ius ad bellum* are strictly intertwined, which is why a definition of unlawfulness of a certain territorial situation is likely to have an important impact on the way international actors can resort to force. By contrast, the *ius in bello* regulating the rights and duties of an occupant is deeply entrenched in the idea of effective control, thus leaving the question of legality of the occupation in the first place outside the scope of its application. Also the access of statehood in the cases of denied self-determination analysed – Guinea-Bissau, Palestine, Western Sahara - was impaired by the lack of effective enforcement mechanisms and the role played by effectiveness in the definition and creation of states. The case of Bosnia and Herzegovina is provided as an example of how a 'one-step approach' to statehood by the international community may represent a solution to instances where the international community is not able to translate its non-recognition of an illegal territorial occupation in a fully-fledged entitlement to statehood.

This aspect ties up with the question of state responsibility for unlawful occupation of territories. Again, whereas nothing prevents an overall question of state responsibility from arising out of an unlawful territorial situation, in practice judicial decisions and state practice are very scanty. In cases where the contested territorial situations crystallise in a territorial dispute, states have often decided to refer their dispute by agreement to an international tribunal. They have normally requested the mere withdrawal of the allegedly unlawful occupant. The recent case of *Cameroon/Nigeria* shows that, even when a territorial dispute is referred to a tribunal unilaterally and the claimant presents a claim of state responsibility, tribunals are reluctant to overburden the losing state with anything beyond the mere withdrawal of the military and civil administration. It has been argued that, as much as it is possible to define a framework of illegality of unlawful territorial situations, the consequences of the existence of a continuing internationally wrongful act should be also addressed. In fact, defining a framework of state responsibility for adverse occupations also contributes to refine the analysis of the primary norms concerning territorial sovereignty, in particular the *uti possidetis* principle and the principle of self-determination, thus to better define what constitutes an unlawful territorial situation. Bad faith, malicious conduct and magnitude of the alleged violation are the main elements to be taken into consideration to decide whether the principles of *uti possidetis* and self-determination as norms protecting a state's or a people's territorial sovereignty have been breached, thus leading to a situation of territorial unlawfulness and the international responsibility of the occupying state.

Finally, the chapter has analysed the concept of legitimacy, as it regulates the consequences of unlawful territorial situations. Legitimacy tested against the fundamental principles of the international community has been found to be the key both to reconcile occasionally contradicting legal principles and to transform an unlawful effectiveness in a lawful state of affairs. In other words, legitimacy of a claim or legitimacy conferred by an authoritative body have been found to be the main factors behind the recognition of originally unlawful territorial situations. The recent case of Iraq has represented a useful test for this proposition.

In sum, the principles of legality analysed in Chapter 4 work at an important but unsophisticated level, both in terms of invalidity and in terms of impact on other areas of international law. These shortcomings, rather than proving an 'irrelevance' of international law to territorial situations, show how international law can only play its role of 'gentle civilizer', if upheld through collective measures and international involvement. Where, on the contrary, a net of bilateral and contractual approach is preferred, this will result in deficiencies and lack of substantive legal relevance. Bargaining power, effectiveness on the ground and unbalanced political support will make international law one of the products on the market place, with the risk that the violating state may turn the law to its advantage. In that respect, the legitimacy of the claims of the 'violating' party, tested against the fundamental principles of the international community, or the legitimation of the effective situation through authoritative bodies, will represent an important factor in the way effectiveness will be tolerated, acquiesced, recognised and legalised or, on the contrary, rejected as mere usurpation of the stronger.

The next chapter completes the analysis of unlawful territorial situations considering the territorial competence of UN authoritative bodies, in particular the SC. Again, legality and legitimacy are considered as two distinct but inter-related concepts, which help us define a coherent analytical framework to review the action of the SC and its impact in the establishment, continuation and extinction of territorial situations.

CHAPTER 6

TESTING LEGALITY AND LEGITIMACY IN UN TERRITORIAL COMPETENCE

1. Introduction

The UN has actively engaged in the last decade in projects of territorial administration such as in Bosnia, East Timor and Kosovo. This type of UN intervention has been described as addressing inter-related but distinctive problems of 'sovereignty' and 'governance'.[1] The involvement of international organisations in administering territories has a long-standing history dating back to the start of the League of Nations. Furthermore, the UN has exercised in the past and still exercises today territorial competencies not only by providing the means and resources for direct territorial administration, but also deciding upon issues of formal territorial status, and endorsing territorial situations on the ground.

The underlying idea is that global governance in the name of global interests can represent the solution to irreconcilable clashes of local interests in local governance. The perceived role of the world organisation as the vehicle for fundamental interests of the international community as a whole, be it in the promotion of the right of self-determination of non-self governing territories, or in the maintenance of peace and security in a certain disputed area, make questions of legality as secondary to the concept of effectiveness of the world organisation. The question is not so much how to make the UN decision-making process in conformity with the positive norms of the instituting treaty, but to render the organisation as effective as possible in view of the political challenges of the Post Cold-War era. In an age where conflicts and unilateralism seem to represent the main threat to a system of global governance, to assess the action of the UN in terms of legality sounds pretentious to a pragmatic mind. The willingness of the UN founding states not to create a system of judicial review of the internal organs' acts and the consequential presumption of legality of those acts developed by the ICJ since the *Certain Expenses* case makes the realist argument even stronger. However, even the pragmatist and realist must bear in mind the fact that the activity of an international organisation neither exists in a legal *vacuum*, nor represents a water-tight compartment of international law. As stated by Judge Percy Spender his separate opinion in the *Certain Expenses* advisory opinion, the

---

[1] Wilde, 'From Danzig to East Timor and Beyond: the Role of International Territorial Administration' 95 *AJIL* (2001), 583.

ICJ may be called to decide on the competence of a certain organ of the UN to act in a certain way, and, in that case, it will be only legal considerations that must be taken into account.[2] In other words, the UN does not act as an absolute world sovereign situated above the rule of law. Abidance by international law makes UN organs more legitimate, thus more effective thanks to what Franck calls the 'pull towards compliance'.[3] But this is not the only role played by legitimacy. Legitimacy may also play a fundamental role in shaping the very broad powers of international legality, as embodied in the theory of implied and inherent powers of international organisations. Furthermore, the legitimacy derived by the promotion of the UN broad ends and aims provided by Article 1 of the UN Charter may be able to accommodate the tension between original Charter violations and *de facto* territorial situations produced on the ground.

This chapter expands the analysis of unlawful territorial situations articulated in the previous chapters to consider UN territorial powers and competencies. Such powers have been with different aims and purposes exercised in the past by the GA and are nowadays mostly exercised by the SC. It assesses the limits in terms of legality and legitimacy to the action of the SC in this respect. The chapter reviews how a situation of territorial unlawfulness can be reinforced by *ultra vires* actions by the SC. As an example of a partly unlawful territorial situation under the authority of the UN the case of Kosovo is considered. On the other hand, the role of legitimacy provided by UN endorsement of post-conflict unlawful territorial situations and by different forms of recognition by the affected state shows how effectiveness and legality can be also reconciled in the long run. Finally, the legitimacy factor can also represent a restraining factor in the way the SC acts and justifies its choices, enhancing its accountability towards the international community and the direct addressees of its actions. The question of sovereignty and final status of Kosovo and the way these two issues have been so far addressed by the UN administration shows the important role that legitimacy plays in this respect.

2. UN competence and powers in territorial situations

The exercise by the UN of territorial competencies and powers is multi-faceted, and, albeit conceptually not entirely new, it represents one of the most innovative and interesting developments in international governance of the last ten years. Bosnia and Herzegovina, Kosovo and East Timor represent three

---

[2] *Certain Expenses of the United Nations*, Advisory Opinion, ICJ Reports 1962, 151, Sep. Op. Judge Percy Spencer, 182, at 184.
[3] Franck, 'Legitimacy in the International System' 82 *AJIL* (1988), 705.

situations where the UN has set up *ad interim* administrations under the ultimate authority of UN personnel and the SC with the aim of solving local conflict, re-establishing international peace and security in the region, ensuring sounds standards of governance and eventually settling pending issues of territorial sovereignty. In all three cases, the SC has provided a mandate to a UN civil administration for the exercise of legislative and executive competencies; the legally binding force underlying those competencies has been derived from a delegation of binding powers under Chapter VII.[4] More specifically, Bothe and Marauhn have argued that the establishment of a civil administration with a view to re-establishing a situation of peace and security in the interested region can be considered within the SC powers under Article 41, whereas Article 42 would support the endorsement or direct establishment of a military presence.[5]

Although being normally reported under the same heading of 'UN administrations', the three above-mentioned cases present some important differences, which unveil different underlying models of the exercise of territorial competencies and powers. The most extensive territorial competence was that exercised by UNTAET; SC Resolution 1272 authorised the establishment of both a civil and a security UN authority.[6] In the case of Kosovo and Bosnia and Herzegovina the SC, while creating a UN civil administration, has not established its own military presence, but has limited itself to endorsing previous agreements, whereby a regional organisation, namely NATO, would undertake the task of ensuring a safe environment in the two regions.[7] This shows that the SC may exercise its territorial competence either setting up and engaging directly in civil and military administration, or mandating those tasks to other actors, be it a state or another international organisation, while still retaining ultimate legal authority, or, lastly, adopting both models at the same time as in the cases of Bosnia and Kosovo.

Both models are not historically unprecedented. For instance, after World War I, the town of Danzig, mostly inhabited by Germans but within Polish territory, was transformed into a Free City under the protection of the League of Nations.[8] The Council of the League of Nations appointed a High Commissioner

---

[4] See SC Res. 1031 (1995) endorsing the content of the Dayton Agreements for Bosnia and Herzegovina; SC Res. 1244 (1999) setting up UNMIK, the UN administration for Kosovo; SC Res. 1272 (1999) setting up UNTAET, the UN administration for East Timor.

[5] Bothe, Marauhn, 'UN Administration of Kosovo and East Timor: Concept, Legality and Limitations of Security Council-Mandated Trusteeship Administration', in Tomuschat (ed.), *Kosovo and the International Community: a Legal Assessment* (2002), 217, at 232.

[6] SC Res. 1272 (1999), paras. 1, 3 (c).

[7] SC Res. 1244 (1999), Annex 2 and Military Technical Agreement recalled therein; SC Res. 1031 (1995) and Annex 1-A to the Dayton General Framework Agreement, in 35 *ILM* (1996), 91.

[8] Treaty of Versailles, Article 103, in Bevans (ed.), *Treaties and Other International Agreements of the United States of America 1776-1949* (1969), Vol. 2, 43.

who would reside in Danzig and would be competent to provide binding interpretations on the existing legal instruments binding upon Danzig and Poland, to authorise amendments to the constitution and to prepare an annual report to be presented to the League of Nations Council.[9] The latter was also competent to decide upon a series of territorial obligations concerning the Free City such as the establishment of military or naval bases, the erection of fortifications and the manufacturing of war materials in its territory.[10] In other words, the Free City of Danzig is possibly the first case where the world organisation begins to exercise some level of direct territorial administration, albeit considerably limited.

A much more pervasive system of direct UN administration was envisaged for the city of Trieste by the Permanent Statute for the Free Territory of Trieste.[11] The city's appurtenance was inextricably linked to the fixing of the border between Italy and Yugoslavia; the creation of a neutral, de-militarised territory had been considered by the Allied Powers as the best way in the long run to ensure a peaceful border settlement. Potentially, the main innovation was to be the appointment by the SC, after consultation with Italy and Yugoslavia, of a Governor for the Free Territory as a guarantor of the Statute. The Governor's powers according to the Statute were surprisingly similar to those today exercised by the Office of the High Representative in Bosnia and Herzegovina, as he was supposed to exercise civil authority jointly with the local administration. Its competence included the powers to refuse the approval of legislation passed by the local assembly in violation of the Statute, to adopt executive acts when necessary to exercise its functions, to appoint the Chief of the police forces and take control over them in case of threat to the Territory's territorial integrity, and to conclude international agreements jointly with the local government.[12] The Governor was directly accountable to the SC, which retained the power to suspend him and appoint a new one.[13] The Statute was never implemented due to the lack of agreement between Italy and Yugoslavia for the appointment of the Governor, and the lack of will of the SC to push forward a candidate without the states' approval.[14] The Allied Administration over Zone A of the Territory was

---

[9] See Lewis, 'The Free City of Danzig' 5 *BYIL* (1924), 94.
[10] Constitution of the Free City of Danzig, Article 5, in *League of Nations Official Journal*, Special Supplement No. 7, 1922.
[11] Permanent Statute for the Free Territory of Trieste, Annex VI, Treaty of Peace between Allied and Associated Powers and Italy (1947), in 42 *AJIL* (Supplement of Documents) (1948), 97. See SC Res. 16 (1947).
[12] *Ibidem*, Arts. 16, 17, 20, 22, 24.
[13] *Ibidem*, Article 11. See also Crawford, *The Creation of States in International Law* (1979), 161-163.
[14] Another case where the UN attempted to exercise directly governmental functions in a territory is the case of the creation by the GA of the UN Council for Namibia (GA Res. 2248 (XXI)). Also in

substituted by an Italian administration in 1954, whereas the Yugoslav administration maintained its control over Zone B.[15] The border was finally settled in 1975 through the Treaty of Osimo according to the extension of the respective administrative areas.[16] Despite the lack of implementation, the experience of Trieste showed a possible legal framework within which the SC could directly exercise territorial competence. Many of its elements have indeed inspired the legal framework in Bosnia after 1995. Moreover, its shortcomings, such as the lack of a system of compulsory arbitration in case of irresolvable differences between interested parties and the non-use of the SC powers under Chapter VII, have been corrected.

The other model of involvement of the UN in the exercise of territorial competence with regard to a territory is also not unprecedented. For instance, the establishment after World War II according to Chapter XII of a series of Trusteeship Administrations was effected through agreement between the UN and the administering state. In particular, both the GA and the SC – the latter for those territories defined as 'strategic areas' in Article 83 of the Charter – mandated the administration of those territories detached from enemy states during World War II and those previously held under Mandate to a particular state. Article 75 specifically stated that the administration of the trust territory was to be exercised on behalf of the UN. A particular organ, the Trusteeship Council, was created with a view to assisting the GA in supervising the Trusts' administration.[17] The aim of the Trusteeship Administrations was to promote self-government or independence of the inhabitants, and to further international peace and security in those regions.[18] A much debated and interesting aspect was whether the GA had ultimate authority over those territories, or whether its power of disposing of a Trusteeship Administration was subject to the consent of the administering power.[19] Whereas the purpose and overall aims of the Trusteeship system, as confirmed by Chapter XII, suggested an ultimate territorial competence of the GA, the fact that the GA did not possess under the

---

this case the Council never exercised any degree of actual authority because of the unwillingness by South Africa to release its control over Namibia.

[15] London Agreement between Italy, Yugoslavia, UK and US, 5 October 1954, in 235 UNTS 99.

[16] Treaty of Osimo, 10 November 1975, in 60 *Rivista di diritto internazionale* (1977), 674.

[17] For the institutional aspects regarding the Trusteeship system see Rauschning, 'United Nations Trusteeship System', in Bernhardt (ed.), *EPIL* (1983) (Vol. V), 369.

[18] UN Charter, Article 76.

[19] See Vedovato, 'Les accords de tutelle' 76 *Recueil des Cours* (1950), 613; Kohen, *Possession contestée et souveraineté territoriale* (1997), 84-86.

Charter any legally binding power over states casts some doubt as to how this competence could be possibly exercised. The ICJ in the *Northern Cameroons* case seemed to leave no doubt that GA Resolution 1608 (XV), whereby the Assembly terminated the British administration over Northern Cameroon, 'had definitive legal effect'.[20] Crawford reconciled this passage of the Court and the incapacity of the GA to create legal obligations by saying that 'the Assembly's function here is a determinative one – that it is designated by the Charter to decide particular matters of political fact, applying principles of self-determination implicit in the Trusteeship instruments.'[21] This interpretation was also supported by the ICJ advisory opinion in the *Namibia* case.[22] As a response to South Africa's claim that the GA did not have a power to revoke its Mandate over Namibia, the Court argued that the GA by adopting Resolution 2145 (XXI) declaring the mandate terminated was only making a determination of a legal situation which had been produced by South Africa's material breach of the Mandate's terms. By analogy between the Trusteeship and the Mandate systems, this reasoning can be also extended to the former. In practice, the problem of unilateral revocation never emerged with regard to Trusteeship agreements, as the bilateral agreements between the GA and the administering power always preceded GA resolutions of termination.

In conclusion, a review of legality concerning a territorial situation where ultimate authority is vested with the UN will depend, in the first place, upon a review of legality of the way the particular UN organ exercises its competence. A second level will be added in those cases where the UN is directly administering the territory, and it will concern the legitimacy of the way the UN acts with regard to that territorial situation. Such legitimacy can be construed with reference to UN action in those territories assessed against some of the fundamental principles of the Charter, such as the maintenance of peace and security, the principle of self-determination and the promotion of human rights.[23] This review of legitimacy is all-important for two reasons. Firstly, it allows a check on the very broad powers envisaged by the Charter and by state practice for the SC; secondly, it explains the way some unlawful territorial situations can become in the long run accepted and recognised by the international community. The next sections respectively consider the question of legality and legitimacy of UN organs' exercise of their powers, in particular that of the SC, as the SC is nowadays exercising the most pervasive powers with regard to territorial situations.

---

[20] *Northern Cameroon Case* (Cameroon/UK), ICJ Reports 1963, 15, at 32.

[21] Crawford, *supra* n. 13, 343-344.

[22] *Legal Consequences for States of the Continued Presence of South-Africa in Namibia notwithstanding Security Council Resolution 276*, Advisory Opinion, ICJ Reports 1971, 6.

[23] Bothe, Marauhn, *supra* n. 5, 235-239.

2.1 Failing the test of legality: the 'impossible task' from the doctrine of *ultra vires* acts to the doctrine of inherent powers

The action of the GA and SC in territorial matters has been shaped through an extensive interpretation of the powers expressly accorded by the Charter. The problem however lies in understanding how broad and extensive such interpretation may be, and what is the limitation placed upon the GA and the SC by international law, possibly by those principles of legality seen in Chapter 4. This problem is particularly strong with regard to the SC, which can adopt enforcement measures which are legally binding upon member states. The Charter is clear in stating in Article 24(2) that 'the Security Council shall act in accordance with the Purposes and Principles of the United Nations.' Among the purposes of UN Article 1(1) also includes 'to bring about by peaceful means, *and in conformity with principles of justice and international law*, adjustment or settlement of international disputes or situations which might lead to a breach of the peace' (emphasis added). Finally, Article 103 creates a normative hierarchy between obligations deriving from the Charter and obligations arising out of international agreements to the effect that the former shall prevail.

It is the present author's view that these provisions, albeit general, provide some considerable guidance to the understanding of the relation between the powers of UN political bodies, in particular the SC, and international law. The problem has lain, however, in the fact that the UN lacks a system of judicial review of internal acts, which would make its principal organs accountable according to the principles of international law. A Belgian proposal to vest with the ICJ the ultimate authority to interpret the Charter was defeated during the *travaux preparatoires*.[24] Unlike the European Court of Justice, which can hear claims of natural and legal persons to review Community acts according to the EC Treaty, the ICJ can only render a decision on the legality of acts of UN organs, if requested so by any other internal organ or authorised specialised agency under Article 65 of the Statute, or if such legal issue arises in contentious proceedings between states under Article 36 of the Statute. In the former case, the decision is advisory, as such non-binding, whereas, in the latter, the matter arises incidentally to the main legal dispute, and the decision is binding only upon the parties to the dispute. However, the authority exercised by the World Court as the main judicial organ of the UN in conjunction with Article 38 of the Statute should ensure that any finding of the Court represents strong evidence of existing international law. The few instances where the Court has pronounced on these issues highlight some of the most important legal principles developed by its judicial policy of review concerning acts of UN bodies. This jurisprudence shows

---

[24] UN Doc. 2, G/7 (k)(1), 3 UNCIO Docs. 335, 336 (1945).

a high degree of judicial restraint by the ICJ, but also the elaboration of some useful legal principles for the understanding of the relation between the SC and international law.

2.1.1 Case law

The first opportunity for the Court to review the relation between the UN Charter and the powers of its organs was given in the advisory opinion on the *Reparation* case of 1949.[25] The Court was asked by the GA to render its opinion whether in the event of a UN agent suffering injuries in the performance of his duties involving the responsibility of a state, the UN could bring a claim on his behalf. The Court stated for the first time the so-called doctrine of implied powers.[26] The Court argued that an analysis of the functions of organisation as spelled out in the treaty becomes the precondition of an assessment of legality of a certain activity, which does not depend upon an express provision of the constituent treaty. This vision of the legal competence of the UN organs was embedded in the recognition by the court that the international organisation has international legal personality, thus it is in its power to adopt all necessary measures to pursue its treaty goals.[27] Using Bowett's words the test of legality 'is a functional one', even if some authors such as Schermers, Blokker and White have warned about the ambiguities inherent in the expression 'implied powers'.[28] Unfortunately, the Court did not proceed to consider such treaty goals and reached its conclusion without that assessment.

In the advisory opinion *Certain Expenses* of 1962 the ICJ had to declare whether the GA was entitled to claim jurisdiction in matters related to peace and security, and whether it could establish peace-keeping forces in view of the SC deadlock.[29] After finding that 'each organ must, in the first place at least, determine its own jurisdiction', the Court stated that 'when the Organization takes action which warrants the assertion that it was appropriate for the fulfilment of one of the stated purposes of the United Nations, the presumption is that such action is not *ultra vires*.'[30] The Court was asserting that in order to ensure the effective functioning of UN organs, and to avoid challenges of legality by member states creating an operational deadlock, a presumption of legality should be given to

---

[25] *Reparation for Injuries Suffered in the Service of the United Nations*, Advisory Opinion, ICJ Reports 1949, 174.
[26] *Ibidem*, 178.
[27] *Ibidem*, 174.
[28] Bowett, *The Law of International Institutions* (1982, 4th ed.), 337; Schermers, Blokker, *International Institutional Law* (1995), 159; White, *The Law of International Organisations* (1996), 131.
[29] *Certain Expenses*, *supra* n. 2, 151.
[30] *Ibidem*, 168.

any act of UN organs. This would not prevent a court from declaring an act *ultra vires* and a doctrine of non-justiciability of UN political organs' acts was clearly rejected by the Court in this important passage:

> 'It has been argued that the question put to the Court is intertwined with political questions, and that for this reason the Court should refuse to give an opinion. It is true that most interpretations of the Charter of the United Nations will have political significance, great or small. In the nature of things it could not be otherwise. The Court, however, cannot attribute a political character to a request which invites it to undertake an essentially judicial task, namely, the interpretation of a treaty provision.'[31]

Yet the difficulty that an international tribunal engages in reviewing SC acts, makes the presumption of legality very strong. The expansionist policy of the Court with regard to the implied power doctrine was then complemented by embracing cases of procedural irregularity.[32] The functional test became all-encompassing, moving from substantive irregularities to procedural ones. Furthermore, the doctrine of implied powers was expanded to consider the absence of any provision prohibiting the exercise of such power by the GA, rather than the positive existence of provision justifying those powers. The only limitation on the power of the GA in respect to matters of peace and security was that only the SC could order coercive action.[33]

An especially relevant case, due to the subject matter of territorial sovereignty involved, was the *Namibia* case (1971).[34] South Africa objected to SC Resolution 276 and GA Resolution 2145 (XXI). This had first declared the South African mandate terminated, on the ground that a) the Covenant of the League of Nations did not confer on the Council the power to terminate a mandate for misconduct of the mandatory, and that, according to the principle *nemo transferre potest quod non habet*, the UN could not succeed in a non-existing competence; b) *quod non datur*, even if the Council had possessed the power of revocation of the Mandate, such power could not have been exercised unilaterally, but only in co-operation with the mandatory power; c) that the GA could not act as a judicial body determining questions of fact and that it could not issue binding decisions transferring territory; d) that SC Resolution 276 did not invoke Chapter VII of the Charter, thus it could not represent a binding decision on South Africa.[35] The Court's approach resembled closely that adopted in *Certain Expenses*. By passing Resolution 276, the SC was acting in pursuance of its task of maintenance of peace and security, its decisions were taken in conformity with purposes and

---

[31] *Ibidem*, 155.
[32] *Ibidem*, 168.
[33] White, *supra* n. 28, 130.
[34] *Namibia*, *supra* n. 22, 16.
[35] *Ibidem*, 21-51.

principles of the Charter, and under Article 25 it was for states to comply with those decisions.[36] It is important to recall the whole passage of the Court on this issue:

'Article 24 of the Charter vests in the Security Council the necessary authority to take action such as that taken in the present case. The reference in paragraph 2 of this Article to specific powers of the Security Council under certain chapters of the Charter does not exclude the existence of general powers to discharge the responsibilities conferred in paragraph 1. Reference may be made in this respect to the Secretary General's Statement, presented to the Security Council on 10 January 1947 to the effect that 'the powers of the Council under Article 24 are not restricted to the specific grants of authority contained in Chapters VI, VII, VIII and XII...[T]he Members of the United Nations have conferred upon the Security Council powers commensurate with its responsibility for the maintenance of peace and security. The only limitations are the fundamental principles and purposes found in Chapter I of the Charter.'[37]

The Court's rationale therefore followed that of *Reparations* and *Certain Expenses* on the doctrine of implied and inherent powers. Since it is the task of the SC to deal with matters of peace and security, then all its decisions, even if falling short of spelling out clearly any legal basis in the Charter, produce legal effects according to Articles 24 and 25. The only limitations to the powers of the SC in the field of peace and security can be found in the fundamental principles and purposes of the UN embodied in Chapter I.

Another important case is the *Lockerbie* affair case.[38] In 1992 Libya requested the Court to indicate provisional measures that would ensure that no step was taken by the SC that would prejudice Libya's rights under the Montreal Convention with specific regard to the Lockerbie terrorist attack.[39] Three days before the end of the oral hearing, the SC passed under Chapter VII Resolution 748 that demanded Libya's compliance with the US and UK requests for extradition of the alleged terrorist.[40] The resolution also imposed a series of economic sanctions upon Libya.[41] In a rather laconic passage of its decision, the Court held that 'at the stage of proceedings on provisional measures, [it] considers that *prima facie*' the obligation of member states to carry out decisions of the SC under Article 25 'extends to the decision contained in Resolution 748 (1992) and that according to Article 103 of the Charter 'the obligations of the

---

[36] *Ibidem.*
[37] *Ibidem*, 52.
[38] *Case Concerning Questions of Interpretation and Application of the Montreal Convention arising out of the Aerial Incident at Lockerbie (Provisional Measures)* (Libya/US, Libya/UK), ICJ Reports 1992, 3.
[39]*Ibidem*, Application by Libya of 3 March 1992, in <http://www.icj-cij.org/icjwww/idocket/ilus/ilusframe.htm>.
[40] SC Res. 748 (1992), paras. 2-3.
[41] *Ibidem*, paras. 4-5.

Parties in that respect prevail over their obligations under any other international agreement, including the Montreal Convention.'[42] The *Lockerbie* decision on provisional measures is relevant to the question of legality of UN organs' acts in respect to two main aspects. The first one is the confirmation concerning the presumption of legality accorded to acts of UN political organs already defined in previous decisions. Since provisional measures can be ordered with regard to disputes where the Court appears to have *prima facie* jurisdiction, and the rights of the applicants have been or are likely to be prejudiced in the continuation of the dispute, it is clear that the refusal of the Court to accede to Libyan requests signifies a confirmation of this presumption of legality. The burden of proof to reverse this presumption was upon the Libyan government, and such full review had to be considered by the Court only at the merit stage. The second aspect is that spelled out in Article 103 of the Charter, that in case of conflict between obligations arising out of the Charter and obligations deriving from an international agreement, the former shall prevail. This helps defining the legality limitations to the powers of the UN, in the sense that international treaties cannot limit the action of the organisation under Chapter VII.

However, Article 103 does not provide a solution to the possibility of the conflict being between obligations under the Charter and obligations under customary international law. Consequentially, this raises the third main aspect of the *Lockerbie* decision, that is to what extent, despite such presumption of legality and Article 103, the SC is limited in its actions by general international law. The problem is only touched upon in some of the separate and dissenting opinions. Judge Bedjaoui in his dissenting opinion reiterates the principle that the SC should act 'in conformity with principles of justice and international law', before moving to a substantive criticism of the Court's decision;[43] Judge Shahabuddeen poses the different legal questions surrounding the relation between the SC and the ICJ by means of a series of rhetorical questions;[44] Judge Weeramantry after having analysed the *travaux preparatoires* concerning the competencies of the SC states that

> 'a clear limitation on the plenitude of the SC's powers is that those powers must be exercised in accordance with the well established principles of international law. It is true, this limitation must be restrictively interpreted and is confined only to the principles and objects which appear in Chapter I of the Charter…The restriction nevertheless exists and constitutes an important principle of law in the interpretation of the United Nations Chapter.'

---

[42] *Lockerbie, supra* n. 38, 15.
[43] *Ibidem*, Diss. Op. Judge Bedjaoui, 143, at 156.
[44] *Ibidem*, Sep. Op. Judge Shahabuddeen, 140, at 142.

The Judge then reaches the conclusion that the Court's review cannot extend to actions within the powers conferred to the SC by Chapter VII, such actions being entirely within the discretion of the Council.[45]

Quite surprisingly, the latest thorough investigation and review of the SC's powers under Chapter VII has come from an *ad hoc* tribunal, the International Criminal Tribunal for Former Yugoslavia (ICTY), in its very first decisions rendered by the Trial Chamber and the Appeals Chamber on jurisdiction in the *Tadic* case.[46] The Defence filed a motion disputing the jurisdiction of the Court on a series of grounds, including the unlawfulness of the creation of the ICTY by SC Resolution 827.[47] In response to the Defence's claim, the ICTY recalled the powers entrusted to the SC by Article 24(1) and the decision made during the *travaux préparatoires* to apply a theory of implied and inherent powers to the competence of the SC. After having recalled that, the Court made the following controversial statement: 'The broad discretion given to the Security Council in the exercise of its Chapter VII authority itself *suggests that decisions taken under this head are not reviewable*' (emphasis added).[48] Further, the ICTY mentioned *Namibia*, where the ICJ stated that it did 'not possess powers of judicial review or appeal in respect of the decisions taken by the United Nations organs concerned', and Judge Weeramantry's dissenting opinion in *Lockerbie* where he stated that 'the determination under Article 39 of the existence of any threat to the peace…is one entirely within the discretion of the Council' and that 'the Council and no other is the judge of the existence of state of affairs which brings Chapter VII into operation.'[49] The Trial Chamber finally raised the principle of non-justiciability to maintain that a determination by the SC under Article 39, and the decision to adopt binding measures according to Article 41 and 42 to remedy a situation of threat to peace and security are totally within the political discretion of the SC, and a court cannot sit in judgement of those decisions.[50]

Despite reaching quite the same outcome, the approach taken by the Appeals Chamber in its decision of 2 October 1995 was considerably different.[51] The Court rightly rejected the way the Trial Chamber had reviewed the SC's powers. It correctly pointed out that the *dicta* of the ICJ in *Namibia* quoted in the decision of the Trial Chamber 'address the hypothesis of the Court exercising such judicial

---

[45] *Ibidem*, Diss. Op. Judge Weeramantry, 160, at 176.
[46] *Prosecutor v. Dusko Tadic A/K/A "Dule"* (Decision on the Defence Motion of Jurisdiction), ICTY, 10 August 1995, 105 ILR (1997), 427.
[47] *Ibidem*, Preamble.
[48] *Ibidem*, 429.
[49] *Ibidem*, 431.
[50] *Ibidem*, 434-435.
[51] *Prosecutor v. Dusko Tadic A/K/A 'Dule'* (Decision on the Defence Motion for Interlocutory Appeal on Jurisdiction), ICTY, 2 October 1995, in 105 ILR (1997), 453.

review as a matter of "primary" jurisdiction' but they 'do not address at all hypothesis of examination of the legality of the decisions of other organs as a matter of "incidental" jurisdiction, in order to ascertain and be able to exercise its "primary" jurisdiction over the matter before it.'[52] Furthermore, the Appeals Chamber went on to dismiss the theory of non-justiciability as applied to actions carried out by the SC pursuant to Chapter VII and it recalled the decision of the ICJ in *Certain Expenses*.[53] Having declared justiciable the action of the SC, the Appeals Chamber rejected the approach of the Trial Chamber to consider the SC as *legibus solutus,* and it correctly claimed that a finding of the Council under Article 39 should be in accordance with the purposes and principles of the UN Charter.[54] Moreover, Judge Sidhwa, in his separate opinion, also added that the SC, when acting under Chapter VII, should be also bound by the fundamental norms of the international community, such as the rules of *ius cogens*.[55] Having reversed the Trial Chamber's approach on the issue of legality and justiciability of SC actions, the Appeals Chamber confirmed the validity of the doctrine of implied powers. It concluded that the establishment of a criminal court as a means of addressing a threat to international peace and security was completely within the discretionary power granted to the SC by Article 41 of the Charter, which did not provide for an exhaustive list of actions, but only a number of examples.

2.2 Assessment: limits of legality and territorial powers of the SC under Chapter VII

An analysis of the way tribunals have tried to review the actions of UN political organs shows an on-going tension between two approaches. On the one hand, a realist approach has tended to put the efficacy of the action of the UN political organs, in particular the SC, as a priority and to situate actions under Chapter VII beyond any check-and-balance mechanism, if not those already

---

[52] *Ibidem*, 462.

[53] *Ibidem*, 463.

[54] *Ibidem*, 465.

[55] *Tadic, supra* n. 51, Sep. Op. Judge Sidhwa, 555. A judicial recognition and elaboration of the limits imposed by *ius cogens* on the SC's Ch. VII powers was made by the Court of First Instance of the European Communities in the *Ali Yusuf* case. In that case, the Court reviewed a number of SC resolutions and, more specifically, of decisions by the 1267 Sanctions Committee, enlisting Mr Ali Yusuf and the Al Barakaat International Foundation among suspects collaborating with Al-Qaeda. Such measures involving the freezing of financial funds have been implemented by the EU Council through a number of regulations. The Court, while considering judicial review of SC resolutions beyond its competence within Community law, went on to consider the compatibility of SC resolutions with fundamental human rights of the applicants, such as the right to property, the right to a fair hearing and the right to an effective judicial remedy. The Court found no breach of these rights. See Case T-306/01, Judgment of 21 September 2005, especially paras. 277-347.

inherent in the working procedure of these organs, and in particular the veto power as regards the SC. On the other hand, a legalist approach has stressed the supremacy of law over politics, more specifically the need to anchor the political organs of the UN to the respect of UN Charter provisions and general international law. The jurisprudence developed by the ICJ has tried to strike a balance between these two opposing trends. The doctrines of implied and inherent powers has provided a very extensive means of interpreting the Charter, however recalling the frame of the purposes and principles of the UN. As a matter of scholarly treatment, such balance is easily comprehensible, and it may represent a flexible understanding. However, at the same time, such flexibility in legality discourse has been worked out too vaguely and too broadly to provide for a satisfactory tool of analysis of such delicate issues. This major flaw can be seen in a number of respects.

Despite paying lip-service to the 'principles and purposes of the UN Charter', the ICJ has not tried to spell them out while analysing the legality of acts of UN organs, and its defence of legality has been rather timid. This is hardly surprising. José Alvarez is right in arguing that such principles and purposes can be among the most contradictory international law has ever tried to reconcile: state sovereignty and human rights, territorial integrity and self-determination.[56] Not one single concrete example has been provided by the ICJ, or, for that matter, by the ICTY, of a SC action which could be deemed outside the realm of legality because contrary to the principles and purposes of the UN Charter, including the settlement of disputes according to principles of justice and international law. We may, however, think that an action by the SC preventing a people from exercising their right of self-determination under international law would be against the 'principles and purposes of the UN Charter'. Likewise, an action by the SC endorsing and legalising a *de facto* territorial situation resulting from a war of aggression would be also against the principles and purposes of the UN Charter. In both instances, the SC would act beyond its powers derived from the Charter, and its endorsement would not transform the previously unlawful territorial situation into a lawful territorial situation by virtue of the Council's powers under Chapter VII. In other words, some of the principles of legality considered in Chapter 4 would become relevant to the possibility of reviewing the action of the SC in territorial issues.

This raises a further important problem concerning the relation between the SC powers and international law, which has not been considered by the ICJ and the ICTY. Article 103 creates a normative hierarchy between obligations arising out of the Charter and obligations arising out of international agreements. This provision was used by the ICJ in *Lockerbie* to limit the possibility to review the

---

[56] Alvarez, 'Judging the Security Council' 90 *AJIL* (1996), 1.

action of the SC in derogation of the 1987 Montreal Convention. As another example, one can also argue that the duties of the occupying powers in Iraq under the Hague Regulations and the 1949 Geneva Convention IV, with regard to the exercise of governmental authority, were relaxed by SC Resolution 1483 in accordance with Article 103.[57] Furthermore, even if the case of conflict between obligations under the Charter and customary international law was not foreseen in Article 103, it is possible to use the general rules of interpretation on the relation between custom and treaty, and in particular the *lex specialis* principle and the *lex posterior derogat legi priori* principle, together with the doctrines of implied and inherent powers, to conclude that obligations arising out of a Chapter VII SC resolution would normally prevail over those deriving from a customary norm. Little, both in theory and in practice, supports the assertion that the SC should always act in accordance with general international law.[58]

However, the problem still remains whether *ius cogens* norms may represent a limit of international legality to the action of the SC. A positive inference can be made by extension of the UN Charter's principles and purposes.[59] In fact, the two hypothetical examples made above of breach of a right of self-determination, or endorsement of an act of aggression, would count as violations of *ius cogens* norms too. A number of writers support such limits.[60] Moreover, if the purpose of *ius cogens* norms is to protect the interests and values of the international community

---

[57] SC Res. 1483 (2003), in particular para. 4 where the SC '[c]alls upon the Authority, consistent with the Charter of the United Nations and other relevant international law, to promote the welfare of the Iraqi people through the effective administration of the territory[…].' See, however, para. 5 calling upon 'all concerned to comply fully with their obligations under international law including in particular the Geneva Conventions of 1949 and the Hague Regulations of 1907'. Bowers argues that '[i]n the case of Iraq, the main purpose of obtaining a mandate in the form of a Security Council resolution was to evade legal difficulties if the occupying powers sought to move beyond the limited rights conferred by the Hague Regulations and Geneva Convention IV to vary existing arrangements.' Bowers, *Iraq: law of occupation*, June 2003, 25, in House of Commons Research Paper 03/51. See also Kaikobad 'Problems of Belligerent Occupation: The Scope of Powers exercised by the Coalition Provisional Authority in Iraq, April/May 2003 – June 2004', 54 *ICLQ* (2005), 253, at 260-264.

[58] On this view see Orakhelashvili, 'The Impact of Peremptory Norms on the Interpretation and Application of United Nations Security Council Resolutions' 16 *EJIL* (2005), 59, at 88, and authors cited in *ibidem*, footnote 57, supporting the same view.

[59] See Judge *ad hoc* Lauterpacht in *Genocide case* who argued that SC Res. 713 of 1991 providing for an arms embargo against the whole of Yugoslavia would prevent Bosnia from defending itself against genocide, thus it should be considered null and void. *Application of the Convention on the Prevention and Punishment of the Crime of Genocide*, Order of 13 September 1993, ICJ Reports 1993, 325, at 439. See also Professor Alain Pellet statement before the ILC in A/CN/. 4/SR. 2257, 16.

[60] E.g. Franck, 'The "Powers of Appreciation": Who Is the Ultimate Guardian of UN Legality?' 86 *AJIL* (1992), 519; Graefrath, 'Leave to the Court What Belongs to the Court. The Libyan Case' 4 *EJIL* (1993) 184; Watson, 'Constitutionalism, Judicial Review, and the World Court' 34 *Harvard International Law Journal* (1993), 1.

as a whole, one wonders why those collective bodies, created with the aim of promoting and taking responsibility for the protection of such interests and values, should be allowed to derogate from them. Secondly, it cannot go unnoticed that the SC is not only an institutional world body aiming at the protection and enforcement of global interests, but it is inevitably also a negotiating forum between different sovereign states. Its action can at best represent the compromise between these sovereign states, at worst the interest of those able to impose, in some way or the other, their will upon other states. To think that such a body should be left 'unchecked' by the fundamental principles of international law is tantamount to leaving unchecked the powers of member states.[61]

Thirdly, one should certainly be wary of making sweeping characterisations of international obligations as *ius cogens* norms, in particular in the field of human rights law and international humanitarian law. On the other hand, once the characterisation is made with due caution, and the applicability of the *ius cogens* norm to the situation at hand is proved, the normative scope of the peremptory obligation should not be overly restricted to accommodate a liberal conception of the powers of the Council under Chapter VII. The same should apply to the principles and purposes of the UN Charter, and their application in the legality evaluation of Chapter VII powers. It could be argued that, if the Council endorsed an act of annexation in defiance of the right of self-determination, or a territorial situation produced by an illegal use of force, for the sake of stabilising the situation in the interest of international peace and security, the Council would not breach itself any *ius cogens* norm, but only recognise the effects of that breach by a state or group of states. The argument is not far-fetched, but it is based on a narrow definition of the obligation of the Council to discharge its function in accordance with the principles and purposes of the Charter and with *ius cogens* norms. Such narrow definition does not keep into account the quasi-constitutional role that the Council plays in international affairs. Moreover, it leads to the inevitable conclusion that the legal limitations construed in the powers of the Council would be devoid of most of their practical impact. It is, indeed, hardly conceivable that the Council may itself wage an illegal war, as any SC authorised military intervention will be, by definition, legal; it is also hardly conceivable that the Council may itself decide to annex territory to an occupying power in defiance of the right of self-determination. A broader interpretation also finds support in draft Article 12 on the responsibility of international

---

[61] On the characterisation of the SC as exercising both an executive and diplomatic function and the need for the Council to exercise its authority in accordance with the law, and the member states to implement the Council's will in accordance with the law too, see White, 'The Will and Authority of the Security Council after Iraq' 17 *LJIL* (2004), 645.

organisations provisionally adopted by the ILC in 2005: an international organisation may be held responsible for aiding or assisting a state or a group of states in the commission of an internationally wrongful act, if it did so with knowledge of the circumstances of the internationally wrongful act, and if that act would be internationally wrongful if committed by the international organisation.[62] Another problematic question concerning such recognition by the SC is that powerful states within the Council may decide to disregard their obligation of non-recognition of the effects of serious breaches of peremptory norms by using the Chapter VII powers of the SC.[63] While the special powers and prerogatives the Council enjoys are here acknowledged, international lawyers should be opposed to the idea that the Council may be used by powerful states and their allies to avoid international obligations, in particular when fundamental values of the international community are at stake.

But even if we consider such action *ultra vires*, and we limit its legal impact to a long term legitimacy effect of the sort analysed in the previous chapter,[64] we still do not solve the legal conundrum that a third state might concretely face: would state X be legally entitled to enter into legal relations with the illegal occupant, without breaching its duty of non-recognition under the law of invalidity and the law of state responsibility? The answer is not an easy one. As we have seen, a Chapter VII resolution carries with it a presumption of legality. In the absence of a determination of illegality of the resolution recognising the authority of the illegal occupant, state X may make its own assessment of the legality of the resolution, bearing in mind this presumption of legality. Should it determine that the resolution is legal, it will simply have to invoke the change of situation determined by the SC recognition or endorsement of the new territorial *status quo*; in other words, because of the legality effect of the resolution, the duty of non-recognition will no more apply. A similar scenario is represented by the situation where the SC, while avoiding the recognition or endorsement of the authority of the occupying power, would create an obligation upon member states to enter into certain dealings with the new authority: in this case, the SC resolution would derogate from the general application of the duty of non-recognition, thus state X would have to comply with it.

Should state X instead consider the resolution *ultra vires*, it may find itself in different situations, according to the content of the resolution, in particular, whether or not it creates obligations for member states. If the SC resolution does

---

[62] See ILC Third report on responsibility of international organizations (2005), Special Rapporteur Giorgio Gaja, A/CN.4/553, paras. 25-29; see also Report of the International Law Commission, Fifty-seventh session (2005), A/60/10, 96-99.
[63] For a discussion of the scope and extent of the obligation of non-recognition under the law of state responsibility see *supra* Ch. 5, section 7.
[64] See *supra* Ch. 5, section 8.

not create obligations for state X to enter into legal relations with the illegal occupant, state X may simply abstain from any form of recognition, thus complying with its duty under the law of state responsibility: no state has under general international law an obligation to enter into relations with another state, government or authority. If the SC does create obligations for state X to enter into relations with the illegal occupant – hypothetically, to provide funds for the re-organisation of the national army - state X may face a dilemma: either to abide by its Article 25 obligation under the Charter to comply with SC resolutions; or to abide by its general international law obligation of non-recognition of an illegal situation. Such legal dilemma may be solved under positive international law in favour of the duty of non-recognition, by recalling that the duty to 'agree and carry out the decision of the Security Council' is limited to decisions adopted 'in accordance with the present Charter'.[65] By reason of its *ultra vires* nature, the obligation to comply with the SC resolution would not apply in the present case.

However, one may immediately sense the dangers inherent in a practice of subjective assessments of SC resolutions; should such practice become widespread, the whole authority of the Council as the UN body exercising primary responsibility in the field of international peace and security would be at stake. On the other hand, such practice would represent more the symptom than the cause of the crisis: it may only become inevitable, as long as there is no possibility of judicial review, and as long as the Council adopts legally controversial resolutions. In the shorter term, one should not overlook the policy implications, for the state itself, of refusing to comply with a Chapter VII resolution, in particular if its refusal is isolated. This is where the legitimacy effect comes into play: notwithstanding its *ultra vires* assessment, state X may decide that it is less costly to abide by the constitutional authority of the Council, and violate its duty of non-recognition owed to the lawful sovereign.[66] In other words, we may have a situation of legitimate recognition, whose contingent legal consequence is a violation of an international obligation, and whose long term consequence may become a legalisation of effectiveness.

One further question concerning the powers of the SC, never dealt with by the ICJ, is the extent to which the Council could adopt a Chapter VII resolution to impose a binding settlement in a dispute. With regard to the present study, the question may be made even more specific, by asking ourselves whether the SC

---

[65] See on this aspect Delbrück, 'Article 25', in Simma (ed.), *The Charter of the United Nations: a Commentary* (2002), Vol. I, at 458-460.

[66] In such a scenario, the UN may be jointly held responsible for the violation by state X of the duty of non-recognition, by reason of the binding nature of the resolution and the lack of room for manoeuvre for the state. See Third Report on responsibility of international organizations (2005), *supra* n. 62, paras. 30-34.

could lawfully impose a territorial settlement, or even change an international boundary, by using its Chapter VII powers. The question is not new, but it is certainly becoming more controversial, insofar as the legislative and quasi-judicial functions of the Council become more and more evident. International legal doctrine is predominantly in favour of considering such action *ultra vires*, with possibly the exception of two authors.[67] Different reasons are brought forward to sustain this position, some more convincing than others. They include: the lack of explicit powers in the Charter;[68] the lack of implied quasi-judicial powers leading to a final determination of the rights and duties of states;[69] the lack of specific competence by the Council to impose a boundary delimitation, and the positions in that regard taken by states within the Council;[70] the violation of the principle of sovereign equality of states under Article 2(1) of the Charter that such exercise of powers would imply.[71]

It is submitted that an appropriate starting point to tackle this legal question is the *Namibia* advisory opinion on the Council's inherent powers: member states have conferred on the Council, through Article 24 of the Charter, commensurate powers to the effective performance of its task of maintaining international peace and security.[72] The only limitation is that any action should be in accordance with the principles and purposes of the United Nations found in Articles 1 and 2. The *Namibia* opinion seems to dispose of supposed limitations on the powers of the Council to determine territorial rights and duties based on the lack of explicit or implict quasi-judicial powers, and the practice of the Council in terms of legal determinations effected through its Chapter VII powers confirms this approach. As for the violation of the principle of sovereign equality under Article 2(1), it is difficult to grasp how that principle may become relevant to a territorial delimitation: any decision determining the rights and duties of states may indeed end up favouring a state in a dispute, at the detriment of the other. But that would in no way undermine the formal legal equality of the two actors, as long as they are given equality in the procedure leading to the decision.

A powerful objection is that put forward by Suy with regard to the lack of specific competence by the Council to impose a boundary delimitation, as shown by the attitude of states in the discussion leading to the adoption of SC res. 687

---

[67] Subedi, 'The Doctrine of Objective Regimes in International Law and the Competence of the United Nations to Impose Territorial or Peace Settlements on States' 37 *GYIL* (1994), 162, at 205; Matheson, 'United Nations Governance of Postconflict Societies' 95 *AJIL* (2001), 76, at 85.

[68] Bowett, 'The Impact of Security Council Decisions on Dispute Settlement Procedures' 5 *EJIL* (1994), 89, at 96.

[69] Frowein, Krisch, 'Ch. VII: Introduction', in Simma, *supra* n. 65, at 708.

[70] Suy, 'Le Conseil de Sécurité et la frontiere entre l'Iraq et le Koweit', in Rama-Montaldo (ed.), *El derecho internacional en un mundo en transformacion* (1994), 441, at 443-448.

[71] Wet, de, *The Chapter VII Powers of the United Nations Security Council* (2004), 365-366.

[72] *Supra* section 2.1.1.

and the creation of the United Nations Iraq-Kuwait Boundary Commission.[73] As a matter of fact, countries as diverse as the US, Cuba, India, Yemen, the UK, China expressed their opposition to the idea that the Council might use its Chapter VII powers to decide a new international boundary between Iraq and Kuwait.[74] The evidence of the existence of a widespread *opinio iuris* in this sense appears significant. On the other hand, one should consider those statements with particular attention. India stated that it 'will never support any decision whereby the Council would impose *arbitrarily* a boundary line between two countries. Boundaries are an extremely sensitive issue and must be settled by the countries freely in the exercise of their sovereignty' (emphasis added). The US stated that it 'does not seek, nor will it support, a new role for the SC as the body that determines international boundaries. Border disputes are issues to be negotiated directly between States or resolved through other pacific means of settlement available, as set out in Chapter VI of the Charter.' The UK stated that it had 'no desire and no intention of overturning the principle that it is for the parties in question to negotiate and reach agreement […].' China stated it 'did not favour United Nations involvement in any form in a boundary dispute.'[75] One can certainly infer from these statements the following propositions. The Council should not play a role in delimiting international boundaries, as boundary delimitation should be left to the agreement of states. The Council should not arbitrarily impose a boundary line between two countries. What, however, cannot be incontrovertibly inferred is the expression of an *opinio iuris*, to the effect that such action would be always *ultra vires*, even in exceptional cases in which the continuation of the boundary dispute is endangering international peace and security, and there is no room left for a peaceful solution between the two states.

There are indeed some arguments to support the contrary. The exercise of such powers would not run contrary to the theory of inherent powers elaborated by the Court in *Namibia*. The Council would be legally bound to comply with the principles and purpose of the UN set out in Articles 1 and 2 of the Charter. In particular, the Council would have to impose a settlement of the territorial dispute 'in conformity with principles of justice and international law' (Article 1).[76] In this latter respect, any territorial settlement manifestly favouring one of the parties in the dispute, both in the outcome, and in the procedure leading to the decision, or breaching fundamental human rights of the populations affected by the territorial change, or the right of self-determination of an affected people,

---

[73] SC Res. 687 (1991). On the UNBDC's creation and functioning see *infra* section 3.
[74] See Suy, *supra* n. 70.
[75] Statements cit. in *ibidem*, 444-445.
[76] Frowein, Krisch, *supra* n. 69, 712.

could be indeed considered *ultra vires*. However, the principle of territorial integrity does not represent a *ius cogens* norm.[77] States normally dispose of territorial rights by agreement, and the SC occasionally does it too, with regard to the exercise of territorial sovereignty by states, by using its Chapter VII powers.[78] The exercise of boundary delimitation should be exceptional; such power should be used only when the dispute threatens to escalate in a breach of the peace, and there is no room left for agreement between the parties. After all, there is little sense in arguing that the Council would have no legal power to impose an international boundary in the exercise of its primary responsibility in the field of international peace and security, even when the delimitation of the boundary may prevent an international armed conflict between the two states, or even only contain its effects. One last point in this regard is that the Council should indicate in the resolution the possibility for the parties to change the boundary by agreement, to avoid a subsequent normative conflict between the SC resolution and a future treaty of boundary delimitation.

A final major gap in the case law of the ICJ and the ICTY seen above is the failure to spell out what would be the legal effects of a finding of illegality of a SC resolution. This casts many difficulties, since, according to the realist view, such niceties as the difference between absolute nullity and voidability can only arise in developed legal systems, where there is a whole machinery of judicial review of private and governmental acts. However, the 'incidental' jurisdiction of the ICJ and its 'inherent' powers could give it the opportunity in the future to pronounce on that; equally, where SC resolution impinge on the rights of individuals or corporations, domestic or regional courts may find jurisdiction and judge upon the legality of a resolution. In the *IMCO* case, the ICJ interpreted in a rather restrictive way its role of 'legal advisor', and it only declared that the Maritime Safety Committee of IMCO was not constituted in accordance with the Convention, which established the Organisation. It did not specify what could be the legal consequences of that finding.[79] The issue was only cursorily dealt with by Judge Sidhwa in his separate opinion in the *Tadic* Trial Chamber's decision, where he stated that, were the Tribunal to find any illegality in its own establishment, it may make 'a simple declaration to that effect and leave it to the SC to correct the situation, or having made such a declaration, continue as an ad-hoc tribunal till the said body or Organisation comes to its aid.'[80] In case of UN endorsed or administered unlawful territorial situations, Judge Sidhwa suggestion may be translated into a duty by the SC to correct the situation with a

---

[77] *Supra* Ch. 4, section 5.
[78] See the case of Kosovo, *infra* section 4.
[79] *Constitution of the Maritime Safety Committee of the Inter-Governmental Maritime Consultative Organization*, Advisory Opinion, ICJ Reports 1960, 150.
[80] *Tadic, supra* n. 46, Sep. Op. Judge Sidhwa, 555.

new action under Chapter VII. At a further conceptual level, territorial action by the SC in defiance of its powers may represent an internationally wrongful act, and to that extent entail the international responsibility of the UN as such. This may result in a claim by the victim state or states against the UN for restitution or reparation. At a practical level, to the difficulties associated with a claim for state responsibility related to unlawful territorial situations, one should add the procedural difficulties inherent in such a claim in particular with regard to the forum competent to adjudicate the dispute.[81]

To conclude, Professor Seyersted's view of international organisation, worked out in 1966, as having full international legal personality and as being entitled to exercise whatever functions and powers are within the aim and scope of the organisation and are not expressly prohibited by its constitution, has been accepted consistently in the jurisprudence of the ICJ and by the ICTY.[82] This gives strong support to those who argue that international organisations are 'sovereign' entities, like states, with the only difference represented by the limitation of their capacity to their scope. This analysis is possibly undermined by the very fact that international organisations derive their functions and powers from an international legal instrument, whereas the attribute of sovereignty is commonly associated with the very nature of the state. However, states also do have a constitution which can limit their freedom of actions in international relations,[83] and the scope and purpose of the SC's actions has been broadened to include direct territorial administrations such as in Kosovo and East Timor, which is usually considered one of the prerogatives *par excellence* of sovereign states. In this latter respect, paradoxically, principles of international legality appear to apply to a more limited extent than they do for states. The concept of effectiveness shows in this specific respect its ambivalent nature: by stressing the need for the *efficacy* of their action, multilateral bodies can often overcome the limits imposed by international law upon states. To claim that the SC is a political body and its driving force is effectiveness rather than legality is undoubtedly true, but it begs the question of the legal limitations to the exercise of this power. Once more, that raises the issue of how these multilateral bodies such as the UN can be 'used' by the states to circumvent those legal norms and boost their effective power in the international arena.

---

[81] On the issue of responsibility of international organisations for the commission of internationally wrongful acts see First report on the responsibility of international organizations (2003), Special Rapporteur Giorgio Gaja, A/CN.4/532; Second report on the responsibility of international organizations (2004), Special Rapporteur Giorgio Gaja, A/CN.4/541; Third report, *supra* n. 62; Report of the International Law Commission (2005), *supra* n. 61, 73-105.

[82] Seyersted, *United Nations Forces in Law of Peace and War* (1966).

[83] E.g. Article 11 of the Italian Constitution. See Cassese, 'Wars Forbidden and Wars Allowed by the Italian Constitution', in *Studi in onore di Giorgio Balladore Pallieri* (1978), Vol. II, 131.

Failing legality to often represent a significant limit, one seems to rest with the unpleasant option of dealing with international political crises around the world with the three likely alternatives: bully unilateralism, bully UN multilateralism, inaction.[84] Excluding the first and the third option for the scope of this chapter, it is submitted that the principle of effectiveness can be retained without making UN multilateralism 'bully' by addressing the question of legitimacy of UN actions. The next section will revolve around the concept of legitimacy within the law, as defined in the previous chapter for the purpose of elaborating further than the simple divide lawfulness/unlawfulness of SC endorsed or administered territorial situations.

3. Illegitimacy within the law: substantive and procedural illegitimacy in SC actions

Questions of substantive and procedural illegitimacy in the way the SC acts may arise in many respects. One could assert that SC powers are in principle unlimited *ratione materiae*, as long as they are deemed to address a threat to peace and security. The reserved domain clause set out in Article 2(7) of the Charter does not apply to enforcement measures under Chapter VII. One could possibly argue that enforcement measures are not the only kind of measures envisaged under Chapter VII, however, the possibility to distinguish such measures from 'preventive' measures is not always feasible, given the all-encompassing nature of practice of the SC.[85] So, for instance, the activism of the SC in the last decade has engaged this organ with territorial settlements and endorsement of territorial status. Commentators have questioned the legality and legitimacy of these actions. The two terms have been often confused. It has been here submitted that the legality of these actions can most of the times hardly be questioned, however the application of principles of substantive and procedural legitimacy makes the issue more problematic. Whereas legality only requires SC actions to be consistent with the principles and purposes of the UN Charter and not in violation of *ius cogens* norms, a legitimacy test requires the SC to justify its actions in terms of preference of certain principles and purposes and values of the Charter rather than others. Whereas, a legality test does not require the SC to prove that a certain action was necessary to promote certain values sacrificing others, a legitimacy test would require the SC to justify the necessity and proportionality of a certain action, if certain values of the Charter have to be

---

[84] See Chinkin, 'The State that Acts Alone: Bully, Good, Samaritan or Iconoclast?' 11 *EJIL* (2000), 31.
[85] See Kirgis, 'Security Council Governance of Postconflict Societies: A Plea for Good Faith and Informed Decision Making' 95 *AJIL* (2002), 579, at 580.

sacrificed.[86] The analysis of some important cases can highlight the relevance of this distinction.

One example is SC Resolution 687, which put a formal end to the hostilities between Iraq and the alliance of states which rescued Kuwait from Iraqi's aggression. *Inter alia* SC Resolution 687 demanded Iraq to respect the boundary established by a 1963 agreement signed by both Iraq and Kuwait and later challenged by Baghdad, and created a UN Boundary Demarcation Commission (UNBDC) entrusted with the task of marking the existing frontier.[87] As is cogently argued elsewhere, this agreement had been validly subscribed to by Iraq, and its later challenge to it lacked a sound legal basis.[88] The SC, aware of the continuing threat to peace and security that the Iraq-Kuwait frontier dispute represented, decided to act as a quasi-judicial body by endorsing a legal instrument defining the frontier and proceeding to demarcate the boundary, in order to practically ensure the inviolability of this frontier.

The resolution was adopted by 12 votes in favour, one contrary (Cuba) and two abstaining (Ecuador, Yemen). During the discussion which led to the adoption of the resolution, concerns of legitimacy of the SC's action were raised by the Iraqi, the Cuban and the Yemenite representatives. They questioned the substantive legitimacy of Resolution 687 on its boundary settlement as being in contradiction with previous Resolution 660, which had called upon Iraq and Kuwait to settle the dispute by negotiations and peaceful means.[89] To impose a solution under duress and to sacrifice the principle of sovereignty of one of the parties to the dispute would be contrary to the principles and purpose of the UN Charter. The Indian representative took the same theoretical approach, however in practice it held that such illegitimacy was cured by the fact that the SC had endorsed an agreement which was already in force.[90] Questions of selectivity were also raised by the Cuban representative. Despite these objections Iraq formally accepted Resolution 687 and its boundary settlement a few days after the adoption of the resolution.[91]

It is here submitted that Resolution 687 was in principle legitimate, since the SC was entitled to make a choice between the principle of state sovereignty and the guarantee of peace and security in the region, which a final demarcation

---

[86] For the application of a legitimacy test to four recent questions concerning the SC Ch. VII powers see Frowein, 'Issues of Legitimacy around the United Nations Security Council' in Frowein (ed.), *Verhandeln für den Frieden: Liber Amicorum Tono Eitel*, 2003, 121.

[87] SC Res. 687 (1998), para. 2.

[88] Mendelson, Hulton, 'La Revendication par l'Iraq de la souveraineté sur le Koweit' 36 *Annuaire Français de Droit International* (1990), 195.

[89] S/PV.2981, Statement of Iraq 32, Statement of Yemen 41, Statement of Cuba 61.

[90] *Ibidem*, Statement of India 77-78.

[91] S/22453, 5 April 1991; S/22456, 6 April 1991.

would bring about. Further, the change of policy since Resolution 660 was justified by Iraqi reluctance to reach an agreement by peaceful means, as proved by the invasion of August 1990. Iraq's consent may well have been superfluous and, despite the fact that Article 52 VCLT did not apply as a result of the duress being imposed against an aggressor state according to Article 75 VCLT and, as a consequence of that, Resolution 687 could not be claimed to be invalid, such consent did not add further legitimacy to the action of the SC.

What, however, would make such legitimacy controversial is the lack of clarity and transparency in what the SC was doing. Apparently, the SC was solely reaffirming an already existing delimitation and the scope of the SC's action would be to 're-start' from such a legal basis and proceed to demarcation. However, the problem exactly lay in the solution the SC provided and the SC could not have ignored that. Indeed, the 1963 Agreement[92] recalled and endorsed an exchange of letters dating back to 1932 between the Iraqi government and the British Ruler of Kuwait.[93] Such agreement recalled in its turn an exchange of letters of 1923 between the British mandatory authorities in Iraq and the Ruler of Kuwait, such exchange of letters providing for a somewhat imprecise definition of the boundary.[94] Despite the attempt by the British authorities to clarify these imprecisions in 1940 and 1951, Iraq never agreed to them, and the 1963 Agreement also did not provide for a solution. All in all, it was clear that the UNBDC would not be engaged solely with demarcation, but part of its task would be to delimit the boundary. Such reality became even more clear during and after the works of the UNBDC.[95] One can definitely conclude that much of the result reached by the UNBDC and endorsed by SC Resolution 833 was corresponding to the British claims of 1940 and 1951, which, however, were never accepted by Iraq. Despite statements to the contrary in SC Resolution 773 and 833 and by the President of the SC, the SC re-apportioned territory in the North Sector in favour of Kuwait, which contained important oil wells exploited for years by Iraq, and parts of the Umm Qasr port complex too. This casts serious doubts on the transparency and good faith of the SC action under Chapter VII. Despite having the legal power to effect a delimitation similarly to a boundary determination carried out by a judicial body,[96] it did not spell out clearly what it was actually doing in order to not convey the impression that it

---

[92] Agreed Minutes between the State of Kuwait and the Republic of Iraq Regarding the Restoration of Friendly Relations, Recognition, and Related Matters, 4 October 1964, 485 UNTS 321.
[93] The document can be found in Lauterpacht, Greenwood, Weller and Bethlehem (eds.), *The Kuwait Crisis, Basic Documents* (1991), Vol. I, 49-50.
[94] *Ibidem.*
[95] Mendelson, Hulton, 'The Iraq-Kuwait Boundary' 64 *BYIL* (1993), 135.
[96] See *supra* section 2.2.

was, for the very first time, dealing with the most sacred idol of states' sovereignty, that is territory. Had it spelled out clearly what was the task of the UNBDC, it should have justified more thoroughly why it was necessary for the maintenance of peace and security in the region to change the pre-invasion *de facto* boundary line between Iraq and Kuwait, and the reason why it was adopting an interpretation of treaty instruments, which was mostly coincident with that always rejected by Iraq. This might have been a more difficult task, yet it does not excuse the way the SC acted and, above all, it can hardly fill a gap of legitimacy that characterised the action of the SC.

The issue of good faith with respect to Resolution 687 recalls a wider problem of good faith in the way the SC ascertains 'a threat to peace and security' under Article 39. In its creative interpretation of its powers under Chapter VII, the SC has declared to represent 'a threat to peace and security' not only classic inter-state armed conflicts, but also internal upheavals,[97] legal disputes about extradition,[98] gross violations of human rights[99], post-conflict situations,[100] humanitarian crises.[101] As Kirgis rightly states 'Article 39 calls on the Council to make a *determination*, not just a recitation.'[102] In some instances, it is self-evident that a certain situation represents a threat to peace and security, such as in the case of the Iraqi invasion of Kuwait. In others, however, it is highly questionable whether the Council was acting in good faith, or was rather being bended to accommodate the national interests of powerful member states, without the existence of a genuine threat or breach of international peace and security. Many legitimate doubts can be expressed whether a legal dispute over extradition like in Lockerbie was a threat to peace and security four years after the criminal act and two weeks before the ICJ was to pronounce on a request by Libya for *interim* measures protecting Libya's rights under the Montreal Convention. Also, it is questionable whether the US decision not to extend the mandate of its own peace-keeping forces in the Balkans, unless covered by absolute immunity from the jurisdiction of the ICC, was indeed a threat to peace and security under Article 39 justifying an action under Chapter VII.[103] Another example is the adoption of SC Res. 1559, where the presence of Syrian troops and intelligence in Lebanese territory, and fears of influence by Damascus over the regular holding of elections was truly the core of the dispute between, the US and France,

---

[97] SC Res. 1199 (1999) on Kosovo.
[98] SC Res. 748 (1992) on the *Lockerbie* affair.
[99] SC Res. 217 (1965) on Southern Rhodesia.
[100] SC Res. 1031 (1995) on Bosnia and Herzegovina.
[101] SC Res. 794 (1992) on Somalia.
[102] Kirgis, *supra* n. 85, 580.
[103] SC Res. 1422 (2002). See comment in Stahn, 'The Ambiguities of SC Res. 1422 (2002)' 14 *EJIL* (2003), 85.

on the one hand, and Syria, on the other, but could hardly be seen, at that point in time, as a threat to international peace and security.[104]

As proposed by Kirgis, in such cases the SC could make use of Article 28 of its Provisional Rules of Procedure, which allows it to 'appoint a commission or committee or a rapporteur for a specified question.'[105] Such group of experts could both investigate the situation on the ground, thus really determining whether such situation amounts to a threat to peace and security, and, if such determination occurs, consider the best course of action. The reality is that more and more often the decisions of the SC under Chapter VII are just reactive, rather than pro-active, if not just an endorsement of actions taken by a concert of powers. The good faith requirement is therefore often ignored, leaving aside all too easily a fundamental legal principle. This may cast an important doubt over the legitimacy of such SC actions and, more importantly, of the legitimacy of the SC as the authority entrusted in the international community with the maintenance of peace and security. Further, the rationale of decisions is hardly mentioned in the preamble of the resolutions, and even the minutes of meetings often do not represent any satisfactory guidance in this respect. For example, the policy of sanctions towards Iraq left for years a big question mark on the legitimacy of the choice for a strict regime of sanctions giving preference to a concern for peace and security in the region over the need to guarantee basic human rights to the local populations.[106]

The question of good faith and of justification of decision-making recalls another significant legitimacy gap of some SC actions. Such a gap relates to procedural guarantees in favour of interested parties, in particular when the Council engages in a quasi-adjudicative function. Procedural unfairness may eventually make the whole decision illegitimate and *ultra vires*.[107] One simple principle is that, if the Council is to decide upon a dispute between two or more parties, procedural fairness would require both parties to be given the opportunity to be heard. Such requirement is usually complied with by the SC. For example, during the work of the UNBDC, such principle was generally applied, and it was Iraq's own choice often not to provide the commission with its views. However, more specifically, a problem of procedural fairness arose with respect to an on-site visit to a part of the boundary, of which allegedly only the Kuwait's expert was informed in due time.[108]

---

[104] SC Res. 1559 (2004). See S/PV.5028 and critical positions over the adoption of the resolution held by Russia, China, Pakistan, Algeria, Brazil and the Philippines.

[105] *Supra* n. 85, 581.

[106] E.g. articles on the issue of sanctions by Craven *et al.*, in the Symposium 'The Impact on International Law of a Decade of Measures on Iraq', 13 *EJIL* (2002), 43.

[107] See *supra* section 2.2.

[108] Mendelson, Hulton, *supra* n. 88, 154.

A more significant problem of procedural fairness is related to the particular role that the SC may play in a particular dispute. If, as in Lockerbie, the SC limits itself to endorsing decisions taken unilaterally elsewhere, it goes without saying that formal procedural guarantees do not protect adequately the position of interested parties. Professor Graefrath raises this point with reference to the adoption of Resolution 731:

> 'This kind of procedure, if applied by any court to an individual, would raise an allegation that the right to fair trial had been breached. However, the procedural rules of the Security Council, a political organ which "shall act in accordance with the Purposes and Principles of the United Nations" (Article 24(2) of the Charter), do not contain any procedural safeguards which a State would automatically enjoy if involved in Court proceedings.'[109]

Despite the well-established practice of both national and international bodies that the decision-making process can be influenced and determined in the course of informal meetings, the fact that the SC limits itself to endorsing such decisions, and the fact that it does not make any efforts to protect the interests of one of the parties to the dispute, may well be not only beyond the principles of legality enshrined in the Charter, but also cast serious problems of procedural fairness, hence of the legitimacy of the decision itself.

3.1 Problems of selectivity and 'ad-hocism' of SC actions

Dworkin and Franck have pointed out that a norm or a certain legal code of conduct is legitimate when it is applied coherently, in other words when like cases are treated alike.[110] The failure to apply norms in a consistent way makes the law selective. A certain action may not be necessarily illegal, but certainly illegitimate, if such selectivity is not justified by reference to another, general or specific, overriding principle of the international legal system. Selectivity can certainly prevent the creation of a customary norm, and, when occurring after its creation, it can slowly lead to the desuetude of a customary norm. As such, selectivity can also affect the legality of a certain behaviour. As to treaty norms, these do not derive their validity from a consistent state practice and *opinio iuris*, but from a validly expressed consent. Once entered into force treaty norms are valid, even if applied incoherently. However, if they are applied selectively and such selectivity is not justified by recourse to other legal principles, international actors will perceive them as illegitimate.

One example of a claim of selectivity is the one advanced by Cuba in the discussion related to the Iraqi-Kuwait boundary leading to the adoption of Resolution 687. Cuba argued that the SC's policy was selectively defined in that

---

[109] Graefrath, *supra* n. 60, 191.
[110] Dworkin, *Law's Empire* (1986); Franck, *Fairness in International Law and Institutions* (1995), 38-41.

it considered such a territorial dispute as a threat to peace and security in the region justifying a binding decision under Chapter VII; yet in similar regional cases such as the Israeli occupation of the Golan Heights and the Palestinian territories, the SC had kept a low profile, without taking any measures under Chapter VII.[111] As seen, it was in the legal competence of the SC to decide those measures under Resolution 687, yet the fact that in similar cases, such as the Middle East, no action was taken, makes any justification invoking the need to protect regional peace and security less legitimate. This raises a broader problem of legitimacy concerning the veto power of permanent members of the SC, which still remains untouched after 60 years since the end of World War II and after a series of dramatic changes in the state of international relations. This problem is strictly speaking procedural, but it obviously entails a substantive dimension as the veto-power always prevents any action against a direct interest of the permanent members.[112]

The question of selectivity is also connected to a broader problem of legitimacy of the way the SC has recently acted. This problem has been called by Bianchi 'ad-hocism'.[113] It is here shared the view of that writer, that the lack of development of general principles and standards of conduct, not to talk about the lack of reference to international legal principles, and a pragmatic approach based on ad-hoc solutions to 'exceptional' circumstances have led the SC to lose the Post-Cold War momentum. The SC, far from becoming a genuine guarantor of world peace and security, has invested major resources in trying to avoid being marginalised by the unilateral action of the only Super-Power, the US, and not to be condemned in a new era to the inaction of Cold War. The US and those countries supporting it in specific situations have been very cautious in allowing the development of invocation of internal normative standards, aware of the fact that such normative standards could one day backfire on them. This has resulted in the SC being perceived as mostly guarantor and endorser of their interests and creating a gap of legitimacy not only in the way it deals with specific actions, such as the regimes of sanctions against Iraq and Libya, or the creation of UN territorial administrations in Europe, but more in general as an institution itself. Further, as argued by Bianchi, the lack of internal normative standards has made

---

[111] S/PV. 2981, Statement of Cuba 61.

[112] E.g. Winkelmann, 'Bringing the Security Council into a New Era: Recent Developments in the Discussion on the Reform of the Security Council' 1 *Max Planck Yearbook of United Nations Law* (1997), 35. Despite the recent discussion leading to the 2005 World Summit and the definition of two models for reform in the 2005 Secretary-General's Report 'In Larger Freedom' (A/59/2005, paras. 167-170), no consensus has been reached so far. The final document adopted by the Heads of States and Government on 15 September 2005, albeit reiterating support for the Council's reform, does not deal substantively with the issue (2005 World Summit Outcome, A/60/L.1).

[113] Bianchi, '*Ad-hocism* and the Rule of Law' 13 *EJIL* (2002), 263.

impossible the development of a framework of accountability of the SC and states involved in its decision-making.[114] Lack of accountability also leads to the perceived illegitimacy of the SC and its actions. More in general, illegitimacy of the SC and illegitimacy of its actions may have the disturbing outcome of rendering any genuinely multilateral framework of co-operation ineffective, and measures being complied with thanks to the stick of the Prince, rather than the awareness and consensus of its members. There is little doubt that a system of that kind may not be sustainable in the long run.

4. The territorial status of Kosovo: legitimacy outside of the law?

As an example of UN-led territorial administration it is worth considering the case of Kosovo. Kosovo, a province within the Union of Serbia and Montenegro (until recently Federal Republic of Yugoslavia), has been placed since 1999 under the authority of the SC and directly administered by a UN civil presence under the leadership of the Secretary General Special Representative for Kosovo (hereinafter SGSR).[115] Kosovo is particularly interesting in order to show how a framework of UN territorial unlawfulness can be defined with regard to a specific situation. The case of Kosovo also encapsulates the two main models of exercise of UN territorial authority seen above. On the one hand, the UN exercise their territorial competence by endorsing the establishment of a NATO-led security presence in the province through the powers of the SC under Chapter VII. On the other hand, the UN, through a Chapter VII authorisation by the SC, directly administer the province. Both models can be reviewed through the legality and legitimacy framework developed above, which clearly shows how the problems faced by each of the two models in terms of international legality and legitimacy are peculiar and distinct; at the same time, the example of Kosovo shows the inter-action of effectiveness and legitimacy in bypassing positive legality and 'curing' unlawful territorial situations. This section will first review the legality of Kosovo's territorial situation as of today, and it will then consider the question of

---

[114] *Ibidem*, 270.

[115] The FRY has changed in 2003 its constitutional structure to a looser form of federation and its official name is now Union of Serbia and Montenegro (*hereinafter* USM). Articles 14, 59 and 60 of the new constitution adopted on 4 February 2003 imply the continuation in the USM of the international legal personality of the FRY. See The Constitutional Charter of Serbia and Montenegro, in <http://www.mfa.gov.yu/Facts/charter_e1.html>. When referring to events prior to the entry into force of the new constitution, I will continue using the acronym FRY, when referring to subsequent events, I will use the acronym USM .

sovereignty over the province in the light of 2001 Delineation Treaty dispute and the policy adopted in that respect by the SGSR.

4.1 The events leading to the international administration of Kosovo

Kosovo had been since 1974 a province of Serbia within the Socialist Federal Republic of Yugoslavia (SFRY) constitutional framework.[116] The 1974 constitution endowed Kosovo with a substantial autonomy, in view of the distinctive ethnic composition represented by a majority of ethnic Albanians. After Milosevic took power in Serbia in 1989, the degree of autonomy granted by Belgrade to Kosovo was substantively reduced, and the participation of ethnic Albanians in public office was actively discouraged. In response, Kosovo Albanian leaders withdrew from all public institutions, created parallel administrative structures and on 19 October 1991 declared Kosovo a sovereign and independent state. Kosovo's statehood was not recognised by any state and, apart from the parallel administrative structures, it did not fulfil the effective control test set out by the Montevideo Convention. The second part of the 1990s saw, on the one hand, the pursuit by most ethnic Albanians of a policy of civil and peaceful disobedience, and, on the other, also the uprising of different local armed groups under the banner of the Kosovo Liberation Army (KLA).[117] In the course of 1997 and 1998, the level of violence was intensified by the KLA with attacks on both military and civilian targets, which led to increasing reaction by the Yugoslav security forces. This also led to an increasing number of refugees and internally displaced persons.

The first definition by the SC of the Kosovo internal conflict as a threat to international peace and security dates back to the beginning of 1998, when, on 31 March, it adopted Resolution 1160, which condemned 'the use of excessive force by Serbian police forces against civilians and peaceful demonstrators in Kosovo, as well as acts of terrorism by the KLA'[118]. Acting under Chapter VII, the SC imposed an arms embargo on the FRY.[119] On 23 September the SC through Resolution 1199 again became seized of the matter, and it called for a cease-fire. The cease-fire was agreed three weeks later. Under the terms of the agreements struck thanks to the mediation of the US envoy Richard Holbrooke, the number of Yugoslav troops in Kosovo was significantly reduced by Belgrade, at the same time allowing 2,000 unarmed OSCE verifiers to step in, in order to oversee compliance with the cease-fire agreement and the establishment of an air

---

[116] 1974 SFRY Constitution, Article 1.
[117] For an historical account of the events of the 1990s in Kosovo which led to the crisis see Malcolm, *Kosovo: a Short History* (1998).
[118] SC Res. 1160 (1998), para. 2.
[119] *Ibidem*, para. 8.

verification mission over Kosovo by NATO forces.[120] Such agreements were endorsed by the SC through Resolution 1203, which was also adopted under Chapter VII. Despite a short standstill in armed activities, by the end of December violations of the cease-fire by the KLA started to intensify once again, leading to initial proportionate responses by Yugoslav forces,[121] but a few weeks later to the massacre of 45 civilians in the village of Racak.[122]

This sparked the diplomatic reaction of NATO countries which led, under the threat of air strikes, to an international peace conference in Rambouillet, France, at the beginning of February 1999. The negotiations lasted for one month and revolved around a draft agreement proposed by the Western members of the Contact Group, under the name of Rambouillet Agreements, providing for an interim substantial autonomy for Kosovo, the possibility of a referendum in three years for full independence from Belgrade, the withdrawal from Kosovo of all Yugoslav security forces and the establishment of an international security force led by NATO. The deal was accepted by the Kosovo leaders, but refused by Belgrade.[123] On 24 March 1999, NATO started an aerial bombing campaign on the FRY, immediately followed by a retaliatory offensive of Yugoslav forces against the Albanian population in Kosovo. The campaign continued until 9 June 1999, when the FRY accepted at Kumanovo the withdrawal of any security presence from Kosovo and the deployment of a NATO-led military force.[124] The following day the SC adopted SC Resolution 1244 (hereinafter 1244) under Chapter VII, which endorsed the Kumanovo Agreement and the Agreement on Political Principles of 3 June 1999, between the FRY, and the EU and Russian envoys, Martii Ahtisaari and Victor Tchernomyrdine. The resolution decided the establishment of a UN civil administration, in charge of governing over Kosovo with a view to implementing self-administration of the province and to facilitating a political process designed to determine Kosovo's future status.[125] No mention

---

[120] Agreement on the OSCE Kosovo Verification Mission, 16 October 1998, S/1998/278; KVM Agreement Between NATO and the FRY, 15 October 1998, S/1998/991.

[121] OSCE, KVM, Press Release n. 08/99, 9 January 1999.

[122] Independent International Commission on Kosovo, *The Kosovo Report: Conflict, International Responses, Lessons Learned* (2000).

[123] For an account of the Rambouillet Conference see Weller, 'The Rambouillet Conference on Kosovo', 75 *International Affairs* (1999), 211; Decaux, 'La Conférence de Rambouillet: Négociation de la dernière chance ou contrainte illicite', in Tomuschat, *supra* n. 5, 45. See also letter of FRY to the SC of 1 February 1999 (S/1999/107) condemning the practice of NATO to seek a political solution under military threat.

[124] Military-technical Agreement between the International Security Force (KFOR) and the Governments of the Federal Republic of Yugoslavia and the Republic of Serbia, signed in Kumanovo, FYROM, 9 June 1999 (usually referred to as 'Kumanovo Agreement'), in 38 *ILM* (1999), 1217.

[125] SC Res. 1244 (1999), paras. 6, 10-11.

was made in 1244 of any deadline for such a determination. Ultimate authority was vested with the UN administration (UNMIK) for a transitional but indefinite period.[126] This was confirmed by the very first regulation of the Secretary-General Special Representative (SGSR), who assumed all executive and legislative powers within Kosovo, the right to appoint judges and civil servants and to remove them from their position, and asserted his authority to administer all funds and properties of the FRY within Kosovo.[127] Since then, Kosovo has been an internationalised territory.[128]

4.2 1244 and its underlying agreements: the application of coercion as invalidating ground of the Kumanovo Agreement

4.2.1 The legal basis of the international presence in Kosovo

The legal basis of the involvement of the international community in Kosovo is more complex than normally claimed. Reading through UNMIK documents and SC resolutions, one may first get the idea that UNMIK and KFOR authority under international law is provided by 1244, adding to the perceived legality and legitimacy of Kosovo's territorial administration. However, an in-depth analysis of the events which led to the end of NATO's campaign and a contextual reading of 1244 tend to muddy the seemingly transparent waters of UN legality and legitimacy. As a starting point, a contextual reading of 1244 in relation to the other legal instruments recalled in its operative part is necessary.

As in previous resolutions concerning Kosovo, 1244 starts in the preamble by recalling the humanitarian tragedy taking place in Kosovo and the need to comply with all previous SC resolutions; it reaffirms the sovereignty and territorial integrity of the FRY; and it condemns all acts of violence against the Kosovo population and all terrorist activities. The first important element of the resolution is also in the preamble and it states:

'Welcoming the general principles on a political solution to the Kosovo crisis adopted on 6 May 1999 (S/1999/516, annex 1 to this resolution) and welcoming also the acceptance by the Federal Republic of Yugoslavia of the principles set forth in points 1 to 9 of the paper

---

[126] *Ibidem*, para. 19.

[127] UNMIK/REG/1999/1, UNMIK Official Gazette, 25 June 1999.

[128] The definition of Kosovo as an internationalised territory can be drawn from an analogy with past regimes such as the Free City of Danzig, the Free Territory of Trieste (this latter was never implemented), and contemporary arrangements such as Bosnia and Herzegovina and East Timor. Such definition can be applied to those territorial arrangements where international organisations exercise full or partial jurisdiction in respect to the legislative, executive or judicial functions. See Marazzi, *I territori internazionalizzati* (1959); Ydit, *Internationalised Territories* (1961); Beck, *Die Internationalisierung von Territorien* (1962); more recently Wilde, *supra* n. 1, 583.

presented in Belgrade on 2 June 1999 (S/1999/649, annex 2 to this resolution), and the Federal Republic of Yugoslavia's agreement to that paper'.

These two instruments are then recalled in operative paragraph 2, where the SC, after invoking Chapter VII, decides that a political solution will be based on these two agreements. As also indicated in the same paragraph, the first instrument was a unilateral statement adopted by the G-8 Foreign Ministers conference on May 6, enunciating those political principles which were then elaborated in detail in the second agreement, the 3rd of June Agreement. Its repetition in the resolution as Annex 1 does not play any self-evident function, since that statement was only a broad unilateral political basis for the accord of June 3. Such role may well be the one of reiterating the novel authority of the G-8 as a body competent for the maintenance of international peace and security, given that the draft resolution was the result of political negotiations within the G-8 in June, or providing a basis for a more conciliatory approach by the SC towards Yugoslavia, thus accommodating Russian and Chinese demands. However, this is only speculation, since no mention is to be found of this in the discussion leading to the adoption of 1244.

As to the 3rd of June agreement, this was a more significant instrument both from a formal and a substantive point of view. From a formal point of view it can be seen as an agreement binding upon Yugoslavia. This is the way at least the FRY considered it, given that it went through the normal process of ratification of treaty by the Serbian Assembly.[129] Further, it may have served the important purpose of giving a consensual basis to a resolution, whose legal effects upon the FRY could have been found to be controversial, given the uncertainty surrounding the FRY status at the UN at that time.[130] From a substantive point of view the 3rd of June Agreement provided for the establishment of a UN civil presence entrusted with the task of providing 'a transitional administration while establishing and overseeing the development of provisional democratic self-governing institutions.'[131] Such civil presence may act under Chapter VII of the Charter in the manner decided by the SC.[132] Indeed, this legal basis for the UN

---

[129] On the events within FRY leading to the ratification of the 3rd of June agreement see Mijatovic, 'A Hard Loss to Spin', Report on the Balkans' crisis, 5 June 1999, Institute for War and Peace Reporting.

[130] See the ICJ decision of 3 February 2003 on the FRY request for a review of the Court's decision on jurisdiction in the case on genocide between Bosnia and Herzegovina and the FRY (*Case Concerning Application of the Convention on the Prevention and Punishment of the Crime of Genocide*, ICJ Reports 1996, 595) in accordance with Article 61(1) of the Statute (*Application for the Revision of the Judgement of 11 July 1996*, in <http://www.icj-cij.org/idocket/iybh/iybhframe.htm>). See also commentary by Craven, 'The *Bosnia* Case Revisited and the 'New' Yugoslavia', 15 *LJIL* (2002), 323.

[131] 3rd of June Agreement, UN Doc. S/1999/649, para. 5.

[132] *Ibidem*, para. 2.

civil authority over Kosovo was superseded by 1244. The referral in its preamble to Chapter VII gives the authority to the SRSG to act as civil authority in Kosovo in the *interim* period, whose length is left undefined.[133] That would be one form of authority to decide non-coercive measures according to Article 41, however the fact that reference is made to the maintenance of law and order and establishment of police leads to the conclusion that probably Article 42 also represents a legal basis of these specific powers. Enforcement measures under Articles 41 and 42 are not subject to the domestic jurisdiction exception of Article 2(7) of the Charter. Further, such basis is complemented by UNMIK Regulation 1 and by the 2001 Constitutional Framework, which specify the powers entrusted to the SRSG by 1244. These two instruments clearly show how the SRSG is the supreme authority in Kosovo, and also that Kosovo institutions are subject to these powers.[134] The practice of the SC to back the establishment of a UN civil administration through its powers under Chapter VII had already been experimented within Bosnia and Herzegovina, and it was eventually rendered explicit in East Timor.[135]

As to the military arrangement, the 3rd of June Agreement provided for the withdrawal of *all* Yugoslav security forces from Kosovo before a limited amount of personnel would be permitted to return, whereas the G-8 statement of May 6 did not specify the 'quantity' of forces to be withdrawn.[136] The agreement recalled the deployment of international military presence under Chapter VII, whereas in the previous statement no mention to Chapter VII was made.[137] It demanded that such military presence would be established 'with substantial NATO participation ... under unified command and control', whereas in the G-8 statement mention was made only of a military presence 'endorsed and adopted by the United Nations'.[138] It is important to note that, as confirmed by the preamble, Yugoslavia accepted only points 1 to 9 of the political agreement of June 3. It did not accept point 10 that would have committed Yugoslavia to accept a timetable for withdrawal of forces agreed in a military-technical agreement, and the condition that military activities would stop only after the verification of the beginning of such activities. Further, such military agreement

---

[133] SC Res. 1244 (1999), para. 19.

[134] UNMIK/REG/1999/1, *supra* n. 127, Sections 1, 4, 6; Constitutional Framework for Provisional Self-Government, UNMIK/REG/2001/9, UNMIK Official Gazette, 15 May 2001, Arts. 12, 14(3).

[135] SC Res. 1031 (1995); SC Res. 1272 (1999). For a comparative analysis of these instruments see Wilde, *supra* n. 1; Bothe and Marauhn, 'UN Administration of Kosovo and East Timor: Concept, Legality and Limitations of Security Council-Mandated Trusteeship Administration', in Tomuschat, *supra* n. 5, 217.

[136] See para. 2 Agreement 3 June, compare with point 2 of the G8 declaration.

[137] Para. 3, compare with point 3.

[138] Para. 4, compare with point 3.

would also decide the timetable and limits of returns of Yugoslav/Serb personnel with the role spelled out in paragraph 6.

The military-technical agreement is given a very low profile in 1244.[139] However, its signature on the 9th of June in Kumanovo by KFOR chiefs and Yugoslav army officers can hardly be overestimated and, indeed, its legal significance has been underestimated.[140] In Article 1(2) it states that the FRY authorities

> 'understand and agree that the international security force ("KFOR") will deploy following the adoption of the SCR (1244) … and operate without hindrance within Kosovo and with the authority to take all necessary action to establish and maintain a secure environment for all citizens of Kosovo and otherwise carry out its mission.'

Article 1(4) then spells out the purposes of the agreement: a) establish a durable cessation of hostilities; b) ensure the withdrawal of all Yugoslav and Serb forces and prevent any re-entry without prior consent by the KFOR commander; c)

> 'to provide for the support and authorisation of the international security force ("KFOR") and in particular to authorize the international security force ("KFOR") to take such actions as are required, including the use of necessary force, to ensure compliance with this Agreement and protection of the international security force ("KFOR"), and to contribute to a secure environment for the international civil implementation presence, and other international organisations, agencies, and non-governmental organisations….'[141]

The suspension and termination of the bombing campaign by NATO is then conditioned upon the verification of a very detailed schedule of withdrawal of all Yugoslav forces.[142] The final important provision is Article 5 which establishes that KFOR commander is the final authority regarding interpretation of the Agreement.

The Kumanovo Agreement (hereinafter KA) is thus fundamental to the understanding of the legal framework created by 1244 despite its very low profile. It complements 1244 in a crucial respect for the territorial status of Kosovo, that of security and effectiveness. This had been the most disputed issue at the Rambouillet negotiations and it had led to the refusal by the FRY to sign the agreements and the beginning by NATO of the bombing campaign.[143] The 3rd of June Agreement, through its vague formula of end of all violence and repression

---

[139] The agreement is re-called in Annex 2, through para. 10 of the 3rd of June Agreement.
[140] With one recent notable exception: Guillaume, 'Le cadre juridique de l'action du KFOR au Kosovo', in Tomuschat, *supra* n. 5, 243.
[141] See also KA, Article II, para. 3c); Appendix B, paras. 2, 5.
[142] *Ibidem*, Article II, III.
[143] Cfr. Weller, *supra* n. 123.

in Kosovo and withdrawal of all military and paramilitary forces from Kosovo and the subsequent return of limited personnel for such purposes such as 'liaison with the international civil mission and the international security presence', provided a basis for interpretation that would justify a gradual return to Belgrade's control over Kosovo. In addition, paragraph 4 referred to NATO substantial presence in the security presence, but not to NATO authority over such military presence. Any more detailed commitment implicit in paragraph 10 was refused by the Yugoslav leadership. It was only one week after that consent was given to vest final security authority over Kosovo with KFOR commander. And it was only 24 hours after such consent was given that the SC approved the same draft resolution mentioned in Article 1(2) KA. Further, 1244, despite being adopted under Chapter VII and despite authorising the establishment of an international security at paragraph 7, neither recalls any issue concerning the composition of the military force if not for paragraph 4 of the 3rd of June Agreement, nor mentions the fact that the international security force is put under the ultimate and exclusive authority of a NATO commander. The KA, however, comes in 1244 through the back door of paragraph 10 of Annex 2. To think of it as a mere military technical agreement of cease-fire, movements and re-deployment of troops, and, perhaps, as argued elsewhere,[144] of establishment of a regime of belligerent occupation is too restrictive. Its importance for a general political settlement is witnessed by the fact that suspension of military activities occurred only after its entry into force. 1244 and the KA recall in many respects SC Resolution 687, whose acceptance by Iraq had been a pre-condition to the cessation of hostilities in 1991.

4.2.2 Is the VCLT applicable to the Kumanovo Agreement?

Once established the fundamental importance of the KA as legal basis for KFOR's security presence, the present analysis must briefly deal with the question of the applicable law, i.e. whether the coercion of states as a ground of treaty invalidity can be applied to the KA. The answer must be sought in the treaty law applicable to the KA.

The first striking element with regard to the KA is that it was entered into by the KFOR commander as representative of KFOR *qua* security presence under direct and effective control of NATO. While it is possible to consider both NATO and NATO members states jointly responsible for *Operation Allied Force*, it is clear that the KA is an international agreement binding upon a state, the FRY, and an international organisation, NATO. Article 52 of both 1969 VCLT and

---

[144] Cerone, 'Minding the Gap: Outlining KFOR Accountability in Post-Conflict Kosovo' 12 *EJIL* (2001), 469.

the 1986 Vienna Convention on the Law of Treaties between States and International Organizations or between International Organizations provides for the nullity of treaties whose 'conclusion has been procured by the threat or use of force in violation of the principles of international law embodied in the Charter of the United Nations.' However, given the circumstances, the VCLT as a treaty does not apply, as it is intended to regulate only treaties concluded by states.[145] The 1986 VCLT is not applicable either, as it has not entered into force yet; nor it has been ratified by NATO.[146] The crucial question becomes whether Article 52 of the 1986 VCLT may be considered a codification of customary international law: in which case, coercion would apply as a ground of invalidity to the KA.

The question may be answered positively for the following reasons. Article 52 of the 1969 VCLT has been considered by both the ICJ and the ILC a codification of customary international law.[147] Such uncontroversial qualification has been the result of the argument that the invalidation of agreements coerced through the unlawful use of force is a corollary of the prohibition of the use of force, later held a *ius cogens* norm by the ICJ.[148] There is little sense in creating a collective security system based on the the prohibition of the use of force, and then allowing the legalisation of the treaty effects of an illegal military coercion. While the ILC could not point to many instances of state practice in this respect, the strength of the *opinio iuris* appears to be the main factor behind the characterisation of the principle as general international law by the ILC and the ICJ. On this account, it is hardly tenable to differentiate the law of treaties between states and the law of treaties between states and international organisations, in order to argue that coercion as a ground of invalidation does not apply to treaties binding upon states and international organisations such as the KA. The lack of differentiation under general international law between coercion by states and coercion by international organisations was supported by the ILC in its preparation of Article 52 of the 1986 VCLT.[149] We therefore refer to Article 52 of both VCLTs as a codification of general international law applicable to the KA.

---

[145] Article 1, 1969 Vienna Convention on the Law of Treaties.

[146] 1986 Vienna Convention on the Law of Treaties between States and International Organizations or between International Organizations. The convention has been so far ratified by 40 parties, but it has not reached the minimum of 35 states required by Article 85(1).

[147] *Fisheries Jurisdiction case* (UK/Iceland), ICJ Reports 1973, 3, at 14; *Yearbook of the International Law Commission* (1966-II), 268.

[148] *Military and Paramilitary Activities in Nicaragua* (Nicaragua/US), ICJ Reports 1986, 13, at 100.

[149] *Yearbook of the International Law Commission* (1979-I), 128-132.

4.2.3 Were the Kumanovo Agreement and the 3rd of June Agreement procured by the threat or use of force?

The possible existence of coercion as an objective element affecting the validity of the KA and the 3rd of June Agreement, and the impact of this coercion on the adoption of 1244 have been analysed only *en passant* by some writers. Cerone only recalls this possibility and he makes the point that even if coercion was proved the invalidation by Article 52 would only apply if NATO intervention was found contrary to the rules of *ius ad bellum*.[150] Zappalà derives from the Chinese non-opposition to the adoption of 1244 on the basis that consent was given by the FRY, that such consent was not coerced through an unlawful intervention. His assertion seems, however, to imply the existence of an objective element of coercion.[151] Kohen is right in asserting that 1244 did not authorise the NATO intervention *ex post facto*. It is however difficult to agree with him that some parts of 1244 do not represent a deal coerced through the use of force upon the FRY.[152] As seen, the KA is an integral part of 1244. It is true that the content of the Rambouillet differs from that of 1244 plus KA in the three important respects mentioned by Kohen: no unrestricted right of movement by KFOR throughout the *whole* of the FRY territory;[153] no deadline for the holding of a referendum;[154] no reference to the will of Kosovo's people.[155] However, that does not mean that 1244 plus KA was not an attempt of legalisation of the conditions imposed by NATO. It is just that those conditions were different as of the beginning of June 1999 from those of 18 March 1999. This may indicate a partial political achievement in Milosevic's strategy, however those conditions were in any case imposed and the consent extorted through the use of force. This was made clear by the Yugoslav representative during the SC meeting of 10 June 1999, which led to the adoption of 1244, and confirmed by the representatives of other states, even NATO states.[156] More explicitly, some important elements in

---

[150] *Ibidem*, 484.

[151] Zappalà, 'Nuovi sviluppi in tema di uso della forza armata in relazione alle vicende del Kossovo' 82 *Rivista di diritto internazionale* (1999), 975, at 988, note 57.

[152] Kohen, 'L'emploi de la force et la crise du Kosovo: vers un nouveau désordre juridique international' 32 *Revue belge de droit international* (1999), 122, at 141.

[153] Rambouillet Agreement, Annex B, para. 8.

[154] *Ibidem*, Ch. 8, Article 1(3).

[155] *Ibidem*.

[156] Statement of the FRY representative Mr. Jovanovic: 'I must note with regret that the draft resolution proposed by the G-8 is yet another attempt to marginalize the world Organization aimed at legalizing *post festum* the brutal aggression to which the Federal Republic of Yugoslavia has been exposed in the last two and a half months. In doing so, the Security Council and the international community would become accomplices in the most drastic violation of the basic principles of the Charter of the United Nations to date and in legalizing the rule of force rather than the rule of international law…The solutions which are being tried to be imposed on the Federal Republic of

the KA tend to support this interpretation: Article II talks explicitly at points a) and e) about suspension and cessation of the bombing campaign only once the withdrawals would comply with the agreement's requirements. The statements of NATO political representatives were very clear on the fact that, if the FRY wanted military action to halt, it should accept NATO's demands.[157] Furthermore, it is arguable that it is not the imposition itself which makes an agreement null and void, but the extortion of the consent through the use of force.[158] In other words, a direct causality link ought to be proved. Claims of imposition can be evidence of a situation fitting into Article 52, but imposition is in itself insufficient. It may have economic and financial connotations rather than military ones, and it could lead states to denounce treaties whenever they perceive them as politically unequal.[159]

As to the 3rd of June Agreement the existence of coercion is more controversial. The G-8 proposal presented by the Russian and the EU envoys did not fully embody NATO's demands, and they represented a compromise between NATO's original demands, on the one side, and Russia and the FRY, on the other side.[160] The political principles established were rather broad and they were apt to support a rather favourable interpretation for the FRY. The reference to the suspension of military activities being conditioned to the acceptance of a detailed schedule of withdrawals, as seen, was not accepted by Belgrade. Further, no agreement was reached on the number of Yugoslav armed

---

Yugoslavia set a dangerous precedent for the international community.... They provide a broad authority to those who have conducted a total genocidal war against a sovereign and peace-loving country and legitimize the policy of ultimatum and diktat.' See also statements of the USA representative Mr. Burleigh, of the UK representative Mr. Greenstock (S/PV. 4011). And statement by the Cuban representative Mr. Rodriguez-Parrilla (S/PV.4011, Resumption 1).

[157] E.g. NATO's spokesman's, James Shea, statement of 6 June 1999 referring to the KA negotiations. 'These talks ... could take some time to conclude, but I must stress it is in the interest of the Serbs for the signing to be as rapid as possible. The linkage is simple: we will not stop until they start, and as they are not starting their withdrawal, we are not stopping out operations.' At <http://www.cnn.com/world/europe/9906/06/kosovo.04/index.html>.

[158] Bothe, 'Consequences of the Prohibition of the Use of Force-Comments on Arts. 49 and 70 of the ILC's 1966 Draft Articles on the Law of Treaties', 27 *ZaöRV* (1967), 507, at 513.

[159] To be noticed is the fact that the inclusion of the 'inequality' of treaties as a ground for invalidation was ruled out by Western states during the diplomatic conference which led to the adoption of the VCLT. A compromise was reached in allowing a Declaration on the Prohibition of the Threat or Use of Economic and Political Coercion in Concluding a Treaty, which, however, is not a legally binding instrument (UN Conference on the Law of Treaties, Official Records, Documents (1968-1969), 285, A/CONF. 39/1/Add. 2 (1971)).

[160] See Black, 'Talks raise hope of breakthrough', *The Guardian*, 2 June 1999.

personnel allowed to return to Kosovo. It is true that the 3rd of June Agreement represents the first acceptance by the FRY of the deployment of international troops with substantial NATO presence under Chapter VII, and that such consent possibly would not have been given without NATO's military action. However, it seems that the causality link between NATO's use of force and the acceptance of the G-8 principles is not easily proven. Even if it was proved, the significance of the 3rd of June agreement is superseded by the KA as regards its security provisions, and by 1244 as regards the deployment of the UN civil administration.

4.2.4 Was the use of force by NATO in violation of principles of international law embodied in the UN Charter? Some exercises in 'lateral thinking'

At this stage the relationship between the law of treaties and the *ius ad bellum* becomes crucial. Was the NATO intervention according to Article 52 'in violation of the principles of international law embodied in the Charter of the United Nations'?

It is not the purpose of this section to re-start a lengthy examination of the alleged existence of a right of humanitarian intervention without SC authorisation.[161] It only engages in an exercise of 'lateral thinking', by focusing the discussion on the basic tenets of the *ius ad bellum* and the legal claims put forward by NATO states in order to justify their action. It is well established that the UN Charter drafters provided only for one case of unilateral use of force: that of self-defence in accordance with Article 51. It did not provide for any exception based on human rights. As of 1986 the main judicial organ of the UN, the ICJ, stated in *Nicaragua* that 'while the United States might form its own appraisal of the situation as to the respect for human rights in Nicaragua, the use of force could not be the appropriate method to monitor or ensure such respect.... The Court concludes that the argument derived from the preservation of human rights in Nicaragua cannot afford a legal justification for the conduct of the United States.'[162] It may well be that after the Cold-War the increasing sensitivity

---

[161] Supporting to different degrees the right of humanitarian intervention see Fonteyne, 'The Customary Law Doctrine of Humanitarian Intervention: its Current Validity Under the UN Charter' 4 *California Western International Law Journal* (1974), 203; Teson, *Humanitarian Intervention: An Inquiry into Law and Morality*, 1997; Lillich, 'Kant and the Current Debate Over Humanitarian Internvention' 6 *Journal of Transnational Law and Policy* (1997), 397; Charney, 'Anticipatory Humanitarian Intervention in Kosovo' 93 *AJIL* (1999), 834; Zappalà, *supra* n. 151; Greenwood, 'International law and the NATO intervention in Kosovo', *4th Report of the House of Commons Foreign Affairs Committee (1999)*, reprinted in 49 *ICLQ* (2000), 926. For a meaningful appraisal of the debate over the question of humanitarian intervention see Chesterman, *Just War or Just Peace? Humanitarian Intervention and International Law* (2001).

[162] *Military and Paramilitary Activities in Nicaragua* (Nicaragua/US), ICJ Reports 1986, 14, at 134.

of the international community for the protection of human rights has developed a new customary norm and, as asserted by the UK government, one important precedent could be the implementation of a no-fly zone in Northern Iraq in 1991 in protection of the Kurdish minority.[163] However, when international law is about the creation of customary norms, counter-claims should not be easily discounted, in particular when the claimant is willing to bring about a modification of a norm of *ius cogens* like the one on the prohibition of the use of force. Opposition to the doctrine of humanitarian intervention and to the claim of legality of the Kosovo intervention was made clear in important fora during and after the NATO campaign. During the discussion within the SC of 24 March and 26 March 1999 claims of illegality of the NATO action were expressed, apart from the FRY, by Russia, Namibia, China, Belarus, India, Ukraine, Cuba.[164] At the 13th meeting of the Human Rights Commission claims of non-conformity of the NATO action with UN principles were further voiced by Mexico, Uruguay, Peru, Mauritius, Chile, Venezuela, Colombia, Sri-Lanka, Ecuador, South Africa, Botswana.[165] Condemnation of all military actions outside the UN Charter framework and without authorisation by the SC was also expressed in the Final Document issued at the XIII Ministerial Conference of the Non-Aligned Movement (NAM) on 8-9 April 2000. The NAM is composed by 114 states from five continents.[166] Even more outspoken was in this sense the Group of 77 South Summit, which made a clear differentiation between humanitarian assistance and humanitarian intervention:

> We stress that the need to maintain a clear distinction between humanitarian assistance and other activities of the United Nations. We reject the so-called "right" of humanitarian intervention, which has no legal basis in the United Nations Charter or in the general principles of international law… Furthermore, we stress that humanitarian assistance should be conducted in full respect of the sovereignty, territorial integrity, and political independence of host countries, and should be initiated in response to a request or with the approval of these States.[167]

---

[163] See Brownlie, 'Kosovo Crisis Inquiry: Memorandum on the International Law Aspects'; Chinkin, 'The Legality of NATO's Action in the Former Republic of Yugoslavia (FRY) under International Law'; Greenwood, 'International law and the NATO intervention in Kosovo', in *4th Report of the House of Commons Foreign Affairs Committee, supra* n. 161, at 878-925.

[164] S/PV. 3988, Statement of FRY 13; Statement of Russia 2; Statement of India 15; Statement of Belarus 15; Statement of Namibia 10; S/PV. 3989, Statement of China 9; Statement of Ukraine 10; Statement of Cuba 12.

[165] E/CN.4/1999/SR. 30, Statement of Mexico 13; Statement of Uruguay 14; Statement of Peru 14; Statement of Mauritius 14; Statement of Chile 14; Statement of Venezuela 14; Statement of Colombia 15; Statement of Sri Lanka 15; Statement of Ecuador, 15; Statement of South-Africa 17; Statement of Botswana 17.

[166] The Document can be found at <http://www.nam.gov.za/xiiiminconf/final1.htm>.

[167] Group of 77 South-Summit, Havana, Cuba, 10-14 Apr 2000, Final Declaration, at http://www.g77.org/Docs/Declaration_G77Summit.htm.

It is true that the whole picture of illegality may be considered blurred by a SC draft resolution proposed by Russia and Belarus condemning the NATO action, which was defeated by 3 to 12;[168] and by a Human Rights Commission draft resolution of the same tenor proposed by Russia, which was defeated by 11 to 24 with 18 states abstaining.[169] However, lack of condemnation cannot be interpreted as an implied *opinio iuris* supporting an expansion of the right to use force unilaterally beyond the Charter's principles. Further, some of the countries abstained from voting on those draft resolutions because of the unbalanced approach and the lack of condemnation of Yugoslav grave violations of human rights and because of serious misgivings in the wording. Yet they agreed that action without SC endorsement should not be supported.[170] What can at best be said is that the international community was divided on the question of the right of humanitarian intervention without SC authorisation, and that there was a measure of tolerance and support towards Operation Allied Force in some sectors of the international community such as the West and Islamic countries. However, the largest and most populated countries China, India, Russia, most of Latin American countries and some African countries opposed the action and the invocation of a right of humanitarian intervention. That can hardly be seen as confirmation of an already existing customary norm or as crystallising an existing trend to a relaxation or reform of a norm of *ius cogens*, unless we are easily ready to discount the universality of international law.[171]

The alleged right of humanitarian intervention did not stand alone in the justifications given by NATO countries for their action. Another important argument was that of the implied authorisation given by Resolution 1160, 1198 and 1203. As already seen, those resolutions were all passed under Chapter VII, however no authorisation was given by their wording. Russia and China expressly stated that they would not veto the resolution 1203, because of the lack of such authorisation.[172] In Resolution 1160 and 1198, the SC only recalled the possibility to take further action, were the SC's requests not met by the FRY. Christine Gray rightly claims that '[t]his argument of implied authorization is open to serious criticism on the facts'.[173] To open the door for such kind of implied authorisation would prevent the SC from taking any type of policy and

---

[168] S/1999/328.

[169] E/CN.4/1999/L.2/Rev.1.

[170] See E/CN.4/1999/SR.50, Statement of Sudan 3; Statement of Nepal 5; Statement of South-Africa 5.

[171] For similar conclusions see Chesterman, *supra* n. 161; Gray, 'From Unity to Polarization: International Law and the Use of Force Against Iraq', 13 *EJIL* (2002) 1 .

[172] S/PV. 3937, Statement of Russia 12; Statement of China 14-15

[173] Gray, *supra* n. 171, at 17.

actions within Chapter VII but short of forcible measures. Further, as the Iraq experience shows the UK and US are isolated in claiming such right to act, in defiance of the literary sense of Chapter VII resolutions and of the debates preceding those resolutions.[174]

As a further ground of justification for its participation in the NATO action, Belgium claimed the state of necessity.[175] Such necessity would consist of the need to avert a humanitarian catastrophe. The state of necessity is in the law of state responsibility one of the circumstances which can preclude the wrongfulness of a certain action otherwise unlawful. However, the ILC Commentary on the 2001 Articles on State Responsibility clearly states that a plea of necessity cannot cover forcible measures of humanitarian intervention, since these are regulated in principle by the primary obligations.[176] In any case, even considering the law of state responsibility, NATO action does not fit into the criteria for the application of the state of necessity as spelled out by Article 25 and 26 of the ILC Articles on State Responsibility, which have been characterised as customary norm by the ICJ in *Gabcikovo-Nagymaros*.[177] The first requirement is that the action must be the only means to pursue the protection of an essential interest. It is debatable whether that was the case in Kosovo. It seems that if the essential interest was the protection of the Kosovo Albanians from gross violations of human rights, such as the violation of the right to life or freedom of movement, NATO bombing could not be possibly the only means to protect such interest, and, considering the dramatic and foreseeable aggravation of the human rights' situation on the ground during the campaign, one wonders whether the action was trying to protect such interest at all. If, on the contrary, the essential interest was the protection of the Kosovo Albanians as a minority and thus their right to enjoy a meaningful autonomy in the FRY, there are good grounds to maintain that at that stage of diplomatic *impasse* that was the only means to ensure this objective. However, such requirement is tied to the condition, also provided by Article 25, that the alleged violator has not contributed itself to the creation of the state of necessity. NATO means of negotiation through the threat of the use of force

---

[174] *Ibidem*; Gazzini, 'NATO Coercive Military Activities in the Yugoslav Crisis', 12 *EJIL* (2001) 391; Sicilianos, 'L'autorisation par le conseil de sécurité de recourir à la force: un tentative d'evaluation', 106 *RGDIP* (2002) 5.

[175] *Legality of Use of Force case (Provisional Measures)*, Oral Pleadings of Belgium, 10 May 1999, CR 99/15; S/PV. 3988, 24 March 1999, Statement of the UK 11.

[176] Crawford (ed.), *The International Law Commission's Articles on State Responsibility: Introduction, Text and Commentaries*, 2002, 185. In other words, a plea of necessity should be assessed within the more general question of the existence of a right of humanitarian intervention (*ius ad bellum*) and not as an 'excuse' precluding the wrongfulness of a certain conduct (law of state responsibility). As seen *supra*, the reactions in the international community to *Operation Allied Force* do not seem to support a relaxation of Article 2(4) on humanitarian grounds.

[177] *Case Concerning the Gabcikovo-Nagymaros Project* (Hungary/Slovakia), ICJ Reports 1997, 7, at 40.

since October 1998 contributed to the sidelining of moderate fringes of the Kosovo Albanians more keen on seeking a feasible diplomatic solution with Belgrade. Internally, it increased the power of the KLA, and it provided new fuel to their strategy of raising the levels of military activities in order to cause Yugoslav responses. At the levels of distrusts and violence reached in March 1999, it may well have been that NATO action was the only means to provide protection to the ethnic Albanian minority, yet the case can be made that such levels of distrusts and violence were also caused by NATO strategy. Article 25 also provides that the action should not impinge on an essential interest of the State. Obviously, territorial integrity and political independence represented essential interests of the FRY. Finally, Article 26 states that the state of necessity shall not be invoked when the action is in violation of a norm of *ius cogens*, and this is obviously the case here. Thus, even invoking the state of necessity as a way to avoid responsibility does not find support in international law.[178]

Some authors have also argued that 1244 did provide for an *ex post facto* endorsement of the NATO action.[179] Nowhere in 1244 is NATO's action condemned, however, in the same manner, nowhere does the resolution afford any endorsement of the action. Lack of condemnation can hardly be seen as an approval of the action by the SC. It is true that in Annex 2 there is reference to the acceptance of military-technical agreement (i.e. the KA) as a condition for the cessation of military activities. But this is exactly the point in question. Was the procurement of the KA in violation of principles of international law as embodied in the Charter? This determination turns on the legality of NATO intervention, which may eventually turn on the existence of an *ex post facto* endorsement by the SC of this intervention. The circle may become vicious. It is incorrect to argue that the existence of such reference to the KA can be seen as an implied endorsement. The only referral of the agreement in the annex does not provide any clear evidence of such intention. Further, it is clear from the discussion preceding and following the adoption of the resolution that the resolution only aimed at restoring the authority of the SC starting from the *de facto* situation created by NATO intervention. It did not aim in any way to legalise and legitimise such intervention, but only to legalise and legitimise the effects of such intervention. The above-question should be rephrased. Was the SC acting within the boundaries of international law by doing that? Or are we rather facing a classic operation of effectiveness in international law?

---

[178] For the same conclusion see Kohen, *supra* note 152, at 137; Chesterman, *supra* n. 161, at 214.

[179] See Henkin, 'Kosovo and the Law of "Humanitarian Intervention"' 93 *AJIL* (1999), 824; Wedgwood, 'NATO's Campaign in Yugoslavia', 93 *AJIL* (1999), 828; Franck, 'Lessons of Kosovo' 93 *AJIL* (1999), 857.

Another possible way of interpreting the use of force by NATO countries as being within the boundaries of UN legality is to conceive the intervention as a way to ensure the achievement of the right of self-determination of the Kosovo-Albanians. Firstly, it is noteworthy that no NATO country has justified its action on these grounds. Further, by adopting this approach, two main complications have to be faced. The first one is the question whether the Kosovo-Albanians could be considered a people, having a right of self-determination within the FRY administrative boundaries. If this question is answered in the affirmative, the second question would be whether foreign states can lawfully intervene in an internal armed conflict, in order to support militarily the group striving for self-determination.

As shown by Julie Ringelheim, the first question was at the core of the political dispute between Belgrade and the Kosovar leaders: the former would claim that the Kosovo-Albanians represented an ethnic minority, hence they were entitled to the protection of their individual human rights as members of a minority; the latter would claim that they ought to be considered a people entitled to self-determination and statehood within the territorial boundaries of *uti possidetis* as previously applied to former Yugoslav republics.[180] The response of the international community was in principle halfway between the two, promoting the right of Kosovo to substantial autonomy within the framework of FRY territorial integrity. However, the degree of self-government and autonomy was itself at the core of the divisions within the international community. As to the Kosovo-Albanians' claim, it is clear that Kosovo cannot fall in the definition of Article 73 UN Charter defining non-self-governing territories under colonial administration. Thus, the classic enunciation of the right of self-determination under GA Resolution 1514 cannot apply to Kosovo. As to the Kosovo Albanian leadership's claim that Kosovo would be entitled to self-determination and secession, exactly as the former Yugoslav republics had been entitled to, some observations are of paramount importance. Looking at the UN and EU practice of recognition of the former Yugoslav republics, it is arguable that the legal concept of self-determination was not adopted at UN debates, and that even the Badinter Commission leaned towards a legal solution of *de facto* collapse of the federal institutions and dismemberment of the old FRY.[181] A right of self-determination, even if not explicitly mentioned, could have been implied if a secession argument had been proposed by the Badinter Commission. But this was not the case. Further, the *uti possidetis* principle was applied by the EC

---

[180] Ringelheim, 'Considerations on the international reaction to the 1999 Kosovo crisis' 32 *Revue Belge de Droit International* (1999), 475, at 484-486.
[181] Arbitration Commission, EC Conference on Yugoslavia, Opinion no. 8, 4 July 1992, in 92 *ILR* 199.

Commission only with respect to the federated republics, but not the autonomous provinces of such republics.[182] Even if such differentiation casts some doubts over its legitimacy, it is highly dubious that such *vacuum* of legitimacy could fill the gap of legality of the Kosovo Albanians' claim. The Canadian Supreme Court decision of 1997 on the right to secession of Quebec under international law reinforces this conclusion.[183] As to the right to substantial autonomy, there is no precedent in this sense in terms of legal entitlement, and, in any case, even where the international community has promoted measures of self-government and autonomy, these have not sacrificed the co-operation between local and central institutions.[184] *Quod non datur*, even if the Kosovo Albanians' were to be found to have a right of external self-determination, Western states have always opposed the developing states' view that there would be a right to foreign military assistance by means of military action, once the non-self-governing territory is subject to an armed attack.[185]

In conclusion, the analysis of the arguments actually employed by NATO countries to justify the action, and other possible arguments such as the *ex post facto* endorsement and the enforcement of a right of self-determination reveal that NATO intervention was in violation of the principles of international law embodied in the Charter, hence illegal coercion as a ground of treaty invalidity would apply to the KA.

4.2.5 Can the SC endorse an agreement which is invalid because of illegal coercion?

At this stage one should ask whether the SC can cure the invalidity of an illegally coerced international agreement, by using its powers under Chapter VII of the Charter. If such power is acknowledged, it may become a purely academic exercise to review the validity of the KA under the law of treaties, since the KA is endorsed in Annex 2 of 1244.

As seen, international tribunals have defined very broadly the competence of the SC to act within the powers provided by Chapter VII. Due to the lack of an institutionalised system of judicial review of the acts of the political organs of the UN, the SC would have the authority to decide its own competence in a particular matter by declaring that matter a threat to international peace and security, and to decide which kind of coercive or non-coercive measures to adopt. Such actions would enjoy a presumption of legality. The only legal limitation to the authority of the SC would be the compliance with the principles and purposes

---

[182] *Ibidem.*, Opinion no. 2, 11 January 1992, in 92 *ILR* 167.
[183] *Re Reference by the Governor in Council concerning Certain Questions Relating to the Secession of Quebec from Canada*, 115 *ILR* 535.
[184] Ringelheim, *supra* n. 180, at 526-527.
[185] Cassese, *Self-Determination of Peoples* (1995), 150-158.

of the UN and norms of *ius cogens*. Given the scope of this authority conferred to the SC, one should possibly rephrase the initial question in the negative, that is whether the SC would be acting contrary to the purposes and principles of the UN Charter, if it endorsed a treaty which is 'procured by the threat or use of force in violation of the principles of international law embodied in the Charter of the United Nations.' The answer may seem self-evidently affirmative.

However, it is worth looking at the practice of the SC in endorsing through Chapter VII imposed territorial settlements, in order to ensure peace and security in a certain area. Such practice is relatively recent. Despite not being originally envisaged, it may represent one of the new creative developments of the way the SC has acted since the end of Cold War and it may find legal support in the doctrine of inherent powers.[186] Yet, the precedents do not speak in favour of the development of any new normative standard enabling the SC to validate an agreement otherwise invalid under Article 52. Resolution 687 imposing a binding territorial settlement upon Iraq by way of endorsement of a conventional instrument was coerced by the military operation *Desert Storm*, however such military action had been authorised by the SC.[187] Article 75 of the 1969 VCLT and Article 76 of the 1986 VCLT indeed exempt from the application of Article 52 any 'treaty which may arise for an aggressor State in consequence of measures taken in conformity with the Charter of the United Nations with reference to that State's aggression.' Resolution 1031 endorsed the Dayton Peace Accords for Bosnia and Herzegovina, however a direct causality link between the signature of the agreements by the Bosnian-Serbs and *Operation Deliberate Force* cannot be easily proved. What can at best be said is that the NATO bombing of Bosnian Serb positions in the summer of 1995 created the momentum for the military offensive of Bosnian and Croat forces on the ground, which then led to a general cease-fire. Such cease-fire was a starting point for a meaningful negotiation in Dayton, but it did not determine the final outcome of the negotiations.[188] Further, it is still generally held that NATO military action in Bosnia was lawful.[189] In other

---

[186] White, *Keeping the Peace* (1997, 2nd ed.), 99.

[187] SC Res. 678 (1990). On the question of application of Article 52 to the consent given by Iraq see Mendelson and Hulton, *supra* n. 95, 149.

[188] See Holbrooke, *To End a War* (1999).

[189] On *Operation Deliberate Force* see White, *supra* n. 186, 99; Sarooshi, *The United Nations and the Development of Collective Security: the Delegation by the Security Council of its Chapter VII Powers* (2000), 262-263; Gray, *supra* n. 171, 4. These authors all reach a conclusion of lawfulness of that operation. See, however, *contra* Gazzini, *supra* n. 174, 428-430. The controversial point is whether the UN Secretary-General, who had been entrusted by the SC with the authority to order air strikes, still had ultimate control over the start, continuation and termination of military operations. Former UN Secretary General Boutros-Boutros Ghali suggests that, despite the delegation of his 'dual-key' authority on 26 July 1995 to the NATO and UN military commanders on the ground, he received a formal commitment by a letter of NATO Secretary General General Claes that he would be still

words, coercion as a ground of invalidity does not apply to these agreements, as, in the case of Iraq, the use of force was not in defiance of the principles and purposes of the UN Charter; in the case of Bosnia, even if we admitted the illegality of the action, the element of coercion is far from clear. More problematic is the understanding of Resolution 1203 related to Kosovo. In this resolution, the SC, acting under Chapter VII, endorsed the agreements of October 15 and 16, 1998 between the FRY and OSCE, and the FRY and NATO respectively, which were concluded after the issuance of an activation order by NATO Secretary General.[190] Such threat of the use of force without SC authorisation was clearly in defiance of international law, however reservations as to the validity of the agreements were never raised. It seems that some delegations were more concerned with avoiding an escalation of the internal conflict and preventing any *actual* use of force by NATO, which was claimed to be contrary to international law and the UN Charter. They saw the Belgrade agreements as the means to avert such developments.[191] Despite that, the lack of reference to international law, the *ad hoc* solution provided and the uniqueness of the precedent hardly speak in favour of the development of new normative standards relaxing the obligation of the SC to abide by the principles and purposes of the UN Charter.

The conclusion claims the illegality of the KA and the *ultra vires* nature of parts of 1244 recalling and endorsing it. Hence, the legal basis of NATO security presence in Kosovo seems to be shaky, *prima facie* making the territorial status of Kosovo unlawful as far as NATO's security presence is concerned.

4.3 Consequences of invalidity: the role of legitimacy in legalising the *status quo*

Once arrived to a finding of invalidity of a part of the legal framework provided by 1244 plus KA, one should ask what are the legal consequences of

---

in a position to take back the authority delegated whenever he considered it necessary (see Boutros-Boutros Ghali, *Unvanquished: a US-UN Saga* (1999), 236-248). See, however, the American envoy Richard Holbrooke's reading of the events supporting different conclusions as to where the ultimate decision-making power in the operation would lie (Holbrooke, *supra* n. 188).

[190] S/1998/978; S/1998/991. The US representative at the SC stated quite frankly at the debate of 24 October 1998 which led to the adoption of Res. 1203 that '[w]e must acknowledge that a credible threat of force was key to achieving the OSCE and NATO agreements and remains key to ensuring their full implementation.' S/PV. 3937, Statement of the US 15.

[191] *Ibidem*, Statement of Ukraine 4; Statement of Costa Rica 6; Statement of Brazil 10; Statement of Russia 11; Statement of China 14.

such invalidity. As seen above, one of the main difficulties in 'legalising' the powers of the SC is the little definition of what would be the legal consequences of a finding of illegality of a SC resolution. One possible consequence is that of the responsibility of the UN, if parts of 1244 were considered as an endorsement of KFOR's illegal presence. As already mentioned, the ILC is supporting the idea that an international organisation may be held internationally responsible for the aid and assistance to the commission of an internationally wrongful act by another international organisation.[192]

Furthermore, there is no reason why one should not apply the VCLT framework, which is expression of customary international law, if the substantive basis of invalidity is a treaty such as the KA. The first question to be asked is whether Article 52 provides for a ground of absolute or relative invalidity. In other words, whether the KA ought to be considered as null and void *ab initio*, or whether it can still produce some legal effects and/or be cured by the coerced party's subsequent acquiescence or acceptance. The wording and the location of Article 52 within the VCLT seem to support the view that coercion describes a ground of absolute nullity.[193] Also the ILC Commentary leans towards this solution. The *ratio* of this finding is that the protection against the threat of use of force is of such fundamental importance for the international community, that any juridical act concluded against such principle ought to be fully invalidated. When discussing the loss of a right to invoke a ground of treaty invalidity by way of acquiescence or subsequent consent (Article 45), the ILC is unambiguous in stating that

> 'the effects and implications of coercion in international relations are of such gravity…that a consent so obtained must be treated as absolutely void in order to ensure that the victim of the coercion should afterwards be in a position freely to determine its future relations with the state which coerced it. To admit the application of the present article in cases of coercion might, in its view, weaken the proposition given by article 48 and 49 [then 51 and 52] to the victims of coercion….'[194]

By contrast, both ILC Special Rapporteurs Fitzmaurice and Waldock thought that the coercion would vitiate the consent of the state, thus the state would be entitled to express subsequent implicit or explicit consent to the execution of the treaty provisions, once coercion had ceased.[195] According to such premises, the Swiss delegation to the 1969 Vienna Diplomatic Conference proposed an

---

[192] See *supra* section 2.2; and ILC Third report on responsibility of international organizations, *supra* n. 62, para. 28.
[193] See Arts. 48-50 and compare with Arts. 51-53 VCLT.
[194] *ILC Yearbook*, 1966 II, 239.
[195] *ILC Yearbook*, 1958 II, 26; *ILC Yearbook*, 1963 I, 50-67, 227-230; *ILC Yearbook*, 1966 I, 22-37, 122-125.

amendment to the draft article to the effect that the coerced state would be entitled to waive the invalidity of the treaty. The proposal was defeated 63-12, thereby supporting the idea that only a subsequent treaty would be able to confirm the validity of that legal regime.[196] It should be noticed that, apart from one author,[197] the absolute nullity thesis has found acceptance in all writings.[198]

Despite a general claim of imposition, the FRY/USM has neither claimed that the KA was null and void because of coercion, nor that parts of 1244 could be found invalid as a consequence of that. In the case brought against ten NATO member states before the ICJ, the FRY/USM never amended its original application and claimed that, as a consequence of the illegality of the use of force by NATO, the KA and parts of 1244 should be declared invalid.[199] This may seem to imply a form of acquiescence towards the 'legalisation' of the KA. However, the formula of absolute nullity embodied in both the 1969 and in the 1986 VCLT hardly supports the idea that acquiescence can cure the invalidity of an agreement which has been illegally coerced. That finds expression in both conventions, in particular in light of Article 45(b)'s non-extension to coercion.[200] Likewise, the Declaration of the Parliament of the Republic of Serbia of 27 August 2003, in which a constitutional organ of the USM 'provides full support to the consistent implementation of [...] The Military-Technical Agreement on Kosovo and Metohia of June 9, 1999' should be considered as not affecting the absolute invalidity of the agreement.[201] The only way the FRY/USM could cure the substantive invalidity of the KA would be through subsequent agreement to

---

[196] See Cahier, 'Le caractéristique de la nullité en droit international et tout particuliérment dans la Convention de Vienne de 1969 sur le droit des Traités' 76 *RGDIP* (1972), 645.

[197] Rozakis, 'The Law on Invalidity of Treaties' 16 *Archiv des Völkerrechts* (1973), 150.

[198] Cahiers, *supra* n. 196; Malawer, *Imposed Treaties and International Law* (1977); Napoletano, *Violenza e trattati nel diritto internazionale* (1977); Aust, *Modern Treaty Law and Practice* (2000); Dinstein, *War, Aggression and Self-Defense* (2001, 3rd ed.).

[199] *Legality of Use of Force (Provisional Measures)* (Yugoslavia/Belgium and others), ICJ Reports 1999, 124. See also Judgment of 15 December 2004 on jurisdiction in <http://www.icj-cij.org/icjwww/idocket/iybe/iybeframe.htm>.

[200] Article 45 states that a 'State may no longer invoke a ground for invalidating, terminating, withdrawing from or suspending the operation of a treaty under articles 46 to 50 or articles 60 and 62 if, after becoming aware of the facts: a) it shall have expressly agreed that the treaty is valid or remains in force or continues in operation, as the case may be; or b) it must by reason of its conduct be considered as having acquiesced in the validity of the treaty or in its maintenance in force or in operation, as the case may be.'

[201] *Ibidem*. Declaration 2435 of the Parliament of the Republic of Serbia, 27 August 2003, in <http://www.mfa.gov.yu/Facts/declarationKIM_e.html>. Apart from the fact that Article 45(a) does not apply to the present Declaration, further problematic constitutional issues are raised by the possibility of the parliament of Serbia expressing an internationally relevant consent for the purpose of the USM's international obligations. Whatever the answer to this latter question, it seems that the importance of the Declaration lies in the conferral of legitimacy to NATO's presence by the sovereign state.

which it has freely consented. However, despite the political re-approaching between Belgrade and NATO, such agreement has never been concluded. The UNMIK-FRY Common Document of 5 November 2001 only reiterated the acceptance of 1244's *basic* principles, and it addressed areas of co-operation between the FRY/USM and UNMIK in the field of Kosovo's *civil* administration, not military control.[202] Hence, the nullity of the KA and the *ultra vires* nature of relevant parts of 1244 are not affected by subsequent agreement of the FRY/USM.[203]

Notwithstanding such conclusion, one has to face the reality that international law is a system largely based on self-help. The fact that the FRY/USM does not challenge the validity of the KA, even once it has ceased to be under coercion, makes international law ineffective in re-addressing the results of its own breaches. On the other hand, the *de facto* situation originated by a violation of international law - such as KFOR's security administration in Kosovo – may produce juridical effects which are recognised at the international level. This phenomenon can be explained through the role played by the principle of effectiveness together with the international legitimacy acquired by NATO's security presence as evidenced by SC support for such presence as well as, more recently, by the Parliament of Serbia. In other words, the role played by NATO in terms of peace-keeping and peace-enforcement in the province makes KFOR's presence legitimate, as the presence is seen as protecting some of the fundamental interests of international community, that of maintenance of peace and security, as an end and means to promote in turn self-governance, human rights and, from the point of view of Serbia, the territorial integrity of the USM and the security of the Serb minority in Kosovo. In that sense, effectiveness on the ground, recognition by the affected state, and legitimacy in the wider community ensure the recognition of the juridical effects produced by the originally unlawful territorial situation. In conclusion, despite the shaky legal basis for NATO's presence, and despite the lack of legal 'continuity' between, on the one hand, a

---

[202] The UNMIK-FRY Common Document of 14 November 2001 can be found in <http://www.ecmi.de/ops/download/kosovo%20UNMIK-FRY.PDF>.

[203] Given recent USM's efforts to enter NATO's Partnership for Peace Program, one possibility to bridge this gap of legality may lie in the signature of a SOFA between Belgrade and NATO. Annex B of the KA in Art 3 provided for the conclusion of a SOFA in a short period of time. This provision has not been followed-up as yet. See FRY Foreign Ministry's Statement of November 2002, 'Foreign Political Position of the FR of Yugoslavia with Emphasis on the Accession to the Partnership for Peace Program', in <http://www.mfa.gov.yu>. See also Guillaume, *supra* n. 140, 253. Rather, it has been superseded by the UNMIK-KFOR Common Document of 17 Aug 2000 and by UNMIK Reg. 2000/47 of 18 Aug 2000, which have spelled out in detail the immunities enjoyed by KFOR personnel. The regulation can be found in <http://www.unmikonline.org/regulations/2000/reg47-00.htm>. It is interesting to note that the KA is never re-called in Reg. 2000/47.

violation of international law and an invalid competence based on that violation, and, on the other hand, the possibility of 'normalisation' and recognition of legal status by the international community, Kosovo represents another case where a (partly in the specific case) unlawful territorial situation is in the long run transformed in a lawful territorial situation, thanks to the joint action of effectiveness and legitimacy.[204]

4.4 Schizophrenic views of state sovereignty: the 2001 Yugoslav-Macedonian delineation agreement

Another problematic aspect with respect to the status of Kosovo is the issue of the USM sovereignty. In the preamble, 1244 reaffirms 'the commitment of all Member States to the sovereignty and territorial integrity of the Federal Republic of Yugoslavia'. Such assertion of principle is highly problematic from a legal point of view and hardly compatible with Judge Huber's famous definition in *Island of Palmas*, who stated that '[s]overeignty in relations between States signifies independence. Independence in regard to a portion of the globe is the right to exercise therein, to the exclusion of any other State, the functions of a State.'[205] If the substantive meaning of sovereignty is independence, and independence means a general *right* to exercise therein the functions of a state, it is clear that the USM under 1244 plus KA does not have such *right* to exercise civil and security functions with respect to Kosovo. If the lack of effectiveness can be seen as evidence of the lack of sovereignty of the USM over Kosovo, the conclusive element is exactly the lack of *compétence-de-la-compétence*. Such powers are vested with UNMIK and with the KFOR commander.[206] Even the partial return of hundreds of FRY forces' units to the border between Kosovo and FYROM in 2001 was effected through KFOR request and consent.[207] One can certainly describe the situation in Kosovo as a situation of 'suspended sovereignty' as in the

---

[204] Ultimately, the Declaration by the Parliament of Serbia – although it does not *per se* provide a legal basis for NATO's presence - is the final and decisive factor in a process of 'accumulation' of legitimacy, that transforms the territorial situation from unlawful to lawful. This is in particular the case because of the representative nature of that institution, and because it represents the actor directly affected by the unlawful territorial situation. In an article based on events before the Declaration, I still argued for the illegality of NATO's presence in Kosovo. See Milano, 'Security Council's Action in the Balkans: Reviewing Kosovo's Territorial Status' 14 *EJIL* (2003), 999.

[205] *Island of Palmas* case (1928), RIAA (Vol. II), 829, at 831.

[206] See UNMIK/REG/2001/9, Section 7; Article 5, KA: 'The international security force ("KFOR") commander is the final authority regarding interpretation of this Agreement and the security aspects of the peace settlement it support. His determinations are binding on all Parties and persons.'

[207] Article 1(4)(a) KA.

case of a belligerent occupation,[208] still one should not overlook that the very issue of sovereignty and independence was and still is, at the time of writing, at the heart of the Kosovo crisis.

The confusion surrounding the substantive meaning of USM sovereignty over Kosovo was highlighted by the signature by Belgrade of a boundary agreement with FYROM. The Agreement Between the Republic of Macedonia and the Federal Republic of Yugoslavia on Delineation of State Border was signed on 23 February 2001.[209] After ratification by the two assemblies, the agreement entered into force on 16 June 2001. The agreement represented the outcome of the work of a Joint Diplomatic Expert Commission established by Skopje and Belgrade in accordance with Article 2 of an agreement regulating the relationship and the co-operation between the FRY and FYROM signed in Belgrade on 6 April 1996.[210] It delineates the frontier between the FRY and FYROM, but at the same time it represents a formal instrument of delimitation of the frontier between Kosovo and FYROM. It is more correct to define the agreement as a treaty of delimitation, rather than demarcation, even if it follows for 95% of its course the *uti possidetis* identified by the previous administrative boundary.[211] Physical demarcation of the boundary is entrusted to a Joint Commission according to Article V.

Despite its simplicity, the agreement caused unease in the international community and vibrant protest by Kosovo Albanians. The question revolved around the competence to enter into a frontier agreement on behalf of Kosovo. As the conclusion of a boundary treaty is a matter essentially within the scope of foreign affairs, the main question was whether such issues were vested with Belgrade's authority, with UNMIK, or with Kosovo's institutions. As to the reactions of the international community the EU's Commissioner for Foreign Affairs, Chris Patten, gave uncontroversial support to the agreement immediately after its conclusion.[212] Also the SC, notwithstanding the use of ambiguous language, endorsed the agreement through a presidential statement on 7 March 2001.[213] On their part, UNMIK and KFOR did not pronounce any statement

---

[208] For a review of the concept of suspended sovereignty see Yannis, 'The Concept of Suspended Sovereignty in International Law and Its Implications in International Politics' 13 *EJIL* (2002), 1037.

[209] An unofficial translation of the agreement can be found in *IBRU Boundary and Security Bulletin*, Summer 2001, 97-98.

[210] Agreement Regulating the Relationship and the Co-operation between the FRY and FYROM, 35 *ILM* (1996), 1246.

[211] Milenkoski, Talevski, 'Delineation of the State Border Between the Republic of Macedonia and the Federal Republic of Yugoslavia', Summer 2001, *IBRU Boundary and Security Bulletin*, 93, at 94.

[212] *Ibidem*, 95.

[213] 'The Security Council recalls the need to respect the sovereignty and territorial integrity of the former Yugoslav Republic of Macedonia. In this context it emphasizes that the border demarcation

until the beginning of 2002. Between January and February 2002 UNMIK and KFOR officials were reported to doubt the legality of the FRY-FYROM agreement.[214] As a response to those statements, both the FRY and FYROM issued formal complaints to UN Secretary General Kofi Annan and NATO.[215] As to the reaction of the Kosovo Albanians', this was of strong opposition to the agreement. According to some analysts, the agreement was among the main causes which triggered the spill-over of armed militias from Kosovo to Macedonia and the beginning of the conflict between FYROM's forces and Albanian rebel groups in northern and western Macedonia in March 2001.[216] After the general elections of November 2001 and the creation of provisional self-government institutions in Pristina, the Assembly of Kosovo passed a resolution on 23 May 2002 declaring the Delineation Agreement between the FRY and FYROM null and void. The same day UNMIK's head Michael Steiner declared and decided the action of the Assembly to be in violation of Kosovo's Constitutional Framework and that the resolution would be null and void, since Kosovo's institutions are not competent to conduct foreign relations. That agreement would be clearly within such competence, which would be vested solely with UNMIK.[217] A few hours later, the SC President in a press statement declared the SC opposition to the Assembly resolution and expressed full support for UNMIK's decision.[218] The FRY and FYROM also expressed in two letters to the SC the opinion that the Assembly's resolution was legally null and void.[219]

This diplomatic row underlines how the question of sovereignty is crucial to the understanding of the legal framework created by 1244.[220] Taking literally and

---

agreement, signed in Skopje on 23 February 2001, and ratified by the Parliament of the former Yugoslav Republic of Macedonia on 1 March 2001, must be respected by all.' S/PV.4290.

[214] Statements by UNMIK spokesman Perhan Haak and KFOR Brigadier General Keith Huber reported by Deliso, 'Blurring the Boundaries in Macedonia', in <http://www.antiwar.com/orig/deliso33.html>.

[215] 'Yugoslav President Asks Kofi Annan to Exert his Influence on KFOR and UNMIK' and 'Macedonian Government Stunned, Will Send Demarche to United Nations', *Yugoslav Daily Survey* (22 February 2002), in <http://www.mfa.gov.yu/Bilteni/Engleski/b220202_e.html>.

[216] Milenkowski, *supra* n. 211, 96.

[217] UNMIK News 23 May 2002, in <http://www.unmikonline.org/news.htm>.

[218] SC/7412.

[219] S/2002/585; S/2002/609.

[220] *Mutatis mutandis* the situation reminds us of the dispute over the legality of the East Timor Gap Treaty. See *Case Concerning East Timor* (Portugal/Australia), ICJ Reports 1995, 90. See also Chinkin, 'The East Timor Case (Portugal v. Australia)' 45 *ICLQ* (1996), 712; and Ong, 'The Legal Status of the 1989 Australia-Indonesia Timor Gap Treaty Following the End of Indonesian Rule in East Timor', 31 *NYIL* (2000), 67.

formally 1244's assertion of FRY sovereignty over Kosovo was a diplomatic and juridical fiction used by the UN to claim that despite preventing any form of effectiveness in government of Kosovo, the territory was still part of the FRY and the UN was not endorsing any state's split-up. Such a radical position was tenable as long as Milosevic was in power in what became to be considered a *pariah* state ruled by alleged war criminals, whose leadership was even prevented from participating in SC debates.[221] Since a new leadership came to power, a partial shift has occurred in the approach of the UN to the participation of the USM in the decision-making of Kosovo. From a policy of exclusion, UNMIK has started to consider Belgrade as an active interlocutor. The involvement of FRY forces in March 2001 in patrolling the border with FYROM has been the first tangible sign of this policy. More importantly, the creation in Pristina of the Co-ordinating Centre for Kosovo and Metohia and the signing by its President of an UNMIK-FRY Common Document in November 2001 has gone in the direction of putting on an equal footing the USM and Kosovo's institutions in negotiations related to Kosovo's Serb minority and Kosovo's future status.

Yet decision-making power remains in this respect with the ambit of competence of Kosovo's institutions and UNMIK, and UNMIK respectively. The issue of the 2001 FRY-FYROM agreement reveals how the picture is blurred. If the USM is entitled to delimit and demarcate boundaries with respect to Kosovo, one would assume that the USM is entitled to conduct foreign relations as it happens in the looser forms of federal state (Bosnia and Herzegovina being one example). However, it is clear from UNMIK's statements concerning the above-mentioned Kosovo Assembly's resolution and from previous practice of UNMIK, that foreign policy competence is in general under the authority of the SGSR. The basis of this power seems to be the general authority conferred to the SGSR through 1244 and more specifically through Article 8(1) points i), m), n), o) of Kosovo's Constitutional Framework enacted on 15 May 2001.[222] It seems that the delimitation and demarcation of boundaries is an exception to this rule, yet its legal basis is controversial given that according to Article 8(1)(i) the SGSR should exercise 'powers and responsibilities of an international nature in the legal field.' The only way to reconcile this is to imply it from the general statement of 1244 regarding the FRY sovereignty over Kosovo. However, even conceded the legality of such differentiation, a question of legitimacy arises. The lack of clarity and coherence in the application of USM sovereignty, hence the perceived illegitimacy of the 'boundaries' exception, seems to be at the basis of the Kosovo Assembly's declaration of invalidity of the FRY-FYROM agreement. If foreign policy ought to be conducted by UNMIK, why

---

[221] *Infra* n. 230.
[222] UNMIK/REG/2001/9, Constitutional Framework for Provisional Self-Government of Kosovo.

are such vital issues such as the delineation of a boundary left within the authority of Belgrade?[223] What is the rationale of this choice? The answer to these crucial questions lies beyond the boundaries of legality and it turns to the general legitimacy of UNMIK's role and aims in Kosovo. The final section considers this important issue.

4.4.1 'Hamlet's ghost' and the legitimacy of UNMIK action in Kosovo

Defining Kosovo's formal status is question-begging. Defining it as an internationalised territory provides a doctrinal and descriptive answer to an inextricable political conundrum. Defining the purpose of the UN involvement in Kosovo cannot be simply describing Kosovo's UN administration as addressing problems of 'governance', rather than 'sovereignty'. As seen, the issue of sovereignty is at the very heart of the Kosovo arrangement. Some basic questions should be addressed, in order to consider whether UNMIK's presence is legitimate. What is the international community striving for apart from inter-communal peace? Is it going towards independence and statehood of Kosovo? Is it going towards the incorporation of Kosovo in the loose federation created by Serbia and Montenegro in February 2003?[224] Is it going in the direction of a permanent UN or EU protectorate, which would prevent a return to Belgrade's exercise of authority, but, on the other hand, would also prevent full independence and statehood for Kosovo?

The legal framework on which UNMIK is based does not substantively address the question of the final status of Kosovo. As to the procedures to be followed for the determination of the future status, on which the final outcome may be heavily dependent, 1244 at paragraph 11 decides that among the main responsibilities of the international civil presence there will be also the facilitation 'of a political process designed to determine Kosovo's future status, *taking into account the Rambouillet accords*' (emphasis added). It is clear that the requirement of the Rambouillet agreement, that provided for of a referendum on final status after three years from the establishment of the international administration, was never considered mandatory. That has been confirmed by the preamble of

---

[223] Such choice is confirmed by the agreement on establishment of a joint expert committee by UNMIK and Macedonia, which 'does not deal with demarcation, but only with practical problems on the ground' (S/PV.4498, Statement of SRSG 1) and by the establishment of a Yugoslav-Macedonian joint commission ('Yugoslavia-Macedonian border under jurisdiction of Belgrade and Skopje', Office of Communication of Serbian Government, 13 May 2002.)

[224] The Constitution states in its preamble that 'the state of Serbia [...] comprises the Autonomous Provinces of Vojvodina and Kosovo and Metohija which, under United Nations Security Council 1244, is currently under an international administration.' See The Constitutional Charter of Serbia and Montenegro, in <http://www.mfa.gov.yu/Facts/charter_e1.html>.

Kosovo's Constitutional Framework, which states that 'the determination of Kosovo's future status' will be effected 'through a process at an appropriate future stage which shall, in accordance with UNSCR 1244 (1999), *take full account of all relevant factors including the will of the people*' (emphasis added).[225] In a note released on 25 May 2001, UNMIK Legal Advisor Alexander Borg-Oliver made clear that it was not in the powers of Kosovo's institutions such as the assembly, the government or the judiciary to make such a decision.[226] Paragraph 5 of UNMIK-FRY Common Document is even more adamant in stating that it '[r]eaffirms that the position on Kosovo's future status remains as stated in UNSCR 1244, and that this cannot be changed by any action taken by the Provisional Institutions of Self-Government.'[227] However, no real indication is given to what this decision-making process may look like. The lack of answers to these questions was made emphatically clear in 2001 in one of the statements of Singapore's representative at the SC:

> 'I want to use two metaphors to illustrate some of the difficulties we face as we meet every month to discuss Kosovo. The first metaphor I will use is the one of the play *Hamlet* and the ghost. You cannot stage the play *Hamlet* without having the scene of the ghost. In the same way, every time we meet to discuss Kosovo, there seems to be a ghost hanging around this room, asking us, what is the ultimate destination and how are we going to get there.'[228]

These answers ought to provide a general framework of legitimacy to UNMIK's administration over Kosovo. Such legitimacy should be construed striking a balance between different imperatives embodied in the preamble of 1244, such as the right of self-government of the people of Kosovo, the need to maintain peace and security in the region, the protection of human rights and the preservation of the USM territorial integrity and sovereignty. These imperatives are drawn from the principles and purposes of the UN.

It is arguable that the lack of clarity in the aims of the international community for Kosovo in the long run depends on priority being given to the maintenance of peace and security and the development of good governance in the short run.[229] The basic argument is that as long as a process of normalisation and reconciliation between ethnic communities is not completed, and sound and inclusive standards of self-government have not developed, it is not feasible for the international community to commit itself to a vision for Kosovo. That would cause further tensions between ethnic communities. Such a policy also postpones

---

[225] Constitutional Framework, *supra* n. 222, Preamble.
[226] UNMIK/FR/0040/01, 25 May 2001.
[227] UNMIK-FRY Common Document, *supra* n. 202.
[228] S/PV. 4309, Statement of Singapore 14. See also statement of the same representative in S/PV. 4498, 14.
[229] S/PV.4702, Statement of SRSG 2.

any conflict between different visions on the future of Kosovo within the international community. However, it presupposes on a narrower scale the possibility of success of what was considered failed on a larger scale. It is difficult to grasp why a policy of reconciliation between an Albanian majority and a Serb minority in Kosovo should be necessarily more successful than a policy of reconciliation between a Serb majority and an Albanian minority in Serbia. This assumption gained momentum during the time of Milosevic's nationalist leadership. It led to the adoption of the 'negotiate and threaten' approach before NATO's military action and later to the exclusion of the FRY representatives from any discussions about Kosovo.[230] Such designation became no more tenable with the fall of Milosevic and the appointment of new moderate governments in Belgrade and after the inter-ethnic incidents occurred in Kosovo in March 2004. It is clear that the SGSRs policy of involvement of Serbian authorities in the decision-making over Kosovo, initiated by Michael Steiner and continued until now by Harri Holkeri and Soren Jessen-Petersen, has represented a positive step in reconsidering these weak assumptions. A partial sacrifice of the right of self-government of Kosovo's people, in order to confer a substantive meaning to the USM sovereignty and territorial integrity (as in the case of the FRY-FYROM agreement), seems in this sense legitimate and justified.

Even then, placing UN policies in a legitimacy framework is not likely to make easier the decision on final status. Ideally, the answer will come from an agreement between Belgrade and Pristina; the present author believes that all possible efforts should be made to reach a real consensus between the USM and Kosovo's representatives. Despite the SGSR express opposition to such option,[231] such consensus may even result in the drawing of a new international boundary between Serbia and Kosovo, resulting in the creation of an independent Kosovo and the incorporation of the northern part of the province, mostly inhabited by Serbs, in the USM.[232] However, any solution imposed by the international community, possibly through a SC resolution, may get caught up in a difficult conundrum. A choice to decide for Kosovo's independence and statehood even if backed by a referendum according to the Rambouillet accords, which were never signed by Belgrade, would be unprecedented and legally controversial. A choice to decide for Kosovo's autonomy within the USM with a return to an even

---

[230] During the SC meeting of 23 June 2000 (S/PV.4164) concerning Kosovo, the participation of the FRY representative was refused by 4 votes in favour, 7 against and 4 abstaining on the ground that Mr Jovanovic was representing 'a Government whose senior leadership has been indicted for war crimes and other violations of international humanitarian law.' See statement of the Representative of the US, Mr. Holbrooke.

[231] S/PV.5130, Statement of the SGSR 5.

[232] For a sensible argument to that effect see Johanson, 'Kosovo: Boundaries and the Liberal Dilemma' 73 *Nordic Journal of International Law* (2004), 535.

limited USM's civilian and military control would be likely to find strong opposition from Kosovo's institutions and the large majority of the population. Even the alternative of an open-ended internationalised status under UN or EU protection would have eventually to come to terms with the principles of self-determination and self-government, which also belong to the peoples of the Balkans. The inherent risk is that Hamlet's ghost may be hanging around longer than anticipated.

5. Conclusions

The present chapter has broadened the analytical framework on unlawful territorial situations, to include cases where the UN, in particular through the SC, exercises territorial competencies. It has argued that the broad powers entrusted to the SC in the field of international peace and security by the UN Charter, subsequent practice and judicial decisions can be interpreted as including the exercise of such powers. Territorial competence is normally exercised by the UN according to two models, one of direct territorial administration and one by mandating territorial administration to a state, group of states or another international organisation. In both scenarios, a review of legality of the action taken by the SC can be carried out by assessing its compliance with the principles and purposes of the UN Charter and fundamental norms of international law. Furthermore, these limitations to the territorial powers of the Council under Chapter VII show that, in theory, the Council could act *intra vires*, should it exceptionally decide to create a new international boundary to prevent the continuation and aggravation of an international dispute. Such extreme exercise of territorial competence is subject to the need for the Council to comply with principles of justice and international law, and to the manifest impossibility to settle the dispute by agreement between the parties.

The endorsement by the SC of a territorial competence over Kosovo established by NATO through coercion outside the UN Charter framework of collective security has been held to be beyond the legal competence of the SC. Such default in legal competence has affected the territorial status of Kosovo, which has been found to be unlawful as far as NATO's security presence is concerned at least until August 2003. Yet the cumulative effect of NATO's effectiveness, of the legitimacy of its presence as a result of its action with regard to security in the region in support of UNMIK's operation, and, most importantly, of the endorsement to the implementation of the KA by the Serbian Parliament, seem to have gradually transformed the originally unlawful territorial situation in a lawful territorial situation. The case of Kosovo is indeed paradigmatic in showing how effectiveness and legitimacy work hand-in-hand at present times, in order to shape international law in accordance with the will of the most influential countries.

Finally, a further level of 'legitimacy analysis' has been added to show that, when the legality of a certain action is established – and given the wide-ranging powers of the SC, that will occur most of the times –, the authority and legitimacy of the SC will benefit from the adherence to principles of substantive consistency, good faith and procedural transparency and fairness in the way it acts. More specifically, when the UN engages directly in territorial administration, the legitimacy of its choices will be tested against these principles and the fundamental aims and principles of the organisation itself. The case of UNMIK's action in Kosovo with regard to the controversial 2001 Delineation Agreement has been tested on that basis and found to be legitimate. It has been finally argued that the dispute over the 2001 Delineation Agreement shows that the issue of substantive sovereignty remains at the core of Kosovo's *ad interim* arrangement; and that neither a legitimacy framework established by UNMIK, nor the reaffirmation by SC Resolution 1244 of USM sovereignty and territorial integrity are likely to make future choices, on where ultimate competence will remain, any easier.

CHAPTER 7

CONCLUSIONS: RECONCILING EFFECTIVENESS, LEGALITY AND LEGITIMACY

This concluding chapter recaps the main points developed in the book, and it examines the broader implications of the findings of the book for the current state of international law. More specifically, it reflects on the effectiveness of international law towards unlawful territorial situations, by reverting Jellinek's maxim *die normative Kraft des Faktischen* and looking at *die faktische Kraft des Normativen*. It finally presents some additional considerations on the possible reconciliation between effectiveness, legality and legitimacy in international law and on the enduring vitality of the concept of effectiveness.

1. The state of unlawful territorial situations in the 21st century

The present book has provided some answers to the fundamental questions regarding the state of international law on unlawful territorial situations in the 21st century. Unlawful territorial situations represent an enduring problematic phenomenon in the international community of the 21st century, albeit hardly ever studied in a systematic manner by international lawyers. More and more often, unlawful territorial situations are not related to classic conflicts over borders and territory in the narrow sense, but they tend to underlie disputes over the way in which territorial sovereignty is exercised. This is witnessed by the fact that, despite the existence of numerous instances of territorial occupations, the language of formal status and of the inviolability of international frontiers is fashionable nowadays, sometimes even among occupying powers. The book has shown that the language of 'sovereignty and territorial integrity', rather than being in radical opposition to the language of effectiveness as one may expect, tends to enhance the role of the latter in the way international law 'regulates' – or, sometimes, does not regulate - territorial issues. In fact, such concepts of sovereignty and territorial integrity are deprived more and more often of their original and substantive meaning of exercise of a legal right and competence, to become a bargaining chip to be negotiated, and often sacrificed in the overall political solution of disputes. The cases of Kosovo and Western Sahara stand out in this respect, insofar as both the USM and POLISARIO are currently deprived of a territorial competence, and even their future entitlement risks being undermined in the process of reaching a political solution.[1]

On the other hand, international law does not lack the instruments to go beyond formal designations and effectiveness, and to assess the legality of territorial situations. An assessment of legality of territorial situations should entail a clear conceptual framework on the existing applicable law. To assess the legality of a foreign military and/or civil presence within the territory of a country is a separate exercise from assessing the scope and extent of the applicability of international humanitarian law, or of the legality of the military intervention leading to the occupation. These are legal questions which are often intertwined with the legality or illegality of the occupation, but that are, and should be kept, conceptually differentiated. This separation is often ignored, which leads to the conclusion that international law is irrelevant to the choice to establish and maintain a territorial occupation. Such misconception is as serious as claiming that a state has no legal restraint in the choice to invade a country in the first place, or in the way it acts towards the civilian population once the occupation is established. It is hoped that the present book will contribute to a broader re-appraisal of the role of international law and international institutions with regard to territorial occupations.

The present work has identified and explored the confines of the principles of legality that limit effectiveness in the exercise of territorial sovereignty: these are the prohibition to use force to modify the status of a territory, the principle of *uti possidetis*, the principle of self-determination and the principle of territorial integrity. Despite to different degrees being inconsistently enforced, and for all the uncertainties surrounding the way the *uti possidetis* and self-determination protect states' and peoples' territorial sovereignty, these primary norms have been regularly re-asserted and quite consistently applied by states and international organisations throughout the post-1960 era. In particular, the actions of the GA and the SC in terms of non-recognition of territorial situations established in defiance of these norms has been crucial for the emergence of a clear territorial dimension to these principles. It has been shown how the application of these legal principles to territorial situations can render international law effective with regard to issues of territorial sovereignty. On the one hand, it can render it effective, insofar as it enables a determination of legality or illegality of a territorial situation by any observer, overcoming the vicious circle of evading any assessment by vacillating between looking at the formal status or, alternatively, recognising a *status quo*. This may contribute to a positive and constructive role played by civil society in putting pressure on governments and governmental organisations in acting in accordance with international law, and in taking

---

[1] See *supra* Ch. 5, section 6.4 and Ch. 6, section 4

political action against the perpetuation of unlawful territorial situations. On the other hand, institutional enforcement of those principles of legality can overcome the weaknesses of international law with regard to the consequences that the system draws from a determination of unlawfulness.

The book has shown how state and judicial practice with regard to the inherent invalidity of unlawful territorial situations confirms a preference for a dualist framework of relations between these international legal principles and the legal effects produced by the *de facto* situation. The dualist scheme is due to the still dominant role played by states in international law and the strong impact of the concept of effectiveness in the definition of state, territory and territorial sovereignty under international law. Whereas such framework gives states, international organisations and international tribunals more flexibility in the way they deal with unlawful territorial situations, allowing them to build in 'legitimate' exceptions in their non-recognition policies, it also shifts responsibilities away from tribunals, towards states and international bodies, in particular the SC and the GA. These two bodies may be expected to uphold and enforce principles of legality, by adopting sanctions towards occupying states, or providing for overall or temporary solutions to the territorial disputes often underlying unlawful territorial situations. It is in this latter respect, concerning especially its Chapter VII powers to determine rights and duties of states, that the SC has taken up and may have to take up in the future an enhanced responsibility, that the founders of the UN could not foresee. It is indeed by addressing at an institutional level the legal consequences of unlawfulness in the different areas analysed in Chapter 5, such as the regulation of the use of force, the entitlement to statehood, the right to obtain reparation for the injury derived from the illegal territorial occupation, that the effectiveness of international law may be enhanced. The impact of a definition of unlawfulness on those areas of international law, with the possible exception of the regulation of the *ius ad bellum*, has been most of the times diminished by *ad hoc* solutions influenced by effective situations on the ground, which have not taken fully into account the legal entitlements of the subjects under occupation. One lesson that can be drawn from the present work is that international law is, most of the times, as effective as states and competent international bodies want it to be. The political organs of the UN should aim at a more systematic consideration of the international law implications of their actions. The request of the GA for an advisory opinion on the legal consequences of the construction of the wall in Palestine fortunately goes in this direction, despite the inevitable, acrimonious politicisation from many sides that has surrounded the request and the delivery of that opinion.

Furthermore, international legal considerations should be also internalised, to make the exercise of powers by the Council more accountable. Because of its increasingly important role in territorial disputes and territorial settlements, the SC ought to abide by norms of *ius cogens* and by the principles and purposes of the

UN embodied in the Charter, when enforcing principles of legality related to territorial situations, or when simply aiming at restoring international peace and security. While the present author believes that the proactive role of the Council in the post Cold War era is a welcome development, the Council and its members should be careful not to overstep the constitutional powers that are entrusted to the Council under the Charter. Even when practical action in the aftermath of a crisis - where the Council has been bypassed by states - seems the only way forward, the Council should be able to distance itself from the actors, results and effects of the unlawful military intervention and unlawful occupation. In order to do that, the best practical option would be to establish both a civil and military presence under strict SC's control such as in the case of East Timor, rather than endorse a military presence under the operational and political authority of the occupying power. When this option is not possible because of the reluctance of the occupying power to relinquish powers to the UN, and of the SC's inability or unwillingness to force it to relinquish those powers, the SC should find diplomatic forms of intervention, such as facilitating the process of dispute settlement, rather than use its Chapter VII powers to endorse and/or legitimise *ex post facto* the intervention. Any repetition of the experiences of Kosovo and Iraq may lead to a clear pattern, evidencing the willingness of the SC to rubber-stamp any form of intervention and occupation, whether legal or illegal, as long as carried out by one or more powerful members. Needless to say, such pattern would be devastating for the legitimate and global authority of the SC.

Finally, even within its broad legal powers under Chapter VII, and until such legal powers are rendered more transparent and their exercise more accountable through the elaboration of some criteria of conduct by the SC itself or by the GA, the Council ought to justify the legitimacy of its choices to sacrifice certain legal values, in order to promote others - for example, the principle of self-determination over state sovereignty. The Article 39 determination of the existence of a threat or breach of international peace and security should be a determination in good faith, not just a recitation, such as in the case of SC res. 1559, where the Council practically ordered the withdrawal of all Syrian military and intelligence from Lebanon, despite the explicit support for such presence by the then legitimate Lebanese government.[2] This should be especially important, when the Council is not only ordering enforcement measures or measures having a provisional character, but it is using its Chapter VII powers to play a quasi-judicial role in a political and legal dispute and to determine the rights and duties of member states as well. The necessity of its action and the proportionality in the

---

[2] SC Res. 1559 (2004).

choice of the means to achieve its objectives should be the main parameters behind the elaboration and adoption of such resolutions.

Both the legality and the legitimacy of the SC action will make it more acceptable to the parties disputing the legality of a territorial situation, thus promoting the effectiveness of international law, and the ability of the Council to contribute to the settlement of international disputes in accordance with 'principles of justice and international law'.[3] Any Chapter VII action manifestly out of proportion, and clearly instrumental to espousing the cause of one or more powerful states in a legal dispute against one or more weaker states, would undermine the constitutional authority of the SC in matters of international peace and security, and provide powerful arguments in favour of non-compliance and civil disobedience. A pattern and practice of this kind would have, in the long run, a detrimental effect in a system lacking in-built mechanisms of physical enforcement independent from the states, and largely based on the legal and political authority of the SC and the compliance and implementation of measures by the member states.

2. Reconciling effectiveness, legality and legitimacy

The present work has argued that international law is a set of norms having an objective normative content, equally applicable to all members of the international society and capable of defining issues of territorial sovereignty in a contextual and specific manner. On the other hand, by focusing on the concept of effectiveness, it has also addressed the role of international law in legitimising material processes of status recognition in the international society. The book has unveiled this tension between the egalitarian element and the hegemonic element in the nature of international law, by looking at the issue of unlawful territorial situations. The concept of effectiveness has been found to permeate the discourse on sovereignty in modern international law. Its role as 'fundamental principle' of the international legal system has been reduced only in the second half of the 20th century, with the affirmation of principles of substantive territorial illegality. The book has shown how the concept of effectiveness still plays an important role in the way international law regulates territorial situations, above all when accompanied by a legitimate claim or through external legitimation by authoritative bodies like the SC. The point is not that we need to go back to effectiveness as one of the fundamental principles of international law, in order to make international law more credible, but that effectiveness is still relevant to the understanding of some emergency situations, where powerful states are

---

[3] UN Charter, Article 1(1).

determined to go beyond positive law. The book seems in fact to point in the direction of a concept of effectiveness re-gaining ground with regard to vital issues such as territorial sovereignty and, in part, the use of force, to the detriment of legality discourse. This is probably due to the novel situation of an international society characterised by the existence of a single Super Power, which more and more espouses a Schmittian concept of law as emergency decision, rather than legal norm.

Effectiveness is, however, limited, to a considerable extent, by the need for legitimacy in a society more and more integrated in everyday life; however, legitimacy discourse also has a more sinister task of enhancing the role of effectiveness in international law by providing, compared to legality, looser, less transparent and less objective devices of power acceptance and recognition. Adopting legitimacy as a device of transformation of illegal effectiveness into a legal one, is also a way for the international community to safeguard the integrity of its principles of substantive legality developed in the last 60 years, at least in the short run, despite making them in some cases peripheral to the actual regulation of disputes. In fact, it has been submitted that either we must be ready to accept that a violation of these principles produces *per se* legal effects in the international sphere, or, alternatively, we must find an explanation beyond positive legality in concepts such as effectiveness and legitimacy. The book advocates the latter solution, as the former is simply incompatible with the existence of a rule of law in the international society. It is, indeed, striking that while many states and international lawyers have argued in the last few years against the legality of some forcible interventions leading to changes of territorial status, the same states and international lawyers have then been ready to easily acquiesce and accept the *status quo* produced by those interventions. Starting from this position, an analytical reconciliation between effectiveness and legality is possible, by looking at the concept of legitimacy, and the role it plays in current international law in driving processes of power recognition. Such reconciliation is purely analytical, and in no way it aims at presenting it as a normative, ideal model; on the contrary, the model plays against the sustainability of the rule of law in the international society in the long run.

Moreover, we must concede that there may be a deeper, inescapable reason behind the enduring 'vitality' of the concept of effectiveness in international law. This reason relates to the inherent ambivalence of the concept of effectiveness as either a criterion provided by positive rules or, alternatively, as a legal-normative device situated on the borderline between positive law and social reality. At the outset of the book, it was argued that

'effectiveness is here considered as a *legal-normative* organising concept, which allows the transformation of effective realities into international law. It represents possibly the concept *par excellence* showing the concreteness and material nature of international law. However, its exact nature as a device situated on the borderline between law and social reality, or, alternatively, as a device situated within international legal norms has been disputed. From the latter approach one derives that effectiveness should be kept conceptually separated from overlapping concepts of 'socio-legal' effectiveness, efficacy or compliance. From the former, one may infer that these concepts may end up overlapping.'[4]

The book has shown that in reality the alternative is misleading, and that the concept of effectiveness is both a criterion of positive legality and a device of transformation of factual realities into law, even when departing from violations of international law. In this latter respect, a simple proposition may explain effectiveness' enduring relevance to international law: international law needs to accept social realities, in order to become effective. This point is illustrated through the case of Iraq. Whereas it has been argued that 'using' the SC has been the way for the Coalition states to legitimise and, in the long run, legalise their violating effectiveness, paradoxically, going back to the SC has also meant making international law again relevant, in other words effective. After the initial success, the discussion was not only and not so much whether the SC would recognise the *de facto* occupation of Iraq, but rather whether the Coalition would recognise a 'vital role' or 'central role' to the UN; in other words, whether the occupiers would allow the SC to take effective action.

The roles were dramatically reversed, in the sense that it was a group of states recognising the partial authority of the SC to deal with the matter, rather than the SC recognising the authority of those states to re-build Iraq. 'Allowing' the SC to play a 'vital' role also meant rendering international law again partly relevant and effective in the context of a legitimate process of constitutionalisation and democratisation of the Iraqi society, after months in which a majority of countries and observers argued that international law was being deeply undermined. In fact, whereas the ultimate decision-making power with regard to Iraq remained with the Coalition states, the UN was now involved in the political and physical reconstruction of Iraq, and the SC could demand the Coalition's full compliance not only with international humanitarian law and with international human rights standards, but also with the principles of internal self-determination and popular sovereignty. In a sort of mutual exchange, international institutions decided to sacrifice the sovereignty and territorial integrity of Iraq, despite all formal declarations, and to recognise effectiveness on the ground, in order to become relevant themselves in other areas. That shows how the concept of effectiveness lies on the borderline between the law and social reality, and it affords a continuous exchange between the two. *Die normative Kraft des Faktischen* and *die faktische Kraft des Normativen* are two sides of the same coin, and international law, sometimes, has to recognise power as its material source, in

---

[4] *Supra* Ch. 2, section 2.

order to be able to influence and limit it. This is possibly the main reason behind the enduring vitality of the concept of effectiveness in international law.

In conclusion, there seems to be an inevitable link between hegemony and law, that even the most developed system of rule of law may be unable to avoid, when hegemonic actors decide to bypass legal norms. On the other hand, this concluding note of realism should not prevent us from seeing the paradox inherent in this relation. Should the SC continue in its operations of mere power recognition and sacrifice of fundamental values of the Charter through its Chapter VII powers, the mechanism of reconciliation between effectiveness, legality and legitimacy may break one day. The SC may gradually diminish – and eventually lose - its ability to confer legitimacy upon unlawful territorial situations, and the mechanism of legitimate recognition may come to a halt. That mechanism may be replaced by one of legitimate non-recognition and disobedience that would be destructive for the unity of international law and, ultimately, for the effectiveness of UN institutions. A pre-Charter system of effectiveness and legality will have made successfully its way back into the international community. There is a powerful argument to be made that not even hegemonic states would eventually benefit from such a system, as they could no more rely on what has been, since the end of the Cold War, a very effective collective mechanism of power recognition.

BIBLIOGRAPHY

Books

R. Ago, *Il requisito dell'effettività dell'occupazione,* (Rome: Anonima Romana Publ., 1934).

R. Ago, *Scienza Giuridica e Diritto Internazionale*, (Milan: Giuffrè, 1950).

A. Alvarez, *The Monroe Doctrine: Its Importance in the International Life of the States of the New World*, (New York: Oxford University Press, 1924).

A. Aust, *Modern Treaty Law and Practice*, (Cambridge: Cambridge University Press, 2000).

W. Balekjian, *Die Effektivität und die Stellung Nichtanerkannter Staaten im Völkerrecht*, (The Hague: Martinus Nijhoff, 1970).

R. Beck, *Die Internationalisierung von Territorien*, (Stuttgart: Kohlhammer, 1962).

E. Benvenisti, *The International Law of Occupation*, (Princeton: Princeton University Press, 1991).

M. Berkin, *The Great Tibetan Stonewall of China: the Status of Tibet in International Law and International Policy*, (Chichester: Barry Rose Law Publ., 2000).

F. Bleiber, *Die Entdeckung im Völkerrecht: Eine Studie zum Problem der Okkupation,* (Bamberg: Greifswald, 1933).

B. Boutros-Ghali, *Unvanquished: a US-UN Saga*, (New York: Random House, 1999).

D.W. Bowett, *The Law of International Institutions*, (London: Sweet and Maxwell, 1982, 4th ed.).

J.L. Brierly, *The Law of Nations*, (Oxford: Oxford University Press, 1955, 5th ed.).

I. Brownlie, *Principles of International Law*, (Oxford: Oxford University Press, 2003, 6th ed.).

I. Brownlie, *System of the Law of Nations: State Responsibility (Part I)*, (Oxford: Clarendon Press, 1983).

L.C. Buchheit, *Secession*, (New Haven: Yale University Press, 1978).

M. Byers, *Custom, Power, and the Power of Rules*, (Cambridge: Cambridge University Press, 1999).

A. Cassese, *International Law in a Divided World*, (Oxford: Oxford University Press, 1986).

A. Cassese, *International Law*, (Oxford: Oxford University Press, 2001).

A. Cassese, *Self-Determination of Peoples: a Legal Reappraisal*, (Cambridge: Cambridge University Press, 1995).

S. Chesterman, *Just War or Just Peace? Humanitarian Intervention and International Law*, (Oxford: Oxford University Press, 2001).

B. Conforti, *Le Nazioni Unite*, (Padua: CEDAM, 1986, 4th ed.).

J. Crawford, *The Creation of States in International Law*, (Oxford: Clarendon Press, 1979).

E. De Vattel, *Les droit des gens*, Vol. 1, (1758).

C. De Visscher, *Les effectivités du droit international public*, (Paris: Pedone, 1967).

G. Di Stefano, *L'ordre international entre légalité et effectivité*, (Paris: Pedone, 2002).

Y. Dinstein, *War, Aggression and Self-Defense*, (Cambridge: Cambridge University Press, 2001, 3rd ed.).

D. Donati, *Stato e Territorio*, (Rome: Atheneum, 1923)

J. Dugard, *Recognition and the United Nations*, (Cambridge: Grotius Publications Limited, 1987).

R. Dworkin, *Law's Empire*, (London: Fontana Press, 1986).

T.M. Franck, *Fairness in International Law and Institutions*, (Oxford: Clarendon Press, 1995).

T.M. Franck, *The Power of Legitimacy among Nations*, (Oxford: Oxford University Press, 1990).

C.V. Fricker, *Vom Gebiet und Gebietshöheit*, (Tübingen: Laupp, 1867).

W.G. Grewe, *The Epochs of International Law*, (Berlin: De Gruyter, 2000).

A. Gentili, *De Iure Belli libri tres*, (1598), Vol. I, Holland (ed.), Oxford, 1877.

M. Giuliano, *La comunità internazionale*, (Milan: Giuffrè, 1950).

J. Goebel, *The Struggle for the Falkland Islands*, (Yale: Yale University Press, 1927).

P. Guggenheim, *Traité de droit international public*, Vol. I, (Geneva: Librairie de l'Université, 1953).

H. Hart, *The Concept of Law*, (Oxford: Oxford University Press, 1994, 2nd ed.).

R. Holbrooke, *To End a War*, (New York: The Modern Library, 1999).

D.J. Harris, *Cases and Materials on International Law*, (London: Sweet&Maxwell, 1998, 5th ed.).

R. Ihering, von, *Der Zweck im Recht*, Vol. I, (Leipzig: Breitkopf und Haertel, 1877).

International Military Tribunal in Nuremberg, *Trial of the Major War Criminals before the International Military Tribunal*, (Buffalo: Hein, 1947).

W. Jellinek, *Allgemeine Staatslehre*, (Berlin: J. Springer, 1922).

R. Jennings, *The Acquisition of Territory in International Law*, (Manchester: Manchester University Press, 1963).

G. Jeze, *Etude theorique et pratique sur l'occupation comme mode d'acquérir les territoires en droit international*, (Paris: V. Girard & E. Briere, 1896).

J. Juste Ruiz, *Derecho Internacional Publico*, (Valencia: Ed. Nomos, 1994).

H. Kelsen, *Das Problem der Souveranität und die Theorie des Völkerrecht*, (Tübingen: Verlag von J.C.B. Mohr, 1920).

H. Kelsen, *General Theory of Law and State*, (New York: Russell&Russell, 1961).

H. Kelsen, *Principles of International Law*, (New York: Rinehart&co., 1952).

H. Kelsen, *Principles of International Law*, (New York: Holt, Rinehart and Winston, Inc., 1966, 2nd ed.).

D. Kennedy, *International Legal Structures*, (Baden-Baden: Nomos Verlagsgesellschaft, 1987).

M. Kohen, *Possession contestée et souveraineté territoriale*, (Paris: Presses Universitaires de France, 1997).

K. Korman, *The Right of Conquest: the Acquisition of Territory by Force in International Law and Practice*, (Oxford: Oxford University Press, 1996).

M. Koskenniemi, *From Apology to Utopia: the Structure of the International Legal Argument*, (Helsinki: Lakimiesliiton Kustannus, 1989).

G. Kreijen, *State Failure, Sovereignty and Effectiveness*, (Leiden: Martinus Nijhoff, 2004).

P. La Pradelle, *La frontière. Etude de Droit Internationale*, (Paris: Les éditions internationales, 1928).

A. Lahlou, *Le Maroc et le droit des pêsches maritime*, (Paris: LGDJ, 1990), 173.

R. Langer, *Seizure of Territory*, (Princeton: Princeton University Press, 1945).

H. Lauterpacht, *International Law*, (Cambridge: Cambridge University Press, 1970).

H. Lauterpacht, *Recognition in International Law*, (Cambridge: Cambridge University Press, 1947).

H. Lauterpacht, *The Development of International Law by the International Court*, (London: Stevens&Sons Ltd., 1958).

S.S. Malawer, *Imposed Treaties and International Law*, (Washington: William Hein Publ., 1977).

N. Malcolm, *Kosovo: a Short History*, (New York: New York University Press, 1998).

A. Marazzi, *I territori internazionalizzati*, (Turin: Giappichelli, 1959).

C. Marek, *Identity and Continuity of States in Public International Law*, (Geneva: Librairie Droz, 1968, 2nd ed.).

C. Martens, *Causes célèbres du droit des gens*, Vol. III, (Leipzig: Brockhaus, 1859, 2nd ed.).

A. Miele, *La comunità internazionale*, (Turin: Giapichelli, 2000, 3rd ed.).

A. Mjaja de la Muela, *El Principio de Effectividad en Derecho Internacional*, (Valladolid: Graficas Andrés Martin, 1958).

T.D. Musgrave, *Self-Determination and National Minorities*, (Oxford: Oxford University Press, 1997).

G. Napoletano, *Violenza e trattati nel diritto internazionale*, (Milan: Giuffré, 1977).

G. Nesi, *L'Uti Possidetis Iuris nel diritto internazionale*, (Padua: Cedam, 1996).

E. Nys, *Le droit international, les principes, les théorie, les faits*, (Paris: Pedone, 1912).

L. Oppenheim, *International Law*, Vol. I, (London: Longmans, 1912, 2nd ed.).

L. Oppenheim, *International Law: a Treatise*, (London: Longmans, 1905).

L. Oppenheim, H. Lauterpacht, *International Law: a Treatise*, (London: Longmans, Green & Co, 1947, 6th ed.).

D.P. O'Connell, *State Succession in Municipal Law and International Law*, Vol. I, (Cambridge: Cambridge University Press, 1967).

C. Peck, R.S. Lee (eds.), *Increasing the Effectiveness of the International Court of Justice: Proceedings of the ICJ/UNITAR Colloquium to Celebrate the 50th Anniversary of the Court*, (The Hague: Martinus Nijhoff, 1997).

N.A. Pelcovits, *The Long Armistice*, (Baldor: Westview Press, 1993).

R. Phillimore, *Commentaries upon International Law*, (Philadelphia: Johnson, 1857).

J.S. Pictet (ed.), *The Geneva Conventions of 12 August 1949, Commentary*, Vol. IV, (Geneva: International Committee of the Red Cross, 1958).

S. Pufendorf, *Elementorum jurisprudentiae universalis libri duo*, (Cambridge: Oldfather ed., 1913).

D. Raic, *Statehood and the Law of Self-Determination*, (The Hague: Kluwer Law International, 2002).

J. Rawls, *A Theory of Justice*, (Oxford: Oxford University Press, 1999, 2nd ed.).

S. Romano, *L'ordinamento giuridico: studi sul concetto, le fonti e i caratteri del diritto*, (Pisa: Mariotti, 1917).

B. Roth, *Governmental Illegitimacy in International Law*, (Oxford: Oxford University Press, 2000).

C. Rousseau, *Droit international public*, Vol. III, (Paris: Ed. Sirey, 1953).

D. Sarooshi, *The United Nations and the Development of Collective Security: the Delegation by the Security Council of its Chapter VII Powers*, (Oxford: Clarendon Press, 2000).

H.G. Schermers, N.M. Blokker, *International Institutional Law*, (The Hague: Martinus Nijhoff, 1995, 3rd ed.).

D. Schindler, J. Toman (eds.), *The Laws of Armed Conflict: a Collection of Conventions, Resolutions and Other Documents*, (Alphen aan den Rijin: Sijthoff & Noordhoff, 1981).

C. Schmitt, *Der Nomos der Erde im Völkerrecht des Ius Public Europaeum*, (Cologne: Greven, 1950).

F. Seyersted, *United Nations Forces in Law of Peace and War*, (Leiden: Sijthoff, 1966).

S.P. Sharma, *Territorial Acquisition, Disputes and International Law*, (The Hague: Martinus Nijhoff, 1997).

M.N. Shaw, *Title to Territory in Africa*, (Oxford: Oxford University Press, 1986).

G. Simpson, *Great Powers and Outlaw States*, (Cambridge: Cambridge University Press, 2004).

M. Smedal, *Acquisition of sovereignty over polar area*, (Oslo: J. Dybwad, 1931).

J. Soroeta Liceras, *El Conflicto del Sahara Occidental, reflejo de las contradicciones y carencias del Derecho Internacional*, (Bilbao: Servicio Editorial de la Universidad del Pais Vasco, 2001).

G. Sperduti, *L'individuo nel diritto internazionale: Contributo all'interpretazione del diritto internazionale secondo il principio dell'effettività*, (Milan: Giuffrè, 1950).

G. Sperduti, *La fonte suprema dell'ordinamento internazionale*, (Milan: Giuffrè, 1946).

F.R. Teson, *Humanitarian Intervention: an Inquiry into Law and Morality*, (New York: Trasnational Publ., 1988).

F.R. Teson, *Humanitarian Intervention: An Inquiry into Law and Morality*, (Irvington on Hudson: Transnational Publ., 1997, 2nd ed.).

The Independent International Commission on Kosovo, *The Kosovo Report*, (Oxford: Oxford University Press, 2000).

The Oxford Paperback Dictionary – New Edition, (Oxford: Oxford University Press, 1994).

J. Touscoz, *Le principe d'effectivité dans l'ordre international*, (Paris: Librairie Général de droit et de jurisprudence, 1964).

G.I. Tunkin, *Theory of International Law*, (London: Allen Unwinn, 1974).

M.C. van Walt van Prag, *The Status of Tibet: History, Rights, and Prospects in International Law*, (Boulder: Westview Press, 1987).

A. Verdross, *Universelles Völkerrecht*, (Berlin: Duncker&Humbolt, 1984, 3rd ed.).

J. Verhoeven, *La Reconnaisance internationale dans la pratique contemporaine*, (Paris: Pedone, 1975).

J.H. Verzijl, *The Jurisprudence of the World Court: a Case by Case Commentary*, (Leiden: Sijthoof, 1966).

J.H. Verzijl, *International Law in Historical Perspective*, (Leiden: A.W. Sijthoof, 1968).

J. Westlake, *Principles of International Law*, (Cambridge: Cambridge University Press, 1894).

E. Wet, de, *The Chapter VII Powers of the United Nations Security Council*, (Oxford: Hart, 2004).

H. Wheaton, *Elements of International Law*, (London: Stevens&Sons, 1916, 5th ed.).

H. Wheaton, *Histoire des progrés du droit des gens en Europe et en Amerique depuis la Paix de Westphalie jusqu'a nos jours*, (Leipzig: Brockhaus, 1865, 4th ed.), Vol. II.

N.D. White, *Keeping the Peace*, (Manchester: Manchester University Press, 1997, 2nd ed.).

N.D. White, *The Law of International Organisations*, (Manchester: Manchester University Press, 1996).

M. Ydit, *Internationalised Territories*, (Leiden: Sythoff, 1961).

G. Ziccardi Capaldo, *Le situazioni territoriali illegittime nel diritto internazionale*, (Naples: Editoriale Scientifica, 1977).

Articles, Courses and Contributions in Edited Books

R. Ago, 'Positive Law and International Law' 51 *AJIL* (1957), 691.

C.H. Alexandrowickz, 'The Theory of Recognition *in Fieri*' 34 *BYIL* (1958), 176.

J.E. Alvarez, 'Judging the Security Council' 90 *AJIL* (1996), 1.

A. Anghie, 'Finding the Peripheries: Sovereignty and Colonialism in Nineteenth-Century International Law' 39 *Harvard International Law Journal* (1999), 1.

G. Arangio-Ruiz, 'L'Etat dans le sens du Droit des Gens et la Notion du Droit international' 26 *Österreische Zeitschrift für öffentliches Recht* (1975-1976), 3, 265.

M. Aristodemou, 'Choice and Evasion in Judicial Recognition of Governments: Lessons from Somalia' 5 *EJIL* (1994), 556.

J. Barboza, 'International Liability for the Injurious Consequences of Acts not Prohibited by International Law and Protection of the Environment' 247 *Recueil des Cours* (1994), 291.

M. Barnett, 'Bringing in the New World Order: Liberalism, Legitimacy, and the United Nations' 49 *World Politics* (1997), 526.

J. Basdevant, 'Règles générales du droit de la paix' 58 *Recueil des Cours* (1936), 475.

V. Bellini, 'Il principio generale dell'effettività' 27 *Annuario di diritto internazionale comparato e di studi legislativi* (1951), 225.

K. Bennoune, 'Sovereignty v. Suffering'? Re-Examining Sovereignty and Human Rights through the Lens of Iraq' 13 *EJIL* (2002), 243.

A. Bianchi, '*Ad-hocism* and the Rule of Law' 13 *EJIL* (2002), 263.

R.L. Bindschedler, 'Annexation', in Bernhardt (ed.), *EPIL* (2000) (Vol. I), 168.

I. Black, 'Talks raise hope of breakthrough', *The Guardian*, 2 June 1999.

P.M. Blau, 'Critical Remarks on Weber's Theory of Authority' 57 *American Political Science Review* (1963), 305.

Y.Z. Blum, Yehuda Z., 'The Missing Reversioner: Reflections on the Status of Judea and Samaria' 3 *Israeli Law Review* (1968), 279.

M. Bothe, 'Consequences of the Prohibition of the Use of Force-Comments on Arts. 49 and 70 of the ILC's 1966 Draft Articles on the Law of Treaties' 27 *ZAÖRV* (1967), 507.

M. Bothe, T. Marauhn, 'UN Administration of Kosovo and East Timor: Concept, Legality and Limitations of Security Council-Mandated Trusteeship Adiministration', in Tomuschat (ed.), *Kosovo and the International Community: a Legal Assessment*, (The Hague: Martinus Nijhoff, 2002), 217.

L. Bouchez, 'The concept of effectiveness as applied to territorial sovereignty over sea-areas, air space and outer space' 4 *Nederlands Tijdschrift voor Internationaal Recht* (1957), 151.

P. Bowers, 'Iraq: law of occupation', June 2003, 10, in House of Commons Research Paper 03/51.

D. Bowett, 'International Law Related to Occupied Territory' 87 *The Law Quarterly Review* (1971), 473.

D. Bowett, 'The Impact of Security Council Decisions on Dispute Settlement Procedures' 5 *EJIL* (1994), 89.

I. Brownlie, 'Kosovo Crisis Inquiry:Memorandum on the International Law Aspects', 4th Report of the House of Commons Foreign Affairs Committee, 49 *ICLQ* (2000), 878.

I. Brownlie, '*International Law and the Use of Force by States* Revisited' 21 *Australian Yearbook of International Law* (2001), 21.

M. Brubacher, 'Le mur de la honte', November 2002, *Le Monde Diplomatique*, 20.

P. Cahier, 'Le caractéristique de la nullité en droit international et tout particuliérment dans la Convention de Vienne de 1969 sur le droit des Traités' 76 *RGDIP* (1972), 645.

A. Carty, 'Carl Schmitt's Critique of Liberal International Legal Order Between 1933 and 1945' 14 *LJIL* (2001), 25.

A. Cassese, '*Ex iniuria jus* oritur: Are We Moving towards International Legitimation of Forcible Humanitarian Countermeasures in the World Community' 10 *EJIL* (1999), 23.

A. Cassese, 'Legal Considerations on the International Status of East Jerusalem' 3 *Palestinian Yearbook of International Law* (1986), 13.

A. Cassese, 'The International Court of Justice and the right of peoples to self-determination', in Lowe, Fitzmaurice (eds.), *Fifty years of the International Court of Justice: Essays in honour of Sir Robert Jennings*, (Cambridge: Cambridge University Press, 1996), 351.

A. Cassese, 'Wars Forbidden and Wars Allowed by the Italian Constitution', in *Studi in onore di Giorgio Balladore Pallieri*, Vol. II, (Milan: Giuffré, 1978), 131.

A. Cavaglieri, 'Règles générales du droit de la paix' 26 *Recueil des Cours* (1929), 315.

J. Cerone, 'Minding the Gap: Outlining KFOR Accountability in Post-Conflict Kosovo' 12 *EJIL* (2001), 469.

J.I. Charney, 'Anticipatory Humanitarian Intervention in Kosovo', 93 *AJIL* (1999), 834.

M. Chemillier-Gendreau, 'A propos de l'effectivité dans l'ordre international' 11 *Revue Belge de Droit International* (1975), 38.

C.M. Chinkin, 'The East Timor Case (Portugal c. Australia)' 45 *ICLQ* (1996), 712.

C.M. Chinkin, 'The Legality of NATO's Action in the Former Republic of Yugoslavia (FRY) under International Law', 4th Report of the House of Commons Foreign Affairs Committee, 49 *ICLQ* (2000), 910.

C.M. Chinkin, 'The State that Acts Alone: Bully, Good, Samaritan or Iconoclast?' 11 *EJIL* (2000), 31.

B. Conforti, 'The Theory of Competence in Alfred Verdross' 6 *EJIL* (1995), 70.

M. Cosnard, 'Sovereign equality – "the *Wimbledon* sails on", in Byers, Nolte (eds.), *United States Hegemony and the Foundation of International Law*, (Cambridge: Cambridge University Press, 2003), 117.

M. Craven *et al.*, in the Symposium 'The Impact on International Law of a Decade of Measures on Iraq' 13 *EJIL* (2002), 43.

M. Craven, 'The *Bosnia* Case Revisited and the 'New' Yugoslavia' 15 *LJIL* (2002), 323.

M. Craven, 'The European Community Arbitration Commission on Yugoslavia' 66 *BYIL* (1995), 333.

M. Craven, 'What's in a Name? The Former Yugoslav Republic of Macedonia and Issues of Statehood' 16 *Australian Yearbook of International Law* (1995), 199.

J. Crawford, 'State Practice and International Law in Relation to Secession' 69 *BYIL* (1998), 85.

J. Crawford *et al.*, 'War would be illegal', *The Guardian*, 7 March 2003.

D.D. Caron, 'The Legitimacy of the Collective Authority of the Security Council' 87 *AJIL* (1993), 552.

D.D. Caron, B. Morris, 'The UN Compensation Commission: Practical Justice not Retribution', 13 *EJIL* (2002), 183.

E. Decaux, 'La Conférence de Rambouillet: Négociation de la dernière chance ou contrainte illicite', in Tomuschat (ed.), *Kosovo and the International Community: a Legal Assessment*, (The Hague: Martinus Nijhoff, 2002), 45.

J. Delbrück, 'Article 25', in Simma (ed.), *The Charter of the United Nations: a Commentary* (Oxford: Oxford University Press, 2002, 2nd ed.), Vol. I, 453.

C. Deliso, 'Blurring the Boundaries in Macedonia', in <http://www.antiwar.com/orig/deliso33.html>.

G. Despeux, 'Das Schiedsurteil *Jemen gegen Eritrea II* vom 17. Dezember 1999: Entscheidung ueber die Seeabgrenzung' 60 *ZaöRV* (2000), 447.

Y. Dinstein, 'The International Law of Belligerent Occupation and Human Rights' 8 *Israeli Yearbook of Human Rights* (1978), 104.

C. Drew, 'The East Timor Story: International Law on Trial' 12 *EJIL* (2001), 651.

C. Dyer, 'Occupation of Iraq illegal, Blair told', *The Guardian*, 22 May 2003.

M. Ehrmann, 'The Status and Rights of Indigenous People in New Zealand' 59 *ZaöRV* (1999), 463.

B. Fassbender, 'Uncertain Steps into a Post-Cold War World: the Role and Functioning of the UN Security Council after a Decade of Measures against Iraq' 13 *EJIL* (2002), 273.

J.P. Fonteyne, 'The Customary Law Doctrine of Humanitarian Intervention: its Current Validity Under the UN Charter' 4 *California Western International Law Journal* (1974), 203.

T.M. Franck, 'Legitimacy and the Democratic Entitlement', in Fox and Roth (eds.), *Democratic Governance and International Law*, (Cambridge: Cambridge University Press, 2000), 25.

T.M. Franck, 'Legitimacy in the International System' 82 *AJIL* (1988), 705.

T.M. Franck, 'Lessons of Kosovo' 93 *AJIL* (1999), 857.

T.M. Franck, 'The "Powers of Appreciation": Who Is the Ultimate Guardian of UN Legality?' 86 *AJIL* (1992), 519.

T.M. Franck, 'The Stealing of the Sahara' 70 *AJIL* (1976), 694.

J. Frowein, 'Die Entwicklung der Anerkennung von Staaten und Regierungen in Voelkerrecht' 11 *Der Staat* (1972), 145.

J. Frowein, N. Krisch, 'Introduction to Ch. VII', in Simma (ed.), *The Charter of the United Nations: a Commentary*, (Oxford: Oxford University Press, 2002, 2nd ed.), Vol. I, 701.

J. Frowein, N. Krisch, 'Article 41', in Simma (ed.), *The Charter of the United Nations: a Commentary* (Oxford: Oxford University Press, 2002, 2nd ed.), Vol. I, 735.

J. Frowein, 'Issues of Legitimacy around the United Nations Security Council' in Frowein (ed.), *Verhandeln für den Frieden: Liber Amicorum Tono Eitel*, (Berlin: Springer, 2003), 121.

H. Gasser, 'Protection of the Civilian Population', in Fleck (ed.), *The Handbook of Humanitarian Law in Armed Conflicts*, (Oxford: Oxford University Press, 1995), 209.

A. Gattini, 'Sense and Quasisense of Schmitt's *Großraum* Theory in International Law – A Rejoinder to Carty's "Carl Schmitt's Critique of Liberal International Legal Order"' 15 *LJIL* (2002), 53.

A. Gattini, 'The UN Compensation Commission: Old Rules, New Procedures on War Reparation', 13 *EJIL* (2002), 161.

A. Gattini, 'A Return Ticket to '*Communitarisme*', Please' 13 *EJIL* (2002), 1181.

T. Gazzini, 'NATO Coercive Military Activities in the Yugoslav Crisis' 12 *EJIL* (2001), 391.

D. Georgiev, 'Politics or Rule of Law: Deconstruction and Legitimacy in International Law' 4 *EJIL* (1993), 1.

B. Graefrath, 'Leave to the Court What Belongs to the Court. The Libyan Case' 4 *EJIL* (1993) 184.

A. Gramsci, 'Culture, Hegemony, Ideology, Intellectuals' in Bennet (ed.), *Culture, Ideology and Social Process: a Reader*, (London: Open University Press, 1947), 192.

C. Gray, 'From Unity to Polarization: International Law and the Use of Force Against Iraq', 13 *EJIL* (2002), 1.

C. Greenwood, 'International law and the NATO intervention in Kosovo', 4th Report of the House of Commons Foreign Affairs Committee, 49 *ICLQ* (2000), 926.

C. Greenwood, 'International Law and the Pre-emptive Use of Force' 4 *San Diego International Law Journal* (2003), 7.

C. Greenwood, V. Lowe, 'Unrecognised States and the European Court' 54 *The Cambridge Law Journal* (1995), 4.

W. Grewe, 'Status Quo', in Bernhardt (ed.), *EPIL*,(2000) (Vol. IV), 687.

P. Guggenheim, 'Contribution a l'histoire des sources du droit des gens' 94 *Recueil des Cours* (1958), 5.

P. Guggenheim, 'La validité e la nullité des actes juridiques internationaux' 74 *Recueil des Cours* (1949), 195.

P. Guggenheim, 'Les deux élements de la coutume en droit international', in *La technique et les principes du droit public: Etudes en l'honneur de G. Scelle*, (Paris: Librairie Générale de Droit et de Jurisprudence, 1950), Vol. I, 275.

M. Guillaume, 'Le cadre juridique de l'action du KFOR au Kosovo', in Tomuschat (ed.), *Kosovo and the International Community: a Legal Assessment*, (The Hague: Martinus Nijhoff, 2002), 243.

F. Halliday, 'Culture and International Relations: a new Reductionism', in M. Ebata, B. Neufeld, *Confronting the Political in International Relations*, (London: Millenium, 2000), 47.

L. Henkin, 'Kosovo and the Law of "Humanitarian Intervention"' 93 *AJIL* (1999), 824.

I. Hurd, 'Legitimacy and Authority in International Politics' 53 *International Organization* (1999), 379.

A. Imseis, 'Critical Reflections on the International Humanitarian Law Aspects of the ICJ *Wall* Advisory Opinion' 99 *AJIL* (2005), 102.

R. Jennings, 'Nullity and Effectiveness in International Law', in *Cambridge Essays in International Law*, (London: Stevens&Sons Ltd., 1965), 64.

E. Jimenez de Arechaga, 'The Work and the Jurisprudence of the International Court of Justice 1947-1986' 58 *BYIL* (1987), 24.

M.C. Johanson, 'Kosovo: Boundaries and the Liberal Dilemma' 73 *Nordic Journal of International Law* (2004), 535.

D.H. Johnson, 'Consolidation as a Root of Title in International Law' 12 *Cambridge Law Journal* (1955), 215.

H. Kelsen, 'Theorie du droit coutumier' 1 *Revue international de la théorie du droit* (1939), 253.

H. Kelsen, 'Theorié genéralé du droit international public' 42 *Recueil des Cours* (1932), 121.

B. Kingsbury, 'Sovereignty and Inequality' 9 *EJIL* (1998), 599.

F.L. Kirgis, 'Security Council Governance of Postconflict Societies: A Plea for Good Faith and Informed Decision Making' 95 *AJIL* (2002), 579.

F.L. Kirgis, 'Security Council Resolution 1483 on the Rebuilding of Iraq', in *ASIL Insights* May 2003, at <http://www.asil.org/insights/insigh107.htm>.

M. Kohen, 'L'emploi de la force et la crise du Kosovo: vers un nouveaue désordre juridique international', 32 *Revue Belge de Droit International* (1999), 122.

R. Kolb, 'Etude sur l'occupation et sur l'Article 47 de la IVeme Convention de Genève du 12 aout 1949 relative à la protection des personnes civiles en temps de guerre: le degreé de intangibilité de droits en territoire occupé' 10 *African Yearbook of International Law* (2002), 267.

L. Kopelmanas, 'Custom as a Means of the Creation of International Law' 18 *BYIL* (1937), 127.

M. Koskenniemi, 'Whose intolerance, which democracy?', in Fox, Roth (eds.), *Democratic Governance and International Law*, (Cambridge: Cambridge University Press, 2000), 436.

H. Krüger, 'Das Prinzip der Effektivität, oder: Über die besondere Wirklichkeitsnähe des Völkerrecht', in *Festschrift für Jean Spiropulos* (1957), 265.

J. Kunz, 'Revolutionary Creation of Norms of International Law' 41 *AJIL* (1947), 119.

C.J. Le Mon, 'Legality of a Request by the Interim Iraqi Government for the Continued Presence of United States Military Forces', *ASIL Insights*, June 2004, Addendum, in <http://www.asil.org/insights/insigh135.htm>.

A. Levine, 'The Status of Sovereignty in East Jerusalem and the West Bank' 5 *New York University Journal of International Law and Politics* (1972), 485.

M. Lewis, 'The Free City of Danzig' 5 *BYIL* (1924), 94.

R.B. Lillich, 'Kant and the Current Debate Over Humanitarian Internvention', 6 *Journal of Transnational Law and Policy* (1997), 397.

L.G. Loucaides, 'The Judgment of the European Court of Human Rights in the *Case of Cyprus v. Turkey*" 15 *LJIL* (2002), 225.

P. Malanczuk, 'Israel: Status, Territory and Occupied Territories', in Bernhardt (ed.), *EPIL* (1999) (Vol. II), 1468.

F.A. Mann, 'Present Validity of Nazi Nationality Laws' 89 *Law Quarterly Review* (1973), 201.

M. Marquez-Carrasco, 'Succession d'Etats et questions territoriales', in Eismann, Koskenniemi (eds.), *State Succession: Codification Tested Against the Facts*, (The Hague: Martinus Nijhoff, 2000), 491.

M.J. Matheson, 'United Nations Governance of Postconflict Societies' 95 *AJIL* (2001), 76

M.S. McDougal, 'International Law, Power and Policy: A Contemporary Conception' 82 *Recueil des Cours* (1953), 133.

M.S. McDougal, M. Reisman, 'The Prescribing Function in World Constitutive Process: How International Law is Made' 6 *Yale Studies in World Public Order* (1980), 249.

J. McHugo, 'Resolution 242: A Legal Reappraisal of the Right-Wing Israeli Interpretation of the Withdrawal Phrase with Reference to the Conflict between Israel and the Palestinians' 51 *ICLQ* (2002), 851.

M.H. Mendelson, 'Formation of Customary International Law' 272 *Recueil des Cours* (1998), 165.

M.H. Mendelson, S.C. Hulton, 'La revendication par l'Iraq de la souveraineté sur le Koweit' 36 *Annuaire Française de Droit Internationale* (1990), 195.

M.H. Mendelson, S.C. Hulton, 'The Iraq-Kuwait Boundary' 64 *BYIL* (1993), 135.

W. Meng, 'Stimson Doctrine', in Bernhardt (ed.), *EPIL* (1982) (Vol. IV), 690.

E. Meyer, N.D. White, 'Editorial: The Use of Force Against Iraq' 8 *Journal of Conflict and Security Law* (2003), 1.

N. Mijatovic, 'A Hard Loss to Spin', Report on the Balkans' crisis, 6 June 1999, Institute for War and Peace Reporting.

E. Milano, 'Security Council's Action in the Balkans: Reviewing Kosovo's Territorial Status' 14 *EJIL* (2003), 999.

M. Milenkoski, J. Talevski, 'Delineation of the State Border Between the Republic of Macedonia and the Federal Republic of Yugoslavia', Summer 2001, *IBRU Boundary and Security Bulletin*, 93.

R. Mullerson, 'The Continuity and Succession of States by Reference to the Former USSR and Yugoslavia' 42 *ICLQ* (1993), 473.

S. Nasrawi, 'Arab Nations Won't Recognize Iraq Council', *Associated Press News*, 5 August 2003.

D.M. Ong, 'The Legal Status of the 1989 Australia-Indonesia Timor Gap Treaty Following the End of Indonesian Rule in East Timor', 31 *NYIL* (2000), 67.

Y. Onuma, 'The ICJ: An Emperor Without Clothes? International Conflict Resolution, Article 38 of the ICJ Statute and the Sources of International Law', in Ando et al. (eds.), *Liber Amicorum Judge Shigeru Oda*, (The Hague: Kluwer International, 2002), 191.

A. Orakhelashvili, 'The Impact of Peremptory Norms on the Interpretation and Application of United Nations Security Council Resolutions' 16 *EJIL* (2005), 59.

G. Ottolenghi, 'Il principio di effettività e la sua funzione nell'ordinamento internazionale' 15 *Rivista di diritto internazionale* (1936), 3, 151, 363.

E. Playfair, 'Introduction', in Playfair (ed.), *International Law and the Administration of Occupied Territories: Two Decades of Israeli Occupation of the West Bank and Gaza Strip*, (Oxford: Clarendon Press, 1992), 1.

R. Quadri, 'Cours général de droit international public' 113 *Recueil des Cours* (1963), 245.

E. Radintsky, 'Die rechtliche Natur des Staatsgebiets' 20 *Archiv des öffentlichen Rechts* (1906), 313.

B.G. Ramcharan, 'Recourse to the Law in the Settlement of International Disputes: Western Sahara' 6 *African Yearbook of International Law* (1998), 205.

S.R. Ratner, 'Drawing a Better Line: *Uti Possidetis* and the Border of New States' 90 *AJIL* (1996), 590.

D. Rauschning, 'United Nations Trusteeship System', in Bernhardt (ed.), *EPIL* (1983) (Vol. V), 369.

R. Redslob, 'Völkerrechtlichen Ideen der Französischen Revolution', in *Festgabe für O. Mayer*, (Tübingen: Mohr, 1916), 273.

M. Reisman, 'Humanitarian Intervention and Fledgling Intervention' 18 *Fordham International Law Journal* (1995), 795.

M. Reisman, 'International Lawmaking: A Process of Communication: The Harold D. Lasswell Memorial Lecture' 75 *ASIL Proceedings* (1981), 101.

J. Ringelheim, 'Considerations on the international reaction to the 1999 Kosovo crisis' 32 *Revue belge de droit international* (1999), 475.

A. Roberts, 'What is a Military Occupation?' 55 *BYIL* (1984), 249.

A. Roberts, 'The End of Occupation: Iraq 2004', 54 *ICLQ* (2005), 27

C.L. Rozakis, 'The Law on Invalidity of Treaties' 16 *Archiv des Völkerrechts* (1973), 150.

.J. Salmon, in 'Débats', Corten (ed.), *Démembrements d'Etats et délimitations territoriales*, (Brussels: Bruylant, 1999), 325.

L.I. Sanchez Rodriguez, 'L'*uti possidetis* et les effectivités' 263 *Recueil des Cours* (1997), 161

O. Schachter, 'International Law in Theory and Practice. General Course in Public International Law' 178 *Recueil des Cours* (1982), 143.

J. Schoenborn 'La nature juridique du territoire' 5 *Recueil des Cours* (1929), 85.

N. Schrijver, 'The Changing Nature of State Sovereignty' 70 *BYIL* (1999), 65.

G. Schwarzenberger, 'The Fundamental Principles of International Law' 87 *Recueil des Cours* (1955), 191.

S. Schwebel, 'What Weight to Conquest' 64 *AJIL* (1977), 344.

S. Scott, 'The Australian High Court's Use of the *Western Sahara* case in *Mabo*' 45 *ICLQ* (1996), 923.

A. Sereni, 'Dottrine italiane di diritto internazionale', in *Scritti di diritto internazionale in onore di Tommaso Perassi*, Vol. 2, (Milan: Giuffré, 1950), 281.

S.P. Sharma, 'Boundary Dispute and Territorial Dispute: a Comparison' 10 *Indian Journal of International Law* (1970), 162.

M.N. Shaw, 'Peoples, Territorialism and Boundaries' 8 *EJIL* (1997), 478.

M.N. Shaw, 'The heritage of states: the principle of *uti possidetis juris* today' 67 *BYIL* (1996), 75.

L.A. Sicilianos, 'L'autorisation par le conseil de sécurité de recourir à la force: un tentative d'evaluation' 106 *RGDIP* (2002), 5.

G. Simpson, '*Mabo*, International Law, *Terra Nullius* and the Stories of Settlement: an Unresolved Jurisprudence' 19 *Melbourne University Law Review* (1993), 195.

G. Simpson, 'Two Liberalisms' 12 *EJIL* (2001), 537.

A.M. Slaughter, 'International Law in a World of Liberal States' 6 *EJIL* (1995), 503.

A.M. Slaughter, 'The Real New World Order' 76 *Foreign Affairs* (1997), 183.

C. Stahn, 'The Ambiguities of SC Res. 1422 (2002)' 14 *EJIL* (2003), 85.

J. Stone, 'What Price Effectiveness' *ASIL Proceedings* (1951), 199.

S.P. Subedi, 'The Doctrine of Objective Regimes in International Law and the Competence of the United Nations to Impose Territorial or Peace Settlements on States' 37 *GYIL* (1994), 162.

E. Suy, 'Le Conseil de Sécurité et la frontiere entre l'Iraq et le Koweit', in Rama-Montaldo (ed.), *El derecho internacional en un mundo en transformacion*, (Montevideo: Fundacion de Cultura Universitaria, 1994), 441.

W.H. Taft *et al.*, 'Agora: Future Implications of the Iraq Conflict' 97 *AJIL* (2003), 553.

S. Talmon, 'Recognition of Governments: an Analysis of the New British Policy and Practice' 63 *BYIL* (1992), 231.

S. Talmon, 'The Cyprus Question before the European Court of Justice' 12 *EJIL* (2001), 727.

S. Talmon, 'Luftverkehr mit nicht anerkannten Staates: Der Fall Nordzypern' 43 *Archiv des Völkerrechts* (2005), 39.

P. Tavernier, 'Article 27: Vote', in Cot, Pellet (eds.), *La Charte des Nations Unies*, (Economica: Paris, 1991, 2nd ed.), 505.

P. Tavernier, 'L'Année des Nations Unies' 24 *Annuaire française de droit international* (1978), 520.

F. Teson, 'The Kantian Theory of International Law' 92 *Columbia Law Review* (1992), 53.

'The new men, and women, in charge', *The Economist*, 19 July 2003, 20.

T. Treves, 'La Prévention des Conflits Internationaux dans la Déclaration Adoptée en 1988 par l'Assemblée Géneral de l'O.N.U.' 34 *Annuaire française de droit international* (1988), 437.

R. Tucker, 'The Principle of Effectiveness in International Law', in Lipsky (ed.), *Law and Politics in the World Community*, (Berkeley: University of California Press, 1953), 31.

F.L.M. Van De Craen, 'Palestine (1996 Addendum)', in Bernhardt (ed.), *EPIL* (1997) (Vol. III), 865.

G. Vedovato, 'Les accords de tutelle' 76 *Recueil des Cours* (1950), 613.

F.A. Von der Heydte, 'Discovery, Symbolic Annexation and Virtual Effectiveness in International Law' 29 *AJIL* (1935), 448.

C. Warbrick, 'States and Recognition in International Law', in Evans (ed.), *International Law*, (Oxford: Oxford University Press, 2003), 205.

G. Watson, 'Constitutionalism, Judicial Review, and the World Court' 34 *Harvard International Law Journal* (1993), 1.

R. Wedgwood, 'NATO's Campaign in Yugoslavia' 93 *AJIL* (1999), 828.

M. Weller, 'The Rambouillet Conference on Kosovo', 75 *International Affairs* (1999), 211.

N.D. White, 'The legality of bombing in the name of humanity' 5 *Journal of Conflict and Security Law* (2000), 27.

N.D. White, 'The Will and Authority of the Security Council after Iraq' 17 *LJIL* (2004), 645.

R. Wilde, 'From Danzig to East Timor and Beyond: the Role of International Territorial Administration' 95 *AJIL* (2001), 583.

J. Wildeman, 'The Philosophical Background of Effectiveness' 24 *Netherlands International Law Journal* (1977), 335.

I.Winkelmann, 'Bringing the Security Council into a New Era: Recent Developments in the Discussion on the Reform of the Security Council' 1 *Max Planck Yearbook of United Nations Law* (1997), 35.

A. Yannis, 'The Concept of Suspended Sovereignty in International Law and Its Implications in International Politics' 13 *EJIL* (2002), 1037.

'Yugoslav President Asks Kofi Annan to Exert his Influence on KFOR and UNMIK' and 'Macedonian Government Stunned, Will Send Demarche to United Nations', *Yugoslav Daily Survey*, 22 February 2002, in <http://www.mfa.gov.yu/Bilteni/Engleski/b220202_e.html>.

S. Zappalà, 'Nuovi sviluppi in tema di uso della forza armata in relazione alle vicende del Kossovo' 82 *Rivista di diritto internazionale* (1999), 975.

Y.H. Zoubir, 'The Western Sahara Conflict: a Case Study in Failure of Prenegotiation and Prolongation of Conflict' 26 *California Western International Law Journal* (1996), 173.

INDEX

Developments in International Law

27. V.D. Degan: *Sources of International Law*. 1997   ISBN 90-411-0421-6
28. Mark Eugen Villiger: *Customary International Law and Treaties*. A Manual on the Theory and Practice of the Interrelation of Sources. Fully Revised Second Edition. 1997   ISBN 90-411-0458-5
29. Erik M.G. Denters and Nico Schrijver: *Reflections on International Law from the Low Countries*. In Honour of Paul de Waart. 1998   ISBN 90-411-0503-4
30. Kemal Baslar: *The Concept of the Common Heritage of Mankind in International Law*. 1997   ISBN 90-411-0505- 0
31. C.L. Lim and O.A. Elias: *The Paradox of Consensualism in International Law*. 1998   ISBN 90-411-0516-6
32. Mohsen Mohebi: *The International Law Character of the Iran-United States Claims Tribunal*. 1998   ISBN 90-411-1067-4
33. Mojmir Mrak: *The Succession of States*. 1999   ISBN 90-411-1145-X
34. C.L. Lim and Christopher Harding: *Renegotiating Westphalia*. Essays and Commentary on the European and Conceptual Foundations of Modern International Law. 1999   ISBN 90-411-1250-2
35. Kypros Chrysostomides: *Republic of Cyprus*. A Study in International Law. 200   ISBN 90-411-1338-X
36. Obiora Chinedu Okafor: *Re-Defining Legitimate Statehood*. International Law and State Fragmentation in Africa. 2000   ISBN 90-411-1353-3
37. Rein Müllerson: *Ordering Anarchy*. International Law in International Society. 2000   ISBN 90-411-1408-4
38. Joshua Castellino: *International Law and Self-Determination*. The Interplay of the Politics of Territorial Possession with Formulations of Post-Colonial 'National' Identity. 2000   ISBN 90-411-1409-2
39. Oriol Casanovas: *Unity and Pluralism in Public International Law*. 2001   ISBN 90-411-1664-8
40. Roberto C. Laver: *Falklands/Malvinas Case*. Breaking the Deadlock in the Anglo-Argentine Sovereignty Dispute. 2001   ISBN 90-411-1534-X
41. Guido den Dekker: *The Law of Arms Control*. International Supervision and Enforcement. 2001   ISBN 90-411-1624-9
42. Sandra L. Bunn-Livingstone: *Juricultural Pluralism vis-à-vis Treaty Law*. State Practice and Attitudes. 2002   ISBN (hb) 90-411-1779-2
     ISBN (pb) 90-411-1801-2
43. David Raic: *Statehood and the Law of Self-Determination*. 2002   ISBN 90-411-1890-X
44. L. Ali Khan: *Theory of Universal Democracy*. Beyond the End of History. 2003   ISBN 90-411-2003-3
45. Antony Anghie, Bhupinder Chimni, Karin Mickelson and Obiora Okafor (eds.): *The Third World and International Order. Law, Politics and Globalization*. 2003   ISBN 90-411-2166-8
46. Stéphane Beaulac: *The Power of Language in the Making of International Law*. The Word Sovereignty in Bodin and Vattel and the Myth of Westphalia. 2004   ISBN 90-04-13698-3
47. Sienho Yee: *Towards an International Law of Co-progressiveness*. 2004   ISBN 90-04-13829-3

48. C.G. Weeramantry: *Universalising International Law*. 2004   ISBN 90-04-13838-2
49. R.P. Anand: *Studies in International Law and History*. 2004   ISBN 90-04-13859-5
50. Gerard Kreijen: State Failure, Sovereignty and Effectiveness, 2004
                                                                   ISBN 90-04-13965-6
51. Nico Schrijver and Friedl Weiss (eds.): *International Law and Sustainable Develop-ment*. 2004.   ISBN 90-04-14173-1
52. Markus Burgstaller: *Theories of Compliance with International Law*. 2004.
                                                                   ISBN 90-04-14193-6
53. L.J. van den Herik: *The Contribution of the Rwanda Tribunal to the Development of International Law*. 2005.   ISBN 90-04-14580-X
54. Roda Verheyen: *Climate Change Damage and International Law*. 2005.
                                                                   ISBN 90 04 14650 4
55. E. Milano: *Unlawful Territorial Situations in International Law*. Reconciling Effec-tiveness, Legality and Legitimacy. 2006.   ISBN 90-04-14939-2

MARTINUS NIJHOFF PUBLISHERS – LEIDEN / BOSTON